Law in Ancient Egypt

Law in Ancient Egypt

Russ VerSteeg

Carolina Academic Press
Durham, North Carolina

ISBN 0-89089-978-9
LCCN 2001096605

Cover Art: "The Judgment of the Dead" from Papyrus Ryerson,
Oriental Institute Museum 9787, reproduced courtesy of
The Oriental Institute of The University of Chicago.

Carolina Academic Press
700 Kent Street
Durham, North Carolina 27701
Telephone (919) 489-7486
Fax (919) 493-5668
E-mail: cap@cap-press.com
www.cap-press.com

Printed in the United States of America

To Whitney (15) and Carl (13)

Contents

Preface xi
Map xiii

PART I
OVERVIEW, JUSTICE, ORGANIZATION AND PROCEDURE

Chapter 1 Introduction 3
§1.01 Overview 3
§1.02 The Tale of the Eloquent Peasant 15
§1.03 Chapter Summary 17

Chapter 2 Ancient Egyptian Concepts of Justice & Jurisprudence 19
§2.01 Introduction 19
§2.02 *Ma'at* 20
§2.03 Justice & Jurisprudence 23
[A] Overview 23
[B] Tradition & Security 24
[C] Rhetoric 25
[D] Impartiality & Social Equality 26
§2.04 *Ma'at*, Justice, & Jurisprudence in *The Tale of the Eloquent Peasant* 28
[A] General 28
[B] Judges & Decisionmaking 29
[C] The Role of Rhetoric 30
[D] Man's Control of Nature & Nature Itself 31
[E] Gods 33
[F] Humans 34
[G] Boating 35
§2.05 Chapter Summary 36

Chapter 3 Legal Organization & Personnel 37
§3.01 Introduction 37
§3.02 Court Structure in the Old & Middle Kindgoms 38
[A] Old Kingdom (c. 2700–2200 B.C.) 38
[B] Middle Kingdom (c. 2050–1674 B.C.) 41
§3.03 Court Structure in the New Kingdom (c. 1552–1069 B.C.) 43
[A] Introduction 43
[B] Pharaoh & the Courts 44
[C] Deir El-Medina 47
[D] Special Courts 49
§3.04 The Office of Vizier 50
§3.05 Judges 52
§3.06 Other Court Personnel & Law Enforcement Officials 56
§3.07 Adjudication by Oracle 58
§3.08 Chapter Summary 61

Chapter 4 Legal Procedure 63
§4.01 Introduction 63
§4.02 Adherence to Precedent 66
§4.03 Outline of Litigation Procedure 68
§4.04 Pretrial & Trial Procedure 72
§4.05 Evidence 77
[A] Introduction 77
[B] Witnesses & Oaths 77
[C] Documents & Other Types of Evidence 82
§4.06 Procedure in the Special Courts 84
§4.07 Appeal 87
§4.08 Legal Procedure in The Tale of the Eloquent Peasant 89
§4.09 Enforcement 93
§4.10 Chapter Summary 94

Part II
Substantive Law

Chapter 5 Property 99
§5.01 General 99
§5.02 Some Significant Principles of Property Law 109
§5.03 Sale & Lease of Land, Deeds, & Recordation of Real Property 112
[A] Sales 112
[B] Leases 114

§5.04 Taxation of Property 115
[A] Introduction 115
[B] Administration 118
[C] Tax Exemptions 121
§5.05 Chapter Summary 122

Chapter 6 The Family 125
§6.01 Introduction 125
§6.02 Marriage 126
§6.03 Divorce 132
§6.04 Roles of Parents and Children 134
§6.05 Chapter Summary 135

Chapter 7 Inheritance & Succession 137
§7.01 Intestate Succession 137
§7.02 Testate Succession 140
§7.03 The Concept of a Trustee for an Estate 147
§7.04 Inheritance of Office 148
§7.05 Chapter Summary 149

Chapter 8 Crime & Tort (Damage to Persons & Things) 151
§8.01 Introduction 151
§8.02 Punishment: An Overview 152
[A] General 152
[B] Incarceration 157
§8.03 The Landscape of Egyptian Crime & Tort 158
§8.04 Theft/Conversion 161
[A] General 161
[B] The Great Tomb Robberies 165
[C] International (The Report of Wenamun) 168
§8.05 Conspiracy/Treason & Homicide 169
§8.06 Sexual Conduct: Homosexuality; Prostitution; Rape; Adultery 172
§8.07 Judicial Misconduct 175
§8.08 Extortion by Officials & Tax Collectors 176
§8.09 Miscellaneous Wrongs 177
[A] Battery 177
[B] Trespass to Land 178
[C] Trespass to Chattels/Vandalism (Criminal Mischief) 178
[D] Defamation 179
§8.10 Crime & Tort in The Tale of the Eloquent Peasant 180
§8.11 Chapter Summary 186

Chapter 9 Trade, Contracts, & Commercial Law 187
§9.01 Trade 187
§9.02 Business Organizations 190
§9.03 Contracts 192
§9.04 Foreign & International Aspects 201
§9.05 Commercial Law: Credit, Security, & Standard Media of Exchange 204
§9.06 Customs Tax & Tax on Municipal Office 207
§9.07 Chapter Summary 208

Chapter 10 Personal Status 209
§10.01 General 209
§10.02 Women 210
§10.03 Middle Class 213
§10.04 Peasant-Serfs and Slaves 214
§10.05 Chapter Summary 216

Bibliography 219
General Index 225
Index of Names 239

Preface

This book is intended to serve as a general introduction to law in ancient Egypt. Professional Egyptologists may consider much of this material too general, and they may find fault with my reliance on sources in English (rather than French and German). If so, I hope that its breadth, organization, and simplicity provide a clarity and scope that make up for its shortcomings. In this type of work one always strives to strike a delicate balance between exhaustive specificity on the one hand (to keep the scholars happy) and simplistic generality on the other (to keep the general readers happy). For good or ill that is the balance that I have tried to achieve. This may be as difficult a task as the deceased Egyptian had in pursuing a balance between his soul and the justice of *Ma'at*. Nevertheless, I decided that the game was worth the candle. Therefore, I have endeavored to present a work that is both sufficiently detailed and extensive to interest and assist scholars and also sufficiently general yet simple enough to educate and enlighten students and generalists. In short, I hope that Egyptologists, historians, legal historians, students, and educated layreaders find this book beneficial.

Several individuals have helped me in the preparation of this book. Dr. Janet Johnson of the Oriental Institute of the University of Chicago and Dr. Richard Jasnow of Johns Hopkins University read an early draft and provided me with helpful comments and criticisms. My father, Bob VerSteeg, read the manuscript when it was near completion, and set me straight on many matters of prose style, grammar, punctuation, and the like. I did an appreciable amount of my work while on sabbatical at the University of London's Institute for Advanced Legal Studies in the Fall of 1999. There the staff and librarians were quite helpful. It was in London also that my son, Carl, encouraged me and kept my spirits afloat even when my laptop went to visit Osiris. To all these people (and many more I'm sure) I owe a great deal of thanks.

More than once the Board of Trustees of New England School of Law and Dean John O'Brien provided funding through Honorable James R. Lawton Summer Research Stipends. This book would not have been possible without those stipends, and I thank the Board and Dean O'Brien for their generous support. Portions of this book have previously appeared in journal articles (or parts thereof). Much of the material relating to *The Tale of the Eloquent Peasant* appeared in *Law in Ancient Egyptian Fiction*, 24 GEORGIA J. OF INT'L & COMPARATIVE LAW 27 (1994). Most of Chapter 3 is taken from *The Machinery of Law in Pharaonic Egypt: Organization, Courts, & Judges on the Ancient Nile*, CARDOZO J. OF INT'L & COMPARATIVE LAW (2001). And most of Chapter 4 is taken from *Legal Procedure and the Law of Evidence in Ancient Egypt*, 9 TULANE J. OF INT'L & COMPARATIVE LAW 233 (2001). I appreciate the editors of those journals allowing me to reuse material originally published by them for the present work.

For the sake of consistency and clarity I have standardized most of the spellings of ancient words and names (even in quoted material and titles of works). For example, I have preferred "Horemhab" to "Har-em-hab"). Similarly, I have referred to Egyptian dynasties (even changing quoted material) with Arabic ordinal numerals (e.g., 4th Dynasty) rather than either Roman numerals (e.g., Dynasty IV) or spelled-out (e.g., Fourth Dynasty). For dates and chronology I generally followed those given by Nicholas Grimal in his A HISTORY OF EGYPT.

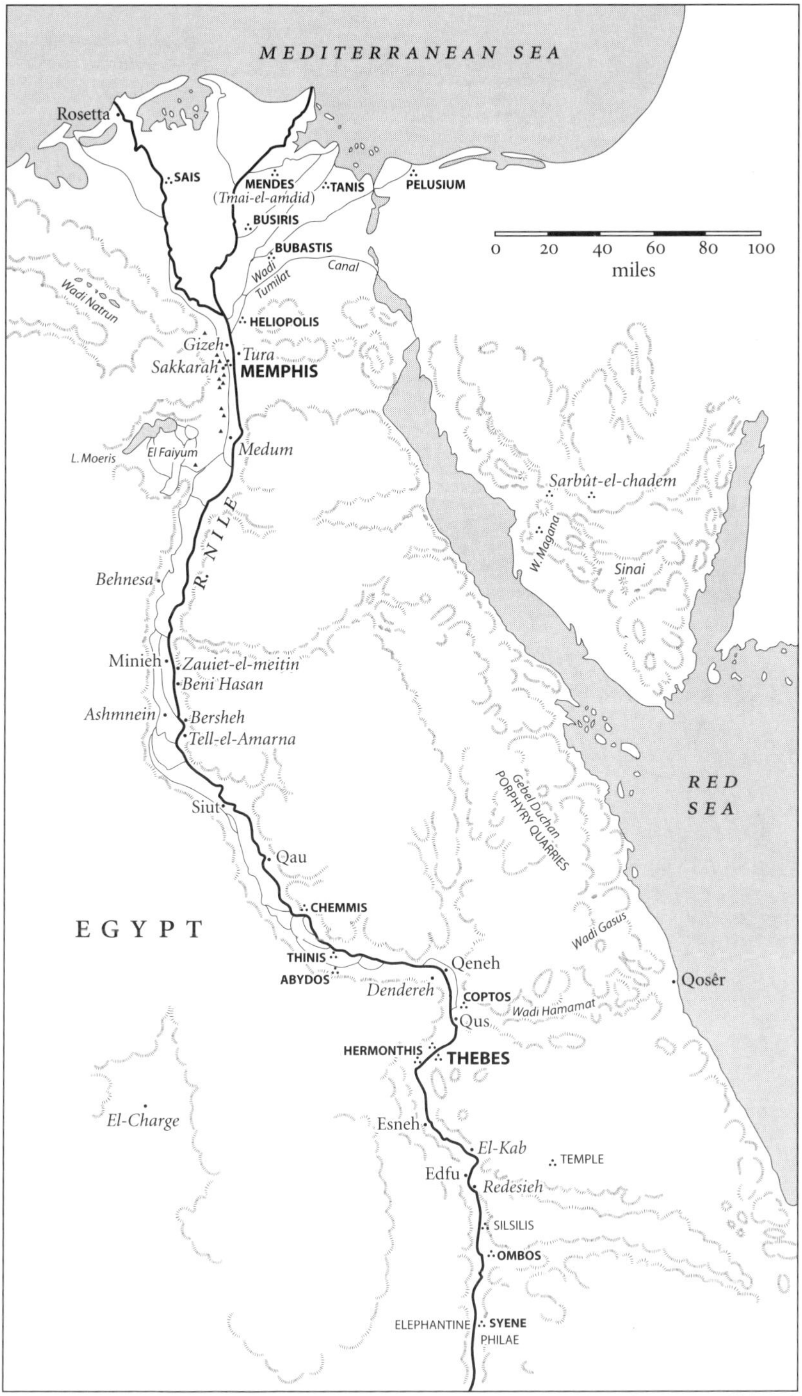

After original in Adolf Erman, Life in Ancient Egypt (tr. Helen May Triard) (1894).

Part I

Introduction, Justice, Organization & Procedure

CHAPTER 1

Introduction

§ 1.01 Overview

The ancient Egyptians knew that law was essential. Egyptian literature routinely contrasts the prosperous life that flourishes when people respect law, with the dismal state of affairs that exists when law has been suspended.[1] The ancient Greeks credited the Egyptians with having a working legal system and laws. In Book I of his *General History*, Diodorus Siculus examined Egypt and discussed justice and Egyptian laws.[2] Diodorus claimed that five ancient Egyptian kings were known as "law-givers."[3] Ac-

1. *See* Sir Alan Gardiner, Egypt of the Pharaohs 109 (1961) [hereinafter "Gardiner, Egypt of the Pharaohs"] (Explaining that lawlessness was rampant in the First Intermediate Period: the 7th, 8th, and 9th Dynasties. This comes from a text in Leyden from "no earlier than the 19th Dynasty"); Nicolas Grimal, A History of Ancient Egypt 138 (Ian Shaw trans. 1992) [hereinafter "Grimal, Ancient Egypt"]; David A. Warburton, State and Economy in Ancient Egypt: Fiscal Vocabulary of the New Kingdom 26 (1997) (Describing this also as a time when the economy faltered.) [hereinafter "Warburton, State and Economy in Ancient Egypt"]; James Hoch and Sara Orel, *Murder in Ancient Egypt, in* Death and Taxes in the Ancient Near East 87, 105 (Sara Orel ed., 1992) (Referring to the Admonitions of Ipuwer.).

2. *See* David Lorton, *The Treatment of Criminals in Ancient Egypt*, 20 J. Economic & Social Hist. Orient 2, 4–5 (1977); Gardiner, Egypt of the Pharaohs 5–6 ("Of great interest are the last thirty paragraphs of his first book, which deal with a variety of topics—the ritually regulated life of the kings, administration of the provinces and the caste system, justice and laws, medicine...."); James H. Breasted, A History of Egypt 241–242 (1905) [hereinafter "Breasted, History of Egypt"] ("The great body of this law was undoubtedly very old, and some of it, like the old texts of the Book of the Dead, was ascribed to the gods; but Horemhab's new regulations were new law enacted by him. Diodorus tells of five different kings before Persian times who enacted new laws, and in the Middle Kingdom even a nobleman relates having made laws, meaning, of course that he had formulated them at the king's request.") (footnotes omitted).

3. *See* David Lorton, *The Treatment of Criminals in Ancient Egypt*, 20 J. Economic & Social Hist. Orient 2, 5 (1977); Janet H. Johnson, *The Legal Status of Women in*

cording to Breasted: "The social, agricultural and industrial world of the Nile-Dwellers was not at the mercy of an arbitrary whim on the part of either King or Court, but was governed by a large body of long respected law embodying principles of justice and humanity."[4]

The ancient Egyptians prized rhetorical skill. Certainly the art of persuasion is critical for anyone hoping to influence a judge or jury. Rhetoric and law clearly go hand-in-hand. And we really cannot be certain which affected the other more: whether law influenced rhetoric more or rhetoric influenced law more. It is not surprising that a people who were infatuated with persuasive speaking would also develop a sophisticated legal system.[5] Nor is it surprising that a civilization that developed an adversarial legal system would also learn to exploit rhetoric. But unlike the ancient Romans who created specialized legal vocabulary and terminology, the Egyptians generally used ordinary, everyday words and phrases to record, describe, and explain legal matters.[6] The ancient Egyptians used commonplace language for legal documents and had only a few imprecise technical terms relating to law.[7] "The Egyptian word that corresponds most closely to our word *law*...is *hp*. This word can also connote custom, order, justice, or right, according to its usage."[8]

Ancient Egypt, in MISTRESS OF THE HOUSE MISTRESS OF HEAVEN: WOMEN IN ANCIENT EGYPT 175, 215, n.17 (Anne K. Chapel and Glenn E. Markoe eds., 1996); GIRGIS MATTHA, THE DEMOTIC LEGAL CODE OF HERMOPOLIS WEST XII (1975, preface, additional notes, and glossary by George R. Hughes)[hereinafter "MATTHA, THE DEMOTIC LEGAL CODE OF HERMOPOLIS WEST"].

4. BREASTED, HISTORY OF EGYPT 242.

5. *See* GARDINER, EGYPT OF THE PHARAOHS 115 (Gardiner refers to the Middle Kingdom instruction text, The Instructions for Merikare, which advise the student to learn rhetoric. Gardiner says: "Stress is laid upon ability to speak well and persuasively, and imitation of ancient models is strongly recommended."); GRIMAL, ANCIENT EGYPT 146–147.

6. *See* ANDREA MCDOWELL, JURISDICTION IN THE WORKMEN'S COMMUNITY OF DEIR EL-MEDINA 13 (1990) [hereinafter "MCDOWELL, JURISDICTION"] ("The Egyptians did not have a specialized legal vocabulary. The phrases used in legal documents were almost all current in everyday speech, and there is no evidence that they acquired a more technical meaning when used in a legal context.").

7. *See* Jac Janssen, *Rules of Legal Proceeding in the Community of Necropolis Workmen at Deir el-Medina*, 32 BIBLIOTHECA ORIENTALIS 291, 294 (1975) ("It is obvious that in ancient Egypt there has not been a well defined juridical language...."); Aristide Théodorides, *The Concept of Law in Ancient Egypt, in* THE LEGACY OF EGYPT 291 (J.R. Harris ed., 2d ed. 1971) ("in their legal deeds the Egyptians use everyday language with the addition of only a few technical terms...."); *Id.* at 315 ("Everyday vocabulary could...embrace legal notions, with the result that one must beware of concluding from the apparent absence of technical terms that there were no juridical concepts.").

8. Janet H. Johnson, *The Legal Status of Women in Ancient Egypt, in* MISTRESS OF THE HOUSE MISTRESS OF HEAVEN: WOMEN IN ANCIENT EGYPT 175, 176 (Anne K.

As early as the Old Kingdom (*c.* 2700–2200 B.C.), the Egyptians envisioned the god Osiris as a judge.[9] And, apparently, there was already a legal system in place before then; perhaps by the 1st and 2nd Dynasties (*c.* 3150–2700 B.C.).[10] The kings of this period received kingship from the gods with the understanding that they were to rule in accordance with the laws of the land. To this end, the early kings issued decrees. Because the Egyptians considered the king a god, he represented an unquestioned source of law.[11] In short, the king's word had the force of law.[12]

In this formative period, although the new State needed rules and regulations for administrative procedure and precedent, it is unlikely that there were any written laws. As Warburton recognizes, "Laws need not be written down, but the administration must be assumed to be run using certain guidelines, either traditional or *ad hoc*."[13] The king and/or *ma'at* (roughly translated "justice"[14]) were responsible for laws. There was no legislative body and no legislation as such.[15] Indeed, the earliest Egyptians must have thought that written laws were unnecessary in a world where the king was conceived of as a god incarnate. Thus, the king's word expressed divine law that was in harmony with the concept of *ma'at*. Clearly, they must have assumed that their god-king would follow the precepts of *ma'at*. Presumably,

---

Chapel and Glenn E. Markoe eds., 1996). *See* R.O. FAULKNER, A CONCISE DICTIONARY OF MIDDLE EGYPTIAN 158 (1981) (Faulkner defines *hp* as "law, ordinance."). *See also* ELLEN BEDELL, CRIMINAL LAW IN THE EGYPTIAN RAMESSIDE PERIOD (Brandeis University, Ph.D. Dissertation) 11 (1973) [hereinafter "BEDELL, CRIMINAL LAW"]("In the Egyptian language the word *hp*, which appeared in the Middle Kingdom, signified 'law,' or 'regulation.' ").

9. *See* BREASTED, HISTORY OF EGYPT 173 (Osiris "had already been known as a judge in the Old Kingdom. . . .").

10. *See* GRIMAL, ANCIENT EGYPT 57–58.

11. *See* John A. Wilson, *Authority and Law in Ancient Egypt*, Supplement to 40 J. AM. ORIENTAL SOC. 1 (1954).

12. *See* GRIMAL, ANCIENT EGYPT 58 ("on condition that he governed with respect for the laws of the land, which were actually identical to the laws of the universe. In order to fulfil this role, the king issued decrees. In a sense every word uttered by the king constituted a decree with the full force of the law, whether it was fixed in writing or not. . . . It seems that the interpretation of these decrees comprised, along with recourse to written laws and the consultation of jurisprudence, the basis of the Egyptian legal system.").

13. WARBURTON, STATE AND ECONOMY IN ANCIENT EGYPT 315.

14. *See infra* § 2.02.

15. *See* Janet H. Johnson, *The Legal Status of Women in Ancient Egypt*, *in* MISTRESS OF THE HOUSE MISTRESS OF HEAVEN: WOMEN IN ANCIENT EGYPT 175, 176 (Anne K. Chapel and Glenn E. Markoe eds., 1996). *See also* WARBURTON, STATE AND ECONOMY IN ANCIENT EGYPT 38 (Discussing the relationship between the State, law, and *ma'at*.).

the vizier and local judges based their decisions on custom.[16] And, theoretically, custom derived from the word of the god-king and his three divine qualities of *Hu*, *Sia*, and *Ma'at* (Authority, Perception, and Justice).[17] In turn, the vizier and local judges must have rationalized that the omniscient will of the king dictated local custom. *Ma'at* was the one unifying, impersonal factor that influenced the judges' decisions. The god-king was both subject to and the earthly interpreter of *Ma'at*.[18]

Thus, through the Old Kingdom (*c.* 2200 B.C.), the situation was very different from the condition in Mesopotamia at the same time, where a tradition of written laws on public display was already evolving. Since there were no written laws available for the early viziers[19] to consult and follow, the kings instructed them to judge impartially and to avoid allowing favoritism to influence their decisions.[20]

The Middle Kingdom (*c.* 2040–1674 B.C.) was a period of increased communication and information recording. The Middle Kingdom scribes recorded a large number of judicial documents.[21] During the New Kingdom (*c.* 1552–1069 B.C.), a community of workers, who were employed to build tombs for the pharaohs, lived at Deir el-Medina. We have numerous contracts and records of lawsuits that those workers recorded on ostraca (pieces of broken pottery).[22] After the political upheaval of the Amarna period (*c.* 1350 B.C.), the pharaoh no longer could claim his word as law. Instead, he came to be subject to impersonal law.[23] Also priests began asserting their control over the civil courts.[24] At the end of the 18th Dynasty, the pharaoh Horemhab (*c.* 1323–1295 B.C.) promulgated a well-known edict that contains a great deal of information about law. But his edict was not a law code per se. Instead, it was "a series of police regulations directed

16. *See infra* § 3.04 regarding the office of the vizier.

17. *See* JOHN WILSON, THE CULTURE OF ANCIENT EGYPT 172–73 (1951) [hereinafter "WILSON, CULTURE OF ANCIENT EGYPT"].

18. *See Id.* at 49–50.

19. *See infra* § 3.04.

20. *See* WILSON, CULTURE OF ANCIENT EGYPT at 172–173; *Id.* at 173 (According to Wilson: "Of course there were royal ordinances to fit specific instances, and of course there were precedents out of past judication; but there was nothing in Egypt corresponding to the Mesopotamian codes, detailed written law, publicly displayed as the symbol of impersonal justice. In Egypt, the law was personally derived from the god-king and was tailored as justice and equity to the individual appellant.").

21. *See* GARDINER, EGYPT OF THE PHARAOHS 60.

22. *See Id.* at 275 (Gardiner mentions records of barter and lawsuits on the ostraca of the workers at Deir el-Medina.). *See infra* §§ 3.01, 3.03[C].

23. *See* WILSON, CULTURE OF ANCIENT EGYPT 234.

24. *See Id.* at 239.

against specific malpractices and also a reorganization of the administrative machinery in the land, in order to control future abuses."[25] Shortly after Horemhab's Edict, Seti I (*c.* 1294–1279 B.C.) issued his Nauri Decree. Written in stone (literally) the Nauri Decree was eventually discovered in Nubia.[26] Seti I's Nauri Decree "gave privileges and exemptions to the temple of Osiris at Abydos, but it outlined a series of possible crimes against persons and property belonging to the Estate, and very specific punishments for the perpetrators of these offenses."[27] A decree that bears similarities to the Nauri Decree has been found at Elephantine. It is likely that Ramses III (*c.* 1186–1154 B.C.) promulgated that decree. It contains protections for the temple there dedicated to Khnum.[28]

Scholars have debated whether the ancient Egyptians used a written code or collection of laws.[29] We have not yet discovered, as we have from the same period in Mesopotamia, any written law collections from ancient Egypt prior to about 700 B.C. Some Egyptologists have maintained, nevertheless, that they did have written laws. For example, Breasted, in his monumental *A History of Egypt* remarks: "There was a body of highly elaborated law, which has unfortunately perished entirely."[30] Erman comments: "The laws which guided the king and courts in their decisions are unfortu-

---

25. *See Id.* at 237. *See also* GRIMAL, ANCIENT EGYPT 243 ("He set out in this edict the measures with which he was addressing the abuses that had taken place due to over-centralization in Amenhotep IV's reign." "To this end Horemhab appointed judges and regional tribunes....Legal power was split between Upper and Lower Egypt, shared between Thebes and Memphis respectively."); *Id.* at 74–75 (Noting that the 4th Dynasty King Shepsekaf also issued "a decree—the earliest known edict—which safeguarded the funerary estates of the earlier kings...."); BEDELL, CRIMINAL LAW 2 (Referring to Horemhab giving judges laws to consult and also referring to his reorganization of the courts.); *Id.* at 151–152; BREASTED, HISTORY OF EGYPT 406 ("All these enactments were recorded by Horemhab on a huge stela some sixteen feet high and nearly ten feet wide, which he set up before one of his Karnak pylons....") (footnotes omitted).

26. *See* BEDELL. CRIMINAL LAW 13; William F. Edgerton, *The Nauri Decree of Seti I: A Translation and Analysis of the Legal Portion*, 6 J. NEAR EASTERN STUD. 219 (1947).

27. BEDELL, CRIMINAL LAW 18. *See also Id.* at 151 (Referring to the Nauri Decree.).

28. *See Id.* at 18–19.

29. *See* David Lorton, *The Treatment of Criminals in Ancient Egypt*, 20 J. ECONOMIC & SOCIAL HIST. ORIENT 2, 5 (1977); James Hoch and Sara Orel, *Murder in Ancient Egypt, in* DEATH AND TAXES IN THE ANCIENT NEAR EAST 87, n. 2 (Sara Orel ed., 1992) (Citing Barry J. Kemp, *Old Kingdom, Middle Kingdom and Second Intermediate Period c. 2686–1552* B.C., *in* ANCIENT EGYPT: A SOCIAL HISTORY 83–84 (Trigger *et al* eds., 1983).

30. BREASTED, HISTORY OF EGYPT 81. *See also Id.* at 165 ("The law...has not survived...."); *Id.* at 242 ("Unfortunately the code...has perished.").

nately unknown to us.... Diodorus informs us expressly of laws made by certain wise kings, and in fact the old chief judge Mentuhotep boasts that he had 'given laws.' Under the 12th Dynasty the canon of the old laws was not considered finally closed, and the same is probably true of later times."[31] "Diodorus... says... that he was informed that the sacred books of law had been composed by Thoth the god of wisdom."[32] Some of the early scholars who assumed that the Egyptians did have written laws once based that assumption, at least in part, on the belief that the forty objects depicted in artistic representations of the vizier were scrolls containing written laws to which the vizier could refer for help in his decision making. More recent study suggests that these objects were not scrolls of written laws but rather "were forty leather thongs which were the symbols of his disciplinary authority."[33] Indeed, a number of Egyptologists have argued that the Egyptians did not have written laws in the most ancient times. Théodorides, for example, expresses his skepticism, stating: "We have, after all, collections of Sumerian, Akkadian, Hittite, and Neo-Babylonian laws—but nothing of the kind from Egypt." "The Nile valley has given us no code, nor any copious theoretical treatises, but the application of law is coherent, despite peculiar features of procedure—the important point being that there was a procedure, with laws to organize it."[34] According to Wilson, "Despite all the written documents which have come down to us from ancient Egypt, we possess neither a body of law which is comparable to the Asiatic codes, nor any textual references to such laws elsewhere...."[35] Shu-

---

31. Adolf Erman, Life in Ancient Egypt 141 (original English trans. 1894 by H.M. Tirard, 1971) (footnotes omitted) [hereinafter "Erman, Life in Ancient Egypt"]. *See also* David Taylor, *Law under the Pharaohs* 6 Pol'y Rev. 66 (1980) ("Although no actual code of ancient Egyptian law has been preserved there can be no doubt that there was a highly elaborate body of law and it is very probable that some sort of code was in existence as early as the 12th Dynasty (*c.* 2,000 BC) if not before. There were certainly statutes as long ago as 3,000 BC but it is not known precisely what those statutes enacted."). *See also* Lexikon der Ägyptolgie, Vol. 5 (1984), "Recht" 185.

32. Erman, Life in Ancient Egypt 141 (footnote omitted).

33. Wilson, Culture of Ancient Egypt 172 (footnote omitted).

34. Aristide Théodorides, *The Concept of Law in Ancient Egypt*, *in* The Legacy of Egypt 291, 320 (J.R. Harris ed., 2d ed. 1971) (footnote omitted). Théodorides also states: "Even documents relating to the legal practice are rare...." *Id.* at 291. *See also* Rudolf Anthes, *The Legal Aspect of the Instruction of Amenemhet*, 16 J. Near Eastern Stud. 176, 180 (1957) ("No codification of laws existed in Egypt, to our knowledge.").

35. John A. Wilson, *Authority and Law in Ancient Egypt*, Supplement to 40 J. Am. Oriental Soc. 5 (1954) (citing Diodorus, 1.79). *See also* Mattha, The Demotic Legal Code of Hermopolis West XII; Breasted, History of Egypt 547 (According to Breasted, the Greeks credited an Egyptian king named Bocchoris in the late Eight Century b.c. for having been "a wise lawgiver who revised the laws of the land

pak adopts a practical approach on this issue: "Was there a codex similar to those of Egypt's neighbors Mesopotamia, Israel, and the Hittites? This question is as yet unanswerable, although the possibility must be given serious consideration."[36] Shupak states further, "No codex has so far been found even though the classical writers mention the existence of one; it is also alluded to in Egyptian writings."[37] Recently, however, Lorton has positively maintained that "we now know for a certainty that law codes did exist in Pharaonic times, thanks to the fact that a recently published papyrus of 12th Dynasty date cites by subject matter five laws dealing with fugitives."[38] It is significant also that there exists a collection of laws from Hermopolis (the so-called "Hermopolis Legal Code") that may date from the first millennium B.C. Indeed, it represents the first concrete evidence for written laws in ancient Egypt and appears to date from the 24th Dynasty (*c.* 700 B.C.). Our copy is probably from the third century B.C.[39] It is the only extant Egyptian analogue to the great law collections from Mesopotamia. And, like its Mesopotamian cousins, it may be a collection of case decisions (or summaries) rather than a law "code" per se.[40] Consequently, this book refers to the Her-

---

and himself rendered legal decisions of the most remarkable shrewdness." Bocchoris became king around 718 B.C.).

36. Nili Shupak, *A New Source For the Study of the Judiciary and Law of Ancient Egypt: "The Tale of the Eloquent Peasant"*, 51 J. NEAR E. STUD. 1, 9 (1992) (footnote omitted) (Citing myriad references in footnote 34 for the existence of a law code.). *See Id.* at 8 ("The term for law in Egyptian is *hp*. The application of the law is in the hands of a judge who, should 'guide' (*sšm*) 'according to the law (*r hpw*).'"); Aristide Théodorides, *The Concept of Law in Ancient Egypt, in* THE LEGACY OF EGYPT 291, 319 (J.R. Harris ed., 2d ed. 1971) (Stating that when the Persians overtook Egypt, "tradition... attributed to Darius a new codification of the existing laws.").

37. Nili Shupak, *A New Source For the Study of the Judiciary and Law of Ancient Egypt: "The Tale of the Eloquent Peasant"*, 51 J. NEAR E. STUD. 1, 9 (1992).

38. David Lorton, *The Treatment of Criminals in Ancient Egypt*, 20 J. ECONOMIC & SOCIAL HIST. ORIENT 2, 5 (1977) (footnote omitted).

39. *See generally* MATTHA, THE DEMOTIC LEGAL CODE OF HERMOPOLIS WEST. *See also* C.J. Eyre, *Crime and Adultery in Ancient Egypt*, 70 J. EGYPTIAN ARCHAEOLOGY 92 (1984) ("There is, indeed, no certain indication that any form of codified law existed before the Third Intermediate Period, and the earliest preserved set of laws [is] from the Ptolemaic Period...." (footnotes omitted)); WILSON, CULTURE OF ANCIENT EGYPT 172 ("[W]e have no evidence of written codes of law... in Egypt, until the time of Bak-en-renef of the 24th Dynasty."); PIETER WILLEM PESTMAN, MARRIAGE AND MATRIMONIAL PROPERTY IN ANCIENT EGYPT IX (1961) [hereinafter "PESTMAN, MARRIAGE & MATRIMONIAL PROPERTY"]; James Hoch and Sara Orel, *Murder in Ancient Egypt, in* DEATH AND TAXES IN THE ANCIENT NEAR EAST 87 (Sara Orel ed., 1992).

40. *See* Janet H. Johnson, *The Legal Status of Women in Ancient Egypt, in* MISTRESS OF THE HOUSE MISTRESS OF HEAVEN: WOMEN IN ANCIENT EGYPT 175, 177 (Anne K. Chapel and Glenn E. Markoe eds., 1996). *See also* C.J. Eyre, *Crime and Adultery in Ancient Egypt*, 70 J. EGYPTIAN ARCHAEOLOGY 92 (1984) (Eyre describes this text as having "the appearance rather of a practitioner's handbook than a code

mopolis document not as a "code" but rather as "the Law Collection of Hermopolis." It contains sections relating to matters such as leasing real estate, contracts relating to a husband's marital obligations, family law, and inheritance.[41] Nevertheless, whether they had written laws or not, it seems certain that law played a significant role in the daily lives of the ancient Egyptians.[42]

Since no written laws (*i.e.*, statutes) survive (at least from before the 24th Dynasty), scholars traditionally have turned to contracts, wills, deeds, family archives, and accounts of criminal trials as sources for ancient Egyptian law.[43] "The legal documents which have been preserved are less numerous than one might have expected. Some wills were discovered..., as well as deeds of sale, census-lists, &c."[44] Such sources enable us to recon-

---

proper."); Bedell, Criminal Law 2 ("Indeed, there is no evidence of a law code in Egypt until the country became a satrapy of the Persian Empire.") (footnote omitted); *Id.* at 15 ("There is absolutely no evidence of a law code in Egypt until the Persian period."). And Bedell warns, "Even this, strictly speaking, was not a law code, but rather a collection of all the existing laws." *Id.* at 16.

41. *See* Janet H. Johnson, *The Legal Status of Women in Ancient Egypt, in* Mistress of the House Mistress of Heaven: Women in Ancient Egypt 175, 177 (Anne K. Chapel and Glenn E. Markoe eds., 1996); S. Allam, *Egyptian Law Courts in Pharaonic and Hellenistic Times*, 77 J. Egyptian Archaeology 109, 118 (1991).

42. *See* Aristide Théodorides, *The Concept of Law in Ancient Egypt, in* The Legacy of Egypt 291, 320 (J.R. Harris ed., 2d ed. 1971) ("[T]he entire day-to-day business of existence in the Nile valley... [was] regulated by law.").

43. *See* David Lorton, *Legal and Social Institutions of Pharaonic Egypt, in* 1 Civilizations of the Ancient Near East 345 (Jack M. Sasson ed., 1995) ("But legal disputes could then arise over possession and transfer of usufruct lands, so families kept archives of documents of appointments to office, transfer of lands, wills that could prove inheritance, and the like."); David Lorton, *The Treatment of Criminals in Ancient Egypt*, 20 J. Economic & Social Hist. Orient 2, 5 (1977) ("Most of the legal material which has survived from ancient Egypt consists of royal edicts and private contracts of sale, endowment, marriage, and the like."); Jac Janssen, *Rules of Legal Proceeding in the Community of Necropolis Workmen at Deir el-Medina*, 32 Bibliotheca Orientalis 291, 295 (1975); Pestman, Marriage & Matrimonial Property 83 ("The Egyptian keeps and stores all the documents in writing relating to agreements in a family archive".) (footnote omitted); *Id.* at 85 ("all deeds by which rights are conferred used carefully to be kept in a family archive and put safely away, hidden under the floor of the house or tomb.") (footnote omitted); Nili Shupak, *A New Source For the Study of the Judiciary and Law of Ancient Egypt: "The Tale of the Eloquent Peasant"*, 51 J. Near E. Stud. 1 (1992) ("Most of the material available regarding the legal aspects of life in ancient Egypt pertains to contracts and other legal documents, as well as to literary works not directly connected with the legal system."); John A. Wilson, *Authority and Law in Ancient Egypt*, Supplement to 40 J. Am. Oriental Soc. 5 (1954) ("We do have legal documents, such as testaments and transfers of property, as well as abbreviated records of court proceedings.") (footnote omitted).

44. Sir Alan Gardiner, Egyptian Grammar 23 (3d ed. 1978) (footnote omitted)[hereinafter "Gardiner, Egyptian Grammar"]. *See also* Taylor, *Law under the Pharaohs*, 6 Pol'y Rev. 66 (1980) ("Most often the nature of the law has to be deduced

struct a sketch of ancient Egyptian law. This sketch reveals both complexity and evolution.[45] We see rules relating to such diverse topics as criminal law, succession, wills, marriage and family law, property, contracts, and taxes. On balance, the substantive laws appear to have been designed to empower individuals and, to some degree, to promote fairness and equality. We even have evidence regarding international law.[46] As Théodorides remarks: "[W]hat is striking is the modernity of this law. It gives Egyptian civilization, though remote in time, a structure close to that with which we are familiar."[47]

In addition to the legal documents available, literary evidence is also helpful. For example, in one Middle Kingdom text, *The Admonitions of an Egyptian Sage*, the protagonist describes the disorderly nature of Egypt during the First Intermediate Period when chaos reigned and the judicial system was not functioning:

> Indeed, the laws / of the council chamber are thrown out; indeed, men walk on them in public places, and poor men break them up in the streets.
>
> Indeed, the poor man has attained to the state of the Nine Gods, and the erstwhile procedure of the House of the Thirty is divulged.
>
> Indeed, the great council-chamber is a popular resort, and poor men come and go in the Great Mansions.[48]

There are many other surviving works of ancient Egyptian literature, specifically Middle Egyptian fiction,[49] that also provide valuable insight

---

from the legal documents of which a small number has survived from the Old Kingdom (2686–2160 B.C.).").

45. *See* Nili Shupak, *A New Source For the Study of the Judiciary and Law of Ancient Egypt: "The Tale of the Eloquent Peasant"*, 51 J. NEAR E. STUD. 1 (1992) ("In the light of the available sources, it is possible to reconstruct the judiciary and law of the land of the Pharoahs [*sic*]."); Aristide Théodorides, *The Concept of Law in Ancient Egypt, in* THE LEGACY OF EGYPT 291, 320 (J.R. Harris ed., 2d ed. 1971) (Indeed, the law in ancient Egypt "did not remain identically the same over the centuries. Human aspirations conditioned by new circumstances caused it to change, and it evolved between the pole of equality and liberty and that of inequality....").

46. *See* Aristide Théodorides, *The Concept of Law in Ancient Egypt, in* THE LEGACY OF EGYPT 291, 316 (J.R. Harris ed., 2d ed. 1971) (In about 1270 B.C. during the reign of Ramses II, the Egyptians concluded a treaty with the Hittites that provided for non-aggression, a defensive alliance, and extradition of political refugees.). *See also infra* §§ 8.04[C], 10.04.

47. Aristide Théodorides, *The Concept of Law in Ancient Egypt, in* THE LEGACY OF EGYPT 291, 320 (J.R. Harris ed., 2d ed. 1971).

48. THE LITERATURE OF ANCIENT EGYPT 218 (William K. Simpson ed., 1972) (footnotes omitted) [hereinafter "SIMPSON, THE LITERATURE OF ANCIENT EGYPT"].

49. *See* GARDINER, EGYPTIAN GRAMMAR 1 ("Middle Egyptian, as here understood, is the idiom employed in the stories and other literary compositions of the Middle Kingdom (9th–13th Dynasties, roughly from 2240 to 1740 B.C.), as well as in

into law.[50] Therefore, this book incorporates some literary evidence to supplement the detached legal documents.[51] Indeed, in discussing the reliability of historical sources for the Middle Kingdom, Gardiner states:

> If it be asked where our best historical material is to be found, our answer may seem to be almost a contradiction in terms; it is to be found in Egyptian fiction, where the authors were able to depict existing conditions and to vent their feelings with a freedom impossible when the predominant intention was that of boasting.[52]

Because of the utility of literary evidence, in addition to traditional legal sources (contracts, deeds, wills, *etc.*), I have relied on one work of Middle

---

the public and private monumental inscriptions of that period and also far down into the 18th Dynasty (1573–1314 B.C.)."); *Id.* at 2 ("[T]he period covered by Middle Egyptian may be considered the classical age of Egyptian literature."); Grimal, Ancient Egypt 171 ("The Middle Kingdom... is the time when Egyptian language and literature reached their most perfect forms.").

50. *See e.g.* James Hoch and Sara Orel, *Murder in Ancient Egypt, in* Death and Taxes in the Ancient Near East 87 (Sara Orel ed., 1992) (Hoch and Orel use a great deal of literary evidence to support their discussion of murder.).

51. Despite certain weaknesses inherent in using literature as a source for legal study (*See* Edmund S. Meltzer, Book Review, 104.2 J. Am. Oriental Soc'y 363 (Reviewing Robert Parant, L'affaire Sinouhe. Tentative d'approache de la justice repressive égyptienne au debut du II millenaire av. J.C. (1982).), many scholars have argued rather convincingly that such a law and literature approach is sound. *See e.g.*, T.G.H. James, Pharaoh's People: Scenes From Life in Imperial Egypt 74 (1984) ("Indeed, the evidence provided by literature is often of a particularly significant kind; for it may incorporate attitudes of mind and descriptions of procedures which are quite specific and very informative."); Richard Posner, Law And Literature: A Misunderstood Relation 1–17 (1988) (Discussing and citing numerous works validating literature as an appropriate field from which to mine legal insight.); James B. White, The Legal Imagination: Studies in the Nature of Legal Thought and Expression (1973); Sanford Levinson, *Law as Literature*, 60 Tex. L. Rev. 373 (1982); Richard Weisberg, *Coming of Age Some More: "Law and Literature" Beyond the Cradle*, 13 Nova L. Rev. 107 (1988); Robert H. Weisberg, *The Law-Literature Enterprise*, 1 Yale J.L. & Human. 1 (1988); Richard Weisberg, *Family Feud: A Response to Robert Weisberg on Law and Literature* 1 Yale J.L. & Human. 69 (1988); Marijane Camilleri, Comment, *Lessons in Law From Literature: A Look at the Movement and a Peer at Her Jury*, 39 Cath. U. L. Rev. 557 (1990).

52. Gardiner, Egypt of the Pharaohs 61; Georges Posener, *Literature*, in The Legacy of Egypt 220, 251 (J.R. Harris ed., 2d ed. 1971) ("Egyptian literature was... essentially secular in its *raison d' être*. It had an independent existence and was cultivated for its own sake, for the mere pleasure it gave, and for the benefit of society and mankind."). *See also Id.* at 252.

Nevertheless, any reconstruction of this type is tentative. Gardiner reminds us that even with respect to what we might call Egyptian History: "It must never be forgotten that we are dealing with a civilization thousands of years old and one of which only tiny remnants have survived. What is proudly advertized as Egyptian history is merely a collection of rags and tatters." Gardiner, Egypt of the Pharaohs 53.

Egyptian fiction in particular: *The Tale of the Eloquent Peasant.*[53] This delightful story is especially useful in the study of the Egyptian view of justice in the abstract[54] and legal procedure.[55] Therefore, in order to provide a meaningful context for the reader, and since I refer to it on numerous occasions throughout, this chapter concludes with a brief summary of *The Tale of the Eloquent Peasant.*

The balance of Part I (chapters 2–4) examines ancient Egyptian justice and jurisprudence (including an analysis of justice and jurisprudence in *The Tale of the Eloquent Peasant*), legal organization, institutions, and procedure. Part II (chapters 5–11) surveys legal doctrines and principles in a number of categories of substantive law (Property law, Family law, Inheritance, *etc.*). Admittedly, these categories are modern constructs. "We do not know how the Egyptians defined their various legal categories, but they seem to proceed as though they had defined them as we do...."[56] Egyptian law, moreover, was imbued with custom, religion, magic, and complex power hierarchies that

---

53. *See* Russ VerSteeg, *Law in Ancient Egyptian Fiction*, 24 GA. J. INT'L & COMP. L. 37 (1994). In another article, Nili Shupak persuasively argues that:

> [a]n analysis of [*The Tale of the Eloquent Peasant*] from the point of view of content, form, and terminology, on the one hand, and a comparison with other works involved with the judiciary, on the other, will demonstrate that this work should be added to the body of sources which, although already far from meager, can benefit from additional information about the law of ancient Egypt.

Nili Shupak, *A New Source For the Study of the Judiciary and Law of Ancient Egypt: "The Tale of the Eloquent Peasant"*, 51 J. NEAR E. STUD. 1, 1–2 (1992) (footnote omitted). According to Shupak, this tale is especially useful for legal study because it "has a well founded juridical background." *Id.* at 1. *See also Id.* at 18. Neither Shupak nor I, however, was the first to recognize that this tale could be particularly useful in the study of law. *See* WILSON, CULTURE OF ANCIENT EGYPT 120–122; T.G.H. JAMES, PHARAOH'S PEOPLE: SCENES FROM LIFE IN IMPERIAL EGYPT 74–78 (1984); PESTMAN, MARRIAGE & MATRIMONIAL PROPERTY 59. Furthermore, since the Middle Kingdom was a period of significant change, the fiction of this age seems especially appropriate for legal analysis. Breasted remarks that the writers of this era "were perfectly conscious that they were thinking upon new lines, and that they had departed far from the wisdom of their fathers." BREASTED, DEVELOPMENT OF RELIGION AND THOUGHT 199–200. Posener relates that the "conflicts and upheavals" of the First Intermediate Period (*c.* 2200–2040)—the period that immediately preceded the Middle Kingdom—were reflected in the literature. *See* Georges Posener, *Literature*, in THE LEGACY OF EGYPT 220, 227 (J.R. Harris ed., 2d ed. 1971).

54. *See infra* § 2.04. *See also* Vincent Tobin, *Ma'at and Dike: Some Comparative Considerations of Egyptian and Greek Thought*, 24 J. AM. RESEARCH CENTER IN EGYPT 113–114 (1987).

55. *See infra* § 4.08.

56. Aristide Théodorides, *The Concept of Law in Ancient Egypt, in* THE LEGACY OF EGYPT 291, 320 (J.R. Harris ed., 2d ed. 1971).

perhaps influenced law more than independent legal categories such as property, torts, or contracts.[57] Even as late as the 19th Dynasty, magic, for instance, could play an important role in law and legal interpretation.[58] Nevertheless, modern American legal categories and their separate substantive classifications serve as useful pedagogical analogues. References to modern American law can provide abstract points of comparison which may help us correlate the unfamiliar ancient concepts with the more familiar modern ones. Lastly, I present much of the material synthetically rather than chronologically. Egyptologists have often adopted a synthetic approach to the study of law because it is very difficult to sort the material chronologically.[59]

---

57. *See* Jac Janssen, *Rules of Legal Proceeding in the Community of Necropolis Workmen at Deir el-Medina*, 32 Bibliotheca Orientalis 291, 294 (1975) ("Juridical matters were far more than we are, unconsciously, inclined to accept aspects of social and religious life.").

58. *See* Wilson, Culture of Ancient Egypt 242 (Explaining that the decrees of Seti I show another interesting factor, the invocation of magic to support law.). *But see* Aristide Théodorides, *The Concept of Law in Ancient Egypt, in* The Legacy of Egypt 291, 320 (J.R. Harris ed., 2d ed. 1971) ("The law is independent in the sense that it is not smothered by a host of primitive religious notions.").

59. *See* McDowell, Jurisdiction 10 ("And yet we will perforce draw on all our legal sources as though they reflect on one and the same state of affairs. There is no alternative; the texts are too few and far between to even think of a diachronic analysis.").

§ 1.02 The Tale of the Eloquent Peasant[60]

The Tale of the Eloquent Peasant is a "long work preserved in four papyrus copies, all dating from the Middle Kingdom."[61] In the story, Khunanup, the peasant protagonist, finds trouble waiting for him on the road. Khunanup leaves his wife at home in the Wadi Natrun and heads for Ninsu in Egypt[62] taking with him his donkeys and a variety of goods to trade.[63] As Khunanup approaches the house of Nemtynakhte (a tenant of Rensi, "the High Steward"[64]), Nemtynakhte spies Khunanup and immediately covets

---

60. The following is a summary of the tale by Miriam Lichtheim:

> The text consists of a narrative frame and nine poetic speeches. It is both a serious disquisition on the need for justice, and a parable on the utility of fine speech. The connection between the two themes is achieved by means of an ironic device in the narrative frame: after the peasant has been robbed and has laid his complaint before the magistrate in a stirring plea, the latter is so delighted with this unlearned man's eloquence that he reports it to the king; and on the king's orders the magistrate goads the peasant to continue pleading until the poor man is completely exhausted. Only then does he receive justice and ample rewards.

MIRIAM LICHTHEIM, ANCIENT EGYPTIAN LITERATURE VOLUME I: THE OLD AND MIDDLE KINGDOMS 169 (1975) [hereinafter "LICHTHEIM, ANCIENT EGYPTIAN LITERATURE"]. The tale is also summarized in GARDINER, EGYPT OF THE PHARAOHS 112 and Nili Shupak, *A New Source For the Study of the Judiciary and Law of Ancient Egypt: "The Tale of the Eloquent Peasant"*, 51 J. NEAR E. STUD. 1, 3 (1992).

See also BREASTED, DEVELOPMENT OF RELIGION AND THOUGHT 216–26. Breasted interprets the story in macroscopic terms as evidence that Egypt was evolving towards attaining social justice for the lower classes. *Id. See also Id.* at 353; Georges Posener, *Literature*, in THE LEGACY OF EGYPT 220, 228–229, 254–55 (J.R. Harris ed., 2d ed. 1971); GARDINER, EGYPTIAN GRAMMAR 24*a*; GRIMAL, ANCIENT EGYPT 148–149.

61. LICHTHEIM, ANCIENT EGYPTIAN LITERATURE 169 (Lichtheim notes that "[t]he individual copies are incomplete, but together they yield the full text, which comprises 430 lines."). *See also* Nili Shupak, *A New Source For the Study of the Judiciary and Law of Ancient Egypt: "The Tale of the Eloquent Peasant"*, 51 J. NEAR E. STUD. 1, 2 (1992) ("This work was written at the beginning of the Middle Kingdom and was preserved on four papyri of that time.") (footnote omitted).

62. *See* SIMPSON, THE LITERATURE OF ANCIENT EGYPT 32, n. 3 (Simpson says that Ninsu is Herakleopolis in Middle Egypt.). The trip from Wadi Natrun to Herakleopolis is about 100 miles.

63. According to the text:

> So the peasant went down to Egypt, and he loaded his asses with reeds, *redemet*-plants,/ natron, salt, wood from the [Hes]-tiu country, wands of *awent*-wood from the Farafra Oasis,/ panther skins, jackal hides, *nesha*-plants, *kheperur*-plants,/ *sahut*, *saksut*-pellets, *misut*-plants, *senet*-stones, *aba*-stones,/ *ibsa*-plants, *inbi*-plants, pigeons, *naru*-birds (ostriches?), *weges*-birds,/ *weben*-plants, *tebes*-plants, *gengenet*-pellets, hair fruit, and *inset*-pellets,/ being full measure of all goodly products of the Wadi Natrun.

SIMPSON THE LITERATURE OF ANCIENT EGYPT 31–32. (footnote omitted).

64. *See Id.* at 32. (footnote omitted).

his possessions. "O that I had some potent idol, that I might steal the peasant's goods from him!"[65] exclaims Nemtynakhte.[66] So, Nemtynakhte devises a plan. He spreads a piece of cloth on the narrow road so that it overlaps the river on one side and his field of barley on the other. Thus, when Khunanup reaches the cloth with his donkeys, he is forced to go into the river, onto the cloth, or into Nemtynakhte's barley. Confronted by this predicament, Khunanup appeals to his adversary's sense of reason: "the bank is high and the (only other) way is under barley, and you are obstructing our road with your clothes. Will you not let us pass upon the road?"[67] However, it is too late. No sooner does Khunanup ask Nemtynakhte to clear the road than one of his animals, obviously tempted by the grain, takes a bite of barley.[68] Immediately, the two argue over the appropriate remedy. Nemtynakhte threatens to take the donkey "because of its eating my barley...."[69] The peasant counters: "My way is good,[70] and one (wisp only) has been damaged. It is for its (the wisp's) price that I will buy back my donkey if you take possession of it/ for a (mere) filling of its mouth with a wisp of barley."[71] At this point, Nemtynakhte invokes the imprimatur of his landlord (the High Steward), beats Khunanup with a stick, and, finally, takes "away his [donkeys] and dr[ives] them to his estate."[72]

Khunanup first argues with Nemtynakhte for ten days, trying to persuade him to listen to reason. After getting nowhere with Nemtynakhte,

---

65. *Id.*

66. Apparently, such an idol would give him only the physical strength to take Khunanup's goods, not the legal right.

67. Simpson, The Literature of Ancient Egypt 33.

68. *See Id.* ("Now when he had finished uttering [this] speech, one of these asses filled/ his mouth with a wisp of barley.").

69. *Id.*

70. Simpson footnotes this phrase as follows: "I.e. I am ready to oblige you." Simpson, The Literature of Ancient Egypt 33, n. 5. Nevertheless, the sense of the phrase seems almost legal. The peasant uses it on a number of occasions as if to say: "I intend no wrongdoing." Shupak interprets this line, "'My way is good' (*nfr mṯn.i*)" as "meaning, my intentions are pure, I am an honest person." Nili Shupak, *A New Source For the Study of the Judiciary and Law of Ancient Egypt: "The Tale of the Eloquent Peasant"*, 51 J. Near E. Stud. 1, 10 (1992) (footnote omitted).

71. Simpson, The Literature of Ancient Egypt 33. See also 1 Corinthians 9:9, Deuteronomy 25.4, and 1 Timothy 5:18 (Hebrew prohibition against muzzling the ox).

72. *Id.* Presumably, he also took all of the peasant's goods that the donkeys were carrying. In *The Admonitions of an Egyptian Sage*, we find conduct that is nearly identical described: "Indeed, the ways are [...], the roads are watched; men sit in the bushes until the benighted traveler comes in order to plunder his burden, and what is upon him is taken away. He is belabored with blows of a stick and murdered." *Id.* at 217 (footnote omitted).

Khunanup next takes his case to the High Steward, Rensi. Rensi confers with the king, who tells him to have scribes transcribe Khunanup's arguments. The central portion of the story, then, consists of Khunanup's nine petitions. At the tale's end, when the High Steward, Rensi, finally delivers his judgment in the case, he grants all of Nemtynakhte's possessions to Khunanup, including his house, as damages.

> Then [the High Steward] Rensi, son of Meru, caused two apparitors to go to [fetch Nemtynakhte], / and he was brought in. An inventory was made of [all his goods...], his [servants], six persons, apart from [...] his barley, his emmer, [his] asses, his pigs, and [his flocks,] and Nemtynakhte's [house was given to the] peasant, / [together with] all his [goods].[73]

Although Nemtynakhte was apprehended, the last few words of the text are lost. Thus, we never learn the ultimate fate of Nemtynakhte.[74]

§ 1.03 Chapter Summary

Although the ancient Egyptians had a functional legal system, it appears that they had little in the way of written law until about the eighth century B.C. Even then, the written law may not have been statutory, in the modern sense. We have abundant evidence for law in Egypt. Contracts, wills, accounts of trials, and records of taxation provide useful information. Evidence from rhetoric and literature supplement these traditional sources too. *The Tale of the Eloquent Peasant*, in particular, adds a great deal to our understanding. Still, the Egyptians did not develop a technical legal vocabulary, but instead used ordinary language to express law and legal concepts.

In the Old Kingdom, the god-king established law simply through his presence on earth and his own volition. Custom and *Ma'at*, the Egyptian

73. *Id.* at 49. For more regarding the forfeiture of property as a criminal punishment, *see infra* § 8.02[A].

74. Faulkner's translation closes as follows: "[Then...] said [...] to Nemtynakhte [...] which is in [...] (*Last word or words of story lost.*) It has come to an end." SIMPSON, THE LITERATURE OF ANCIENT EGYPT 49. There is evidence that the Pharaoh Horemhab (1323–1295 B.C.) punished this type of behavior severely. In circumstances where "ordinary citizens ... [were] ... deprived of their boats and their cargoes, or again ... [were] beaten and robbed of the valuable hides of their cattle ... the malefactors in the worst cases ... [were] ... docked of their noses and banished to the fortress town of Tjel on the Asiatic border, and the lesser cases punished with a hundred strokes and five open wounds." GARDINER, EGYPT OF THE PHARAOHS 244–245. *See infra* § 3.03[B] for more on Horemhab's Edict.

abstract sense of justice, guided the king's command. By the time of the New Kingdom, courts such as the local court at Deir el-Medina served communities to provide objective arbitration for citizens. Also in the New Kingdom, pharaohs such as Horemhab and Seti I issued edicts and decrees to address specific problems and to institute sweeping changes throughout Egypt.

CHAPTER 2

Ancient Egyptian Concepts of Justice & Jurisprudence

§2.01 Introduction

In the Egyptian "judgment of the dead," the god Horus (the falcon-headed god) weighs the heart of the deceased (the heart symbolically represents the "soul"—*ba*) in the scales against an ostrich feather. The woman who accompanies Horus is the goddess Ma'at, who symbolizes justice. The ostrich feather is Ma'at's symbol. She is often depicted wearing this "feather of truth" on her head, as something like a hat. The scene of Horus and Ma'at weighing the heart of the departed is the judgment in the underworld; and, as far as the ancient Egyptians were concerned, this was *the judgment*. If the heart is heavier than the feather, that means that it is heavy with evil deeds (*i.e.*, not full of truth and justice). When that happens, a special beast (the "devourer") summarily eats the departed. On the other hand, if the heart balances with the feather (*i.e.*, if it is in balance with justice), that means that the soul is full of righteousness, goodness, truth, and justice, and ought not be terminated.[1] Thoth, the sacred god of scribes, also attends this weighing-in ceremony as evaluator (a court reporter, perhaps) and records the results. This visual representation provides an introduction to at least some aspects of how ancient Egyptians might have perceived justice.[2] It seems simplistic. But it was so important to the ancient Egyptians that they made it a central part of their theology.[3]

1. *See* Grimal, Ancient Egypt 153.
2. *See* Breasted, Development of Religion and Thought 35 (Noting that when the tribunal of gods at Heliopolis restored Osiris' throne "to him against the claims of Set," Osiris was given the epithet "justified."). *See also Id.* (Breasted asserts that the term "justified" "must have been a legal term already in use when this episode in the myth took form."); *Id.* at 147.
3. *See* David Lorton, *The Treatment of Criminals in Ancient Egypt*, 20 J. Economic & Social Hist. Orient 2, 4 (1977).

To a certain degree, it is inappropriate for us 4,000 years later, based on the small amount of evidence that we have, to try to generalize about what an ancient Egyptian thought, on a deep level, about right and wrong. As James says: "The precise definition of law in ancient Egypt is difficult to achieve because the evidence is both thin and scattered over many centuries. It has, in addition, an elusive quality which hinders precision of definition.... Egyptian law was an integrated system of statute, precedent, practice and, to a limited extent, religious principle."[4] Indeed, as a rule, it is often impossible to separate the secular from the religious in analyzing ancient Egypt.[5] There are strong religious overtones in nearly everything that the Egyptians did. Therefore, although this judgment scene is, strictly speaking, a religious representation, it still serves as a useful starting point for reflecting on and appraising the ancient Egyptians' sense of law and justice.

§2.02 Ma'at

We must begin the discussion of justice and jurisprudence by considering *ma'at*. As a goddess, *Ma'at* held an important place in the Egyptian pantheon.[6] As an abstract concept, *ma'at* significantly influenced individual and collective conduct in the daily life of the Egyptians. In mythology, *Ma'at* was the daughter of the sun god, Re. As mentioned before, when a person was judged after death, Ma'at's symbol, the ostrich feather of truth, was weighed against the deceased's heart.[7] The goddess *Ma'at* was also important to

---

4. T.G.H. JAMES, PHARAOH'S PEOPLE: SCENES FROM LIFE IN IMPERIAL EGYPT 62 (1984).

5. *See generally* Jan Assman, *When Justice Fails: Jurisdiction and Imprecation in Ancient Egypt and the Near East*, 78 J. EGYPTIAN ARCHAEOLOGY 149 (1992).

6. *See* J. Gwyn Griffiths, *Isis as Maat, Dikaiosune, and Iustitia, in* 3 HOMMAGES A JEAN LECLANT 255, 256 (1994) ("On the one hand, she is said to have had no cult-places according to the Coffin Texts nor any temple of her own prior to the New Kingdom. On the other hand, she is said to have been venerated by her own priesthood 'from the 5th Dynasty at the latest'.") (footnotes omitted).

7. *See Id.* at 257. *See also* GRIMAL, ANCIENT EGYPT 47; Erik Iversen, *The Hieroglyphic Tradition*, in THE LEGACY OF EGYPT 170 (J.R. Harris ed., 2d ed. 1971) (Explaining that this curious admixture of myth and reality in the form of *Ma'at* may, in part, be explained by "the particular 'pre-Aristotelian' logic of the Egyptians, based on an indomitable faith and belief in the magical nature of things and the aetiological reality of myths."); BREASTED, DEVELOPMENT OF RELIGION AND THOUGHT 173 (Breasted recognizes the "legal form and legal process" by which the deceased was judged.); *Id.* at 299 (Furthermore, "[w]hereas the judgment hereafter is mentioned as far back as the Pyramid Age, we now [in the New Kingdom] find a full account and description of it in the Book of the Dead.").

Furthermore, the Egyptian habit of concretizing what we today would consider

judges and to their sense of duty. Judges were considered "priests of *Ma'at*," and some wore a small figure of the goddess as a pendant around their necks to symbolize their judicial office.[8] To the ancient Egyptians, the concept *ma'at* was a central overriding principle in law. *Ma'at* represented a universal harmony and order—the way that things are supposed to be.[9] *Ma'at* became the focal point of the legal system. *Ma'at* represented the natural order and balance of life in ancient Egypt. It had a religious, ethical, and moral connotation. It was the guiding principle for all aspects of life and represented the values that all people sought.[10] According to Wilson, *ma'at* "is an attribute which imposes responsibilities upon the king, since it involves conformance with principles of the universe which come down from the creation or it involves right-dealing among humans. This *ma'at* is the most important of the divine attributes of the king.... [*M*]*a'at*, in this sense of truth, order, or regularity, belonged to the world which the gods set up at creation."[11] "On a cosmic scale it represented order as opposed to primeval chaos; an order maintained through truth, justice, balance, tradition, and the virtually whole inventory of Egyptian principles."[12]

Grimal observes: "Ma'at occupies a unique place in the Egyptian pantheon: she is not so much a goddess as an abstract entity. She represents the equilibrium which the universe has reached through the process of creation, enabling it to conform to its true nature. As such, she is moderator of all things, from justice to the integration of a dead man's soul into the universal order at the time of the final judgment."[13]

---

abstract is not surprising: "The most striking feature of Egyptian [*i.e.*, the Egyptian language] in all its stages is its concrete *realism*, its preoccupation with exterior objects and occurrences to the neglect of those more subjective distinctions which play so prominent a part in modern, and even in the classical, languages." GARDINER, EGYPTIAN GRAMMAR 4.

8. *See* Nili Shupak, *A New Source For the Study of the Judiciary and Law of Ancient Egypt: "The Tale of the Eloquent Peasant"*, 51 J. NEAR E. STUD. 1, 15 (1992) (footnote omitted). *See also* BEDELL. CRIMINAL LAW 10; ERMAN, LIFE IN ANCIENT EGYPT 139.

9. *See* LEXIKON DER ÄGYPTOLGIE, Vol. 5 (1984), "Recht" 183; GRIMAL, ANCIENT EGYPT 75; BEDELL. CRIMINAL LAW 11 ("Maat, as one of the attributes of the Egyptian state, was expressed in right-dealing in relation to persons and situations, it was not recorded in statutes and precedents.") (footnote omitted); ERMAN, LIFE IN ANCIENT EGYPT 139; BREASTED, DEVELOPMENT OF RELIGION & THOUGHT 166.

10. *See* LEXIKON DER ÄGYPTOLGIE, Vol. 5 (1984), "Recht" 183.

11. John A. Wilson, *Authority and Law in Ancient Egypt*, Supplement to 40 J. AM. ORIENTAL SOC. 2 (1954). *See also* Jan Assman, *When Justice Fails: Jurisdiction and Imprecation in Ancient Egypt and the Near East*, 78 J. EGYPTIAN ARCHAEOLOGY 149, 151 (1992) ("the Egyptian term *Maat* could refer both to cosmic and social order, truth and justice.") (footnote omitted).

12. MCDOWELL, JURISDICTION 23 (footnote omitted).

13. GRIMAL, ANCIENT EGYPT 47.

Perhaps the most lucid and insightful explanation of *ma'at* as an abstract principle is Wilson's discussion in his book *The Culture of Ancient Egypt*. Wilson describes *ma'at* as a concept that is:

> variously translated as "truth," "justice," "righteousness," "order," and so on. Each of those translations may be apt in a certain context, but no one English word is always applicable. *Ma'at* was a quality which belonged to good rule or administration, but it cannot be translated as "rule," "government," "administration," or "law." *Ma'at* was the proper quality of such applied functions. Basically, *ma'at* had some of the same flexibility as our English terms "right," "just," "true," and "in order." It was the cosmic force of harmony, order, stability, and security, coming down from the first creation as the organizing quality of created phenomena and reaffirmed at the accession of each god-king of Egypt. In the temple scenes the pharaoh exhibited *ma'at* to the other gods every day, as the physical evidence that he was carrying out his divine function of rule on their behalf. Thus there was something of the unchanging, eternal, and cosmic about *ma'at*. If we render it "order," it was the order of created things, physical and spiritual, established at the beginning and valid for all time. If we render it "justice," it was not simply justice in terms of legal administration; it was the just and proper relationship of cosmic phenomena, including the relationship of the rulers and the ruled. If we render it "truth," we must remember that, to the ancient, things were true not because they were susceptible of testing and verification but because they were recognized as being in their true and proper places in the order created and maintained by the gods. *Ma'at*, then was a created and inherited rightness, which tradition built up into a concept of orderly stability, in order to confirm and consolidate the *status quo*, particularly the continuing rule of the pharaoh. The opposites of *ma'at* were words which we translate as "lying," "falsehood," and "deceit." That which was not consonant with the established and accepted order could be denied as being false. *Ma'at* comes closest to the moral connotation of our word "good."[14]

---

14. Wilson, Culture of Ancient Egypt 48. *See also* Warburton, State and Economy in Ancient Egypt 56 (Discussing *ma'at* as "a concept of 'justice' as opposed to dominance [that] must play a role in the concept of the state, being subsumed under the rubric of 'custom', as the concept evolves through time."); Nili Shupak, *A New Source For the Study of the Judiciary and Law of Ancient Egypt: "The Tale of the Eloquent Peasant"*, 51 J. Near E. Stud. 1, 15 (1992). According to Shupak:

> *Ma'at* is a central conception of the legal world of ancient Egypt, denoting order, honesty, and justice. It relates not simply to the activities of human life but to the cosmos in general. *Ma'at* was the order of the universe ever

Tobin sums it up well when he states: "To the Egyptian mind, *ma'at* bound all things together in an indestructible unity: the universe, the natural world, the state, and the individual were all seen as parts of the wider order generated by *ma'at*."[15] In many respects, it is a concept that reminds us of what we refer to as "natural law."[16]

§ 2.03 Justice & Jurisprudence

[A] Overview

In addition to the universal concept of *ma'at*, several other precepts and values that were important in the minds of the ancient Egyptians helped to shape the character of justice and legal philosophy. In his tomb inscription, the vizier Rekhmire (*c.* 1479–1425 B.C.) articulated his approach to the administration of justice. Here we see aspects of his legal philosophy manifest in his recorded deeds:

> I judged both [the insignificant] and the influential; I rescued the weak man from the strong man; I deflected the fury of the evil man and subdued the greedy man in his hour... I succoured the widow who has no husband; I established the son and heir on the seat of his father. I gave [bread to the hungry], water to the thirsty, and meat, oil and clothes to him who had nothing... I was not at all deaf to the indigent. Indeed I never took a bribe from anyone....[17]

Prominent among the influential precepts and values in Egyptian jurisprudence are the following: 1) a strong preference for tradition as opposed to change (and a belief closely linked to tradition—the conviction that the world was basically secure and operating in a fixed, regular, routine, and natural order—*ma'at*); 2) a view that rhetorical skill should be esteemed; and, 3) as Rekhmire's inscription illustrates, a desire to achieve impartiality and social equality.

---

since its creation by the god Ra'; and the Egyptian king, as Ra''s representative on earth, was responsible for the preservation of *ma'at*.

15. Vincent Tobin, *Ma'at and Dike: Some Comparative Considerations of Egyptian and Greek Thought*, 24 J. AM. RESEARCH CENTER IN EGYPT 113 (1987).

16. *See infra* § 2.04[D].

17. T.G.H. JAMES, PHARAOH'S PEOPLE: SCENES FROM LIFE IN IMPERIAL EGYPT 57 (1984). *See also* BEDELL, CRIMINAL LAW 20 (Referring to the instructions for Rekhmire when he was installed as vizier. According to Bedell, "the vizier, as supreme judge, and the judges of local courts throughout Egypt were equipped with laws and instructions given directly by Pharaoh."). For other references to Rekhmire, *see infra* §§ 3.04, 4.01, 4.02, 5.01, and 5.04[B], note 107.

[B] Tradition & Security

No civilization has ever been so attached to tradition as the ancient Nile dwellers. They were conservative in the extreme.[18] One explanation of why traditional things were settled and immutable is that nature supplied the Egyptians a secure world with fixed, harmonic routines. First, the topography of the Nile valley provided inherent protection from foreign invasion. Second, the consistent annual inundation of the river fostered a confidence in the orderliness of life and dictated recurring rituals, farming practices, and legal proceedings (*e.g.*, redrawing property boundaries).[19] This reverence for the past influenced the development of law in at least two ways that are actually interconnected. First, judges kept records of their legal decisions in the vizier's archives so that they could consult them later as precedent.[20] Consequently, and this is the second result of the Egyptian veneration for tradition, Egyptian law was very slow to evolve.[21] The convention of vigorously following precedent meant that laws tended to remain in force without modification for extremely long periods of time.[22]

---

18. *See* Christopher J. Eyre, *Peasants and "Modern" Leasing Strategies in Ancient Egypt*, 40 J. ECONOMIC & SOCIAL HIST. ORIENT 367, 367–68 (1997); GARDINER, EGYPT OF THE PHARAOHS 56 ("one of the most characteristic traits of the Egyptian habit of mind... [was] the extraordinary attachment to the traditional as opposed to the actual, in fact a conservatism of expression without parallel elsewhere in the world. No other people has ever shown a greater reverence for what was by them termed 'the time of the ancestors' 'the time of the god', or 'the first occasion'. Occasionally this love of the time honored and the typical led to downright falsification."). *But see infra* § 2.04[A] n. 39 (Discussing the flexible nature of *Ma'at*).

19. *See* GRIMAL, ANCIENT EGYPT 17 ("The internal geographic unity... contributed to the apparent lack of change."); *Id.* at 51 (Regarding the regularity of the Nile's flooding.); GARDINER, EGYPT OF THE PHARAOHS 37 ("Taking all in all, Egypt in her early days was about as happily isolated as any continental country could be to develop her own highly individual culture."). *See also Id.* at 27 (In Chapter III, "The Land, its Neighbors, and Resources," Gardiner discusses the regularity of the Nile's inundation. The regularity of the annual inundation must have had a positive effect on the Egyptians' sense of law and order and their respect for law.); WILSON, CULTURE OF ANCIENT EGYPT 13 (Wilson describes the regularity of the inundation and discusses its positive effects on the collective perception of security of the ancient Egyptians.).

20. *See* Aristide Théodorides, *The Concept of Law in Ancient Egypt, in* THE LEGACY OF EGYPT 291, 308 (J.R. Harris ed., 2d ed. 1971). *See also* BEDELL, CRIMINAL LAW 15 (Noting that we do not know whether records of cases were kept in small town and village courts.). *See also infra* § 4.02.

21. *See* GARDINER, EGYPT OF THE PHARAOHS 56.

22. *See* Aristide Théodorides, *The Concept of Law in Ancient Egypt, in* THE LEGACY OF EGYPT 291, 294 (J.R. Harris ed., 2d ed. 1971) (Noting that, in the Old Kingdom, the "king was in supreme control of legislation, but laws were conceived as expressions of

[C] Rhetoric

The Egyptians valued the ability to speak persuasively.[23] Many works of Middle Kingdom literature teach the importance of skillful speech. The Egyptians of the Middle Kingdom (*c.* 2040–1674 B.C.) recognized that one's ability to speak could make or break a case. For example, in one work that was probably composed in the Middle Kingdom—but set in the First Intermediate Period—*The Teaching for Merikare*, "[s]tress is laid on the ability to speak well and persuasively, and imitation of the ancient models is strongly recommended...."[24] King Khety III (*c.* 2150 B.C.) advises Merikare: "Be skillful in speech, that you may be strong; [...] it is the strength of [...] the tongue, and words are braver than all fighting...."[25] However, there is a duality here too, for in the same text, Merikare is counseled: "A talker is a mischief-maker; suppress him, kill [him], erase his name, [destroy] his kinfolk, suppress the remembrance of him and his partisans who love him."[26] In another Middle Kingdom work of fiction, *The Shipwrecked Sailor*, the sailor says: "For the speech of a man saves him, and his words gain him indulgence."[27] The sailor's statement, however, could also be translated, "It is the speech of a man which takes him away" (*i.e.*, a man's speech can get him carted off to forced labor or prison). The verb *nḥm* can mean both "save, rescue" as well as "take away, carry off."[28] Thus, assuming that the sailor's use of *nḥm* is intended as a *double entendre* for both "save" and "take away," the sailor's assertion recognizes that a rhetorician can win his case with persuasive advocacy but that he can also lose his case (and his freedom) without it.[29]

---

ideal justice. A law promulgated...remained in force so long as it was neither modified nor abrogated....").

23. *See* Wilson, Culture of Ancient Egypt 123 ("We wish to emphasize the high value which the period put upon speaking out on one's own behalf."). For more on the Egyptian regard for skillful speaking, *see Id.* at 302.

24. Gardiner, Egypt of the Pharaohs 115. *See also* Grimal, Ancient Egypt 146–147.

25. Simpson, The Literature of Ancient Egypt 181. *See* Grimal, Ancient Egypt 146 (Grimal asserts that Khety III was probably the author of *The Teaching for Merikare* even though "he is not actually named, but he is known to have been the predecessor of Merikare, for whom the advice was intended.").

26. Simpson, The Literature of Ancient Egypt 181.

27. *Id.* at 51.

28. R.O. Faulkner, A Concise Dictionary of Middle Egyptian 136 (1981).

29. In many respects a *double entendre* seems entirely consistent with the clever personality of the sailor. There is something in his wry character that gives us the impression that he is often speaking with tongue-in-cheek. For example, at one moment, he tells us that the sailors aboard his ship could predict a storm even before the clouds

To a great extent, the legal process itself is fundamentally an attempt to reach a result that both parties involved in a controversy are willing to accept. In order to function fairly, a legal process must also allow adversaries to explain their conflicting points of view. The Egyptian zest for rhetorical craft facilitated a robust legal process and enhanced the capacity for Egyptian courts to reach just results.

[D] Impartiality & Social Equality

Impartiality and equality are core concepts and essential components of basic fairness. These notions dictate that persons who are situated similarly ought to be treated similarly before the law. In the history of Egypt, the pinnacle of concern for legal neutrality occurred during the late First Intermediate Period (*c.* 2200–2040 B.C.) and Middle Kingdom (*c.* 2040–1674 B.C.).[30] The instructions for the vizier Merikare (mentioned above) emphasize the importance of judging objectively:

---

had gathered. Yet, immediately we discover that a storm overtakes the ship before they are able to make port.

From a linguistic standpoint, it is entirely possible that the sailor's use of *nḥm* here was meant and was understood as a *double entendre*. In his *A Concise Dictionary of Middle Egyptian*, Faulkner cites several examples of *nḥm* from *The Admonitions of an Egyptian Sage, The Eloquent Peasant,* and *Sinuhe* (all of which are most certainly of Middle Kingdom origin, and, therefore, roughly contemporary with *The Shipwrecked Sailor*). R.O. FAULKNER, A CONCISE DICTIONARY OF MIDDLE EGYPTIAN 136. In these examples, there are some in which *nḥm* is used to mean "save, rescue" (clearly with positive overtones) and others in which it means "take away, carry off" (with decidedly negative or pejorative connotations). In *The Admonitions of an Egyptian Sage*, *nḥm* occurs once. In that instance it means "save, rescue": "Is he brave and does he save himself?" (*in ḳni-f nḥm-f sw*) (*Admonitions of an Egyptian Sage* 13,3). In *The Eloquent Peasant nḥm* twice means "take away, carry off": "Behold, Peasant, I am going to take away your donkey!" (*mk wi r nḥm '3-k sḪty*) (*Eloquent Peasant* B1,11); and "You take away the very complaint from my mouth." (*nḥm-k rf nhwt m r-i*) (*Eloquent Peasant* B1,28). The author of *Sinuhe* uses *nḥm* three times. Twice it means "save, rescue": "I saved the man who was robbed." (*nḥm-n-i 'w3y*) (*Sinuhe.* B97); and "You who have saved me from death." (*nḥm wi m mt*) (*Sinuhe* B203). Once it has the meaning "take away, carry off": "Their food was taken" (*nḥm wnmt-sn*) (*Sinuhe* B104). These examples clearly show that both meanings were well understood in the Middle Kingdom. That the literate audience of that period was aware of both possible meanings for *nḥm* is best illustrated in *Sinuhe* where the author uses the same word but in both contexts (*i.e.*, to mean "save" and "take away.").

30. *See generally* WILSON, CULTURE OF ANCIENT EGYPT 114–124 (Wilson characterizes the First Intermediate Period and beginning of the Middle Kingdom as a time when the Egyptians first embraced the concept of social justice.). *See Id.* at 115 (Wilson remarks that "a concept of equality was theoretically possible."); *Id.* at 114 ("Before 2000 B.C., many centuries before the prophets Amos and Hosea, Egypt came close to the realization that the individual man had personal rights to just treatment. If she

> The abomination of the god is a show of partiality. So this is the instruction; thou shalt act accordingly: thou shalt look upon him whom thou knowest like him whom thou dost not know, upon him who is close to thy person like him who is distant from thy house. As for the official who acts thus, he will flourish here in this office.[31]

In the same instruction, "the creator-god states that he has made all men equal in opportunity and that, if there be any violation of this equality, the fault is man's."[32] The early Middle Kingdom was a time when the Egyptians developed in their legal perspective a:

> disregard of political or economic barriers in the belief that all men have equal rights and opportunities—or should have such. It seems clear...that there was a belief in social justice for everybody at this time and that even the poorest man had rights to the gifts of the gods because the creator-god "made every man like his fellow."[33]

Wilson interprets this outlook as unique in human history, commenting: "When we consider that they stood more than a thousand years ahead of similar thinking by the Hebrews and the Greeks, we must give them all credit for a sublime vision."[34]

---

fell short of realization of that great dream or if she soon abandoned her search for social justice, we may still recognize that the ancient Egyptian had the capacity to see a broader base for human good and can only regret that her discovery was too early in human history to gain any lasting root."); *Id.* at 123 ("This was Egypt's democratic age." "By 'democracy' in our context we do not mean a form of government in which the sovereign power resided or was thought to reside with the people at large; we are using, rather, the secondary but common meaning of social equalitarianism, the disregard of political or economic barriers in the belief that all men have equal rights and opportunities—or should have such. It seems clear...that there was a belief in social justice for everybody at this time and that even the poorest man had rights to the gifts of the gods...." "[T]his age insisted that *ma'at* reached down to embrace the lowliest Egyptian and that he had a right to insist upon such democratic coverage from his rulers.").

31. *Id.* at 173 (footnote omitted).

32. *Id.* at 117. *See also* Aristide Théodorides, *The Concept of Law in Ancient Egypt, in* The Legacy of Egypt 291, 307–308 (J.R. Harris ed., 2d ed. 1971) (The Instructions for the Vizier, whose "composition must go back to the 13th Dynasty," say that "justice is to be rendered in public and in such a way that every individual shall always secure his rights. To this end, appeal is made to a sense of equity and also, by implication, to jurisprudence....") (footnote omitted).

33. Wilson, Culture of Ancient Egypt 123. *See also Id.* at 314 ("[T]he Egyptians discovered the worth of the common man and insisted upon his sacred right to justice.").

34. *Id.* at 124.

§ 2.04 Ma'at, Justice, & Jurisprudence in *The Tale of the Eloquent Peasant*

[A] General

The Tale of the Eloquent Peasant[35] offers a wealth of material relating to ancient Egyptian notions of justice and jurisprudence. Three jurisprudential principles in the story stand out from the rest. First, justice is something that should be available to the poor and disadvantaged on a basis equal with the rich. Secondly, the story suggests that law is fundamentally a natural force, like the sun, wind, wild animals, or current in the Nile. Third, it implies that a judge's primary duty is to control the natural force of law. Careful examination of these specific themes and concrete images in the peasant's rhetoric help us to better appreciate the sophistication and subtleties of his opinions about justice and legal philosophy.

In an attempt to recover his livestock, Khunanup first pleads with Nemtynakhte for ten days in vain.[36] He then takes his case to Nemtynakhte's landlord, Rensi, the High Steward of Ninsu. The majority of the story is actually Khunanup's nine speeches wherein he appeals to Rensi. After Khunanup's first speech, Rensi tells the King, Nebkaure, about Khunanup's appeal. Nebkaure, in turn, commands that Rensi pretend to ignore Khunanup, thereby causing him to return on a daily basis to plead his case. Meanwhile, Nebkaure also tells Rensi to enlist scribes to transcribe Khunanup's arguments for posterity, and the king also makes sure that Khunanup's family is cared for while he remains in Ninsu to plead his case.[37]

Khunanup's speeches employ multiple arguments which beseech the judge, Rensi, to act justly. As such, his entreaties reflect ancient Egyptian legal philosophy. These arguments, however, have nothing to do with the merits of Khunanup's case against Nemtynakhte.[38] They are predomi-

---

35. *See supra* § 1.02.

36. SIMPSON, THE LITERATURE OF ANCIENT EGYPT 34 ("And the peasant spent a period of ten days appealing to Nemtynakhte, but he paid no attention to it.").

37. At the story's end, Rensi has someone read aloud all nine entreaties for Khunanup to hear: "Well, stay here that you may hear your petitions. And he had [them] read out from a new papyrus-roll, each petition according to [its] contents." SIMPSON, THE LITERATURE OF ANCIENT EGYPT 48–49.

38. Apparently, as a matter of procedure, Khunanup had already argued the facts and relevant points of law when he presented the case to Rensi's "servant of choice." Nevertheless, Shupak argues that "[t]he work is written in the form of a complaint made before a judge...." Nili Shupak, *A New Source For the Study of the Judiciary and*

nantly plain and simple appeals to the judge to act justly and in accordance with law. He frequently implores Rensi not to be tempted by bribes and not to be influenced by the fact that he (*i.e.*, Khunanup) is a poor man. Thus, macroscopically, this tale is an exhortation to the judiciary to ignore class distinctions in decisionmaking and to concentrate, rather, on what is right.[39] Indeed, in the Middle Kingdom (*c.* 2040–1674 B.C.) "[i]t was... not only religious belief and social axiom, but also formally announced royal policy, that before the bar of justice the great and the powerful must expect the same treatment and the same verdict accorded to the poor and the friendless."[40]

The peasant's rhetoric invokes a number of themes and concrete images to drive home his points. It will be useful for us to evaluate the peasant's use of these themes and images; namely: 1) the proper role of judges in decisionmaking; 2) the role of rhetoric itself; and, 3) the various metaphors that he weaves together involving: a) nature; b) the gods; c) humans; and, d) boating.

[B] Judges & Decisionmaking

In his fourth petition, Khunanup advises Rensi that justice comes through patience: "be / patient, that you may learn justice...."[41] Indeed, this

---

Law of Ancient Egypt: "The Tale of the Eloquent Peasant", 51 J. Near E. Stud. 1, 4 (1992).

39. *See* Wilson, Culture of Ancient Egypt 120 (Wilson observes that *The Tale of the Eloquent Peasant* "gives us the clear argument that *ma'at*- justice was not a neutral maintenance of past order or a negative repair of breaches of order but a positive search for new good."); *Id.* at 120–122 (Wilson interprets *The Tale of the Eloquent Peasant* and other Middle Kingdom texts as important for our understanding of *ma'at* and the broadened scope of that concept in the Middle Kingdom.); *Id.* at 122 ("*Ma'at* in the texts of this age did not carry its customary connotation of static order; it was not a matter of the pharaoh offering *ma'at* to the gods in token of the fact that the god-given order was stable and unchanging. *Ma'at* here was the positive force of social justice, of man's humanity to man. It was a magistrate who could be likened to the ferryman who carried over the poor widow without exacting a fare. It was a king who could be likened to a herdsman who wearied himself on behalf of his flock. In this near-democratic age, the emphasis was not upon the rights of the ruler but upon the rights of the ruled.").

40. Breasted, Development of Religion and Thought 252. *Cf.* Jon Manchip White, Everyday Life in Ancient Egypt 131 (1963) (White makes the dubious claim that "questions of right and wrong were civil questions, not religious ones. Morality was a social and legal matter, whereas religion was mainly concerned with magic.").

41. Simpson, The Literature of Ancient Egypt 42.

is somewhat humorous since Rensi surely must be patient to listen to Khunanup's multiple petitions. Also in the fourth petition, Khunanup offers yet another tidbit of wisdom regarding management of a judge's caseload. "Pass over a case, and it will become two."[42] In addition, a judge who fails to do his job sets a bad example: "As for the judge who ought to be punished, he is a pattern for the wrongdoer."[43] The sixth petition begins with several positive images of the good judge. Good judges "lighten (the weight of) falsehood, foster truth, foster all good and destroy evil...."[44] Khunanup also generalizes about justice: "The purloiner diminishes justice, so render good and full account; then justice will be neither filched from nor excessive."[45] Khunanup characterizes justice as a universal concept, not confined to life on earth: "But justice is for eternity, and it goes down with him who does it into the realm of the dead... his name is not obliterated on earth and he is remembered for goodness...."[46] When Khunanup says "his name," he arguably refers to the name of a conscientious judge. As his arguments draw to a close in the ninth petition, Khunanup bluntly asserts that punishment is an appropriate remedy in particular situations: "Deal punishment to him who ought to be punished, and none shall resemble your rectitude."[47] This suggests that determining guilt and meting out punishment are precisely what judges are supposed to do.

[C] The Role of Rhetoric

In the second petition, Khunanup offers an interesting observation about the plasticity of rhetoric. He says: "It means that a twister of speech from its exact sense / makes a travesty of it...."[48] The importance of oral advocacy for Khunanup is paramount. His rhetoric is, after all, the skill that has caused Rensi and the King to treat him with special care and respect. The significance of Khunanup's rhetorical ability calls to mind references to speech and its importance in other Middle Egyptian texts.[49]

---

42. *Id.* Faulkner footnotes this sentence explaining that "a problem shelved becomes doubly difficult." *Id.* at 42, n.54. Perhaps we would say "a stitch in time saves nine."

43. *Id.* at 43.

44. *Id.*

45. *Id.* at 44.

46. *Id.* at 46–47.

47. *Id.* at 47.

48. *Id.* at 37.

49. *See supra* §§ 1.01 and 2.03[C].

[D] Man's Control of Nature & Nature Itself

In his second speech, Khunanup addresses the judge, Rensi. He calls him the "Steering Oar of heaven, beam of earth, plumbline which carries the weight! O Steering oar, do not diverge; O Beam, do not tilt; O Plumbline, do not swing awry."[50] These metaphors are illuminating. Each—an oar, a beam, and a plumbline—is a man-made, physical device used by humans to control or measure natural forces. An oar makes it possible for people to direct their path in the water and temporarily to subvert the current and the wind. A wooden architectural beam contains the force of gravity.[51] A plumbline uses gravity as a means to achieve or test verticality. Similarly, a judge is one who controls the law. Thus, these metaphors suggest that Rensi, like the oar, beam, and plumbline, is in a position to control a natural force too: namely, law. Perhaps, then, the ancient Egyptians viewed justice as being something like the forces of nature; a river's current, wind, or gravity. These images imply that Khunanup viewed law as a universal constant: a natural law.[52] It would be understandable if the ancient Egyptians perceived law as a natural phenomenon. As has been noted earlier,[53] the regularity of the Nile's annual inundation must have instilled in the minds of the ancient Egyptians a confidence in the natural order of the universe.[54]

Again in his third petition, Khunanup portrays justice as a physical device used to control or measure the natural order, like scales which are controlled by the force of gravity: "Will the balance deflect? Will the stand-balance incline to one side?"[55] Similarly, in the third petition, the peasant asserts:

---

50. SIMPSON, THE LITERATURE OF ANCIENT EGYPT 36.

51. It is also possible that the "beam" is the central piece of a scale. *See infra* § 2.04[D], note 54 and accompanying text.

52. *See generally* JEROME HALL, FOUNDATIONS OF JURISPRUDENCE 21–53 (1973).

53. *See supra* § 2.03[B].

54. *See generally* GARDINER, EGYPT OF THE PHARAOHS 27–44.

55. SIMPSON, THE LITERATURE OF ANCIENT EGYPT 39. Scales are a symbol of impartiality. *See* Nili Shupak, *A New Source For the Study of the Judiciary and Law of Ancient Egypt: "The Tale of the Eloquent Peasant"*, 51 J. NEAR E. STUD. 1, 16, n. 57 (1992) ("As in the case of the scales, which record an incorrect weight as a result of being unbalanced, so does the liar harm the norm of justice. For this reason, the judge overseeing justice is compared to a pair of scales and to a plummet and parts of his body to parts of the scales."). In his discussion of *The Eloquent Peasant*, Breasted notes that the scales "form a symbol which became widely current in Egyptian life, till the scales appear as the graphic means of depicting the judgment of each soul in the hereafter." BREASTED, DEVELOPMENT OF RELIGION AND THOUGHT 221–222. Breasted also relates a story of a vizier who perhaps went too far in his attempt to appear impartial:

In the Feudal Age [*i.e.*, the Middle Kingdom], a thousand years after the rise

> The true balancing of the land is the doing of justice; do not speak falsehood, for you are great; / do not be light, for you are weighty; do not speak falsehood, for you are the balance; do not swerve, for you are rectitude. See, you are on one level with the balance; if it tilt, then you may tilt.[56]

Also, in the third petition, he tells Rensi: "Your tongue is the plummet, your heart is the weight,[57] your lips are its arm."[58] In the sixth petition, he continues this motif, describing a good judge as clothing for nakedness and a fire to cook raw food.[59]

Khunanup persists in using scale imagery to describe the judiciary: "Is he a balance? It does not tilt. Is he a stand-balance? It does not incline to one side." "Does a balance tilt? It is its scalepans which weigh things..."[60] Finally, he continues with scale images in the ninth petition: "Their tongue is men's stand-balance, and it is the balance which searches out deficiencies."[61] The prevalence of imagery representing man-made objects that are used to control and harness nature is striking. Such images imply that the ancient Egyptians considered law a natural force and considered that a judge's task was to manage and direct that natural force.

Khunanup perceives justice as a natural function, like breathing, shade, shelter, food, warmth, water, and a flooding river. He says: "'The doing of justice is breath to the nose.'"[62] "Shade, do not act as the sun-heat; Shelter, do not let the crocodile take." The statement, "his possessions are (the very) breath to a poor man, and to take them away is to stop up his nose,"[63] echoes the peasant's earlier references to those who provide support for children, wives, and other dependents. A good judge is satiety for hunger, the sky's warmth for the cold, and water for thirst.[64] In the eighth petition,

---

> of the Old Kingdom, at the installation of the vizier, that official used to be referred to the example of an ancient vizier who had already become proverbial in the Pyramid Age. The cause of his enduring reputation was that he had decided a case, in which his relatives were involved, against his own kin, no matter what the merits of the case might be, lest he should be accused of partial judgment in favor of his own family.

Id. at 167 (footnote omitted). *See also Id.* at 243–244.

56. SIMPSON, THE LITERATURE OF ANCIENT EGYPT 40.
57. Perhaps this is *Ma'at* personified.
58. SIMPSON, THE LITERATURE OF ANCIENT EGYPT 40.
59. *Id.* at 44.
60. *Id.* at 47.
61. *Id.*
62. *Id.* at 39.
63. *Id.* at 43.
64. *Id.* at 43–44.

Khunanup characterizes good judges as "shelter from the aggressive."[65] The petitions also, not surprisingly, contain references to the inundation of the Nile. In the third petition, Khunanup argues that Rensi must "[r]estrain the robber, take counsel for the poor man... [and that he must]... not become an inundation against the petitioner."[66] The end of the fifth petition returns to the theme that Rensi is failing to do his duty as judge.

> You were appointed to hear pleas, / to judge between suitors and to repress the robber, but see, what you do is to support the thief! Men trust in you, and you have become a transgressor. You were appointed to be a dam for the poor man; beware lest he drown, for see, you are a swift current to him.[67]

Here, Khunanup has defined what he perceives the judge's role should be, and has used yet one more image of the river.

[E] Gods

Khunanup opens his third petition by invoking Rensi as both the sun god, Re, and as the Nile god, Hapy.[68] The Pyramid Texts of the Old Kingdom indicate that there was a strong connection between the sun god, Re, and justice.[69] Indeed, "it was the Sun-god... who was the earliest champion of moral worthiness and the great judge in the hereafter."[70] Breasted specifically notes that the Pyramid Texts make clear the nexus between a person's moral conduct on earth and prosperity in the hereafter.[71] The god Hapy represented the river Nile during its inundation phase.[72] Consequently, Khunanup here equates the judge with two gods who represent tremendous natural forces: the sun which brings light; and the Nile at the time that it brings rich soil to fertilize the valley.

He then, in the seventh and eighth petitions, evokes the god Thoth, telling Rensi: "you are the companion of Thoth, who judges without show-

---

65. *Id.* at 46.

66. *Id.* at 39. Apparently, the judge and not the flood itself should be the one who controls the flooding.

67. *Id.* at 43.

68. *Id.* at 39 ("O High Steward my lord! You are Re, lord of heaven, with your entourage, and the sustenance of all men is you, even like the flood; you are Hapy, who makes green the meadows and furnishes the wasted tracts.").

69. *See* BREASTED, DEVELOPMENT OF RELIGION AND THOUGHT 172.

70. *Id.* at 176.

71. *Id.* at 176–98. *See also* GRIMAL, ANCIENT EGYPT 126.

72. MANFRED LURKER, THE GODS AND SYMBOLS OF ANCIENT EGYPT 57 (Barbara Cummings trans., 1980) (1974).

ing partiality."[73] "You pen, papyrus, and palette of Thoth, beware of making trouble...."[74] The reference to Thoth is interesting. According to Breasted, in the judgment scene of the Coffin Texts of the Middle Kingdom, Thoth appears "as an advocate of the accused" "before the Sun-god..."[75] "Thoth having been, according to the Solar myth, the vizier of the Sun-god."[76]

[F] Humans

In his first petition, Khunanup addresses Rensi with a series of human metaphors. In one sense, it is plain that the peasant merely intends to flatter Rensi. Nevertheless, to the extent that a judge personifies justice, these metaphors also reflect what the author of this tale thought about law and justice. Khunanup calls Rensi "a father to the orphan, a husband to the widow, a brother to her who is divorced, a garment to the motherless."[77] The father, husband, and brother in these examples are people[78] who render assistance to a dependent who has had something taken away from them: the orphan has lost his parents and both the widow and divorcee have lost their husbands. Similarly, the garment serves as a substitute for the warmth and protection of a child's mother. In like fashion, although Khunanup has lost neither a parent nor spouse, he has lost his possessions—the very possessions which he had intended to use to support himself and his family. Khunanup sees justice, then, as an instrument

---

73. SIMPSON, THE LITERATURE OF ANCIENT EGYPT 45. *See also* Nili Shupak, *A New Source For the Study of the Judiciary and Law of Ancient Egypt: "The Tale of the Eloquent Peasant"*, 51 J. NEAR E. STUD. 1, 16 (1992)(Shupak cites this line and remarks that "one of the principles of justice is the judge's objectivity. For this reason, Thoth, the Egyptian god of justice, and the ideal judge, 'never inclines sideways.'").

74. SIMPSON, THE LITERATURE OF ANCIENT EGYPT 46.

75. BREASTED, DEVELOPMENT OF RELIGION AND THOUGHT 254–55.

76. *Id.* at 255. Iversen, citing Plato, comments that:

> Thoth, the Egyptian god of learning and writing, had been the first to observe that 'the infinity of sound' could be divided up into distinctive elements such as vowels and consonants, and was therefore considered not merely the discoverer of the concept of letters, but also the inventor of writing as such. And a further passage in Cicero...stated that...'Thoth...was said to have provided the Egyptians with laws and letters'...[and that he] came to be considered in Roman times...the primordial legislator—in Christian circles the Egyptian Moses.

Erik Iversen, *The Hieroglyphic Tradition*, in THE LEGACY OF EGYPT 170, 172 (J.R. Harris ed., 2d ed. 1971).

77. SIMPSON, THE LITERATURE OF ANCIENT EGYPT 35.

78. It is unclear whether the fact that these persons are all male has appreciable significance here.

that fills gaps for those who have been deprived of their means of support. At the close of this first petition, Khunanup makes his earlier analogy (*i.e.*, to a father, husband, brother, and garment) explicit when he emphasizes to Rensi that he too has suffered a loss—obviously correlating his misfortune to that of the orphan, widow, divorcee, and motherless child: "I speak that you may hear: Do justice, O praised one whom the praised ones praise; *do away with / my needs, for see, I am heavy-laden; examine me, for see, I am in a loss.*"[79]

[G] Boating

Given the importance of boat travel on the Nile, it is only logical that the ancient Egyptians would have used boating imagery to convey ideals of law. In the second petition, the peasant uses a great deal of piloting and boating imagery to describe the proper role of a judge. "The face of the helmsman should look forward, but the ship diverges as it will; the king is indoors and the steering oar is [in] your hand...."[80] Next the judge is likened to a safe harbor for boats: "Act as a shelter, that your coast may be clear; see, your abode is infested with crocodiles."[81] "Bringer to shore of all who are drowning, save one who is shipwrecked; rescue me...."[82]

Khunanup continues to exploit this metaphor in subsequent petitions to Rensi: "Steer according to the bunt (of the sail); 'stave off' the inundation so as to do justice; beware lest you run aground because of the tiller rope." "Do not diverge, but steer (aright), pull upon the tiller rope."[83] A judge who neglects his duty is "like a ship in which there is no captain."[84] He then adds more boating imagery in his sixth and seventh petitions: "The sounding pole is in your hand like a 'free' pole when [deep water has been found.]"[85] "You are the steering oar of the entire land, and the land sails in accordance with your command...."[86]

---

79. Simpson, The Literature of Ancient Egypt 35 (emphasis added).
80. *Id.* at 38 (footnote omitted).
81. *Id.*
82. *Id.* at 39 (ellipses original).
83. *Id.* at 40.
84. *Id.* at 41 (third petition).
85. *Id.* at 44. *See also Id.* at 44, n.61 (Faulkner translates this passage in the footnote literally and provides an explanatory note: "'like an open stick, an occasion of water having happened'; the metaphor seems to be that Rensi is in safe waters because his pole cannot touch bottom.").
86. *Id.* at 44–45.

§2.05 Chapter Summary

The scene of the Judgment of the Dead symbolically illustrates some of the fundamental aspects of law in the abstract for the ancient Egyptians. A man's heart—representing his life deeds—must balance with *Ma'at*'s feather. *Ma'at*'s feather represented the totality of justice and truth. The goddess *Ma'at* symbolized the abstract principles of universal harmony and the natural order of the cosmos. *Ma'at* was ethical, moral, religious, and legal truth rolled into one. *Ma'at* represented equilibrium.

To implement *Ma'at*, the ancient Nile dwellers promoted specific values and protected certain interests in their quest to achieve justice. For example, the vizier, the most important judicial official, recognized the need to protect the weak and disadvantaged. He knew also how important it was not only to *be* impartial but also to *appear* impartial as well. The Egyptian sense of jurisprudence prized precedent and tradition. And the Egyptians themselves fully appreciated the dynamic power of rhetoric in law. *The Tale of the Eloquent Peasant* illustrates that they considered: 1) that justice should be available for the poor as well as the rich; 2) that justice was a natural force; and 3) that judges were persons empowered to interpret and channel the tremendous force of the law to benefit humankind.

CHAPTER 3

Legal Organization & Personnel

§ 3.01 Introduction

Lorton asserts that "there were no professional judges or courts in our sense of the term."[1] Thus, it may be best to be skeptical about historical traditions relating to court structures and systems during pharaonic Egypt. Indeed, little is known about the courts during the Old Kingdom (*c.* 2700–2200 B.C.).[2] During the New Kingdom (*c.* 1552–1069 B.C.), the vizier presided over the so-called "Great Court." We also know that ad hoc panels of judges could be commissioned to deal with individual cases such as the harem conspiracy trials or prosecutions of royal tomb robbers.[3] In short, for major crimes like theft of State property, tomb violation, or treason, the pharaoh often employed special investigative commissions.[4] Other local courts handled matters in individual communities.[5] We know a fair amount about one such local court that operated at Deir el-Medina (mostly during the 19th and 20th Dynasties (*c.* 1295–1069 B.C.)) where those who were constructing and furnishing the New Kingdom royal tombs resolved their legal disputes.[6] Typically, senior government officials

1. David Lorton, *Legal and Social Institutions of Pharaonic Egypt*, *in* 1 CIVILIZATIONS OF THE ANCIENT NEAR EAST 345, 355 (Jack M. Sasson ed., 1995).

2. *See* Janet H. Johnson, *The Legal Status of Women in Ancient Egypt*, *in* MISTRESS OF THE HOUSE MISTRESS OF HEAVEN: WOMEN IN ANCIENT EGYPT 175, 177 (Anne K. Chapel and Glenn E. Markoe eds., 1996) ("We do not know enough about courts in the Old and Middle Kingdoms to discuss their composition or functioning.").

3. *See* GAY ROBINS, WOMEN IN ANCIENT EGYPT 137 (1993). *See also infra* §§ 3.03[D], 4.06, 8.04[B], 8.05.

4. *See* MCDOWELL, JURISDICTION 248–249. *See also infra* §§ 3.03[D], 4.06.

5. *See* BEDELL, CRIMINAL LAW 42 ("[I]t is probable that by the Ramesside Period most minor civil suits were debated in a local court.").

6. *See generally* MCDOWELL, JURISDICTION. *See also* S. Allam, *Egyptian Law Courts*

were in charge of the Great Court and the special courts that were convened in the conspiracy and royal tomb robbery trials. For community courts like the one at Deir el-Medina, significant persons in the community such as scribes and crew chiefs usually presided as arbiters (although sometimes laborers and even women took part in the decision making process).[7] Occasionally, to add an extra measure of objectivity, judges from outside the community heard cases along with the local judges.[8] But these local courts ordinarily did not hear cases involving serious crimes such as homicide and rape. It is possible that crimes of that nature were under the jurisdiction of a court of higher authority.[9]

§ 3.02 Court Structure in the Old & Middle Kindgoms

[A] Old Kingdom (*c.* 2700–2200 B.C.)

The Egyptians established a system for dispute resolution even as early as the Old Kingdom (*c.* 2700–2200 B.C.).[10] The Egyptian government created two officials who had judicial responsibilities of some as yet unspecified nature as early as the 1st and 2nd Dynasties (*c.* 3150–2700 B.C.).[11] By

---

in Pharaonic and Hellenistic Times, 77 J. Egyptian Archaeology 109, 110 (1991); David Lorton, *The Treatment of Criminals in Ancient Egypt*, 20 J. Economic & Social Hist. Orient 2, 38 (1977). *See also supra* § 1.01, note 22 and accompanying text, and *infra* § 3.03[C].

7. *See* Janet H. Johnson, *The Legal Status of Women in Ancient Egypt* Mistress of the House Mistress of Heaven: Women in Ancient Egypt 175, 177 (Anne K. Chapel and Glenn E. Markoe eds., 1996). *See also* T.G.H. James, Pharaoh's People: Scenes From Life in Imperial Egypt 88–93 (1984); David Lorton, *Legal and Social Institutions of Pharaonic Egypt*, *in* 1 Civilizations of the Ancient Near East 345, 355 (Jack M. Sasson ed., 1995).

8. *See* S. Allam, *Legal Aspects in the 'Contendings of Horus and Seth'*, *in* Studies in Pharaonic Religion and Society in Honour of J. Gwyn Griffiths 137, 142, 145, n. 34 (Alan B. Lloyd ed., 1992).

9. *See* Jac Janssen, *Rules of Legal Proceeding in the Community of Necropolis Workmen at Deir el-Medina*, 32 Bibliotheca Orientalis 291, 296 (1975).

10. *See* Bedell, Criminal Law 1 ("A system of courts was set up, and various functionaries were given the authority to act on behalf of the state in dispensing justice.").

11. *See* Breasted, History of Egypt 42 ("The officials whom we later find as nobles with judicial functions, attached to the two royal residences of the North and South, Pe and Nekhen, already existed under the earliest dynasties, indicating an organized administration of judicial and jural affairs.").

the 4th Dynasty (*c.* 2625–2510 B.C.), kings were extraordinarily powerful, and a high degree of centralization had developed.[12] Even in this early era, the Old Kingdom government established a royal archive where deeds for land, contracts, wills, and royal decrees were kept.[13] According to tradition, there were six courts of justice, also called the *Great Houses*. Each of the Six Great Courts had a chief justice. There was also a group called the "thirty great men of the south," each of whom supposedly served as a judge and district chief. Apparently, each of these "thirty great men of the south" also served as a judge on one of the Six Great Courts.[14] It was customary, though not required, for a judge to apprentice as a clerk in the court prior to the time that the king promoted him to a judgeship as one of the thirty great men of the south.[15] But the evidence concerning the "thirty" is so thin that we must be cautious in drawing any firm conclusions about them. A body known as the Southern Tens played some unspecified role in adjudication.

The Greeks called the local administrative districts in Egypt "nomes."[16] There were twenty-two nomes in Upper Egypt and twenty in Lower Egypt. The kings of the 4th and 5th Dynasties probably appointed a chief administrator for each nome, and that administrator, who had the title "judge," probably conducted trials in the nome's own law court.[17] That same nome administrator, whom some refer to as a governor or "nomarch," also collected taxes which were exacted not in money, but in grain, cattle, poultry,

---

12. *See* GARDINER, EGYPT OF THE PHARAOHS 60.

13. *See* GRIMAL, ANCIENT EGYPT 91 (Grimal notes that in the Old Kingdom: "The third major department of state, the Royal Archives, looked after the deeds for land ownership. This department also held copies of documents recording civil actions, consisting essentially of contracts and testaments as well as the texts of royal decrees. Such documents provided the statutory basis of the fourth major department, that of Justice, which was concerned with the application of laws (*hepw*)."). I am discomforted by Grimal's use of the word "statutory" here. Technically speaking, it is inaccurate.

14. *See* ERMAN, LIFE IN ANCIENT EGYPT 138.

15. *See Id.* at 138–39.

16. *See* GRIMAL, ANCIENT EGYPT 58 ("representatives of central power dealt with local areas split up into provinces, which the Greeks called 'nomes' and the Egyptians at first called *sepat* and then *gâh* from the Amarna period (c. 1350 B.C.) onwards."); *Id. at* 92 ("The central government was backed up by a system of provincial administration that relied on the division of the country into 'nomes'."). *See also* THE OXFORD CLASSICAL DICTIONARY 1047 (Simon Hornblower and Antony Spawforth, eds. 1996, 3d ed.) Interestingly, this is the same word, *nomos*, in Greek that means "law.".

17. *See* GRIMAL, ANCIENT EGYPT 58 (Noting that the nomarchs were called *adj-mer*, "administrators"); BREASTED, HISTORY OF EGYPT 79 ("At the head of such a district or nome there was in the 4th and 5th Dynasties an official appointed by the crown...." "[H]e...served in a judicial capacity, and therefore bore...the title of 'judge.'"); *Id.* at 80 (Stating that each nome had its own "court of justice.").

and industrial products.[18] The local governors were not primarily judges, but they heard cases as part of their administrative duties. There were no "professional judges" per se.

The vizier was the most important government official and foremost judicial administrator in Egypt.[19] Originally the vizier was chosen from the king's family.[20] By the 5th Dynasty (*c.* 2510–2460 B.C.), however, royal relationship was no longer absolutely necessary. It was in the 5th Dynasty that the vizier acquired the title "Prophet of *Ma'at.*"[21] He supervised the Six Great Courts on which the local judges served.[22] The vizier held regular, formal hearings. He also made himself available daily for petitions by the poor. The king required that the vizier adhere to the laws, precedents, and neutrality.[23] As was mentioned, in addition to the court of the vizier, there were local courts throughout Egypt. These were not standing tribunals but rather they were comprised of local administrative officials in each district who convened to hear cases on an as-needed basis. Commissioners from

---

18. *See* Breasted, History of Egypt 80 ("The chief administrative bond which coordinated and centralized these nomes was the organization of the treasury, by the operation of which there annually converged upon the magazines of the central government the grain, cattle, poultry and industrial products, which in an age without coinage, were collected as taxes by the local governors."). *See also infra* § 5.04[A].

19. *See* S. Allam, *Egyptian Law Courts in Pharaonic and Hellenistic Times*, 77 J. Egyptian Archaeology 109, 110 (1991); T.G.H. James, Pharaoh's People: Scenes From Life in Imperial Egypt 52 (1984) ("At the head of the pyramid authority was the vizier, and he was supported in all his duties by officials who mostly bore scribal titles."). *See infra* § 3.04.

20. *See* Breasted, History of Egypt 119 (Explaining that in the 4th Dynasty, the king's eldest son was the vizier and chief judge.); *Id.* at 126 (With the change in royal line in the 5th Dynasty, the position shifted to another family: "The change in royal line is also evident in the organization of the government. The eldest son of the king is no longer the most powerful officer in the state, but the position which he held in the 4th Dynasty as vizier and chief judge is now the prerogative of another family, with whom it remains hereditary.").

21. *See* John A. Wilson, *Authority and Law in Ancient Egypt*, Supplement to 40 J. Am. Oriental Soc. 3 (1954). *See also* T.G.H. James, Pharaoh's People: Scenes From Life in Imperial Egypt 54 (1984) ("[I]t becomes clear that by the time of the 6th Dynasty the close family links between the king and the highest officers of state had become greatly slackened.").

22. *See* Breasted, History of Egypt 80–81 ("[T]he judicial functions of the local governors were merely incidental to their administrative labours. There was therefore no clearly defined class of professional judges, but the administrative officials were learned in the law and assumed judicial duties. Like the treasury, the judicial administration also converged in one person, for the local judges were organized into six courts and these in turn were under a chief justice of the whole realm.").

23. *See* John A. Wilson, *Authority and Law in Ancient Egypt*, Supplement to 40 J. Am. Oriental Soc. 4 (1954).

the court of the vizier occasionally traveled to a distant town in order to collaborate with these local courts in rendering decisions. In certain circumstances, a petitioner was required to first have a hearing before his local court as a condition precedent to having his case brought before the court of the vizier. We are not sure how many local courts there were, but the local courts operating in Thebes (where the judges varied daily) and in Memphis were surely the most important.[24] Nor are we certain how these local courts related to the court of the vizier. We do know of one case from the New Kingdom (*c.* 1552–1069 B.C.), however, where a slave owner was unsuccessful in a suit (relating to a stolen slave) brought before the vizier, and yet was able to recover the slave later in his local court. Our evidence also shows that the local judges had a reputation for accepting bribes from the rich.[25]

[B] Middle Kingdom (*c.* 2050–1674 B.C.)

By the Middle Kingdom, most of the Old Kingdom court structure had become defunct. Some of the titles of officials continued to be used, but apparently that is all that they were—titles.[26] The court in the Middle Kingdom was different. The judges who served varied from day to day. Nevertheless, the judges were priests and elder officials who presumably

24. *See* BREASTED, HISTORY OF EGYPT 241 ("Besides the vizier's 'hall,' also called the 'great council,' there were local courts throughout the land, not primarily of a legal character, being as we have already explained, merely the body of administrative officials in each district, who were corporately empowered to try cases with full competence. They were the 'great men of the town,' or the local 'council,' and acted as the local representatives of the 'great council.' In suits involving real estate titles, a commissioner of the 'great council' was sent out to execute the decisions of the 'great council' in cooperation with the nearest local 'council.' Or sometimes a hearing before the local 'council' was necessary before the 'great council' could render a decision. The number of these local courts is entirely uncertain, but the most important two known were at Thebes and Memphis. At Thebes its composition varied from day to day....") (footnote omitted).

25. *See Id.* at 241–242 ("It is difficult to discern the relation of these courts to the 'hall of the vizier,' but in at least one case when satisfaction was not obtained at the vizier's hall, the petitioner recovered a stolen slave by suit before one of these courts. They did not, however, always enjoy the best reputation among the people, who bewailed the hapless plight of 'the one who stands alone before the court when he is a poor man and his opponent is rich, while the court oppresses him (saying) 'Silver and gold for the scribes! Clothing for the servants!" For of course the bribe of the rich was often stronger than the justice of the poor man's cause, as it frequently is at the present day.") (footnotes omitted). *See infra* § 3.05.

26. *See* ERMAN, LIFE IN ANCIENT EGYPT 139.

possessed the wisdom and judgment necessary for sound decision making.[27] During the late Middle Kingdom, some individual nomarchs probably established their own law courts that functioned independently of the courts of the king.[28] Also during this period (and probably at other times too) the government divided Egypt into Northern and Southern districts for tax administration.[29]

Breasted describes the judicial organization during the Middle Kingdom as follows:

> Justice, as in the Old Kingdom, was still dispensed by the administrative officials; thus a treasurer of the god boasts that he was one "knowing the law, discreet in exercising it." The six "Great Houses" or courts of justice, with the vizier at their head, sat in Ithtowe. There was besides a "House of Thirty," which evidently possessed judicial functions, and was presided over by the vizier, but its relation to the six "Great Houses" is not clear. There was more than one "Southern Ten," and "Magnates of the Southern Tens" were frequently entrusted with various executive and administrative commissions by the king. As we shall see, they had the census and tax records in charge; but their connection with the judicial administration cannot be determined with clearness. Magistrates with the sole title of "judge," whose tombstones are occasionally found, may have been well-to-do middle class citizens who assumed judicial functions with a restricted local jurisdiction.[30]

The vizier in the Middle Kingdom refers to himself as the person "confirming the boundary records [and] separating a land-owner from his neighbor."[31] As had been the case during the Old Kingdom, the vizier con-

---

27. *See Id.* at 139–40 ("The members varied." "It consisted of 'wise men and princes,' that is of priests and officials who 'formed the great court of justice;' on a certain day they assembled....") (footnote omitted); *Id.* at 140 ("We see by the fact that the court of justice was called the 'court of the day,' that those who were qualified by their official or priestly office to serve did not all sit at the same time, and in fact the composition of the court varied very much.") (footnote omitted).

28. *See* BREASTED, HISTORY OF EGYPT 158 (Explaining that the 12th Dynasty nomarchs functioned like "miniature Pharaohs" and even had their own courts of justice.).

29. *See Id.* at 165 (According to Breasted, in the Middle Kingdom: "For the purpose of carrying on public works, as well as for taxation and census records, the country was divided into two administrative districts of the South and the North....").

30. *Id.* at 164–65 (footnotes omitted).

31. *Id.* at 166 (footnote omitted).

tinued to function as the premier court administrator, overseeing the Six Great Houses (*i.e.*, courts of law) and the "House of the Thirty."[32]

§ 3.03 Court Structure in the New Kingdom (*c.* 1552–1069 B.C.)

[A] Introduction

In the New Kingdom, two bodies which once exercised significant adjudicatory roles during the Old Kingdom and, to a lesser degree, the Middle Kingdom—the Southern Tens and the Six Great Houses (courts)—no longer appear in any court documents and, apparently, were gradually phased out of existence.[33] Because Egypt was such a vast kingdom—600 miles long—it was necessary for the king and the vizier to delegate some judicial responsibility to local bureaucratic officials.[34] Local officials continued to function as judges although, as had been the custom before, they did not serve as judges exclusively. Judging was merely one of a local administrator's duties.[35] Later, when the king appointed an additional vizier (*i.e.*, a Northern vizier in Heliopolis—probably by the early 18th Dynasty[36] (*c.* 1500 B.C.)), he (*i.e.*, the Northern vizier) also heard petitions on

32. *See Id.* ("As formerly, he was also head of the judicial administration, presiding over the six 'Great Houses' and the 'House of Thirty'....").

33. *See Id.* at 239–240 ("In the administration of justice the southern vizier played an even greater role than in the treasury. The old magnates of the Southern Tens, once possessed of important judicial functions, have sunk to a mere attendant council at the vizier's public audiences, where they seem to have retained not even advisory functions. They are never mentioned in the court records of the time, though they still live in poetry and their old fame survived even into Greek times. The vizier continues to bear his traditional title, 'chief of the six great houses' or courts of justice, but these are never referred to in any of the surviving legal documents and have evidently disappeared save in the title of the vizier.") (footnotes omitted).

34. *See* John A. Wilson, *Authority and Law in Ancient Egypt*, Supplement to 40 J. Am. Oriental Soc. 1, 4–5 (1954).

35. *See* Breasted, History of Egypt 240 ("As always heretofore the officers of administration are incidentally the dispensers of justice. They constantly serve in a judicial capacity. Although there is no class of judges with *exclusively* legal duties, every man of important administrative rank is thoroughly versed in the law and is ready at any moment to serve as judge."). *See also Id.* at 237.

36. *See Id.* at 236. *See also* Grimal, Ancient Egypt 167 (Stating that Sesostris I (Senusert I) divided "the vizier's office into two posts.").

a daily basis, as did his Southern counterpart.[37] The viziers probably heard both civil and criminal cases.[38] A permanent court scribe reported lawsuits.[39]

[B] Pharaoh & the Courts

According to Breasted, in the New Kingdom, the king had a recognized judicial function. He determined the punishments for condemned criminals. The vizier prepared a written report and the king, upon reviewing it, sentenced the convicted criminal.[40] But we know of other instances where the pharaoh was careful to exclude himself from the sentencing decision. He did not wish to appear merely vindictive.[41] It is probably a positive sign, for example, that Ramses III (*c.* 1186–1154 B.C.) did not, on simply his own authority, summarily execute the conspirators involved in a plot on his life.[42] The fact that he appointed a special court, and instructed the judges to beware lest they conduct themselves unjustly, indicates that the New Kingdom Egyptians had respect for due process and the rights of the accused.[43]

Some laws are attributed to the pharaoh. For example, tradition reports that the king promulgated laws concerning: 1) inheritance ("It is to the one

---

37. *See* T.G.H. JAMES, PHARAOH'S PEOPLE: SCENES FROM LIFE IN IMPERIAL EGYPT 55 (1984); SALLY L.D. KATARY, LAND TENURE IN THE RAMESSIDE PERIOD 195 (1989) [hereinafter "KATARY, LAND TENURE IN THE RAMESSIDE PERIOD"].

38. *See* BREASTED, HISTORY OF EGYPT 240 ("[W]hen the North received its own vizier such cases there were referred to him at Heliopolis. All crimes in the capital city were denounced and tried before him, and he maintained a criminal docket of prisoners awaiting trial or punishment, which strikingly suggests modern documents of the same sort.") (footnotes omitted).

39. *See* ERMAN, LIFE IN ANCIENT EGYPT 140.

40. *See* BREASTED, HISTORY OF EGYPT 236 ("The punishment of condemned criminals was determined by him, the documents in the case being sent up to him for a decision while the victims awaited their fate in the dungeon.") (footnote omitted).

41. *See* BEDELL, CRIMINAL LAW 24–25.

42. *See infra* §§ 4.06, 8.05.

43. *See* BEDELL, CRIMINAL LAW 23–24 (Referring to the fact that in the harem conspiracy trial under Ramses III, the commission—not the pharaoh—decided the fate of the guilty.). *See infra* §§ 8.02[A], 8.05. *See also* BREASTED, HISTORY OF EGYPT 499 ("The old Pharaoh... appointed a special court for the trial of the conspirators." His charge to the court "lay upon the judges a responsibility for impartial justice on the merits of the case, with a judicial objectivity which is remarkable in one who held the lives of the accused in his unchallenged power and had himself just been the victim of a murderous assault at their hands." Among the charges, Ramses III reminded the court: "Give heed and have a care lest ye execute punishment upon [anyone] unjustly...") (Breasted's brackets).

who buries that property is given, says the law of Pharaoh."); 2) property ("Pharaoh has said, may every man do as he wishes with his belongings."); and, 3) a woman's dowry ("Pharaoh has said give the *sfr* (dowry?) of every woman to her.").[44] Clearly, in the New Kingdom, the pharaoh had the authority to play a significant role in legal affairs if he so desired.[45] Occasionally, the pharaoh acted as the ultimate judge.[46] But in many instances where the pharaoh is credited with having functioned as a judge, scholars suspect that it was actually a palace official who heard the case as the king's designate.[47] According to McDowell, the pharaoh personally acted as judge in some circumstances: "[T]here is one good example from Deir el-Medina and a few from elsewhere in which there can be no doubt that the king personally decided the cases of individuals...."[48] In addition to acting as a judge, he selected court personnel (including the viziers), determined the scope of their authority, and maintained the power to legislate on his own.[49] The pharaoh had the authority to discharge a judge or even the vizier himself.[50]

Horemhab (*c.* 1323–1295 B.C.) is one New Kingdom pharaoh who deserves special mention for his contributions to court structure and the judiciary. In particular, he is known for his famous Edict. Upon taking the throne, Horemhab reorganized the courts first by establishing two permanent "Great Courts." The Great Court in Heliopolis had jurisdiction in Lower Egypt (*i.e.*, the Delta region) and the court in Thebes was responsible for Upper Egypt (*i.e.*, Egypt south of the Delta). The pharaoh's viziers managed and supervised these Great Courts. Quite plainly, the vizier of

---

44. *See* MCDOWELL, JURISDICTION 235 (footnote omitted); WARBURTON, STATE AND ECONOMY IN ANCIENT EGYPT 43 (Noting: "The fact that the mere phrase 'Law of Pharaoh' sufficed to refer to guarantees surrounding property rights underlies that property rights were important in ancient Egypt.") (footnote omitted); *Id.* at 63; J.J. Janssen and P.W. Pestman, *Burial and Inheritance at Thebes*, 11 J. ECONOMIC & SOCIAL HIST. ORIENT 167–168 (1968).

45. *See* BEDELL, CRIMINAL LAW 17 ("The role of the Pharaoh in the New Kingdom Egyptian judicial system placed him at the apex of the organization....").

46. *See* MCDOWELL, JURISDICTION 236. *See also* BEDELL, CRIMINAL LAW 28 ("Pharaoh was the ultimate judge and he could try an individual himself any time he wished.").

47. *See* MCDOWELL, JURISDICTION 237.

48. *Id. See also Id.* at 238–240, 243 (Noting that the Pharaoh played a fairly active role in adjudicating cases in Deir el-Medina.).

49. *See* BEDELL, CRIMINAL LAW 17–19; *Id.* at 18 ("Individual Pharaohs did add laws to the corpus. This was usually in the form of a decree for a specific temple foundation."); *Id.* at 19 ("So it is clear that the Pharaoh could propose laws of both general and limited application.").

50. *See Id.* at 29.

lower Egypt presided over the court in Heliopolis and his counterpart in the south directed the Theban Great Court.[51] The Great Courts only decided important cases or those with potentially grave consequences.[52] In addition, Horemhab founded smaller, local courts to serve the needs of towns and villages.[53] Both the Great Courts and the local courts were sometimes referred to as courts "of hearers."[54] In addition to these standing local courts, some evidence suggests that traveling judges (circuit courts) may have provided adjudication for villages that were too small to have their own courts.[55] For example, judges visited the Delta town of Tjebnet to hear a case involving a thief who stole certain weavers (slaves).[56] In sum, then, Horemhab split legal authority between Upper and Lower Egypt,[57] and he appointed new judges, gave them salaries, provided them with laws to use as precedents, and advised them not to associate with others and not to accept bribes.[58] His new judges were mostly priests and government or mu-

---

51. *See Id.* at 3–4; GRIMAL, ANCIENT EGYPT 243. *See also* S. Allam, *Egyptian Law Courts in Pharaonic and Hellenistic Times*, 77 J. EGYPTIAN ARCHAEOLOGY 109, 115 (1991) (Noting that the *ḳnbt* at Thebes continued to function as a court into the late dynastic period (*i.e.*, the 7th century B.C.)).

52. *See* S. Allam, *Egyptian Law Courts in Pharaonic and Hellenistic Times*, 77 J. EGYPTIAN ARCHAEOLOGY 109, 111 (1991) ("Its members were recruited from among the highest dignitaries, both ecclesiastical and lay, and presided over by the vizier. In judicial matters, it can be regarded as the supreme court. It dealt with serious crimes such as robberies of royal tombs; these were all the more hideous since some high officials were implicated in these grave violations. It also examined lawsuits pertaining to civil law, such as litigation over a large estate. Evidently it dealt only with important cases, which could not so easily be judged by a local council and exceeded its power."); BEDELL, CRIMINAL LAW 9 ("There were local courts which tried both civil and criminal cases within their jurisdiction, and the two Great Courts which dealt with the more serious civil and criminal cases.").

53. *See* BEDELL, CRIMINAL LAW 2–3; *Id.* at 6 ("In addition to the two Great Courts, there were numerous district or local courts which were identified by the name of the town in which they were located.").

54. *See Id.* at 9.

55. *See Id.* at 8 ("While the evidence for a circuit court is certainly not conclusive, it is feasible to assume that magistrates were appointed by the state to serve areas that did not have a permanent court.").

56. *See Id.* at 45–46 (The judges ordered the thief to return the stolen weavers to their rightful owner.); *Id.* at 46 (Bedell says: "It is clear that the judges stayed only long enough to arbitrate this case, and then they departed presumably for another village.").

57. *See* GRIMAL, ANCIENT EGYPT 243 ("Horemhab appointed judges and regional tribunes and reintroduced local religious authorities. Legal power was split between Upper and Lower Egypt...").

58. *See* Kurt Pflüger, *The Edict of Horemhab*, 5 J. NEAR EASTERN STUD. 260, 265 (1944); MCDOWELL, JURISDICTION 161; BEDELL, CRIMINAL LAW 17 (Referring to Horemhab's Edict, stating that he "appointed judges and gave them laws."); *Id.* at 18–19.

nicipal officials.[59] According to his Edict, the "courts have been set up all over the country [to judge] every [man living], to hold court in the towns according to the excellent plans of [My Majesty]."[60] Horemhab's plan also exempted the courts from paying taxes of silver and gold.[61] At the beginning of the 19th Dynasty (*c.* 1295 B.C.—in the period immediately following Horemhab), written laws may have begun to supplant the personal authority of the pharaoh. And, it is clear that the priests gained greater control of the civil courts.[62]

[C] Deir El-Medina

By the 19th Dynasty (*c.* 1295–1188 B.C.), the court system had become a fixed institution.[63] In the New Kingdom (*c.* 1552–1069 B.C.), there were many local courts throughout Egypt which operated under the name of *ḳnbt.*[64] Because of the volume of documents uncovered by archaeologists, modern scholars simply know more about the *ḳnbt* at Deir el-Medina than any other.[65] Deir el-Medina was a relatively small community. "The only inhabitants were the workmen themselves and their families, at most periods from 40–60 households in all."[66] The *ḳnbt* at Deir el-Medina was usually

---

59. *See* Kurt Pflüger, *The Edict of Horemhab*, 5 J. NEAR EASTERN STUD. 260, 268 (1944).

60. *Id.* at 266.

61. *See* WILSON, CULTURE OF ANCIENT EGYPT 237 (Under Horemhab: "Pharaoh further made the courts of law free from any tax of silver and gold, 'in order to prevent an obligation of any kind from being exacted from the courts of Upper and Lower Egypt.'"). *See also infra* § 5.04[C].

62. *See* WILSON, CULTURE OF ANCIENT EGYPT 239 (Wilson comments on Horemhab's Edict: "[N]ow clearly specified and impersonal regulations were drafted to take over pharaoh's personal authority. The edict further shows remarkable control over the civil courts by the priests.").

63. *See* BEDELL, CRIMINAL LAW 1 ("[I]n the Ramesside Period... the courts were firmly entrenched as secular organs of the state.").

64. *See* S. Allam, *Egyptian Law Courts in Pharaonic and Hellenistic Times*, 77 J. EGYPTIAN ARCHAEOLOGY 109, 122 (1991) ("During the New Kingdom besides temples many a locality could set up its own *ḳnbt.*").

65. *See Id.* at 110; MCDOWELL, JURISDICTION 144. *See also* BEDELL, CRIMINAL LAW 221 (Referring to the fact that much of our knowledge about small community courts comes from Deir el-Medina.); Christopher J. Eyre, *The Market Women of Pharaonic Egypt, in* LE COMMERCE EN ÉGYPT ANCIENNE 173, 174 (Nicolas Grimal and Bernadette Menu eds., 1998); The Deir el-Medina Data Base www.leidenuniv.nl.nino/dmd/dmd.html. *See also supra* § 1.01, note 22 and accompanying text, and *supra* § 3.01, note 6 and accompanying text.

66. MCDOWELL, JURISDICTION 2. *See also* GRIMAL, ANCIENT EGYPT 278 ("The total number of workmen... reached 120, meaning that the community as a whole must have numbered about 1200."); WARBURTON, STATE AND ECONOMY IN ANCIENT

composed of persons from the village "and outside authorities connected with Deir el-Medina."[67] The court met "in the open air...."[68] Even the pharaoh himself occasionally acted as a judge in cases involving individuals from Deir el-Medina.[69] McDowell describes the Deir el-Medina corpus as "hundreds of texts" that "span more than two centuries, from the early years of Ramses II to the last years of the 20th Dynasty, and contain useful references to events as far back as the reign of Horemhab."[70]

The workmen's community at Deir el-Medina was an atypical community in ancient Egypt. To begin with, the vizier was directly responsible for it. In time, the High Priest took over this administrative role. In addition, the average level of education was higher there than in other villages. As yet we have not had the good fortune to discover another ancient community as rich in legal documents. Although we tend to assume that the legal information that we draw from Deir el-Medina is representative of law in other ancient Egyptian communities, we cannot be sure.[71] The place called the *ḫtm*, the "enclosure", is the location where the court (*ḳnbt*) probably held its sessions.[72] "Presumably there was also an open space either within the

---

EGYPT 18; Andrea McDowell, *Legal Aspects of Care of the Elderly in Egypt to the End of the New Kingdom, in* THE CARE OF THE ELDERLY IN THE ANCIENT NEAR EAST 199, 208–215 (Marten Stol and Sven P. Vleeming eds., 1998).

67. MCDOWELL, JURISDICTION 2. *See also* S. Allam, *Egyptian Law Courts in Pharaonic and Hellenistic Times*, 77 J. EGYPTIAN ARCHAEOLOGY 109, 110 (1991) ("Officials from outside the locality also occasionally attended the council session."); BEDELL, CRIMINAL LAW 7–8 (Bedell says that the court at Deir el-Medina "can also be classified as a district or local court.").

68. MCDOWELL, JURISDICTION 2.

69. *See Id.* ("the pharaoh...is named in our sources not only as a legislator, but very occasionally as a judge who personally heard litigation involving members of the workmen's community.").

70. *Id.* at 9. *See also* WARBURTON, STATE AND ECONOMY IN ANCIENT EGYPT 135 ("thousands of administrative notes".); William A. Ward, *Some Aspects of Private Land Ownership and Inheritance in Ancient Egypt, ca. 2500–1000 B.C., in* LAND TENURE AND SOCIAL TRANSFORMATION IN THE MIDDLE EAST 63, 67 (Tarif Khalidi ed., 1984) (Ward states that these texts are "thousands of documents of all kinds...mainly short texts dealing with the daily affairs of the villagers mostly written on ostraca and limestone flakes."); GRIMAL, ANCIENT EGYPT 269.

71. *See* MCDOWELL, JURISDICTION 10–11. *See also* William A. Ward, *Some Aspects of Private Land Ownership and Inheritance in Ancient Egypt, ca. 2500–1000 B.C., in* LAND TENURE AND SOCIAL TRANSFORMATION IN THE MIDDLE EAST 63, 67 (Tarif Khalidi ed., 1984) ("These people were...artisans, stone masons, scribes and the like, so they do not represent the population of an ordinary agricultural village.").

72. *See generally* MCDOWELL, JURISDICTION 94–105, 151. *See Id.* at 99 ("[I]t is because various legal events are reported to have taken place at the *ḫtm* that it is relevant to this study; in fact it is the only specific location given for any legal activity in our material. It does not necessarily follow that this was the only or even the usual place for legal events, but as the only one of which we can be certain it naturally attracts our atten-

ḥtm or near it where even a large group of people involved in the proceedings and curious onlookers could assemble."[73]

Allam summarizes the subject matter jurisdiction of the Deir el-Medina *ḳnbt* as follows:

> In civil matters, the majority of cases dealt with related to the fulfillment of obligations (payment, sale and loan of objects, rent and sale of beasts, mostly donkeys, etc.). Some litigation concerned landed property, some family law and inheritance. In penal matters, the theft of objects was treated in some cases. It would seem that violations of sexual mores (adultery in particular) were not rare.[74]

According to McDowell, "most of the cases which came before the *ḳnbt* concerned economic transactions."[75] As a rule, these cases involved allegations of breach of contract. Occasionally, the *ḳnbt* performed the role of a notary; merely witnessing a transaction or a will.[76] A couple of cases from Deir el-Medina may have been heard and decided by a single individual who acted as an arbitrator.[77] There are also a few other disputes that seem to have been adjudicated by small (sometimes three-person) panels, rather than by a full court (*ḳnbt*).[78]

[D] Special Courts

When special courts were convened to handle extraordinary matters, the king usually appointed the highest government and/or municipal officials available as judges.[79] In one such extraordinary criminal trial, the king (Pepi I, *c.* 2325 B.C.) appointed a man named Weni to serve as judge be-

---

tion."); *Id.* at 104 ("If we are correct in believing that most court sessions took place at the *ḥtm*, then this would be another occasion on which many villagers would gather there.").

73. *Id.* at 100.

74. S. Allam, *Egyptian Law Courts in Pharaonic and Hellenistic Times*, 77 J. Egyptian Archaeology 109, 111 (1991).

75. McDowell, Jurisdiction 155.

76. *See Id.*

77. *See Id.* at 146–148. *See also Id.* at 2 ("[I]f the dispute was very minor, the litigants might simply submit it to a single official for arbitration. . . .").

78. *See Id.* at 147.

79. *See* Gardiner, Egypt of the Pharaohs 300 ("These were important state trials, and the judges specially chosen to conduct them were the highest available officials. . . ."). *See also* David Lorton, *Legal and Social Institutions of Pharaonic Egypt*, *in* 1 Civilizations of the Ancient Near East 345, 355 (Jack M. Sasson ed., 1995) ("In extraordinary cases involving theft from temples or tombs or an attempt on the life of the king, the king himself appointed the members of the tribunals."). *See also infra* §§ 8.04 and 8.05.

cause the king held Weni in such high regard. In addition to Weni's other responsibilities, he wrote an opinion to explain the reasons for his decision.[80] The chief justice and one of the judges "attached to Nekhen" occasionally heard special private cases; and, in one particular case involving treason in the royal harem, the king appointed two judges "attached to Nekhen" to hear the case (without the chief justice).[81]

§ 3.04 The Office of Vizier[82]

According to Bedell, the "Pharaoh... appointed the vizier to head the official state legal system, and his primary function was to preside over the two Great Courts of Egypt."[83] In some respects he was like the English Chancellor in medieval England. The vizier headed the entire organization of the government. His office maintained all of the State archives and other important documents such as land records, wills, census administration, and tax registration.[84] The vizier was often called the prophet of *Ma'at*. He

---

80. *See* Gardiner, Egypt of the Pharaohs 95. Regarding Weni's appointment as judge, *see* Grimal, Ancient Egypt 82–83; Breasted, History of Egypt 134. *See also infra* § 8.05.

81. *See* Breasted, History of Egypt 81 ("Special cases of private nature were 'heard' by the chief justice and a judge 'attached to Nekhen,' while in a case of treason in the harem, the accused queen was tried before a court of two judges 'attached to Nekhen,' especially appointed by the crown for that purpose, the chief justice not being one of them.") (footnotes omitted). For more about the phrase "attached to Nekhen," *see infra* § 3.05.

82. *See generally* G.P.F. van den Boorn, The Duties of the Vizier: Civil Administration in the Early New Kingdom (1988).

83. Bedell, Criminal Law 34. For more on the office of the vizier, *see Id.* at 34–42.

84. *See* Grimal, Ancient Egypt 58 ("As early as the 2nd Dynasty the circle of officials around the king included a *tjaty*, but it was not until the 4th Dynasty that the office of *tjaty* seems to have acquired the enormous power that made it comparable to that of the Ottoman vizier."); *Id.* at 90 ("the vizier (*tjaty*)... appears to have first emerged in the 2nd Dynasty."); *Id.* at 91 ("The vizier was in a sense a chief executive, with authority in practically all areas of government...."); Katary, Land Tenure in the Ramesside Period 195 (Katary describes the vizier as "the highest ranking civil servant in the whole of the country."); Warburton, State and Economy in Ancient Egypt 178–181 ("Instructions For The Vizier"); Breasted, History of Egypt 82 ("The immediate head of the entire organization of government was the Pharaoh's prime minister, or as he is more commonly called in the east, the vizier. At the same time he also regularly served as chief justice....") ("His 'hall' or office served as the archives of the government, and he was the chief archivist of the state. **** Here all lands were registered, and all local archives centralized and coordinated; here wills were recorded, and when executed the resulting new titles were issued. The will of a king's son in the 4th Dynasty has been preserved practically complete, and another from the beginnings of the 5th Dynasty, both having been cut in hieroglyphs on the

was the supreme judge, the chief justice.[85] The vizier ordinarily led the discussion in court (*i.e.*, during trial) and asked the litigants more questions than any other judges in the Great Courts of Thebes and Heliopolis. In minor disputes, he often heard matters on his own without the assistance of other judges.[86]

When a case came before the vizier, he was required to issue his decision rather quickly; perhaps within three days. For cases involving land outside of Thebes, he may have had longer, possibly as much as two months.[87] When the king began appointing a second vizier (in the North), the two viziers split their jurisdiction on a geographic basis.[88] It was common for local officials to report suspicious matters to the vizier's office.[89] Scribes and police also routinely reported crimes to the vizier.[90] The viziers heard all criminal trials and decided all cases involving prisoners who were in custody awaiting trial or punishment.[91] In the New Kingdom (*c.* 1552–1069

---

stone wall of the tomb-chapel where they could defy the lapse of nearly five thousand years, while the papyrus archives of the vizier perished thousands of years ago.") (footnotes omitted); *Id.* at 166 (In the Middle Kingdom, "The office of the vizier was thus the central archives of the government as before, and all records of the land-administration with census and tax registration were filed in his bureaus."). *See also* GARDINER EGYPT OF THE PHARAOHS 104 (Gardiner discusses the role of viziers generally.); T.G.H. JAMES, PHARAOH'S PEOPLE: SCENES FROM LIFE IN IMPERIAL EGYPT 66–69 (1984).

85. *See* GRIMAL, ANCIENT EGYPT 91 ("He was also the chief judge...but he did not necessarily deal with all legal matters."); *Id.* at 91–92 (Mentioning that the vizier of the 5th Dynasty was referred to as the "priest of Maat."); BEDELL, CRIMINAL LAW 39 ("[T]he vizier was the president of the Great Court...." "[I]n all the Ramesside documents we have describing trials in the two Great Courts of the land, the vizier is mentioned first in the list of judges."). For a general description of the duties of the vizier, *see* GARDINER, EGYPT OF THE PHARAOHS 104 ("That the vizier was the supreme judge was seen from the inscription of Weni, and is reflected in his frequent epithet 'prophet of Ma'e, i.e. of the goddess of Truth. He prided himself on being accessible to all petitioners, who it was recognized cared more about being allowed to vent their grievances than about having them redressed."). *See also* KATARY, LAND TENURE IN THE RAMESSIDE PERIOD 218 (Katary describes the vizier as the person responsible for appointing judges and the one who "presided over the Great Court...in the capacity of Chief Justice [and who] made judgments in important civil law cases referred to him by local courts....").

86. *See* BEDELL, CRIMINAL LAW 40–42.

87. *See* WARBURTON, STATE AND ECONOMY IN ANCIENT EGYPT 178–79.

88. *See supra* § 3.03[A].

89. *See* MCDOWELL, JURISDICTION 131.

90. *See* BEDELL, CRIMINAL LAW 35. *See also Id.* at 36 (Referring to workers (not just officials) in Deir el-Medina reporting crimes to the vizier.).

91. *See* BREASTED, HISTORY OF EGYPT 240 ("In cases concerning land located in Thebes he was obliged by law to render a decision in three days, but if the land lay in the "South or North" he required two months. This was while he was still the only vizier; when the North received its own vizier such cases there were referred to him at

B.C.), the southern vizier became the most powerful judicial official. When possible, the vizier met with the pharaoh every morning[92] and he prepared criminal trial reports which the king used as a basis for sentencing.[93]

The vizier understood how important it was to allow litigants to speak their piece. The tomb inscription of Rekhmire, the vizier of Thutmose III (*c.* 1479–1425 B.C.), specifically notes that a petitioner is perhaps more anxious to air his grievance than he is, necessarily, to win his case.[94] In the guidelines established for Rekhmire, the pharaoh directs him to be impartial and advises him to admit his mistakes. And when he recognizes that he has made a mistake, the pharaoh advises him to steer the injured party to another judge for assistance.[95] The vizier is told: "A magistrate's refuge lies in acting according to the regulations in doing what is specified. A petitioner who has been judged should not be able to say: 'I have not been allowed to plead my innocence.'" "Do not dismiss a petitioner before you have considered his words." "You should dismiss him only after you have let him hear the reasons why you dismiss him. See! The saying is: 'The petitioner prefers the consideration of his utterance to the judgement on the matter about which he has come.'"[96]

§ 3.05 Judges

Old Kingdom tradition regarded the god Osiris as a judge.[97] In earthly matters, however, the Egyptians had to rely on human judges. Many of the Old Kingdom judges retained the phrase "attached to Nekhen," as part of their official title. This phrase was a vestige of an earlier time when

---

Heliopolis. All crimes in the capital city were denounced and tried before him, and he maintained a criminal docket of prisoners awaiting trial or punishment, which strikingly suggests modern documents of the same sort.") (footnotes omitted). *See also* MCDOWELL, JURISDICTION 247–248 (Referring to criminal procedure.).

92. *See* BREASTED, HISTORY OF EGYPT 235–236.

93. *See Id.* at 236 ("The punishment of condemned criminals was determined by him, the documents in the case being sent up to him for a decision while the victims awaited their fate in the dungeon.") (footnote omitted).

94. *See* GARDINER, EGYPT OF THE PHARAOHS 196 ("a petitioner better likes to be allowed to pour out his grievances than that they should be put right.").

95. *See* BEDELL, CRIMINAL LAW 31.

96. T.G.H. JAMES, PHARAOH'S PEOPLE: SCENES FROM LIFE IN IMPERIAL EGYPT 60–61 (1984). For other references to Rekhmire, *see supra* § 2.03, *infra* §§ 4.01, 4.02, 5.01, and 5.04[B], note 107.

97. *See* BREASTED, HISTORY OF EGYPT 173 (Osiris "had already been known as a judge in the Old Kingdom....").

"Nekhen (Hieraconpolis) was the royal residence of the Southern Kingdom."[98] Since there were no written laws, these judges were left to their own devices. Scholars have conjectured that the early judges relied on their own interpretations of the king's will.[99] "In Egypt, the law was personally derived from the god-king and was tailored as justice and equity to the individual appellant."[100] Thus, it was paramount for the judge to go to great lengths to achieve impartiality in his decision making.[101] Judges ordinarily heard cases as a group, rarely alone.[102] Ancient sources tell us that, occasionally, Egyptian judges endeavored to frighten litigants in an attempt to command respect from them.[103] "What was needed for this very personal justice was the proper blend of authority and sympathy—what we call paternalism."[104]

In an effort to curb bribery among judges, the pharaoh Horemhab (*c.* 1323–1295 B.C.), whom we have previously singled out as an innovator in judicial affairs,[105] exempted judges from taxation for their earnings (as judges).[106] Presumably, the amount saved through tax exemption was sufficient to make taking bribes unnecessary. In concert with providing this tax exemption for the judiciary, Horemhab strengthened the penalty for accepting bribes, making it a capital offense.[107] This same pharaoh, as today's

---

98. *Id.* at 81.

99. WILSON, CULTURE OF ANCIENT EGYPT 172–73 ("What the vizier dispensed was customary law, phrased as the commanding word of pharaoh and arising out of pharaoh's three divine qualities of *Hu*, *Sia*, and *Ma'at*, Authority, Perception, and Justice.") (footnote omitted).

100. *Id.* at 173.

101. *See Id.* ("For that reason, a special charge was laid upon the vizier to be scrupulously fair in dispensing justice. 'The abomination of the god is a show of partiality. So this is the instruction; thou shalt act accordingly: thou shalt look upon him whom thou knowest like him whom thou dost not know, upon him who is close to thy person like him who is distant from thy house. As for the official who acts thus, he will flourish here in this office.'") (footnote omitted). *See also supra* § 2.03[D].

102. *See* S. Allam, *Legal Aspects in the 'Contendings of Horus and Seth'*, *in* STUDIES IN PHARAONIC RELIGION AND SOCIETY IN HONOUR OF J. GWYN GRIFFITHS 137, 138 (Alan B. Lloyd ed., 1992).

103. *See* WILSON, CULTURE OF ANCIENT EGYPT 173 ("The authority of the vizier was very great, and he must inspire immediate and unquestioned respect—called 'fear' in the texts—but his goal must be justice, rather than the search for arbitrary authority.").

104. *Id.*

105. *See supra* § 3.03[B].

106. *See infra* § 5.04[C].

107. *See* BREASTED, HISTORY OF EGYPT 405 (Horemhab then carefully selected two men to serve as viziers. He particularly wanted two good judges. Breasted relates: "In order to discourage bribery among the local judges he took an unprecedented step. He remitted the tax of gold and silver levied upon all local officials for judicial duties, permitting them to retain the entire income of their offices, in order that they might have no excuse for illegally enriching themselves. But he went still further;

American President often does, tried to influence the tide of jurisprudence with his judicial appointments: "Horemhab put into the courts of law individuals of a reactionary type. He tells us that he was at pains to seek out men 'of perfected speech and good character, able to distinguish the innermost thoughts.'"[108]

Scribes were especially important in legal endeavors. Some scribes mentioned in the Deir el-Medina legal documents were from Deir el-Medina itself but many came from the outside; like the scribes of the vizier.[109] Indeed, the scribe of the vizier often served as a judge in significant litigation.[110]

The juridical texts from Deir el-Medina refer to many persons as *srw* ("magistrates") only when those persons were engaged in performing legal duties. For example, when townspeople served as judges, they were called *srw*.[111] In some regards, the term was used in the way that we refer to modern jurors as "ladies and gentlemen of the jury." The title only applies while the jurors are serving. It is not a title that they otherwise retain.[112] "[S]o long as they were members of the court, the local officials and even simple workmen were considered mandatories of royal power and so deserved the

while organizing the local courts throughout the land he passed a most stringent law against the acceptance of any bribe by a member of a local court or 'council'. . . .") (footnote omitted); *Id.* at 406 (In fact he made accepting a judicial bribe a capital offense: "Behold my majesty has done this to improve the laws of Egypt.") (footnote omitted); *Id.* (Demonstrating that Horemhab went out of his way to treat judges well so that they would be beholden to him.).

108. Wilson, Culture of Ancient Egypt 237.

109. *See* S. Allam, *Egyptian Law Courts in Pharaonic and Hellenistic Times*, 77 J. Egyptian Archaeology 109, 112 (1991) ("During trials the scribe did not merely record, he often helped in the interrogations. . . ."); *Id.* at 112–115, 125 ("In the judicial machine of the New Kingdom many a 'scribe' played a positive part. At the local level he used to act in legal proceedings from start to finish; if need be, he had to communicate directly with the highest official of state (the vizier); and at the Great *ḳnbt* he sometimes officiated as a prosecutor. Correspondingly, at the Great *ḳnbt*, a high official with the rank of 'scribe of Pharaoh' joined in its dealings; apparently this official ensured the control of the king over this supreme court."); McDowell, Jurisdiction 69 ("A particularly prominent part in the legal activity of Deir el-Medina was played by scribes, some of whom were 'insiders,' that is, inhabitants of the village and on the payroll of the gang; while others were "outsiders," representatives of some other unit of the administration. The last group is represented principally by the scribes of the vizier, through whom the vizier's office was directly involved in the legal activity of Deir el-Medina.").

110. *See* McDowell, Jurisdiction 72, 85.

111. *See generally Id.* at 65–69. *See also* Bedell, Criminal Law 42–43 (Noting that the term *srw* was used to refer to impaneled judges.).

112. *See* Bedell, Criminal Law 43 (Bedell notes that a judge "was known as a *sr* only as long as he was a member of the court, and it was not afterwards included among his titles.").

name of *srw*. On the other hand, certain outside authorities were called *srw* even in purely administrative roles. These outside *srw* were apparently very high ranking Theban officials. . . ."[113]

We do not know how the Deir el-Medina community selected judges for the court. As McDowell writes: "The members of the court varied from one session to the next according to no discernible pattern . . . , though they generally included the captains of the [workers] gang. These could be joined by lower ranking members of the gang, including simple workmen; also outside authorities such as the scribes of the vizier and the chiefs of police."[114] As was mentioned, in the Great Court in Thebes, the vizier acted as the chief judge.[115] Similarly, in the court at Deir el-Medina, ordinarily there also appears to have been some individual who served as a chairman of the court.[116] Often a scribe functioned as something like a chief judge or foreman who presided over the court.[117] Usually—though not always—at least one captain of the workmen served as a judge on the *ḳnbt*.[118] It is particularly interesting that in nearly two-thirds of the cases in Deir el-Medina, either one of the scribes of the vizier or one of the chiefs of police (*3ʿtw*) (*i.e.*, officials from *outside* of Deir el-Medina) served as judges on the *ḳnbt*.[119] Outsiders frequently served as judges in difficult cases. But occasionally, outsiders were on the court even in mundane, unexceptional trials.[120] It is difficult to state with certainty how many judges served on a typical court

113. McDowell, Jurisdiction 69. *See also* S. Allam, *Egyptian Law Courts in Pharaonic and Hellenistic Times*, 77 J. Egyptian Archaeology 109, 119 (1991) (Allam argues that changes occurred by the late dynastic period which made the courts dedicated, full-time bodies, rather than splitting their responsibilities between administrative and judicial functions.).

114. McDowell, Jurisdiction 144; *Id.* at 148, 159 ("The composition of the court varied from one session to the next."). *See also* Bedell, Criminal Law 6–7 (Referring to the fact that "prominent citizens" ordinarily served on the local courts.); *Id.* at 52 ("[T]he members of the court changed regularly.").

115. *See* McDowell, Jurisdiction 168–169.

116. *See Id.* at 159.

117. *See Id.* at 167, 170. *See also* Bedell, Criminal Law 48 (Bedell states that one of the foremen served as the chief judge on the court.).

118. *See* McDowell, Jurisdiction 160.

119. *See Id.* at 162 ("[S]o far as I can tell there are no 'rules' for when an *3ʿtw* might sit on the court. As a relatively high-ranking authority whose duties often brought him to Deir el-Medina he evidently could join any court which happened to be sitting when he was in the village, or perhaps his visits were even seized upon as suitable occasions for a hearing."); *Id.* at 163 ("The situation with the scribes of the vizier was similar in that they were among the judges in a variety of cases, and there can be no doubt that they had the authority to sit on the court whenever they chose.").

120. *See Id.* at 163–165.

at Deir el-Medina. For instance, the cases show three, four, five, seven, and twelve judges serving in different circumstances. It is possible also that our texts fail to record all of the judges in any given trial. Perhaps the scribes only noted certain judges or only "important" people. In several cases, the texts state that all of the workmen were present for a trial. It is unlikely, in these instances, that the group—in its entirety—actually participated as judges.[121]

The composition of the Great Courts appears to have been more consistent but it too changed. The judges on the Great Courts—unlike the *ḳnbt* at Deir el-Medina—tended to be members of the upper class elite (*e.g.*, the chief priest of Amon, a royal butler, a scribe of the pharaoh, the mayor of Thebes, a military officer) rather than ordinary workers. In the Great Court at Thebes, the vizier and two royal butlers were consistently on the panel. For several years during the reign of Ramses XI (*c.* 1098–1069 B.C.), three individual jurists appear in every case heard by the Great Court. They simply may have been quasi-permanent judges.[122]

§ 3.06 Other Court Personnel & Law Enforcement Officials

There were persons who worked in the courts or assisted in law enforcement other than the judges but we know very few details about them. For example, there were officials who administered beatings and other torture to witnesses.[123] A court officer called a "retainer of the court" or "servant of the court" (*šmsw n ḳnbt*) may have inflicted these beatings.[124] But we know of one case decided by an oracle[125] where it was an "inspector" who "gave a hundred blows of the palm-rib" to a witness.[126] This position (*šms n ḳnbt*) probably was not a full-time job but rather something that the individual did as a low-level, part-time employee. His principal roles

121. *See* S. Allam, *Egyptian Law Courts in Pharaonic and Hellenistic Times*, 77 J. Egyptian Archaeology 109, 110 (1991) ("It was usually composed of up to eight members, although as many as twelve and fourteen are attested. The judges, according to their titles, were the most prominent men in the community, such as chief workmen, scribes, deputies, guardians, policemen, and painters."); Bedell, Criminal Law 48–52.

122. *See* Bedell, Criminal Law 52–56.

123. *See Id.* at 60–61. *See also infra* § 4.05[B] regarding the beating of witnesses.

124. *See* Bedell, Criminal Law 61–62.

125. *See infra* § 3.07.

126. Bedell, Criminal Law 62 (Citing Papyrus British Museum 10335).

were "to carry messages, run errands, and confiscate items in the name of the court."[127] This last duty appears to have been his most important.[128] It seems likely that the persons known as "doorkeepers" served as bailiffs for the court.[129]

Although the term *m'd͟3yw* originally denoted someone from Nubia, by the New Kingdom (*c.* 1552–1069 B.C.), *m'd͟3yw* was the word for "police" or "desert rangers."[130] According to McDowell, "They were employed as policemen, guards, and patrols throughout Egypt, but perhaps particularly in desert and frontier regions."[131] In the vicinity of the Theban necropolis, their primary responsibility was to guard the tombs. And in the investigations concerning the Great Tomb Robberies, it was the *m'd͟3yw* who were dispatched to probe the tombs under suspicion.[132] In theft cases in particular, the *m'd͟3yw* frequently served as witnesses at trial.[133] There was also a group called *3t͟w* whose legal function seems to have been something like detectives.[134] Another group identified as the *rw'd͟w* (usually translated "agents") performed a number of paralegal and quasi-judicial tasks. McDowell identifies no less than six different subgroups of *rw'd͟w*.[135]

---

127. McDowell, Jurisdiction 49 (footnote omitted). *See also* S. Allam, *Egyptian Law Courts in Pharaonic and Hellenistic Times*, 77 J. Egyptian Archaeology 109, 110 (1991) (Stating that, for the *šmsw n ḳnbt*, his "principal role was apparently to carry out tasks such as house-searches and seizure of goods.").

128. *See* McDowell, Jurisdiction 50.

129. *See* McDowell, Jurisdiction 45 ("It comes as no surprise... that doorkeepers were... called upon to act as bailiffs for the court." "There is, in short, a good case to be made for the doorkeeper as a bailiff for the court.").

130. *See Id.* at 51; Bedell, Criminal Law 62 ("The official policemen of the Necropolis were the Medjay, and they provided many of the necessary law enforcement functions in the Theban area."); *Id.* at 64–65. *See also* Grimal, Ancient Egypt 68.

131. McDowell, Jurisdiction 52.

132. *See Id.* at 52–53. For more on the Great Tomb Robberies, *see infra* §§ 4.06 and 8.04[B].

133. *See* Bedell, Criminal Law 65 (Bedell specifically mentions a case involving the theft of "portable chests.").

134. *See* McDowell, Jurisdiction 57 ("These duties resemble those of a plainclothes police officer, the deskbound colleague of the man on the beat."); *Id.* at 58 ("In short, we might roughly describe the *3t͟w* as investigators who dealt with problems of law and order among the villagers themselves....").

135. *See Id.* at 59–65. *See also* Warburton, State and Economy in Ancient Egypt 18.

§ 3.07 Adjudication by Oracle

In addition to using courts for judicial decision making, commencing in the New Kingdom (*c.* 1552–1069 B.C.), the Egyptians also used divine oracles.[136] In some cases, parties made fairly intricate arguments before an oracle (as they might before a panel of judges). In other instances, however, one party merely posed a simple question to the god.[137] A petition for trial by oracle could be either oral or written.[138] We have half a dozen examples of rather involved written petitions seeking a decision from the oracle.[139] "[E]ven within the city of Thebes, cases of petty theft were often tried by oracle."[140] "[A]n image of the deity was placed on a litter and carried about in public, expressing answers to questions by movements of various sorts. The whole operation took place in the open air and the answers were apparently quite unambiguous, often either 'yes' or 'no.'"[141] According to Bedell, "[P]etitions for oracles could only be presented to the deity when he appeared in public on festival days."[142] Tradition has it that Amenhotep I (*c.* 1526–1506 B.C.) established the workers' community at Deir el-Medina. Thus, it was the deified Amenhotep I who, as an oracle, rendered judicial decisions there.[143] Besides Amenhotep I at Deir el-Medina, there were at

---

136. *See generally* McDowell, Jurisdiction 107–141. *See also* Bedell, Criminal Law 69 ("[T]rial by oracle was separate from the regularly established system of courts."); *Id.* at 192 (Noting that the ancient Egyptians began using oracles as a means of dispute resolution early in the 19th Dynasty.); Id. at 192, 200 (Bedell says that the poor were especially likely to use oracles rather than courts, because, according to her, the judges in the courts were prone to accept bribes.); *Id.* at 206–207 (Referring to oracular dispute resolution at Deir el-Medina.); *Id.* at 212 (Explaining that outside of Thebes, small localities sought dispute resolution from oracles of their local deities.). *See generally Id.* ch. 5 (Bedell explains that trial by oracle became more popular after the 21st Dynasty due, in part, to problems with the court system, including bribery, corruption, and unfairness for the commoners.); *Id.* at 273 ("Trial by oracle developed at the beginning of the Ramesside Period as an alternative form of justice to the local courts. Throughout this period it became more and more popular, and continued to be a viable form of justice in Egypt for a long time."); *Id.* at 274 ("[T]he practice of consulting oracles continued in Egypt without interruption from the beginning of the Ramesside Period to the Christian era.").

137. *See* McDowell, Jurisdiction 138–139.

138. *See* Bedell, Criminal Law 233.

139. *See* McDowell, Jurisdiction 139.

140. Bedell, Criminal Law 211.

141. McDowell, Jurisdiction 107.

142. Bedell, Criminal Law 240. *See also Id.* at 238 ("[I]t is clear that petitions for oracles were presented to the deity during the processions.").

143. *See* McDowell, Jurisdiction 108. *See also* Bedell, Criminal Law 206–211 (Referring to the deified Amenhotep I as having been the god of the oracle at Deir el-Medina.).

least two other deified pharaohs who were used for oracular quasi-judicial decisions. In Abydos, the citizens took their cases to the oracle of Ahmose I (Amenhotep's father) (*c.* 1552–1526 B.C.). In the city of This (near Abydos), the deified Ramses II (*c.* 1279–1212 B.C.) served as the oracle. By the 21st Dynasty (*c.* 1069–945 B.C.), the oracle of Amon-Re at Karnak heard cases.[144]

The procedure for oracular decisions was rather complex. Priests carried a statue of the god on a litter. Supposedly, the god inspired the priests to move in response to questions posed. By moving backwards, the god indicated a negative response ("no"). A number of Egyptologists have argued, therefore, that forward movement must have indicated a positive answer ("yes").[145] Technically, however, the extant texts use the word *h3n* ("agree") for an affirmative reply. In addition to using forward and backward movement to signify a response, a number of texts state that the oracle spoke.[146] Just as it was the priests (*i.e.,* the priests who carried the image of the god) who manipulated the litter's movements, in all likelihood it was probably also the priests who actually spoke. Thus, in essence, the litter-bearers acted as judges for the oracular decisions.[147] The oracle could also respond in other ways. For example, it could stop moving at a decisive moment. Other manifestations of an oracle's decision are too speculative for us to interpret with any confidence.[148]

There seems to have been a division of subject matter jurisdiction in Deir el-Medina. The *ḳnbt* decided cases of a criminal nature and either the oracle or the office of the vizier decided cases relating to the ownership of property.[149] The *ḳnbt* did not deal with cases of real estate owner-

---

144. *See* GRIMAL, ANCIENT EGYPT 200; BEDELL, CRIMINAL LAW 213, 216–217.

145. *See* MCDOWELL, JURISDICTION 109. *See also* BEDELL, CRIMINAL LAW 246–247 (A number of scholars have suggested that the oracle walked backwards to signify a negative response and forwards for an affirmative answer.).

146. *See* MCDOWELL, JURISDICTION 109.

147. *See Id.* at 111. *See also Id.* at 127 (Referring to the priests who carried the litter functionally acting as de facto judges: "But in fact the priests who carried the god's litter and indicated his response by moving forwards and backwards probably expressed the popular consensus; that is, a general opinion would emerge about how the god should act which was enough to convince the bearers that they indeed felt him moving this way or that. This meant that the god in effect did no more than ratify the decision made by the local population. . . .").

148. *See* BEDELL, CRIMINAL LAW 248–250.

149. *See* MCDOWELL, JURISDICTION 118 ("'Criminal cases'. . . generally came before the *ḳnbt*." "[A]ll known disputes about property ownership were decided by the oracle, or by the office of the vizier, and none by the local court. This group, which of course includes the questions about the inheritance of real estate, forms the lion's share of cases brought before the god. In addition, the oracle was peculiarly useful for identifying a thief and for setting a price on goods when the parties involved could not reach an agreement. . . ."); *Id.* at 127 ("in practice all land cases seem to have been

ship.[150] According to McDowell, "all litigation about real estate came before the oracle."[151] It is entirely possible that the reason why the oracle had exclusive jurisdiction to decide cases relating to ownership of real property was because buildings and land may have been considered owned by the State or by the pharaoh.[152] Thus, the oracle decided matters involving the inheritance of real property and it also named thieves and established the value of objects. Other officials could deal with issues concerning real property—but only those issues unrelated to ownership.[153] The oracle also decided a number of types of cases other than those related solely to real estate ownership. We have, though, only about a dozen oracle cases that are not related to real estate. Of those non-real estate cases, most either involve establishing the values of goods or the identities of thieves.[154] In theft cases, victims frequently asked the oracle to identify the thief.[155] On those occasions when an oracle was asked to identify a thief, an official read aloud a list of houses in the village. At the instant that the name of the thief was read, the "god" made some sort of movement to signify that that was the name of the thief.[156] "[E]ven though the god accused a person of theft, the witnesses were responsible for evaluating his decision."[157] In Deir el-Medina there were only two cases wherein a victim of private theft sued in the *ḳnbt*.[158] McDowell summarizes the Deir el-Medina oracle cases as follows:

---

heard by the oracle or by the representatives of the vizier."); *Id.* at 249 (Noting that real estate was under the jurisdiction of either the oracle or vizier, whereas the *ḳnbt* handled cases of tort, contract, and minor crime.).

150. *See Id.* at 246.

151. *Id.* at 118. *Cf.* S. Allam, *Egyptian Law Courts in Pharaonic and Hellenistic Times*, 77 J. Egyptian Archaeology 109, 111 (1991) ("Some litigation [in the *ḳnbt*] concerned landed property....").

152. *See* McDowell, Jurisdiction 246; *Id.* at 122 ("In short, when landed property was involved the litigants no longer had a real choice of forum: they could not go to the local court but must try their luck with the oracle or, exceptionally, with the outside authorities."). *See Id.* at 125 (Explaining that, probably, the reason why the oracle and vizier's office were empowered to deal with cases involving real estate—while the *ḳnbt* was not—is that "the houses in the village, the huts in the Valley of the Kings and the graves... [were considered] the property of Pharaoh and it was not up to the workmen of the Necropolis to hand these out or decide a holder's right to them...."). *See also infra* § 5.01 regarding land ownership.

153. *See* McDowell, Jurisdiction 118.

154. *See Id.* at 132–133.

155. *See Id.* at 229.

156. *See* Bedell, Criminal Law 250.

157. *Id.* at 264. *See also Id.* at 260 (Referring to the presence of witnesses for oracles.); *Id.* at 265–267 (Referring to the coordination between the courts and the oracles.).

158. *See* McDowell, Jurisdiction 229.

"It happens that the large majority of cases submitted to the oracle involved property in one way or another. The handful of further cases which came before the oracle have no common feature."[159] On the other hand, "The lion's share of private matters which did not involve real estate—including disputes arising from financial affairs, transactions to be notarized, family quarrels, and various other matters—were taken to the *ḳnbt*, 'court.' "[160] We have a text on a stela from Abydos that also shows a dispute about real property decided by an oracle (the oracle of the deified Amhose I). This text provides evidence from outside Deir el-Medina of an oracle resolving a real estate dispute.[161]

Several Deir el-Medina ostraca refer to "litigation" before the oracle that was related to "ordinary disputes about business transactions."[162] Unfortunately though, these texts are in such a poor state of preservation that scholars cannot really make much sense of them. The oracle rarely, if ever, acted completely on its own. There seems to have been a significant degree of cooperation between the local magistrates and the oracle.[163] The enforceability of oracular decisions may have been on par with the enforceability of court decisions.[164] The people had to accept the decision of either for the ruling to have any real meaning.[165]

§ 3.08 Chapter Summary

Very early in their history, the Egyptians established courts. Unfortunately, for the Old and Middle Kingdoms we have many obscure references but few clear details. According to tradition, the Old Kingdom kings founded Six Great Courts and employed the Thirty Great Men of the South to serve as arbiters of disputes. Each nomarch may have acted as a judge in his own nome. By the Middle Kingdom, the nomarchs definitely functioned as judges. There was also a legal institution known as the Southern Tens.

---

159. *Id.* at 246.

160. *Id.*

161. *See Id.* at 122 ("We might note here also that at least one New Kingdom oracle outside Deir el-Medina also concerned landed property ownership, notably that recorded on a stela from Abydos, whereby the deified Pharaoh Amhose I rules on the ownership of two fields.") (citing Cairo Stela Jd'E 43649).

162. *Id.* at 135.

163. *See Id. See also Id.* at 245 (Referring to the general spirit of cooperation in law in Deir el-Medina.).

164. *See infra* § 4.09.

165. *See* MCDOWELL, JURISDICTION 138, 170–72.

By the New Kingdom, our picture becomes clearer. The pharaoh possessed significant judicial authority. He appointed the vizier(s), and, according to tradition, the pharaoh himself was responsible for creating a handful of laws. He regularly was the final arbiter of criminal punishments and occasionally he served as a judge himself. Horemhab and Seti I are well known, respectively, for their Edict and Nauri Decree which addressed specific problems and reorganized the court system. The viziers—one in the North and one in the South—were the principal judicial administrators. Known as the "prophets of *Ma'at*," they heard petitions on a daily basis and reported directly to the pharaoh. The viziers usually acted as chief justices, leading discussion and questioning in their respective Great Courts. For unusual cases, such as the harem conspiracies and Great Tomb Robberies, pharaohs assigned special ad hoc commissions to investigate and adjudicate. These commissions were granted extraordinary powers and authority. Judges on local courts such as the *ḳnbt* at Deir el-Medina ordinarily heard cases in panels, rarely alone. The *ḳnbt* at Deir el-Medina had a special location, the *ḫtm*, where it conducted its trials in public. The Deir el-Medina court decided cases mostly related to economic transactions. Interestingly, women were allowed to serve on local courts. Most courts had one individual who—analogous to the viziers in the Great Courts—acted as a chief judge to direct and control discussion. Scribes, given their special training, often served as judges and performed other quasi-judicial services for others. In addition to the judges themselves, there were many other legal and court personnel who assisted the legal machinery in a variety of ways. A number of communities, like Deir el-Medina, used divine oracles for legal decisionmaking to supplement the *ḳnbt*. Priests carried an image of the god on a litter and moved in certain directions to signify the god's judgments. In Deir el-Medina, the deified Amenhotep I rendered oracular decisions, mostly concerning the ownership of real property.

CHAPTER 4

Legal Procedure

§ 4.01 Introduction

I begin this chapter by describing one particular lawsuit that provides a curious look at civil procedure and litigation involving a variety of stages.[1] This case provides at least a partial paradigm[2] and reveals a blend of elements that are typical of ancient Egyptian legal procedure: various officials conducting investigations; witnesses testifying; parties using documents (some falsified) as evidence; and, the persistent retrying of the same issues again and again with diverse results. Although the text that we have focuses on a dispute from the time of Ramses II (*c.* 1279–1212 B.C.), many of the relevant facts of the case stretch back to the beginning of the 18th Dynasty (*c.* 1552 B.C.).[3] This case involves a dispute regarding the ownership of a parcel of land. Actually, several disputes occurred and I begin *in medias res.*

The Great Court sitting in Heliopolis, with the vizier presiding, dispatched a commissioner to the district where the property in question was

---

1. *See generally* T.G.H. JAMES, PHARAOH'S PEOPLE: SCENES FROM LIFE IN IMPERIAL EGYPT 93–97 (1984); William A. Ward, *Some Aspects of Private Land Ownership and Inheritance in Ancient Egypt, ca. 2500–1000 B.C., in* LAND TENURE AND SOCIAL TRANSFORMATION IN THE MIDDLE EAST 63, 64–65 (Tarif Khalidi ed., 1984); KATARY, LAND TENURE IN THE RAMESSIDE PERIOD 218–221.

2. *See infra* § 4.03, text accompanying note 44.

3. *See* Schafik Allam, *Women as Owners of Immovables in Pharaonic Egypt, in* WOMEN'S EARLIEST RECORDS FROM ANCIENT EGYPT AND WESTERN ASIA 123, 132 (Barbara S. Lesko ed., 1989); T.G.H. JAMES, PHARAOH'S PEOPLE: SCENES FROM LIFE IN IMPERIAL EGYPT 93; William A. Ward, *Some Aspects of Private Land Ownership and Inheritance in Ancient Egypt, ca. 2500–1000 B.C., in* LAND TENURE AND SOCIAL TRANSFORMATION IN THE MIDDLE EAST 63, 64–65 (Tarif Khalidi ed., 1984) ("The story of this estate began in the mid-sixteenth century B.C. when an ancestor of Mose, the Ship's-captain Neshi, was given a plot by the king as a reward for his services in war.") (footnote omitted).

located. He appointed one of the parties, a woman named Wernero, as trustee to cultivate the land on behalf of her brothers and sisters. One sister objected and apparently convinced the commissioner to change his mind. Now he ordered that the land, which had hitherto been considered indivisible, be split into separate parcels for each of the six heirs. At this juncture, a man named Huy, the father of the principal litigant (whose name was Mose or Mes), and Wernero (Huy's mother) appealed the commissioner's decision to divide the property. When Huy died soon thereafter, his widow, Nubnofre, attempted to use self-help to retake the land by cultivating it. A man named Kha'y ejected her. She then appealed to the Great Court in Heliopolis. That appeal went in favor of Kha'y. Years later, Mose, the son of Huy and Nubnofre (Wernero's grandson), again appealed to the Great Court. Evidently, the Great Court reversed its prior decision, persuaded by witnesses who testified as to Mose's descent. It seems that, in the earlier case between Kha'y and Nubnofre, a commissioner had colluded with Kha'y to falsify the land records.

From this account we can surmise that the Egyptians did not, strictly speaking, adhere to the principle of *res judicata* to the extent that we do today. It is notable that subsequent litigants were able to appeal what appeared to be final decisions to the same court.[4] Regarding the case of Mose, James concludes:

> It demonstrates something of the care with which a case of this kind might be pursued; how documents lodged in official archives might be consulted; how legal decisions taken by such high courts could be challenged and, ultimately, reversed by the introduction of fresh evidence.[5]

In Middle Egyptian (the "classic" period of the ancient Egyptian language), the verb *mdw* was used to describe a legal dispute or litigation.[6] Legal procedure itself was intensely important for the ancient Egyptians. It is likely that they never used a completely arbitrary method of decision

---

4. *See generally* Gardiner, Egypt of the Pharaohs 268–70; Bedell, Criminal Law 4–5.

5. T.G.H. James, Pharaoh's People: Scenes From Life in Imperial Egypt 97 (1984).

6. *See* McDowell, Jurisdiction 20–21 ("The verb *mdw*... is used almost exclusively with the meaning 'dispute' or 'contest.' " "Since in the overwhelming majority of cases the verb *mdw* means to dispute with someone at law, we may fairly translate it with "to litigate against."). *See also* R.O. Faulkner, A Concise Dictionary of Middle Egyptian 122 ("*mdw ḥnʿ* 'dispute with.'... *šm r mdt ḥnʿ* 'to go to law with' ").

making, such as the River Ordeal practiced in Mesopotamia.[7] There may, however, have been occasions when an oracle identified a thief by drawing names by lot.[8] In Deir el-Medina, local officials occasionally handled minor offenses on their own without resorting to the courts or oracle. For example, there is a case (Papyrus Deir el-Medina 26 A recto) involving a workman who stole some lamps. The accusing scribe searched the workman's hut and found them but did not take the case to court.[9] Still, to the ancient Egyptian, having a formal dispute resolution process may have been almost as important as actually winning a case in court. The Egyptians realized that without a formal procedure for resolving disputes, individuals would perceive grave injustice. Working through the dispute resolution process was an essential element of justice.[10] Thus, they acknowledged the importance of something akin to modern "due process."[11] One Middle Kingdom (*c.* 2040–1674 B.C.) instruction text advises the judge: "The petitioner likes attention to his words better than the fulfilling of that for which he came.... It is not (necessary) that everything about which he has petitioned should come to pass, (but) a good hearing is a soothing to the heart.'"[12] Having a legal procedure was particularly vital for

---

7. *See* S. Allam, *Legal Aspects in the 'Contendings of Horus and Seth', in* STUDIES IN PHARAONIC RELIGION AND SOCIETY IN HONOUR OF J. GWYN GRIFFITHS 137, 140 (Alan B. Lloyd ed., 1992).

8. *See* BEDELL, CRIMINAL LAW 252–254.

9. *See* MCDOWELL, JURISDICTION 202 (It is interesting, however, that the accused apparently sought help from the oracle, but got none.).

10. *See supra* § 3.04.

11. *See* Aristide Théodorides, *The Concept of Law in Ancient Egypt, in* THE LEGACY OF EGYPT 291, 308 (J.R. Harris ed., 2d ed. 1971) (Explaining that the concept of due process was important.). *See also Id.* at 320 ("The Nile valley has given us no code, nor any copious theoretical treatises, but the application of law is coherent, despite peculiar features of procedure—the important point being that there was a procedure, with laws to organize it.") (footnote omitted); WILSON, CULTURE OF ANCIENT EGYPT 93 (Wilson discusses the Instruction of Ptah-hotep, and emphasizes the importance of public and persuasive speaking. Note also the advice to the judge: Wilson says, "The interpretation of how *ma'at* was to be applied in the daily activities of the official is intensely practical. It is more important that the magistrate show a sympathetic face than that he take full and final action: 'If thou art one to whom petition is made, be calm as thou listenest to what the petitioner has to say. Do not rebuff him before he has swept out his body or before he has said that for which he came.'").

12. WILSON, CULTURE OF ANCIENT EGYPT 93. *See also* GARDINER, EGYPT OF THE PHARAOHS 196 (According to Gardiner, the tomb inscription of Rekhmire, vizier of Thutmose III, has this to say about the job of vizier: "that a petitioner better likes to be allowed to pour out his grievances than that they should be put right."); Aristide Théodorides, *The Concept of Law in Ancient Egypt, in* THE LEGACY OF EGYPT 291, 308–309 (J.R. Harris ed., 2d ed. 1971) (A good judge must give litigants a chance to have their say and must then explain the reasons for his decisions.). For other references to Rekhmire, *see supra* §§ 2.03, 3.04, *infra* §§ 4.02, 5.01, and 5.04[B], note 107.

the poor and disadvantaged. "That the poor and weak could obtain justice was a fundamental object of the legal process in ancient Egypt...."[13]

Scholars have been unable to detect any clear pattern or schedule that might constitute anything like a court calendar. The *ḳnbt* could convene on practically any day. We have texts that show courts in session on weekdays, weekends, and even during festival days.[14] It is likely that two factors affected the scheduling of the *ḳnbt* sessions the most: 1) the urgency of any given case; and, 2) the availability of the court officials. Interestingly, there is only one instance where two cases were heard on the same day; and the same person was the plaintiff in both cases.[15] As a rule, though, once a court convened, a typical trial lasted for one day only.[16] In the Great Courts, the same panel of judges usually saw a case from start to finish.[17]

Egyptologists hypothesize that the judges reached their decision together; neither the chief judge nor any one judge had the authority to trump the decision of the group.[18] Courts ordinarily gave specific instructions regarding who was to pay whom and how much (or some other remedy). Courts did not, so far as we know, merely declare a winner and loser.[19]

§ 4.02 Adherence to Precedent

Egyptian law was slow to evolve and adhered vigorously to precedent. One factor that contributed to both (*i.e.*, gradual legal evolution and high regard for past decisions) was the typical ancient Egyptian reverence for the past. Gardiner describes this reverence as a cultural trait that manifested it-

---

13. T.G.H. JAMES, PHARAOH'S PEOPLE: SCENES FROM LIFE IN IMPERIAL EGYPT 78. *See also supra* § 2.03[D].

14. *See* MCDOWELL, JURISDICTION 149 ("[T]he dates of the *ḳnbt* sessions form no clear pattern: a proportionately higher number of court sessions took place on weekends and festival days, but a significant number (16 of the 42) were held on workdays. This contrasts with the distribution of oracle sessions, which show a marked preference for weekends, occurring relatively less often than did the court on weekdays and never known on a festival day, oddly enough.") (Citing the work of Vleeming.).

15. *See Id.* at 150–151.

16. *See* BEDELL, CRIMINAL LAW 46.

17. *See Id.* at 53–54 (Bedell notes that this was the case in the Great Tomb Robberies.).

18. *See* MCDOWELL, JURISDICTION 169 (Citing the work of Théodorides.).

19. *See Id.* at 171; *Id.* at 172 ("[T]he court not infrequently gave positive instructions in the form of an order to one party to pay a certain sum to the other." "As a matter of fact, no case ends simply with the verdict 'A is right, B is wrong.'—this is always followed by some action by the court or an oath by one of the parties.").

self as "a conservatism of expression without parallel elsewhere in the world. No other people has ever shown a greater reverence for what was by them termed 'the time of the ancestors' 'the time of the god', or 'the first occasion'. Occasionally this love of the time honored and the typical led to downright falsification."[20] To some extent, then, partially as a consequence of this esteem for the past, judges relied on both custom and precedent to decide their cases.[21] It seems likely that, at certain periods, they also retained written copies of each judicial opinion.[22]

Litigants in the New Kingdom (*c.* 1552–1069 B.C.) occasionally cited the "law of the Pharaoh" as authoritative precedent.[23] Thus, the Egyptians discovered the utility of following precedent, a concept that we today refer to by the Latin term *stare decisis*.[24] The vizier Rekhmire was explicitly advised to follow the precedents available: "As for the office in which you hold audience, it includes a large room which contains [the records] of [all] the judgements, for he who must practise justice before all men is the vizier.... Do not act as you please in cases where the law to be applied is known...."[25]

20. GARDINER, EGYPT OF THE PHARAOHS 56. *See also supra* § 2.03[B].

21. On the topic of the ancient Egyptians using legal precedent, *see* MCDOWELL, JURISDICTION 119, 217. *See also* BEDELL, CRIMINAL LAW 2 ("[I]n most cases, at least in the Ramesside Period, judicial decisions were based on precedent."); *Id.* at 149 (Referring to the Egyptians recognizing precedent.). *See also supra* § 2.03[B].

22. *See* Janet H. Johnson, *The Legal Status of Women in Ancient Egypt, in* MISTRESS OF THE HOUSE MISTRESS OF HEAVEN: WOMEN IN ANCIENT EGYPT 175, 177 (Anne K. Chapel and Glenn E. Markoe eds., 1996) ("Egyptian judges based their decisions on traditions and precedent and kept copies of their decisions.") (footnotes omitted); BEDELL, CRIMINAL LAW 13–15; *Id.* at 13 (Referring to Egyptian use of precedent, Bedell explains: "We know that in the two Great Courts a record of each trial, which included the decision rendered by the judges, was kept on file in the judgment-hall.").

23. *See* Janet H. Johnson, *The Legal Status of Women in Ancient Egypt, in* MISTRESS OF THE HOUSE MISTRESS OF HEAVEN: WOMEN IN ANCIENT EGYPT 175, 177 (Anne K. Chapel and Glenn E. Markoe eds., 1996). *See supra* § 3.03[B].

24. *See* LEXIKON DER ÄGYPTOLGIE, Vol. 5 (1984), "Recht" 186. *See also* Taylor, *Law under the Pharaohs*, 6 POL'Y REV. 66, 67 (1980) ("The principle of *stare decisis* is not a western notion. The Egyptian courts based much of their law on precedent and there are examples of judgements based on decisions many hundreds of years old."); Aristide Théodorides, *The Concept of Law in Ancient Egypt, in* THE LEGACY OF EGYPT 291, 307–308 (J.R. Harris ed., 2d ed. 1971) (Explaining that the Instructions for the Vizier, whose "composition must go back to the 13th Dynasty...", say that "justice is to be rendered in public and in such a way that every individual shall always secure his rights. To this end, appeal is made to a sense of equity and also, by implication, to jurisprudence, since it is pointed out that the records of all judgements are kept in the vizier's archives, where they would certainly have been consulted....") (footnote omitted).

25. Aristide Théodorides, *The Concept of Law in Ancient Egypt, in* THE LEGACY OF EGYPT 291, 309 (J.R. Harris ed., 2d ed. 1971) (ellipses original). For other references to Rekhmire, *see supra* §§ 2.03, 3.04, 4.01, *infra* §§ 5.01, and 5.04[B], note 107.

In practice, in the courts at Deir el-Medina litigants cited precedent when pleading their cases.[26]

By the Middle Kingdom (*c.* 2040–1674 B.C.), the Egyptians ordinarily required that trials be held in public and that records of decisions be kept. Written records of decisions were kept so that later judges could refer to them as precedent. In addition to the private records of the litigants, some official records of cases may have been kept at Deir el-Medina (*i.e.,* during the 19th and 20th Dynasties (*c.* 1295–1069 B.C.)). We have one fragmentary papyrus (Papyrus Deir el-Medina 26) which looks like one such account. The particular locations where several judicial ostraca were discovered may suggest that some sort of archive (where documents relating to the same incidents were stored) existed at Deir el-Medina.[27] But more than likely, most extant judicial ostraca are records preserved by the interested parties whose rights were affected by the litigation. As McDowell says: "It is easy to imagine that a workman would keep a record of a law suit he had won in case the matter was reopened...."[28] Thus, the prevailing party probably kept a record of the legal proceedings and the decision of the oracle or court.[29] "There are no indications, however, that any of the texts dealing with private legal disputes were destined for an official archive, although the possibility remains that some of the contents would be incorporated in an official compendium...."[30]

§ 4.03 Outline of Litigation Procedure

In most Deir el-Medina criminal cases, we see the same procedural sequence of events. A local official discovers some problem, reports it to the vizier, and the vizier, in turn, dispatches personnel to find out more details. Ordinarily, this involves taking suspects to the riverbank for questioning

---

26. *See* T.G.H. JAMES, PHARAOH'S PEOPLE: SCENES FROM LIFE IN IMPERIAL EGYPT 90–91 (1984).

27. *See* MCDOWELL, JURISDICTION 4–5.

28. *Id.* at 6.

29. *See Id.* at 188 ("[I]t is likely that most accounts of the *ḳnbt* and oracle sessions were drawn up for the individual who benefitted from them; that is, that the litigant who won the case kept a record of the hearing and verdict as evidence for his newly established rights. These would be private documents, then, and it is not surprising that they are drawn up on ostraca, the cheapest and most abundant writing materia; they were kept in the village.").

30. *Id.* at 7.

before a decision regarding guilt or innocence is made.[31] We know of at least three criminal cases where suspects were taken to the riverbank for questioning.[32] Although scholars have advanced a number of theories regarding the interpretation of this phrase, McDowell contends, quite plausibly, that it simply means the suspect was brought to the riverbank and interrogated there.[33] "[A]fter a crime against the state, which was to be tried in the Great Court, was reported, the official state bureaucracy took over the investigation and eventual prosecution of the criminal. The person who made the accusation was usually called as a witness for the prosecution."[34]

On the other hand, persons who were the victims of civil wrongs had to bring their defendants to court. Neither police nor State prosecutors were responsible for bringing these non-criminal cases to trial.[35] "Compensation was the main reason for civil actions, and the court did not usually physically punish the offender."[36] The first procedural step for any Egyptian who wished to institute a civil lawsuit against another was to apply to the vizier, who heard petitions daily in the mornings. In the "hall of the vizier," ushers and bailiffs maintained order and lined up the petitioners on a first-come-first-served basis.[37] Thus, to commence a lawsuit, every petitioner had to

---

31. *See Id.* at 157. *See also Id.* at 202 (Referring to local officials discovering crimes and then reporting them to superiors.); *Id.* at 202–208 (McDowell explains the "oath of office" in the Egyptian judicial context, and the duty of officials in Deir el-Medina to report irregularities to their superiors.); *Id.* at 208 ("In sum, the oath of *s'ḏf3 tryt* played an important part in criminal law, in that a work-related offense was thereby made also a violation of the oath of office, and in that everyone, down to the lowest workman, was obliged to report such offenses to his superiors."). For more regarding criminal procedure in general, *see Id.* at 212 ("[I]n the normal course of events a workman would lay his charges before the captains of the gang who would presumably investigate the matter and inform the higher administration if necessary."). For reference to officials of Deir el-Medina reporting criminal conduct to the office of the vizier, *see Id.* at 213. Regarding the obligation to report irregularities, *see Id.* at 216 ("In sum, everyone whose duties brought him into contact with the Necropolis and the work in progress there was responsible for reporting irregularities to his superiors. If there was any substance to these reports they would eventually reach the office of the vizier."). *See also* BEDELL, CRIMINAL LAW 70 (Referring to the duty of any citizen to report crime to the authorities and also noting that the Nauri Decree required reporting of violations.); *infra* § 8.02, note 33.

32. *See Id.* at 221. *See also Id.* at 157 (Referring to taking an accused to the riverbank for interrogation.).

33. *See* MCDOWELL, JURISDICTION 219–223.

34. *Id.* at 76.

35. *See* BEDELL, CRIMINAL LAW 179.

36. *Id.* at 191.

37. *See* BREASTED, HISTORY OF EGYPT 240 ("All petitioners for legal redress applied first to him in his audience hall; if possible in person, but in any case in writing. For this purpose he held a daily audience or 'sitting' as the Egyptians called it. Every morning the people crowded into the 'hall of the vizier,' where the ushers and bailiffs

submit his complaint to the vizier.[38] Originally such complaints may have been merely oral,[39] but the ancient Egyptians probably submitted cases to judges in writing even as early as the Old Kingdom (*c.* 2700–2200 B.C.).[40] The vizier next had to determine whether the petition was legally sufficient, and, if it was, he then notified the defendant. Afterwards, the defendant filed a written answer with the vizier. It is possible that the plaintiff in turn was permitted to reply to the defendant's answer and that the defendant was also given an opportunity to respond to the plaintiff's reply (but the evidence is inconclusive). After all of the "briefs" (*i.e.,* written accusations and responses) were filed, the vizier conducted a hearing. He summarized the parties' arguments and asked them both questions.[41] Of course, as is true in modern litigation, the parties also had the option to settle their dispute before the court rendered its decision. This often happened when one of the parties expressly acknowledged liability in the face of convincing evidence.[42] As Allam paraphrases the judge's order to Horus and Seth in their mythological dispute: "Eating and drinking together is by far the best way for opposed parties to negotiate towards a prospective reconciliation."[43]

Although I began this chapter by stating that the case of Mose was not a perfect or universal paradigm, still, in some respects, it does in fact serve to illustrate a concise summary of basic civil procedure in ancient Egypt. First, the plaintiff filed a complaint with the vizier. That petition explained the basis for the complaint. If the vizier deemed the complaint satisfactory, he

---

jostled them into line that they might 'be heard,' in order of arrival, one after another.") (footnotes omitted).

38. *See Id.* at 240–241 ("Every petitioner to the king was obliged to hand in his petition in writing at the same office.") (footnote omitted).

39. *See* Janet H. Johnson, *The Legal Status of Women in Ancient Egypt, in* MISTRESS OF THE HOUSE MISTRESS OF HEAVEN: WOMEN IN ANCIENT EGYPT 175, 177 (Anne K. Chapel and Glenn E. Markoe eds., 1996) ("Civil lawsuits involved an oral petition to the court by a private individual.").

40. *See* Taylor, *Law under the Pharaohs*, 6 POL'Y REV. 66 (1980).

41. *See* Aristide Théodorides, *The Concept of Law in Ancient Egypt, in* THE LEGACY OF EGYPT 291, 311 (J.R. Harris ed., 2d ed. 1971) (Civil procedure began with "lodging a petition with the vizier...." "When this petition had been declared admissible and notified to the defendant, who in turn made known his case, and after each had replied, the vizier opened the hearing. He directed the proceedings, beginning in all probability by making known the arguments of the two parties, questioning them, referring to the evidence, and reserving the right to require fuller information. The vizier presided over the court....").

42. *See* S. Allam, *Legal Aspects in the 'Contendings of Horus and Seth', in* STUDIES IN PHARAONIC RELIGION AND SOCIETY IN HONOUR OF J. GWYN GRIFFITHS 137, 139–41 (Alan B. Lloyd ed., 1992) ("[M]any a trial came to an end by one of the two litigants making an avowal or acknowledgement.") (footnote omitted).

43. *Id.* at 141.

next notified the defendant who was then given an opportunity to answer the allegations. After this initial pleading stage, the vizier held a hearing at which he could question the litigants and examine evidence.[44]

Even though there were no professional lawyers who, as advocates, pleaded cases on behalf of clients, there were scribes who specialized in legal affairs.[45] These scribes produced legal documents for a fee.[46] Breasted mentions that an ancient Egyptian deceased was expected to "personally represent himself and thus ensure himself the favor of the god in the hereafter."[47] Perhaps the expectation that the dead would plead their own cases merely mirrors the expectation that the living should plead theirs as well. However, in one sense, *The Book of the Dead* itself functioned as a boilerplate brief for the deceased to present to Osiris. This "brief" was intended to persuade Osiris and his fellow judges to permit the deceased to enter the Netherworld. Thus, the scribes who produced the scrolls containing *The Book of the Dead* were like lawyers who represented their clients *via* a written brief before the ultimate judge, Osiris. Breasted speculates: "The general reliance upon such devices [*i.e., The Book of the Dead*] for escaping ultimate responsibility for an unworthy life must have seriously poisoned the life of the people."[48] "In so far as the *Book of the Dead* had become a magical agency for securing moral vindication in the hereafter, irrespective of character, it had become a positive force for evil."[49] Much the same could be said

---

44. *See* Aristide Théodorides, *The Concept of Law in Ancient Egypt, in* THE LEGACY OF EGYPT 291, 311 (J.R. Harris ed., 2d ed. 1971).

45. *See* S. Allam, *Egyptian Law Courts in Pharaonic and Hellenistic Times*, 77 J. EGYPTIAN ARCHAEOLOGY 109, 113 (1991) ("Certainly it was his familiarity with law and administration that attracted those who wanted to arrange their legal affairs....") (footnote omitted); S. Allam, *Legal Aspects in the 'Contendings of Horus and Seth', in* STUDIES IN PHARAONIC RELIGION AND SOCIETY IN HONOUR OF J. GWYN GRIFFITHS 137, 138 (Alan B. Lloyd ed., 1992); David Lorton, *The Treatment of Criminals in Ancient Egypt*, 20 J. ECONOMIC & SOCIAL HIST. ORIENT 2, 4 (1977).

46. *See* Aristide Théodorides, *The Concept of Law in Ancient Egypt, in* THE LEGACY OF EGYPT 291, 311 (J.R. Harris ed., 2d ed. 1971) ("There were no professional lawyers pleading instead and in place of their clients, but legal representation was known, and there must, moreover, have been specialized scribes who placed themselves at the disposal of the interested parties."). *See also* David Lorton, *Legal and Social Institutions of Pharaonic Egypt, in* 1 CIVILIZATIONS OF THE ANCIENT NEAR EAST 345, 355 (Jack M. Sasson ed., 1995) ("There was no legal profession in Egypt; people argued their own cases.").

47. BREASTED, DEVELOPMENT OF RELIGION AND THOUGHT 287. *See also* GRIMAL, ANCIENT EGYPT 126 ("These funerary formulae recount a ritual which was intended to ensure that the deceased passed through into the afterworld and an existence among the blessed.").

48. BREASTED, DEVELOPMENT OF RELIGION AND THOUGHT 309.

49. *Id.*

regarding clever lawyers today who are able to free the guilty on technicalities or with persuasive rhetoric.

§ 4.04 Pretrial & Trial Procedure

In addition to the preliminary steps described in § 4.03, criminal courts routinely took the following measures as part of their pretrial phase. 1) Upon receiving a criminal complaint, officials initiated a preliminary investigation. 2) If the preliminary investigation proved fruitful, the officials intensified their investigation in an effort to identify and arrest suspects. 3) The officials then submitted a list of suspects to the vizier, and they were deposed (*i.e.*, questioned under oath). Officials questioned the suspects during their depositions in an attempt to locate stolen goods and to discover the identities of other criminals.[50]

It is unlikely that the legal system was completely optional. When a plaintiff accused a defendant, the defendant was under some degree of obligation to appear in court.[51] Either private citizens or law enforcement officials had the capacity to bring charges against another.[52] In either case,

---

50. Bedell summarizes pre-trial procedure as follows:

> This pre-trial procedure at least in its essential features was standard among Theban officials. The officials received a report of a crime from some source and they investigated. If they found that a crime had indeed been committed every effort was made to discover the identity of the criminals and arrest them. A list of thieves was then usually submitted to the vizier and a deposition was taken from the culprits. In cases of theft the deposition was mainly to aid in the recovery of the stolen property. In addition to capturing the criminals, there is reason to believe that the investigators uncovered all the information they could about their activities. This information was given to the judges to be used in the trial, and it is evident in the specific nature of their questions.

BEDELL, CRIMINAL LAW 81. *See also Id.* at 78 ("It was also standard procedure in Thebes to take a deposition from thieves before their trial. The main purpose of the deposition was to discover the whereabouts of the plunder so that it could be recovered by state officials."); *Id.* at 79 (Noting that depositions of suspected criminals were taken prior to trial.); *Id.* at 72 (Referring to the *šmsw*—retainers—who "served the accused with some sort of summons that had the force of law behind it.") (footnote omitted).

51. *See* MCDOWELL, JURISDICTION 16 ("When someone says that he...'took' his opponent before the court, this therefore suggests that a certain degree of coercion was involved....") (footnote omitted); *Id.* at 154 ("Some meager evidence that a private person could force his opponent to come before the *ḳnbt* can be found in various statements that one person 'took' another to court." "But on the whole, the evidence that someone could be forced to appear in court is weak.").

52. *See* BEDELL, CRIMINAL LAW 67.

the party who initiated the suit had the responsibility to bring the defendant to court and to prove his case.[53]

Civil trial procedure in the New Kingdom (*c.* 1552–1069 B.C.) ordinarily followed a prescribed sequence of events. 1) With both litigants standing before the seated court judges, the plaintiff asserted his complaint. 2) The court declared the case "heard" and summoned the defendant to answer. 3) The defendant answered. It was crucial for the court to hear the sides of both parties.[54] 4) The court declared its ruling. The litigants then turned to each other and recited ceremonial pronouncements, the winner repeating the court's opinion and the loser agreeing to abide by it.[55] In some cases, at the close of the proceedings, the losing litigant formally promised not to reopen the case.[56] Courts regularly rendered their verdicts in simple terms: A is right, B is wrong: *m3ʿt A ʿḏ3 B*.[57]

At the opening of a trial, the plaintiff usually spoke first. His opening statement ordinarily laid out the relevant facts of the case and explained the basis for his legal claim. In other words, he described the case and explained what he believed the defendant had done to injure him. This statement contained what the Egyptians called the *smi* (*i.e.*, "the formal charge against a person").[58] There seem to have been no idiosyncratic rules about the form nor prescribed content of the plaintiff's opening argument. Plaintiffs simply gave their version of the dispute as best as they could.[59] We have a num-

---

53. *See Id.* at 69 ("It is probable that in local cases there was an official of the court who ensured that the defendant would appear for trial.").

54. *See* S. Allam, *Legal Aspects in the 'Contendings of Horus and Seth'*, *in* Studies in Pharaonic Religion and Society in Honour of J. Gwyn Griffiths 137, 138 (Alan B. Lloyd ed., 1992).

55. *See* McDowell, Jurisdiction 177 ("The loser does not seem to have had any choice in the matter, he swore his oath on order of the court."); Erman, Life in Ancient Egypt 141. *See also* Bedell, Criminal Law 82 ("Legal procedure in Egyptian courts of the Ramesside Period was not standardized, but officials adhered to certain basic principles of justice and the methods of conducting a trial which best served these fundamental beliefs."); *Id.* at 83 (Regarding trial procedure, Bedell writes: "The Egyptians were a pragmatic people and simply did what was expedient in a particular situation. The introduction of evidence was somewhat haphazard, and it mattered little whether the prosecution or the defense presented his arguments first. The oath which the court administered to ensure against false statements was taken either before or after a beating, but sometimes it was not accompanied by a beating.")

56. *See* McDowell, Jurisdiction 37.

57. *See Id.* at 24 ("The standard verdict *m3ʿt A ʿḏ3 B*...means no more than A is 'right' or 'correct' in his claims, while B is 'wrong' or 'incorrect' in his actions.") (footnote omitted).

58. Bedell, Criminal Law 83–84. *See also* R.O. Faulkner, A Concise Dictionary of Middle Egyptian 227 (1981).

59. *See* McDowell, Jurisdiction 165–166.

ber of ostraca that record what appear to have been statements of plaintiffs. These are similar to depositions, or affidavits, that might have been read in court, or, at least, submitted to the court like a plaintiff's brief, explaining his version of the facts of the case.[60] On one rather curious text the defendant's response actually precedes the plaintiffs' complaint.[61] We cannot conclude whether this necessarily means that the defendant really spoke before the plaintiffs as well. In that case, however, the defendant had a higher social standing than his accusers. Thus, his status may have influenced the scribe's decision to enter his statement in the record first. Or as was suggested, it may have influenced the court to allow him to speak first. We simply cannot be certain.[62]

If the *ḳnbt* at Deir el-Medina had fixed rules of court procedure, we do not know what they were. For example, we do not even know how the judges reached their decisions (*i.e.*, whether each judge's vote was equal, whether a simple majority vote controlled, or whether unanimity or consensus was required).[63] McDowell allows that "it need not follow that the court had to return a unanimous verdict; a majority opinion could have been enough, or perhaps some judges' votes counted more than others."[64] Some evidence suggests that judges, at least occasionally, articulated in writing the reasons for their decisions. One papyrus from the time of Thutmose III (*c.* 1479–1425 B.C.) in particular contains the conclusion of a case that was dismissed. In it, the writing states the grounds for the decision and the factors considered.[65]

For criminal trials, the order of proceedings was basically the same as in civil trials, except that a State official, perhaps the vizier, took the place of the plaintiff. For criminal trials in the Great Courts, the plaintiff's opening statement was not required since the judges themselves functioned as prosecutors in those cases.[66] Bedell suggests that the defendant/accused (in a

---

60. *See Id.* at 18.

61. *See* Bedell, Criminal Law 85 (Citing the slander case of the foreman Ḥ3y.). For more on the case of Ḥ3y, *see infra* § 8.09[D].

62. *See Id.* at 85–86.

63. *See* McDowell, Jurisdiction 148, 167, 170.

64. *Id.* at 170.

65. *See* Aristide Théodorides, *The Concept of Law in Ancient Egypt, in* The Legacy of Egypt 291, 310 (J.R. Harris ed., 2d ed. 1971) (Mentioning a case that shows a legal opinion that explains the basis of its the decision. "The statement given as to the grounds of the decision embraces the factors taken into consideration, followed by the legal basis of the sentence and the enacting terms....").

66. *See* Bedell, Criminal Law 84. *See also Id.* at 72 ("In the extant records, a private citizen never acts as prosecutor in a criminal case tried in the Great Court of Thebes.").

criminal case) was required to plead guilty or not guilty at the opening of the trial—just after the accusation was stated.[67] Apparently, an accused criminal defendant was presumed innocent until proven guilty. Bedell maintains that, if an accused refused to confess and the prosecution was unable to produce a witness to testify against him, the accused had to be freed upon swearing an oath of innocence.[68] Ordinarily, criminal courts in ancient Egypt were legitimate deliberative bodies. They were not kangaroo courts staged merely to lend an appearance of authority to punishments. We know of several defendants in criminal cases who pled not guilty and, indeed, were later set free.[69]

Since there were no advocates who represented the parties, the judges took an active role in litigation. They questioned the parties, often probing with great diligence.[70] They were inclined to ask defendants, especially, numerous questions. It was common for judges to ask a defendant whether he could produce a witness to support his claims. More often than not, the judge who is recorded as having asked a question was also the highest ranking member of the judges on the court.[71] In criminal cases where one defendant confessed, the judges sought evidence (through their questioning) that would advance the case against other co-criminals. The court also hoped to discover the whereabouts of stolen property. In addition, they pressed for details regarding how the criminals had accomplished their

---

67. *See Id.* at 88–89 ("The first thing the judges wanted was a plea of guilty or not guilty because the nature of subsequent proceedings would depend on this plea."); *Id.* at 145 ("throughout the tomb robbery texts, the term used for innocent was *w'b*, which literally means 'pure.' ").

68. *See Id.* at 82, 105–106; *Id.* at 142 (According to Bedell: "If a suspect refused to confess to a crime after being subjected to repeated torture, and he had taken an oath in defense of his innocence the judges had to release him."). *See also Id.* at 71 ("[T]he burden of proof in local court actions was always on the accuser whether the crime was perpetrated against him or against the state.").

69. *See Id.* at 90, 131; *Id.* at 133 (Noting that in one case a sailor named Amenhotep was beaten with a stick while testifying. He swore an oath of innocence, and was then declared innocent and set free.).

70. *See Id.* at 10 ("In the Ramesside courts the judges thoroughly interrogated suspects to determine the truth in a particular case."); *Id.* at 54 (Referring to the judges asking witnesses questions during the trial.). *See also Id.* at 86–88 (Referring to judges asking witnesses questions.); *Id.* at 86 ("The judges were responsible for questioning the plaintiff to make certain that his charges were true and that a crime had actually been perpetrated."); *Id.* at 87 (Specifically recounting questions asked by the judges in the Ḥ3y slander case.); *Id.* at 88 ("It is clear... that the judges were obligated to make sure that the accusations of the plaintiff were true. In the local courts this was accomplished by repeatedly questioning the accuser about details of the alleged crime."); *Id.* at 88 (Referring to judges asking defendants questions.).

71. *See* MCDOWELL, JURISDICTION 168.

crime. In that way, the judges hoped to gain information that could help them prevent reoccurrences.[72] Thus, the judges extensively questioned criminals in an attempt to elicit accomplices, amounts stolen, the modus operandi, and the whereabouts of the plunder. In one tomb robbery case, a thief confessed and then told the court exactly how much gold and other valuables had been taken from the mummies in the tomb. In another case involving a theft from a temple of Ramses III, one of the thieves admitted that he had melted some of the gold that he had stolen from the temple. Another thief confessed that he and his cohorts had fenced some of the gold taken from the temple of Ramses II, by purchasing corn with it.[73]

Judges were not confined to asking merely pointed, step-by-step questions (*i.e.*, of the sort that the modern law of evidence often requires on cross-examination). Judges could ask defendants open-ended questions. Such inquiries basically sought a narrative of criminal activity.[74] For example, in one case brought before the Great Court of Thebes, a woman by the name Taaper had witnessed a sale of stolen goods. At trial, one of the judges asked her to tell her version of the blackmarket trafficking: "Come tell the story of this copper which you said was in the possession of... Peikharu...."[75] Thus, the lion's share of the judges' questions were designed to resolve issues of fact. Unlike the cases heard by the oracles, there was very little discussion in the *ḳnbt* relating to applicable laws and precedential cases. McDowell suggests that the paucity of reference to law is "mostly because the laws or customs involved were familiar to all concerned...."[76] In addition to the judges, occasionally scribes—who may have functioned as prosecutors in these cases—also were permitted to ask the witnesses questions.[77]

After the court rendered its decision, the non-prevailing party ordinarily took an oath promising to respect the court's decision. Or, if the court had sentenced the defendant to a punishment, the court itself might implement the penalty (*e.g.*, beatings). For extremely serious cases (particularly in criminal cases), the court usually referred the matter either to the vizier or the pharaoh for final sentencing.[78]

---

72. *See* BEDELL, CRIMINAL LAW 56–58, 91–98 (Referring to judges questioning criminals, who confessed, to discover how a crime was committed and where the stolen goods were hidden.).

73. *See Id.* at 94–98.

74. *See Id.* at 57.

75. *See Id.* at 73.

76. McDOWELL, JURISDICTION 166.

77. *See* BEDELL, CRIMINAL LAW 60.

78. *See* McDOWELL, JURISDICTION 116–117. *See also* ERMAN, LIFE IN ANCIENT EGYPT 141 ("[I]n criminal cases...the accusations were addressed to the governor, who took the place of the plaintiff." Then, instead of pronouncing the sentence itself,

§ 4.05 Evidence

[A] Introduction

The ancient Egyptians often experienced difficulty obtaining solid, credible evidence. It was burdensome, for example, to discover who stole goods or who vandalized property.[79] But, as Bedell remarks concerning the courts in the Ramesside Period, "there was an attempt to base decisions on human experience, perception, and reason, such as testimony and material evidence...."[80] Judges took into account many kinds of evidence including documents and the testimony of witnesses. In fact, the word used for witnesses, *mtrw*, was used not only for human witnesses but also for other types of evidence, such as written documents (*e.g.*, letters).[81] Egyptian courts preferred the testimony of witnesses to other kinds of evidence. And although we cannot be certain whether courts in the Old, Middle, and New Kingdoms had verifiable rules of evidence, by the time of the Law Collection of Hermopolis (*c.* 700 B.C.), it appears that rules of evidence had been formulated.[82]

[B] Witnesses & Oaths

Parties themselves routinely swore oaths to affirm the veracity of their assertions. In civil trials, witnesses could testify regarding the authenticity of documents, such as wills.[83] One provision in the Law Collection of Hermopolis allows—quite logically—that the testimony of the builders who constructed a house was competent to prove that the party claiming ownership was, indeed, the true owner of the dwelling in question.[84] The an-

---

the court often sent the case to the king for sentencing if the court found the defendant guilty.) (footnote omitted).

79. *See* MCDOWELL, JURISDICTION 228.

80. BEDELL, CRIMINAL LAW 123.

81. *See* MCDOWELL, JURISDICTION 21. *See also* R.O. FAULKNER, A CONCISE DICTIONARY OF MIDDLE EGYPTIAN 121 (1981).

82. *See* S. Allam, *Egyptian Law Courts in Pharaonic and Hellenistic Times*, 77 J. EGYPTIAN ARCHAEOLOGY 109, 119 (1991).

83. For example, in the case of Mose, the court took into account "depositions of witnesses in the previous litigation over the land in his grandmother's time and verbal statements of his own contemporaries." William A. Ward, *Some Aspects of Private Land Ownership and Inheritance in Ancient Egypt, ca. 2500–1000* B.C., *in* LAND TENURE AND SOCIAL TRANSFORMATION IN THE MIDDLE EAST 63, 65 (Tarif Khalidi ed., 1984).

84. *See* MATTHA, THE DEMOTIC LEGAL CODE OF HERMOPOLIS WEST 33.

cient Egyptians were very fond of putting a witnesses's testimony into writing. They attached great importance to the permanence of written testimony.[85] It appears likely that a witness was required to affix some sort of signature to his written testimony (as a means of validation) when it was used as evidence in court.[86] The courts may have considered relevant the sheer number of witnesses who testified for or against a party. In one case (Papyrus Cairo 65739), for example, the prosecution produced a relatively large number of witnesses; six, three men and three women.[87] But the content and credibility of the testimony mattered more than numbers alone.

Sources from the New Kingdom (*c.* 1552–1069 B.C.) confirm that both women and slaves were legally competent to testify in court.[88] Witnesses, however, were not always treated with a great deal of respect. Court personnel routinely beat or otherwise tortured witnesses.[89] In the case of the famous Great Tomb Robberies under Ramses IX (*c.* 1125–1107 B.C.), officials bound the hands and feet of at least one witness, beat him with a stick, and forced him to swear an oath or else suffer mutilation. And after this cruel treatment, officials incarcerated the witness for further questioning.[90] Some

85. *See* Erman, Life in Ancient Egypt 136; Mattha, The Demotic Legal Code of Hermopolis West 77.

86. *See* Gay Robins, Women in Ancient Egypt 137 ("Legal documents, which were often drawn up before the court and produced as evidence, had to be signed by witnesses to validate the contents.").

87. *See* Bedell, Criminal Law 118–119.

88. *See* Gay Robins, Women in Ancient Egypt 137 ("While some female witnesses are known, the majority were men."); Wilson, Culture of Ancient Egypt 203 ("Further, such business documents as we possess from the Empire show that women had their own rights to property, to buying and selling, or to testifying in court."); Aristide Théodorides, *The Concept of Law in Ancient Egypt, in* The Legacy of Egypt 291, 307 (J.R. Harris ed., 2d ed. 1971) (Noting that slaves "could acquire property and bear witness at law, even against their masters....").

89. *See* McDowell, Jurisdiction 21 ("The *smtr*, 'examination,' of a witness could be a painful process, involving beatings and other forms of torture to encourage him to confess....") (footnote omitted); Bedell, Criminal Law 59–61 (Referring to beating witnesses to elicit testimony and torture to try to induce a confession.); *Id.* at 90 ("He was examined by beating with the stick; his feet and hands were fettered (?)...."); *Id.* at 97 ("Their examination was made by beating with sticks, and their feet and hands were twisted."); *Id.* at 101 ("Beating the accused and the witnesses was the most common method of checking the truth of their testimony."), *Id.* at 102–103 (Referring generally to the torture of witnesses.); *Id.* at 102 (According to Bedell, "Three instruments of torture were used, the stick, the birchrod, and a device for twisting.").

90. *See* McDowell, Jurisdiction 174 ("[T]hose investigating the Great Tomb Robberies made liberal use of blows in their efforts to extract information from both suspects and witnesses. This suggests that a beating was unpleasant but not unbearable."). *See also* Gardiner, Egypt of the Pharaohs 300–301; *Id.* at 300 (Noting especially the examination of witnesses: "He was examined by beating with a stick, and fetters were placed upon his feet and hands; an oath was administered to him, on pain

of the thieves who testified were "beaten with sticks, and their feet and hands were twisted."[91] Those who were accused and tortured often confessed—but not always.[92] Modern scholars believe that in some cases an accused may have confessed to a crime not due to actual guilt but instead because of pressure and torture.[93] Occasionally the Egyptian judges themselves became concerned that an innocent defendant might confess to a crime simply in an attempt to stop the beatings that were being inflicted.[94]

What makes the torture of witnesses such an interesting phenomenon is that the Egyptian courts did not torture only an accused, but also on occasion ordinary witnesses who were merely offering testimony. In a similar vein, during warfare—almost universally—enemy prisoners are routinely tortured in an effort to extract information. One must wonder whether the goal of such torture is to try to get information out of that particular prisoner. Clearly, to a limited extent the answer is yes. To another degree, however, part of what enemy torture during wartime is intended to accomplish is to try to compel other prisoners to tell the truth. When fellow prisoners of war see one of their comrades being tortured, perhaps that increases the likelihood that they (the ones who see and/or hear their friends being tortured) will tell the truth in an attempt to avoid torture themselves. As an analogy then, perhaps, at least on one level, torturing trial witnesses was meant to send a message to other witnesses that they should tell the truth in order to avoid torture. One must wonder though about the viability of such a scheme. Procedurally it may be efficient. Witnesses may say what others want them to say. Thus, witnesses under threat of torture may make a trial run more smoothly because they say what the prosecutor or plaintiff wants them to say. There may not be very much truth, but it could be procedurally very efficient. The threat of witness-torture might also have the

---

of mutilation, not to speak falsehood." "He was made a prisoner for further examination."). *See also infra* § 8.04[B].

91. J. Capart, A.H. Gardiner, and B. van de Walle, *New Light on the Ramesside Tomb-Robberies*, 22 J. EGYPTIAN ARCHAEOLOGY 169, 172 (1936). *See also Id.* at 187.

92. *See Id.* at 188. *See also* McDOWELL, JURISDICTION 198 (Referring to torture used to elicit confessions.).

93. *See* McDOWELL, JURISDICTION 138 ("[H]e was seized upon and beaten. The evident confusion of the accused and the vehemence of his repeated denials leave the modern reader with the uncomfortable feeling that he was innocent all along and had simply been browbeaten into confessing a crime he had never committed.").

94. *See* BEDELL, CRIMINAL LAW 100 ("It was necessary for the judges to check the reliability of a confession because some suspects... pleaded guilty out of fear of the beatings used to elicit confessions. In Papyrus B.M. 10052 an accused criminal threatened to lie if the severe beatings were not stopped.").

effect of chilling the bringing of frivolous law suits. It might also decrease the willingness of citizens to testify at trial.

Although defendants in criminal trials were permitted to offer the testimony of witnesses into evidence,[95] the witnesses had to swear an oath promising not to commit perjury.[96] The word used for such an oath was *'nḫ*.[97] The witness's oath ordinarily recited that the witness would suffer severe punishments if he committed perjury. It was common for a witness's oath regarding perjured testimony to invoke the same punishment as the wrong at issue in the case itself.[98] In the case of Mose,[99] one woman witness stated that her penalty for perjury would be a demotion in her household ("[I]f I speak falsely, may I be sent to the back of the house."). A male witness in the Mose case said that he would endure mutilation and banishment ("[I]f I speak falsely, may my [nose] and ears be cut off, and may I be sent to Kush."). A female witness in the Great Tomb Robberies trial summoned banishment as her penalty for perjury ("If I speak falsehood, may I be sent to Ethiopia.").[100] In another oath, a witness invoked mutilation and impalement ("[H]e is to have his nose and ears cut off and be placed upon a stake.").[101] It is likely, however, that the penalties recited in the witnesses' oaths were merely formulaic. They served a cautionary function to remind

---

95. *See* Aristide Théodorides, *The Concept of Law in Ancient Egypt, in* The Legacy of Egypt 291, 312–313 (J.R. Harris ed., 2d ed. 1971) (Noting that criminal defendants could use witnesses to try to exculpate themselves.).

96. *See* McDowell, Jurisdiction 198 (Referring to oaths against perjury.); Aristide Théodorides, *The Concept of Law in Ancient Egypt, in* The Legacy of Egypt 291, 299 (J.R. Harris ed., 2d ed. 1971). *See also* Bedell, Criminal Law 129 ("All oaths taken by witnesses and defendants while testifying in Ramesside courts were among those that J. Wilson labeled assertory, confirming the truth of a statement or declaration.") (footnote omitted); *Id.* (Bedell notes two types of witness oaths. First, was the standard oath against perjury. It invoked a penalty for perjured testimony. Second, was an oath that a defendant took *sua sponte* as a declaration of innocence. Essentially, the defendant swore that he had not committed the crime as accused.); *Id.* ("[O]ften a defendant would take both types of oath, one given by the court swearing that he would not give false testimony and one taken specifically as a defense."); *Id.* at 140–141 ("[T]he cases of perjury that we know of seem to give conflicting evidence about the importance of the oath. In some cases perjury was treated as a serious crime and in others it was overlooked.").

97. *See* McDowell, Jurisdiction 33. For more on legal oaths in general, *see Id. at* 36–37. *See also* Bedell, Criminal Law 123 ("An oath taken in a court of law no matter what its purpose was known as an oath of the lord ('nḫ n nb) and sometimes a great oath of the lord ('nḫ '3 n nb).") (footnotes omitted). *See also* R.O. Faulkner, A Concise Dictionary of Middle Egyptian 44 (1981).

98. *See* Bedell, Criminal Law 126.

99. *See supra* § 4.01.

100. *See* Bedell, Criminal Law 126 (footnotes omitted).

101. *See* Id. at 128 (footnote omitted).

the witnesses of the importance of truthful testimony. It is doubtful that witnesses guilty of perjury actually suffered such severe punishments as a consequence of lying under oath in court.[102]

In contested cases, as is often true today, the judges plainly were forced to decide based on their interpretation of which witnesses were telling the truth and which were lying. The credibility of witnesses could play a decisive role in the difference between conviction and acquittal.[103] The status of a witness could affect his credibility. For example, the testimony of important individuals, such as the chief of police in one instance and the vizier, himself, in another, influenced the court nearly to the point of being dispositive.[104]

Interestingly, as an empirical matter, in extant cases more witnesses testified on behalf of the prosecution than for the defense. This may have been because of the prosecution's burden of proof. Without a witness, the prosecution really had no case.[105] There are very few cases where both prosecution and defense witnesses testified.[106] And, in fact, when defendants were able to produce a witness, the courts seem to have been inclined to presume that they (*i.e.*, the defendants) were innocent.[107]

In one tomb robbery case (Papyrus British Museum 10052), the prosecution accused a man by the name of Peikharu of having ferried certain thieves across the Nile (*i.e.*, thereby aiding and abetting the crimes). Peikharu called another ferryman, named Nesamon, as a witness in his defense. In testimony that sounds like something out of the old Perry Mason T.V. series, Nesamon confessed that it was he, not Peikharu, who had provided transport for the robbers. In this instance, the defense witness proved to be critical, indeed.[108]

In a few cases, the widow of a deceased suspect was called as a witness. In these circumstances, the court's motive appears to have been a desire to lo-

---

102. *See Id.* at 127–128.

103. *See Id.* at 110 ("The evidence of other witnesses who testified in the Great Court of Thebes was instrumental in convicting or defending the accused. The character and previous credibility of the witness was apparently important to the judges."). *See also Id.* at 139 ("In many cases the oath of a defendant stood against the testimony of a witness who had also sworn to tell the truth, and the judges had to decide who was lying.").

104. *See Id.* at 111.

105. *See Id.* at 112, 117 ("In cases tried in the local courts the witness was almost a prerequisite for the prosecution.").

106. *See Id.* at 113 ("A witness for the prosecution and a witness for the defense in the same case is a very rare occurrence in extant texts.").

107. *See Id.* at 114 ("We can assume that when a witness for the defendant did testify in court, the judges almost always decided in his favor.").

108. *See Id.* at 112.

cate the husband's share of plunder.[109] But judges sometimes suspected that the widows still had some of the loot that their husbands had stolen. This was especially true if the widow, as of late, had been living beyond her apparent means (*e.g.*, purchasing slaves).[110] We also know of a situation where sons of deceased suspects had to testify regarding what they knew about their fathers' thefts. By the time of the trial, the sons testified that they were mere children back when the thefts had occurred.[111] In one tomb robbery case, although a suspect had died, the court demanded that one of his female servants be taken to the crime scene to ascertain whether she could identify which tomb her former, deceased master had robbed.[112]

We know of at least one instance (Papyrus Mayer A) where testimony that modern law characterizes as hearsay was admitted into evidence. In this tomb robbery case, a prosecution witness, a herald named Perpethew, testified that he had *heard* that a butcher named Pennestytauy had been involved in the robberies in some unspecified fashion. Pennestytauy pleaded innocent. Ultimately, the boss of the thieves testified that Pennestytauy had not been involved. Thus, although hearsay testimony appears to have been admissible, in this particular case, it proved to be untrustworthy (and probably just plain false).[113]

[C] Documents & Other Types of Evidence

Because of the nature of the litigation involved, parties were likely to use documentary evidence in civil cases more than in criminal ones.[114] Documents, in particular, could be important in establishing facts.[115] And as a rule, the testimony of witnesses was rarely used in isolation. It was usually used either to corroborate documentary evidence or to impeach it.[116] Especially in cases involving contract disputes, land ownership, or disagreements over wills, litigants produced the relevant document(s) (or some-

---

109. *See Id.* at 114, 117.
110. *See Id.* at 115.
111. *See Id.* at 116–117.
112. *See Id.* at 101.
113. *See Id.* at 113–114.
114. *See Id.* at 120.
115. *See* PESTMAN, MARRIAGE & MATRIMONIAL PROPERTY 84; *Id.* at 68. *See also* Aristide Théodorides, *The Concept of Law in Ancient Egypt, in* THE LEGACY OF EGYPT 291, 311 (J.R. Harris ed., 2d ed. 1971).
116. *See* Aristide Théodorides, *The Concept of Law in Ancient Egypt, in* THE LEGACY OF EGYPT 291, 311 (J.R. Harris ed., 2d ed. 1971) ("[L]egal decisions were made on the basis of documentary proof, supported by witnesses' evidence.").

times a document purported to be such) as evidence.[117] In the property dispute of Mose,[118] for example, the vizier examined title deeds (documentary evidence). In the same case, other officials examined official records of the granary and treasury at the Northern capital of Pi-Ra'messe.[119] When the officials themselves conspired to falsify those documents, Mose resorted to bringing in witnesses (both men and women) who swore to his lineage and swore that his father had cultivated the land in question and had paid taxes. The court changed its mind on the basis of these witnesses and prior written evidence.[120] As another illustration, the Law Collection of Hermopolis required that a plaintiff actually produce an annuity contract in court as a means of proof.[121] Similarly, a valid receipt was considered competent documentary evidence.[122]

In another case (Papyrus Mayer A) the defendant, named Howtenefer, was accused of robbery. He argued that his financial situation was such that

---

117. *See* BEDELL, CRIMINAL LAW 106; *Id.* at 117 ("[T]he witness was the most common means of proving an allegation."); *Id.* at 122 (Mentioning the case of Mose relating to "the dispute over the ownership of lands between Nebnefret and Khay...."). *See also Id.* at 123 (Referring to problems with litigants attempting to use forged documents as evidence.).

118. *See supra* § 4.01.

119. *See* S. Allam, *Egyptian Law Courts in Pharaonic and Hellenistic Times*, 77 J. EGYPTIAN ARCHAEOLOGY 109, 114 (1991); GARDINER, EGYPT OF THE PHARAOHS 269 ("His deposition was immediately followed by that of the defendant Kha'y, and it is from their combined statements that we learn what had happened. When the Vizier came to examine the title-deeds he could not fail to perceive that there had been forgery on one side or the other. Nubnofre then proposed that a commissioner should be sent with Kha'y to consult the official records of Pharaoh's treasury and granary at the northern capital of Pi-Ra'messe."). *See also* GRIMAL, ANCIENT EGYPT 261 (Referring to the location of Pira'messe.).

120. *See* GARDINER, EGYPT OF THE PHARAOHS 269 ("To Mose, determined to recover his rights, no alternative was now open but to establish with the help of sworn witnesses the facts of his descent from Neshi and of his father's having cultivated the estate year by year and having paid taxes on it. The testimony afforded by the men and women cited by him, taken together with the written evidence previously used, no longer left any uncertainty as to the rightness of his cause, and though the end of the hieroglyphic inscription is lost we cannot doubt that the Great Court together with the lesser one at Memphis delivered a final verdict re-establishing Mose in his inheritance."). *See also* Christopher J. Eyre, *Peasants and "Modern" Leasing Strategies in Ancient Egypt*, 40 J. ECONOMIC & SOCIAL HIST. ORIENT 367, 385, n. 101 (1997); William A. Ward, *Some Aspects of Private Land Ownership and Inheritance in Ancient Egypt, ca. 2500–1000 B.C., in* LAND TENURE AND SOCIAL TRANSFORMATION IN THE MIDDLE EAST 63, 65 (Tarif Khalidi ed., 1984) ("His documentation was impressive: family records going back 300 years; a copy of the official land-register which named his parents as the owners; a copy of the official tax-assessment records showing his family had paid the taxes on the land....").

121. *See* MATTHA, THE DEMOTIC LEGAL CODE OF HERMOPOLIS WEST 100.

122. *See Id.* at 97.

it should be obvious that he had not robbed anyone; he was not living beyond his means. This argument is a savvy one. Many a criminal has been caught when detectives discover that he has an inflated bank account and is spending lavishly. Howtenefer's argument regarding his relative lack of funds certainly seems persuasive. In fact, he was ultimately released after another witness—who had originally testified against him—later recanted his fabricated testimony.[123] Interestingly, the witness who recanted, a slave named Degay, had already admitted guilt himself.[124] But we know from other cases, as well, that when a defendant was charged with robbery, evidence relating to his finances could be especially relevant.[125]

In addition to witness testimony and legal documents, the ancient Egyptians also searched homes and visited crime scenes (sometimes discovering stolen objects in the process) to obtain evidence.[126] Officials were entitled to search houses of persons who had been accused of theft. But we do not know the scope of the suspects' rights. Nor do we know what degree of suspicion was required before such a search could be made. In short, we have very little idea of whether the Egyptians had any protections for individuals' rights analogous to the American Constitution's prohibitions regarding unreasonable searches and seizures.[127] As a means of acquiring additional evidence, occasionally judges required an accused to accompany them to a crime scene (such as a tomb that had been robbed). There, the court asked specific questions about the precise nature of the criminal deeds.[128]

§ 4.06 Procedure in the Special Courts

In certain extraordinary circumstances, the king took it upon himself to appoint a special court to deal with unusually sensitive cases.[129] In those in-

123. *See* Bedell, Criminal Law 90–91, 108.

124. *See Id.* at 108.

125. *See Id.* at 116 (Bedell mentions two suspects in the Great Tomb Robberies, Irinefer and Ese: "the court thoroughly investigated their financial status.").

126. *See Id.* at 123 (Referring to other physical evidence used in court during the Ramesside Period.); Jacke Phillips, *Tomb-robbers and their Booty in Ancient Egypt, in* Death and Taxes in the Ancient Near East 157, 166 (Sara Orel ed., 1992).

127. *See* McDowell, Jurisdiction 134 (McDowell describes a case involving a search for stolen property in the hut of the accused.). The musing regarding the similarity to the American Constitution is my musing, not McDowell's.

128. *See* Bedell, Criminal Law 101.

129. *See Id.* at 74 ("In a few cases serious crimes against the state were reported to Pharaoh. Pharaoh then delegated certain members of his bureaucracy to investigate the alleged offenses." Bedell gives an example of one such case involving the theft of gold and silver from a temple at Medinet Habu.). *See also supra* §§ 3.01, 3.03[D].

stances, the procedures followed may have been ad hoc.[130] There are three kings who appointed famous special courts: 1) Pepi I (*c.* 2325 B.C.); 2) Ramses III (*c.* 1186–1154 B.C.); and, 3) Ramses IX (*c.* 1125–1107 B.C.). The earliest example of these extraordinary procedures comes from the 6th Dynasty during the reign of king Pepi I. Pepi, as was mentioned above, appointed one special prosecutor, a man named Weni, who wrote a report and acted as a single judge for deciding the case.[131]

In an exceptional criminal case (a plot—hatched and developed from within the pharaoh's harem—to assassinate the 20th Dynasty pharaoh Ramses III), the pharaoh selected a special commission to investigate the matter. Ramses III originally appointed fourteen men to serve on the committee to investigate this infamous harem conspiracy.[132] But in this case, the pharaoh expressly ordered the commission to handle all of the details itself, because he did not want to be involved. Apparently, the matter was so personal that Ramses did not want to let his emotions affect the process and, thus, he insulated himself from the proceedings. It was unusual that the same judicial body in this case was empowered both to determine guilt or innocence *and* also to determine the sentence. Often in Egyptian legal procedure, one body decided the merits of a case and another was responsible for sentencing.[133]

---

130. *See* BREASTED, HISTORY OF EGYPT 499 ("The old Pharaoh...appointed a special court for the trial of the conspirators." His charge to the court "lay upon the judges a responsibility for impartial justice on the merits of the case, with a judicial objectivity which is remarkable in one who held the lives of the accused in his unchallenged power and had himself just been the victim of a murderous assault at their hands." Among the charges, Ramses III reminded the court: "Give heed and have a care lest ye execute punishment upon [anyone] unjustly....") (Breasted's brackets). *See also* ERMAN, LIFE IN ANCIENT EGYPT 141 ("There were of course particular cases, which formed exceptions to the usual procedure of justice...."); *Id.* at 142 (Explaining that when unusual circumstances occurred, as when the accused persons were close to the king, he would take control of the case away from the usual system and appoint one or more ad hoc judges/fact finders.).

131. *See supra* § 3.03[D], *infra* § 8.05. *See also* ERMAN, LIFE IN ANCIENT EGYPT 142.

132. *See* BREASTED, HISTORY OF EGYPT 500.

133. *See* Aristide Théodorides, *The Concept of Law in Ancient Egypt, in* THE LEGACY OF EGYPT 291, 313 (J.R. Harris ed., 2d ed. 1971) ("Some cases were tried by extraordinary means." Théodorides gives the example of the "Judicial Papyrus of Turin" from the 20th Dynasty in which Ramses III "appointed a special commission, instructing its members to judge the guilty severely but justly, and without referring the matter to him." This extraordinary procedure was used because the alleged criminals were involved in a plot to assassinate Ramses, and he thought that he should distance himself from the judicial process. This also presents an unusual case in that the special tribunal both conducted the investigation and carried out the sentence. "Usually in criminal cases authority for the examination of a case was distinct from authority to pass judgement."). *See also supra* §§ 3.03[B], 3.04, *infra* § 8.05.

In this case, several members of the royal harem originally formulated the plot. Later, members of the military and other officials conspired with them to assassinate Ramses III. Most of the conspirators were attached to the royal household. Their scheme was to kill Ramses and to instigate a coup. It was actually after the confederates were arrested that Ramses appointed the commission to investigate.[134] The pharaoh wrote special instructions for this ad hoc "court," telling them to execute those who deserved it but not to tell him anything regarding the matter. In order to operate more efficiently, this commission divided itself into two separate subcommittees. A six-member subcommittee dealt with one group of conspirators and a five-member subcommittee dealt with the others.[135] Interestingly, in the midst of the investigation, three members of the six-person subcommittee were arrested because they were becoming friendly with the harem women! The members of the commission who were arrested for cavorting with the women were tried, convicted, and punished by having their noses and ears cut off.[136] When the other members of the commission had completed their work, the guilty conspirators were forced to commit suicide.[137]

To investigate the royal tomb robberies (*i.e.*, the Great Tomb Robberies) that occurred under Ramses IX, the pharaoh instructed the vizier to convene a special commission to inspect the pilfered tombs and to report back to the vizier. The commission was empowered to arrest suspects and to hold them pending trial by the vizier and other high officials.[138] The vizier

---

134. *See* Erman, Life in Ancient Egypt 142 ("We have a more detailed account of a similar lawsuit of later time, concerning the great harem conspiracy under Ramses III." The military, the harem, and other officials were involved in the plot. Ramses "avoided the regular lawcourts, and appointed a number of trusted personages to form a special court of justice, and gave them discretionary powers over the life and death of the criminals." "Certain persons belonging to the royal household (fictitious names are given) had conspired against his majesty and planned an open rebellion. The harem formed the centre of the conspiracy."); *Id.* at 143 (The conspirators were discovered and arrested, "and brought before a kind of court-martial, consisting of officials of high and low rank, whom the king believed worthy of his special confidence.").

135. *See Id.* at 143.

136. *See Id.* at 144 ("[T]heir punishment was fulfilled by cutting off their noses and ears.").

137. For Breasted's account of the Ramses III harem conspiracy, *see* Breasted, History of Egypt 498–500.

138. *See* Aristide Théodorides, *The Concept of Law in Ancient Egypt, in* The Legacy of Egypt 291, 312 (J.R. Harris ed., 2d ed. 1971) (Apparently describing the 20th Dynasty Tomb Robberies, Théodorides says: "In the most serious cases, such as crimes of pillage in the royal necropolis, it appears to have been on royal indictment that the vizier instituted public proceedings. He began by appointing a commission of inquiry which inspected the scene of the crime and reported its conclusions. The suspects, after being arrested and imprisoned, appeared before the court, which apart

personally re-examined the scene of the crime.[139] In these extraordinary cases, the vizier wrote an opinion that delineated which defendants were guilty and which would be acquitted. He then passed his opinion on to the pharaoh who sentenced the guilty.[140]

Based on the case of the Great Tomb Robberies under Ramses IX, McDowell reconstructs and summarizes the procedures of the special courts as follows:

> [T]he standard procedure was for irregularities in the necropolis to be reported to the vizier and other high-ranking officials in Thebes. These would then have sent out a commission to investigate the charges, drawn up a list of suspects, and had them arrested. The vizier and his colleagues themselves would interrogate the suspects, perhaps crossing over to the necropolis to inspect the scene of the crime, and rule on the guilt or innocence of the accused; but the punishment of the thieves was the choice of Pharaoh. A report of the proceedings would be sent to him and the guilty would be imprisoned to await his decision. In all probability he would order their execution.[141]

§4.07 Appeal

The judicial system at Deir el-Medina had no procedure for appeal in its modern sense. We know of no case where a losing party appealed to another authority outside of the community for a second opinion. Nor do our sources indicate—at least ordinarily—that someone who lost a case that had been decided by a court could then appeal the matter to the oracle, or vice versa. In fact, a party who lost his case before the *ḳnbt* routinely swore an oath promising not to reopen the issue. For the most part, cases appear to have been adjudicated in a particular forum (*i.e.*, *ḳnbt* or oracle) on the basis of subject matter.[142] Hence appeal to another forum was virtu-

---

from the vizier was composed of high officials....."); Grimal, Ancient Egypt 188. *See also infra* §8.04[B].

139. *See* Aristide Théodorides, *The Concept of Law in Ancient Egypt, in* The Legacy of Egypt 291, 312 (J.R. Harris ed., 2d ed. 1971).

140. See *Id.* (Explaining that, after this preliminary investigation, the vizier wrote down his conclusions. He then could uphold charges against those whom he deemed guilty and dismiss charges against the others. He sent his written conclusions to the king who ultimately decided the punishments for the guilty.).

141. McDowell, Jurisdiction 192.

142. *See supra* §3.07.

ally inconceivable.[143] There are a number of instances, however, where the prevailing party took his opponent to court a second, third, or fourth time. Apparently, these cases illustrate attempts merely to reinforce the initial trial and to apply public pressure to coerce the loser into complying with the court's original order. In one case from outside of Deir el-Medina, a man who was convicted of theft by an oracle of Amon later appealed his case to two other Amons. In both instances, the "appellate gods" affirmed the prior verdicts.[144] In general, there seems to have been considerable cooperation between the oracle and *ḳnbt* in Deir el-Medina.[145]

Thus, although there is some evidence to the contrary,[146] conventional wisdom teaches that the Egyptian system did not have higher appellate courts. Therefore, parties basically had only one chance to prove their case. Yet, even though appeal was not technically available, the same court could hear the same case again if new evidence came to light.[147] Some Egyptologists maintain that the pharaoh, himself, could and did act as a kind of appeals court. In one case (Ostracon British Museum 5631 recto) for example, after a man was accused of stealing copper objects, a Delta official sentenced him to penal labor. His father then appealed to the pharaoh who ordered the defendant's release.[148] Breasted argues that there were some instances when a litigant could appeal directly to the king as early as the Old Kingdom (*c.* 2700–2200 B.C.).[149]

---

143. There are three cases—each involving a storehouse (*i.e.*, real property that technically was probably owned by the State)—which *may* have been the subject of some sort of appeal, either from an oracle's decision to a court or to some unspecified authority. The fact that each of these three cases involves a storehouse, coupled with a lack of details in these enigmatic texts, renders conclusions about these cases extremely tentative and uncertain. *See* MCDOWELL, JURISDICTION 184–186. *See also infra* § 5.02 text accompanying notes 54–56 (Describing an oracle's decision that may overturn a previous decision by the court.)

144. *See* MCDOWELL, JURISDICTION 183, 185.

145. *See Id.* at 186 ("[B]oth the oracle and the court seem to have reflected the same popular consensus on the rights and wrongs of the matters at issue.").

146. *See* S. Allam, *Legal Aspects in the 'Contendings of Horus and Seth', in* STUDIES IN PHARAONIC RELIGION AND SOCIETY IN HONOUR OF J. GWYN GRIFFITHS 137, 139 (Alan B. Lloyd ed., 1992).

147. *See* Aristide Théodorides, *The Concept of Law in Ancient Egypt, in* THE LEGACY OF EGYPT 291, 310 (J.R. Harris ed., 2d ed. 1971) ("[T]here was no higher jurisdiction to which appeal could be made against a judgment pronounced by an inferior court." But the same court could hear a case again "in light of fresh evidence."). *See also* S. Allam, *Legal Aspects in the 'Contendings of Horus and Seth', in* STUDIES IN PHARAONIC RELIGION AND SOCIETY IN HONOUR OF J. GWYN GRIFFITHS 137, 138 (Alan B. Lloyd ed., 1992); MCDOWELL, JURISDICTION 135; BEDELL, CRIMINAL LAW 267 (Bedell states that decisions by the oracle could be appealed to the courts and vice versa).

148. *See* BEDELL, CRIMINAL LAW 32–33.

149. *See* BREASTED, HISTORY OF EGYPT 81–82 ("Under certain circumstances, not yet clear to us, appeal might be made directly to the king, and briefs in the case sub-

By the 22nd Dynasty (*c.* 945–715 B.C.), the Egyptians did finally institute changes providing for appeals in their civil and criminal procedure. In civil cases, a right of appeal was granted. In criminal cases involving minor offenses, defendants also were permitted to appeal. Interestingly, the appeal was made to an oracle for judgment. As a practical matter, though, it is doubtful whether this right of appeal actually had a significant effect on the administration of justice.[150]

§4.08 Legal Procedure in *The Tale of the Eloquent Peasant*

The Tale of the Eloquent Peasant brings to light a somewhat different version of ancient Egyptian procedure. After Nemtynakhte had taken Khunanup's donkeys, beaten him, and had threatened to kill him, Khunanup still tried to convince Nemtynakhte to return his goods to him: "And the peasant spent a period of ten days appealing to Nemtynakhte, but he paid no attention to it."[151] Consequently, Khunanup decided to take his case to Rensi.[152] Throughout the affair, the peasant represents himself and does not hire a litigator on his behalf.[153] Rensi was on his way out of his house when Khunanup arrived. He was "go[ing] down to his courthouse barge."[154] Thus, Khunanup asked:

---

mitted to him. Such a brief is the document from the Old Kingdom now in Berlin. . . .").

150. *See* Aristide Théodorides, *The Concept of Law in Ancient Egypt, in* THE LEGACY OF EGYPT 291, 317 (J.R. Harris ed., 2d ed. 1971) ("judicial procedure underwent a change to the extent that plaintiffs could appeal to the oracle for judgement in civil cases and those involving minor offences.") (footnote omitted), *Id.* at 318 (But ordinary tribunals continued their work and "criminal cases remained the exclusive province of the vizier's court until the end of the New Kingdom.") (footnote omitted).

151. SIMPSON, THE LITERATURE OF ANCIENT EGYPT 34.

152. *See Id.* at 34 ("So the peasant went to Ninsu to appeal to the High Steward Rensi, son of Meru. . . ."). Shupak offers numerous reasons why Rensi could have been the vizier. *See* Nili Shupak, *A New Source For the Study of the Judiciary and Law of Ancient Egypt: "The Tale of the Eloquent Peasant"*, 51 J. NEAR E. STUD. 1, 5–6 (1992). *See also Id.* at 5 (Shupak notes that "[t]hree representatives of the judicial hierarchy appear in the story [of *The Eloquent Peasant*]: the king, the high steward (*imy-r-pr*), and the *srw*."). For a more detailed account of the administrative organization of the judiciary *see generally supra* Ch. 3; ERMAN, LIFE IN ANCIENT EGYPT 87–88 (Describing and identifying several different types of judges and their respective jurisdictions.); Taylor, *Law under the Pharaohs*, 6 POL'Y REV. 66, at 67–68 (Discussing the various judicial officials and their hierarchy.).

153. *See supra* §4.03, text accompanying notes 45–47.

154. LICHTHEIM, ANCIENT EGYPTIAN LITERATURE 171. Certainly, this phrase

> "May I be allowed to acquaint you with this complaint? Might a servant of your choice be sent to me, through whom I could inform you of it?" So the high steward Rensi, the son of Meru, sent a servant of his choice ahead of him, and this peasant informed him of the matter in all its aspects.[155]

The plaintiff then pleaded his case to the "servant of choice" ("informed him of the matter in all its aspects"). Apparently, it was at this stage of pleading that Khunanup explained the facts of his dispute with Nemtynakhte and argued points of law.[156] We next discover that Rensi takes up the matter with "the magistrates who were with him."[157] Presumably, then, between the time that Khunanup explained his case to Rensi's servant and the time that Rensi began discussing the case with other magistrates, the servant must have related the affair to Rensi. There is an additional procedural lacuna. The author fails to recount at what point Rensi formed his opinion that Khunanup was telling the truth and that Nemtynakhte had acted wrongfully. Perhaps Rensi's servant made some findings of fact and re-

---

could be a metaphor for the "ship of State." Shupak interprets the phrase *ḳ3kw n ʿrryt* as "boat of the court." Nili Shupak, *A New Source For the Study of the Judiciary and Law of Ancient Egypt: "The Tale of the Eloquent Peasant"*, 51 J. NEAR E. STUD. 1, 17 (1992). He explains: "This object is explained by the custom of Egyptian judges of wandering throughout the kingdom to make themselves available to anyone wishing to approach them in legal matters." *Id.* (footnote omitted). "We may therefore assume that the efficient judicial system of Egypt also included mobile law courts located on boats. . . ." *Id.* at 17–18.

155. LICHTHEIM, ANCIENT EGYPTIAN LITERATURE 171. The Federal Rules of Civil Procedure establish the requirements for bringing such a complaint in contemporary American federal courts. A pleading must include:

> (1) a short and plain statement of the grounds upon which the court's jurisdiction depends . . ., (2) a short and plain statement of the claim showing that the pleader is entitled to relief, and (3) a demand for judgement for the relief the pleader seeks.

FED. R. CIV. P. 8(a) (1991).

Khunanup's complaint appears to have included an assumption of Rensi's authority (or jurisdiction) to hear his case. The peasant's pleading may have included his specific complaint as well as a demand for the relief sought, since he described the complaint "in all its aspects."

156. *See* Nili Shupak, *A New Source For the Study of the Judiciary and Law of Ancient Egypt: "The Tale of the Eloquent Peasant"*, 51 J. NEAR E. STUD. 1, 4 (1992) (Shupak recognizes that Khunanup's later arguments to Rensi have nothing to do with either the facts or law pertaining to the merits of the case: "The complaint is not directed at the rapacious official but at the entire corrupt bureaucracy of Egypt. The personal injustice suffered by the peasant serves as an excuse for attacking the administrative establishment headed by Judge Rensi as a whole.").

157. LICHTHEIM, ANCIENT EGYPTIAN LITERATURE 171.

ported them along with his legal conclusions to Rensi?[158] Perhaps Rensi discussed the matter with his servant and then, based on that discussion, reached his conclusion? Perhaps the servant merely transcribed or listened to Khunanup's arguments and then reported them to Rensi, who, in turn, decided the matter alone? In any event, Rensi believed that Nemtynakhte had acted improperly and, upon discussing this case with other magistrates (*srw*), "denounced this Nemtynakht[e]. . . ."[159]

The text, unfortunately, fails to disclose the relationship between Rensi and "the magistrates who were with him."[160] We do not know whether he was obligated to ask their advice. Perhaps he was supposed to reach a consensus with them as part of a formal procedural process? Perhaps his discussions with them were purely informal conversations with other judicial officials? Later, we discover that he "did not answer these magistrates. . . ."[161] In due course, Rensi consulted the king who told Rensi to have the peasant's speeches transcribed.[162] This is consistent with other evidence from ancient Egypt that complaints of this nature were required to be in writing.[163] Additionally, by transcribing Khunanup's speeches, the king may

---

158. In modern American civil procedure, authority to make legal determinations is allocated to the court; however, findings of fact are often made by a jury. *See* FED. R. CIV. P. 38 (1991) (Reiterating the Seventh Amendment preservation of right to trial by jury.). *See also* FED. R. CIV. P. 39 (Trial by Jury or by the Court.).

159. LICHTHEIM, ANCIENT EGYPTIAN LITERATURE 171.

160. *See* SIMPSON, THE LITERATURE OF ANCIENT EGYPT 34. *See also* Nili Shupak, *A New Source For the Study of the Judiciary and Law of Ancient Egypt: "The Tale of the Eloquent Peasant"*, 51 J. NEAR E. STUD. 1, 6 (1992) (Shupak states that "[t]he *srw* were officials in the king's service, and they enjoyed legal autonomy. They acted as advisers to the regional governor in the local courts and were considered authorities on matters involving private property."). It is perhaps instructive to consider a parallel in ancient Egyptian religion. In one version of the *Book of the Dead* (the papyrus of Ani) the judge, Osiris, sits "enthroned at one end of the judgment hall, with Isis and Nephthys standing behind him. Along one side of the hall are arranged the nine gods of the Heliopolitan Ennead, headed by the Sun-god. *They* afterward announce the verdict. . . ." BREASTED, DEVELOPMENT OF RELIGION AND THOUGHT 304. (footnote omitted, emphasis original). Thus, the judge in the underworld was also accompanied by numerous other judges. However, unlike Rensi's magistrates (*srw*), it was the assisting Heliopolitan judges themselves who announced the verdict. Whether it was they who actually made the decision is unclear. Perhaps they were merely the mouthpiece for Osiris, who decided the case of the deceased.

161. SIMPSON, THE LITERATURE OF ANCIENT EGYPT 34.

162. *Id.* at 35. *See* Nili Shupak, *A New Source For the Study of the Judiciary and Law of Ancient Egypt: "The Tale of the Eloquent Peasant"*, 51 J. NEAR E. STUD. 1, 5 (1992) (According to Shupak, "[i]n general . . . the king delegated this right [*i.e.*, the right to make legal decisions] to a lower authority.").

163. *See supra* §4.03, text accompanying note 40. See also Nili Shupak, *A New Source For the Study of the Judiciary and Law of Ancient Egypt: "The Tale of the Eloquent Peasant"*, 51 J. NEAR E. STUD. 1, 5 (1992) ("The erudition in legal matters shown

have been preserving a valuable source for legal precedent.[164] Given that Khunanup's declarations yield an abundance of legal wisdom, the king may have been trying to ensure that the peasant's opinions on jurisprudence were preserved in writing for posterity. Ultimately we learn that the king told Rensi to render the final judgment.[165]

Based upon this literary case, we can infer a number of significant details that may supplement what we know from traditional sources about ancient Egyptian legal procedure. A plaintiff could plead his case (both presenting facts and arguments of law) directly to the High Steward himself. In certain instances, the High Steward could designate a "servant of his choice" to listen to the case in his stead. After the servant presented the case to the High Steward (with or without offering his own impressions, interpretations, and initial conclusions—we simply cannot tell), the High Steward could consult (either formally or informally—again we cannot be certain which) other magistrates (*srw*) and seek their advice. The High Steward was not compelled to follow the magistrates' advice. When in doubt, a High Steward could appeal directly to the king. Lastly, the king, himself, could defer and allow the High Steward to decide the case.[166]

One final remark from the end of Khunanup's ninth petition also may relate to legal procedure. Khunanup voices his concern that Rensi may not redress his wrongs and that he will be forced to appeal to a higher authority, namely, Anubis: "See, I appeal to you, but you do not hear it; I will go, that I may appeal / about you to Anubis!"[167] This may be Khunanup's way

---

by the author of 'The Tale of the Eloquent Peasant' is further evident from his noting the fact that the peasant's complaints were written down, *a required procedure in the law of ancient Egypt*. . . .") (emphasis added). For a more elaborate discussion of the requirement that complaints be in writing in ancient Egypt, *see Id.* at 10.

164. *See supra* § 4.02 regarding precedent.

165. *See* Simpson, The Literature of Ancient Egypt 49 ("And [His Majesty] said: You yourself give judgment, son of Meru.").

166. For discussion of another potential historical source for a description of civil procedure, but during the 16th or 17th Dynasty, *see* Gardiner, Egypt of the Pharaohs 161. In discussing a stela from the reign of King Nebirierau, Gardiner states:

> The main narrative explains . . . all manner of details concerning the judicial proceedings involved, the court of the vizier, and the final oath sworn by the two parties. Certain obscurities remain, but do not prevent this document from being as illuminating a specimen of Egyptian administrative procedure as any that has survived from Pharaonic times.

Id.

For a somewhat fanciful account of a vizier holding court, *see* Jon Manchip White, Everyday Life in Ancient Egypt 123–25 (1963).

167. Simpson, The Literature of Ancient Egypt 48. Khunanup's desire to appeal is here directed to a spiritual rather than mortal authority. It is unclear whether the peasant would be permitted to petition the king for relief were he unhappy with Rensi's

of saying that he will consult an oracle as his final means of appeal.[168] This is interesting since other evidence suggests that the Egyptians probably did not permit appeal to an oracle until about 1200 years after the composition of this tale.[169]

§ 4.09 Enforcement

Generally speaking, one of the key weaknesses of Egyptian procedure was its lack of enforcement mechanisms. As Eyre relates: "One of the most noticeable aspects of the legal texts from Deir el-Medina is the apparent difficulty in getting any enforcement of 'decisions' expressed by the local tribunal."[170] For example. in a handful of Deir el-Medina cases, we know that the party who was found liable (or guilty) managed to elude the authorities and simply never complied with the court's final order.[171] According to McDowell, "[T]he *ḳnbt* had very little actual power to enforce its decisions. It relied on its prestige for its effectiveness, and on the fact that the entire village was often witness to the legal proceedings, which probably put considerable social pressure on the litigants to abide by the court's decision."[172] Contradicting the standard view that the court's decisions had no actual teeth, there is other evidence, however, that suggests that the *ḳnbt* did, in fact, have the muscle to enforce some of its decisions, at least, to a limited degree.[173] It is possible that the court itself was supposed to enforce

---

decision and, if he could make such an appeal, at what stage it would be allowed. American civil procedure generally requires that a final judgment be entered before an appeal may be brought. *See* 28 U.S.C. § 1291 (1989). However, certain judicial determinations provide grounds for an interlocutory appeal. *See* 28 U.S.C. § 1292 (1989).

168. *See supra* § 3.07 regarding trial by oracle. *See also* Nili Shupak, *A New Source For the Study of the Judiciary and Law of Ancient Egypt: "The Tale of the Eloquent Peasant"*, 51 J. NEAR E. STUD. 1, 11 (1992). Shupak remarks in a footnote that his "interpretation differs from that of Perry, who thinks that the peasant is threatening suicide here, as the god Anubis, who is mentioned, is involved with death." *Id.* at n.40.

169. *See supra* § 4.07, note 150 and accompanying text.

170. C.J. Eyre, *Crime and Adultery in Ancient Egypt*, 70 J. EGYPTIAN ARCHAEOLOGY 92, 102 (1984) (footnote omitted). *See also* MCDOWELL, JURISDICTION 2 ("[I]t is by no means clear whether the local bodies had the power to enforce their verdicts.").

171. *See* MCDOWELL, JURISDICTION 177–178 ("I count some half dozen cases in which a litigant is known to have disobeyed the court without penalty, some of which are simply outrageous.").

172. *Id.* at 117. *See also Id.* at 171 ("Evidently the court could decide where justice lay, but could not ensure that it was done.").

173. *See Id.* at 171 ("[T]he local court did have the mechanisms and power to carry out its will even in routine business disputes."); *Id.* at 172 ("[T]he court is occasionally seen to take effective action, both in the form of execution against the prop-

its judgments.[174] Later, in the second century B.C., a "bailiff was empowered to enforce judicial decisions up to the imprisonment of a judgement debtor."[175]

§4.10 Chapter Summary

The ancient Egyptians established fixed procedures for dispute resolution. As is the case with modern American law, they tried to follow precedent, recognized the importance of due process, and kept records of their decisions so that, when similar problems arose, they were able to resolve those problems in a consistent fashion. There was no viable appeal procedure until the first millennium B.C.; or if there was a right of appeal earlier, it was extremely limited in scope. The ancient Egyptian had his day in court (so to speak) and that was it. Indeed, most trials lasted only one day. Although there were no professional lawyers, scribes seem to have specialized in preparing legal documents for pleading, and also wrote wills and other documents of a legal nature. Thus, the scribal class, that is the class that was educated in letters, functioned somewhat like lawyers or quasi-lawyers. But scribes did not plead cases for others as advocates. Most of our evidence points to a relatively simple procedural structure. The plaintiff or the State official acting in the capacity of a prosecutor brought his case, often by means of a written complaint, then argued it. The defendant then answered, arguing his case, followed by a summation. It is clear that both testamentary evidence (*i.e.*, bringing in witnesses to speak on your behalf) as well as documentary evidence (*e.g.*, contracts, wills, deeds, and tax records) were both admissible as evidence in court. Interestingly, however, the Egyptians preferred to have the testimony of their witnesses written down. The judges took an active role at trial, asking questions and interviewing witnesses. Witnesses were threatened with severe penalties for perjury and sometimes were tortured. Officials had authority to search houses and to seize property as evidence. Although the special courts were not bound by

---

erty of the offender and in the form of physical punishment."); *Id.* at 173 ("[T]he court did often phrase its verdict in active rather than passive terms, and...it did have some means to enforce its decision."); *Id.* at 179.

174. *See* S. Allam, *Legal Aspects in the 'Contendings of Horus and Seth', in* Studies in Pharaonic Religion and Society in Honour of J. Gwyn Griffiths 137, 142 (Alan B. Lloyd ed., 1992).

175. S. Allam, *Egyptian Law Courts in Pharaonic and Hellenistic Times*, 77 J. Egyptian Archaeology 109, 124 (1991).

formulaic court procedures, they too relied on traditional judicial mechanisms (*e.g.*, investigation) and standard types of evidence (*e.g.*, witnesses, documents, searches, and visits to the scene of the crime). We are not sure how much power the courts possessed to enforce their judgments.

Part II

Substantive Law

CHAPTER 5

Property

§ 5.01 General

Because property concepts pervade most other substantive law topics, we shall consider laws relating to property first. Ancient Egypt was chiefly an agricultural society.[1] Breasted states the matter succinctly when he says: "The economic foundation of this civilization... in all... periods of Egyptian history, was agricultural."[2] As a consequence, real property was extremely important. Manning claims that "disputes over property can be documented from the 3rd Dynasty... onward."[3] To appreciate the significance of real property, one need only remember the nature of Egyptian topography; there was only a limited amount of land which was useful for cultivation. There was only a narrow strip of land a few miles wide on either side of the Nile that could be farmed. Beyond that, there was mostly dry desert. Also, every year after the inundation property boundaries might have to be redrawn.[4] Indeed, documents suggest "that every plot in Egypt was measured, its ownership, crop-yields and tax payments recorded, and that very extensive archives once existed...."[5]

---

1. *See* Christopher J. Eyre, *Peasants and "Modern" Leasing Strategies in Ancient Egypt*, 40 J. Economic & Social Hist. Orient 367, 368 (1997); David Lorton, *Legal and Social Institutions of Pharaonic Egypt*, *in* 1 Civilizations of the Ancient Near East 345, 353 (Jack M. Sasson ed., 1995); J.G. Manning, *Demotic Egyptian Instruments of Transfer as Evidence for Private Ownership of Real Property*, 71 Chicago-Kent L. Rev. 237, 250 (1995) (Manning characterizes "agricultural wealth" as "the economic engine in Egypt."); Breasted, History of Egypt 28 ("In the fruitful Nile valley we can not think of such a people as other than chiefly agricultural; and the fact [is] that they emerge into historical times as agriculturalists....").
2. Breasted, History of Egypt 92.
3. J.G. Manning, *Demotic Egyptian Instruments of Transfer as Evidence for Private Ownership of Real Property*, 71 Chicago-Kent L. Rev. 237, 237–238 (1995).
4. *See* Christopher J. Eyre, *Peasants and "Modern" Leasing Strategies in Ancient Egypt*, 40 J. Economic & Social Hist. Orient 367, 378 (1997).
5. William A. Ward, *Some Aspects of Private Land Ownership and Inheritance in*

In the predynastic era (*c.* 4500–3150 B.C.), it is likely that the Egyptians held a tribal, or community sense of property.[6] In the earliest historical times, there is good reason to believe that the king, at least theoretically, owned all real property.[7] There has been considerable scholarly debate among Egyptologists regarding the issue of private ownership of real property in pharaonic Egypt. Some argue that the State owned all land while others argue that private individuals were considered owners.[8] For example, Breasted describes the system in the New Kingdom (*c.* 1552–1069

Ancient Egypt, ca. 2500–1000 B.C., in Land Tenure and Social Transformation in the Middle East 63, 65 (Tarif Khalidi ed., 1984). *See also* Warburton, State and Economy in Ancient Egypt 43; J.G. Manning, *Demotic Egyptian Instruments of Transfer as Evidence for Private Ownership of Real Property*, 71 Chicago-Kent L. Rev. 237, 246 (1995) (Manning notes that "the pharaoh retained both a theoretical interest and a real one [in land], since taxes were collected on all land.") (footnote omitted). *But see* Christopher J. Eyre, *Peasants and "Modern" Leasing Strategies in Ancient Egypt*, 40 J. Economic & Social Hist. Orient 367, 372 (1997) ("Yet the administrative effort necessary to operate a consistently efficient centralised system of survey and revenue collection would have been immense, and there is no reason to believe that it was ever achieved in antiquity. The central government was never big enough.").

6. *See* Wilson, Culture of Ancient Egypt 21 (In discussing predynastic Egypt, Wilson remarks: "Apparently the first attempts at village life retained some of the elements of tribal custom: the individual sense of property had not yet replaced the community sense of property.").

7. *See* Grimal, Ancient Egypt 92 ("the whole country theoretically belonged to the king."); Warburton, State and Economy in Ancient Egypt 32 (Citing Menu and Helk.). *But see Id.* at 60–61 ("this does not mean that the new king regarded himself as the sole owner of everything in the country...."); *Id.* at 63 (Suggesting that private property was the norm—not ownership by the monarch.).

8. *See e.g.*, William A. Ward, *Some Aspects of Private Land Ownership and Inheritance in Ancient Egypt, ca. 2500–1000 B.C., in* Land Tenure and Social Transformation in the Middle East 63, 64 (Tarif Khalidi ed., 1984); J.G. Manning, *Demotic Egyptian Instruments of Transfer as Evidence for Private Ownership of Real Property*, 71 Chicago-Kent L. Rev. 237, 239 (1995) ("While the notion of the pharaoh 'owning' all of the land in Egypt is still commonly held by Egyptologists, it was, at most, a 'propriété théorique.'") (footnote omitted); *Id.* at 242–245 (Manning summarizes the arguments pro and con; citing scholars such as Baer and Pirenne, who advocate that private ownership existed, versus Helk, Stuchevsky, and Grunert, who maintain that the State owned all real property.); Katary, Land Tenure in the Ramesside Period 23, 25 (Citing the work of Stuchevsky who argues that the State owned all real estate.), 170 (Noting that Gardiner, like most Western scholars, supports the notion of private ownership in Egypt.), 212 (Citing Baer's position advocating "privately owned" land.); Christopher J. Eyre, *Peasants and "Modern" Leasing Strategies in Ancient Egypt*, 40 J. Economic & Social Hist. Orient 367, 377 (1997) ("In that limited sense the state is 'owner' of all land: it claims the right to tax land, and to assign or donate rights over land to individuals or institutions."); Schafik Allam, *Women as Owners of Immovables in Pharaonic Egypt, in* Women's Earliest Records From Ancient Egypt and Western Asia 123, 133 (Barbara Lesko ed., 1989); Warburton, State and Economy in Ancient Egypt 127 (Citing Helk.); *Id.* at 137.

B.C.) as one where most lands were owned by the king and "were worked by the king's serfs, controlled by his officials, or entrusted by him as permanent and indivisible fiefs to his favourite nobles, his partisans and relatives."[9] Katary, on the other hand, states: "It has long been generally accepted that private ownership of land, or at least something very close to private ownership of land as we know it, existed during the New Kingdom."[10] Warburton emphatically rejects the theory that the State owned most of the land. He bases his model of the Egyptian economy on the principle that private individuals owned land: "It is... clear that the temples and Pharaoh did not even own a significant portion of the land in ancient Egypt...."[11] According to Warburton, "The agrarian economic system in Egypt was...based on taxation and rent in which people were awarded plots in exchange for services, under the condition that they render up part of the surplus to state authorities."[12] Indeed, as early as the 2nd Dynasty (*c.* 2925–2700 B.C.) (and perhaps even earlier)[13] the Egyptians *treated* land as if it were privately owned by individuals themselves. No matter what the *legal technicalities* may have been, the Egyptians *treated* real property in a manner basically equivalent to the way that we today treat private property ownership. For that matter, historically speaking, after William the Conqueror seized and redistributed land in England, he technically retained ownership of all real property. Nevertheless, the persons to whom he granted the land *treated* it functionally as their own private property.[14] Hence, in an analogous manner, even if the Egyptian State was considered the technical owner of real property, we will not be far off the mark if we speak of ancient Egyptian law as having recognized the concept of private property.[15] As such, land owners could transfer their property by sale, in-

9. BREASTED, HISTORY OF EGYPT 237.

10. KATARY, LAND TENURE IN THE RAMESSIDE PERIOD 23. *See also* WARBURTON, STATE AND ECONOMY IN ANCIENT EGYPT 39 (Discussing the notion of private property in emerging states.); *Id.* at 42 ("It is generally agreed that private ownership of land in ancient Egypt emerged after the emergence of the state rather than preceding it."); *Id.* at 139–40 ("Excursus On Land Ownership").

11. WARBURTON, STATE AND ECONOMY IN ANCIENT EGYPT 327.

12. *Id.*

13. *See* Aristide Théodorides, *The Concept of Law in Ancient Egypt, in* THE LEGACY OF EGYPT 291, 292 (J.R. Harris ed., 2d ed. 1971). *Cf.* WILSON, CULTURE OF ANCIENT EGYPT 21.

14. *See* ROGER A, CUNNINGHAM, WILLIAM B. STOEBUCK, AND DALE A. WITMAN, THE LAW OF PROPERTY § 1.6 at 14–21, § 1.7 at 21–22 (1993).

15. *See* William A. Ward, *Some Aspects of Private Land Ownership and Inheritance in Ancient Egypt, ca. 2500–1000 B.C., in* LAND TENURE AND SOCIAL TRANSFORMATION IN THE MIDDLE EAST 63, 64, (Tarif Khalidi ed., 1984) ("[I]f a person worked a plot of land and could personally dispose of that land by sale, through inheritance, or other

heritance, or otherwise.[16] Ward maintains that "throughout Egyptian history, private individuals could own farm land and dispose of it as they chose."[17] Manning says much the same thing: "conceptions and terminology in the private documentation suggest very clearly defined concepts of private ownership. * * * Whether there was legally defined ownership before the Romans or not, there was much land in private hands that individual holders *treated* as their own and transferred to their heirs."[18] Indeed, as Eyre notes, "The earliest surviving text that seems to refer to land purchase is the inscription of *Metjen* from the early Old Kingdom."[19] Warburton even suggests "that the existence of private property was one of the first things guar-

---

means, then that land was privately owned."); *Id.* at 67, 71–72, 76, n. 24; KATARY, LAND TENURE IN THE RAMESSIDE PERIOD 212 ("Regardless of the terminology, they remain 'freeholders' or 'private persons' cultivating plots to which they did not necessarily have full ownership rights. That they were at least 'virtual owners' is certainly indicated by the small quantities of grain that they were assessed as well as the right to inherit the land."); David Lorton, *Legal and Social Institutions of Pharaonic Egypt, in* 1 CIVILIZATIONS OF THE ANCIENT NEAR EAST 345, 353 (Jack M. Sasson ed., 1995) ("There is also evidence for private landownership in all periods, for the selling and renting of land, and for economic exchanges besides barter."); GAY ROBINS, WOMEN IN ANCIENT EGYPT 127 ("[T]he notion of private ownership of property, that is, land owners could dispose of as they wished, had already arisen by the early Old Kingdom.").

16. *See* Aristide Théodorides, *The Concept of Law in Ancient Egypt, in* THE LEGACY OF EGYPT 291, 292 (J.R. Harris ed., 2d ed. 1971) (Even as early as the 2nd Dynasty "the transfer of both personal and landed property from one owner to another was considerable, and... private property must... have existed."); *Id.* ("From the evidence of documents of legal practice..., it thus appears that private property did indeed exist, that it was transferable, and further that there was real equality between man and wife in the eyes of the law."); BREASTED, HISTORY OF EGYPT 237 ("Divisible parcels might also be held by tenants of the untitled classes. Both classes of holdings might be transferred by will or sale in much the same way as if the holder actually owned the land.") (Citing the case of Mose.).

17. William A. Ward, *Some Aspects of Private Land Ownership and Inheritance in Ancient Egypt, ca. 2500–1000 B.C., in* LAND TENURE AND SOCIAL TRANSFORMATION IN THE MIDDLE EAST 63, 72 (Tarif Khalidi ed., 1984). It is perhaps also significant that the each of the laws ascribed to the pharaohs relates directly to property. *See Id.* at 77, n. 24. *See also supra* § 3.03[B].

18. J.G. Manning, *Demotic Egyptian Instruments of Transfer as Evidence for Private Ownership of Real Property*, 71 CHICAGO-KENT L. REV. 237, 267 (1995).

19. Christopher J. Eyre, *Peasants and "Modern" Leasing Strategies in Ancient Egypt*, 40 J. ECONOMIC & SOCIAL HIST. ORIENT 367, 377 (1997) (footnote omitted). *See also* WARBURTON, STATE AND ECONOMY IN ANCIENT EGYPT 33 ("Even in the Old Kingdom... land changed hands in commercial transactions."); *Id.* ("It can... be argued that private property... existed independent of the king from the beginning...."); *Id.* at 42–43 ("The meaning of the M'tn inscription... is however that as far back as the inscriptions go, land could be purchased and sold, and that there were legal arrangements to assure that this was possible....").

anteed by the state...."[20] In addition to the outright sale of real estate, we also know of leasing (by means of a document called a *sḥn*) and sub-leasing as well.[21] But it is worthwhile to note that our present understanding of Egyptian property law is still incomplete. Principles from the late period easily blur our vision and make it difficult to distinguish pharaonic concepts from Ptolemaic.

Warburton puts the issue of private property ownership into perspective:

> Documents relating to land ownership are in short supply, but it is possible to demonstrate that the agricultural land of New Kingdom Egypt was in the hands of the King, temples, officials and private people. The exact rights under which officials and private people could "own" land are however the crux of the problem.[22]

Ward points to the case of Mose,[23] for example, as evidence "to prove beyond a doubt that agricultural land could be privately owned and passed from generation to generation...."[24] In fact, the land at issue in the Mose dispute illustrates another important fact regarding the ownership of real property. Mose's ancestor, a ship captain named Neshi, was originally given

---

20. WARBURTON, STATE AND ECONOMY IN ANCIENT EGYPT 62.

21. *See* KATARY, LAND TENURE IN THE RAMESSIDE PERIOD 11, 16–17, 211, 223 (Specifically identifying leasing and sub-leasing in P. Wilbour and P. Berlin 3047.); J.G. Manning, *Demotic Egyptian Instruments of Transfer as Evidence for Private Ownership of Real Property*, 71 CHICAGO-KENT L. REV. 237, 239 (1995) (Referring to Ptolemaic Egypt, Manning states: "Many Egyptians took on sub-leases of land that were nominally in the hands of Greek reserve soldiers...."); *Id.* at 241 (Noting that the ordinary number of witnesses for a lease was twelve.); *Id.* at 261 (Describing the land lease provisions of the Law Collection of Hermopolis.); Christopher J. Eyre, *Peasants and "Modern" Leasing Strategies in Ancient Egypt*, 40 J. ECONOMIC & SOCIAL HIST. ORIENT 367, 381 (1997) ("Data concerning 'private' leasing is otherwise extremely limited before the end of the New Kingdom. The earliest significant group of written lease agreements appear with a general extension of the habit of using documents in private business matters from the 25th and 26th Dynasties.") (footnotes omitted); *Id.* at 382 ("Characteristically they are one-year arrangements, made at a time of year when the effect of the inundation can be predicted. The rent is a share of the crop—typically ⅓ to be paid at harvest—although provision by the landlord of seed and plough animals may reduce the take of the farmer down as far as ⅓. The landlord consistently makes himself responsible for any tax payment: a measure that would ensure he remained the registered tax-payer and so 'owner'.") (footnotes omitted); Christopher J. Eyre, *The Market Women of Pharaonic Egypt*, *in* LE COMMERCE EN ÉGYPT ANCIENNE 173, 184 (Nicolas Grimal and Bernadette Menu eds., 1998).

22. WARBURTON, STATE AND ECONOMY IN ANCIENT EGYPT 70.

23. *See supra* § 4.01.

24. William A. Ward, *Some Aspects of Private Land Ownership and Inheritance in Ancient Egypt, ca. 2500–1000* B.C., *in* LAND TENURE AND SOCIAL TRANSFORMATION IN THE MIDDLE EAST 63, 65 (Tarif Khalidi ed., 1984).

the tract of land in recognition of his outstanding war record.[25] Indeed, it was common for pharaohs to grant real property as rewards to men after they retired from the military.[26]

Warburton points out that "[t]he fact that the mere phrase 'Law of Pharaoh' sufficed to refer to guarantees surrounding property underlines that property rights were important in ancient Egypt."[27] Property could be owned by an individual or jointly by two or more persons (*e.g.*, property that a married couple accumulated while married or property inherited jointly).[28] Women too could legally own, buy, and sell property.[29] The gov-

---

25. *See Id.* at 64. *See also* GARDINER, EGYPT OF THE PHARAOHS 268 ("[O]n the walls of a tomb at Sakkara...are set forth at length the proceedings in a trial in which the matter at stake was the ownership of a tract of land in the neighborhood of Memphis. This estate, the plaintiff Mose maintained, had been given by king Amosis as a reward to his ancestor Neshi, a ship captain.").

26. *See* WARBURTON, STATE AND ECONOMY IN ANCIENT EGYPT 316 ("Soldiers, scribes, stable-masters, retainers, priests and other state employees were awarded small plots...."); William A. Ward, *Some Aspects of Private Land Ownership and Inheritance in Ancient Egypt, ca. 2500–1000 B.C., in* LAND TENURE AND SOCIAL TRANSFORMATION IN THE MIDDLE EAST 63, 70 (Tarif Khalidi ed., 1984). *See also* GRIMAL, ANCIENT EGYPT 194 (Quoting from the autobiographical tomb inscription of Ahmose, son of Ibana, who received land as a reward for his part in fighting against the Hyksos.); *Id.* at 199; Andrea McDowell, *Legal Aspects of Care of the Elderly in Egypt to the End of the New Kingdom, in* THE CARE OF THE ELDERLY IN THE ANCIENT NEAR EAST 199, 200, 202 (Marten Stol and Sven P. Vleeming eds., 1998).

27. WARBURTON, STATE AND ECONOMY IN ANCIENT EGYPT 43 (footnote omitted). *See also supra* §3.03[B].

28. *See* William A. Ward, *Some Aspects of Private Land Ownership and Inheritance in Ancient Egypt, ca. 2500–1000 B.C., in* LAND TENURE AND SOCIAL TRANSFORMATION IN THE MIDDLE EAST 63, 68 (Tarif Khalidi ed., 1984); KATARY, LAND TENURE IN THE RAMESSIDE PERIOD 16; J.G. Manning, *Demotic Egyptian Instruments of Transfer as Evidence for Private Ownership of Real Property*, 71 CHICAGO-KENT L. REV. 237, 259–260, 263–264 (1995); *Id.* at 264 ("The evidence for the joint control of land between two or more parties is abundant." "In addition to family plots held in common, texts from the Ptolemaic period show that groups associated by profession with status titles like 'herdsmen of Horus of Edfu' or 'Royal Farmers' jointly held plots of land."); *Id.* at 265 ("family property was often worked jointly with profits divided up."); Aristide Théodorides, *The Concept of Law in Ancient Egypt, in* THE LEGACY OF EGYPT 291, 310 (J.R. Harris ed., 2d ed. 1971); Janet H. Johnson, *The Legal Status of Women in Ancient Egypt, in* MISTRESS OF THE HOUSE MISTRESS OF HEAVEN: WOMEN IN ANCIENT EGYPT 175, 177 (Anne K. Chapel and Glenn E. Markoe eds., 1996).

29. *See* GAY ROBINS, WOMEN IN ANCIENT EGYPT 127 ("[W]omen as well as men could own land."); William A. Ward, *Some Aspects of Private Land Ownership and Inheritance in Ancient Egypt, ca. 2500–1000 B.C., in* LAND TENURE AND SOCIAL TRANSFORMATION IN THE MIDDLE EAST 63, 69, (Tarif Khalidi ed., 1984) (Referring to the Adoption Papyrus, Ward asserts, "no Egyptian text states more clearly the right of women to own property in their own name.") (footnote omitted); KATARY, LAND TENURE IN THE RAMESSIDE PERIOD 16 ("There are also numerous women smallholders...."); WILSON, CULTURE OF ANCIENT EGYPT 203 ("[S]uch business documents as

ernment counted all real and personal property (such as livestock) annually for purposes of tax assessment.[30] Of the many individual (*i.e.*, secular) owners mentioned in the Wilbour Papyrus, whom Katary calls "smallholders", we see quite a diverse mix of persons who were subject to property taxation: slaves, women, goatherds, priests, stablemasters, tenant farmers, soldiers, coppersmiths, embalmers, beekeepers, sailors, scribes, cattle-branders, and various foreigners.[31] A little over one-third of smallholders are listed as having had occupations that relate to animal husbandry. About one-fifth were in the military.[32] Male owners (89.2 percent) far outnumber female (10.8 percent).[33]

Special attention must be given to the property which the temples owned and also the land owned by the State and officials such as nomarchs.[34] As Lorton notes, "the state and temples were the major landholding institutions."[35] Warburton explains:

---

we possess from the Empire show that women had their own rights to property, to buying and selling. . . ."); Schafik Allam, *Women as Owners of Immovables in Pharaonic Egypt, in* WOMEN'S EARLIEST RECORDS FROM ANCIENT EGYPT AND WESTERN ASIA 123, 133 (Barbara Lesko ed., 1989); Christopher J. Eyre, *The Market Women of Pharaonic Egypt, in* LE COMMERCE EN ÉGYPT ANCIENNE 173, 183–85 (Nicolas Grimal and Bernadette Menu eds., 1998).

30. *See* William A. Ward, *Some Aspects of Private Land Ownership and Inheritance in Ancient Egypt, ca. 2500–1000 B.C., in* LAND TENURE AND SOCIAL TRANSFORMATION IN THE MIDDLE EAST 63, 65, (Tarif Khalidi ed., 1984); BREASTED, HISTORY OF EGYPT 237 ("Other royal property, like cattle and asses, was held by people of both classes, subject, like the lands, to an annual assessment for its use. For purposes of taxation, all land and other property of the crown, except that held by the temples, were recorded in the tax-registers of the White House, as the treasury was still called. All 'houses' or estates and the 'numbers belonging thereto,' were entered in these registers. On the basis of these, taxes were assessed. They were still collected in naturalia: cattle, grain, wine, oil, honey, textiles, and the like.") (footnote omitted). *See also infra* § 5.04.

31. *See* KATARY, LAND TENURE IN THE RAMESSIDE PERIOD 71–72; WILSON, CULTURE OF ANCIENT EGYPT 272; Schafik Allam, *Women as Owners of Immovables in Pharaonic Egypt, in* WOMEN'S EARLIEST RECORDS FROM ANCIENT EGYPT AND WESTERN ASIA 123, 128–29 (Barbara Lesko ed., 1989).

32. *See* KATARY, LAND TENURE IN THE RAMESSIDE PERIOD 71. *See also* WARBURTON, STATE AND ECONOMY IN ANCIENT EGYPT 166.

33. *See* KATARY, LAND TENURE IN THE RAMESSIDE PERIOD 72. *See also* Schafik Allam, *Women as Owners of Immovables in Pharaonic Egypt, in* WOMEN'S EARLIEST RECORDS FROM ANCIENT EGYPT AND WESTERN ASIA 123, 135 (Barbara Lesko ed., 1989) ("about twelve percent as coming from women".); Christopher J. Eyre, *The Market Women of Pharaonic Egypt, in* LE COMMERCE EN ÉGYPT ANCIENNE 173, 184–85 (Nicolas Grimal and Bernadette Menu eds., 1998); Christopher J. Eyre, *Peasants and "Modern" Leasing Strategies in Ancient Egypt*, 40 J. ECONOMIC & SOCIAL HIST. ORIENT 367, 380 (1997) (Characterizing real property ownership in the New Kingdom, Eyre states that "a significant proportion of holders are women. . . .").

34. *See supra* § 3.02[A].

35. David Lorton, *Legal and Social Institutions of Pharaonic Egypt, in* 1 CIVILIZATIONS OF THE ANCIENT NEAR EAST 345, 353 (Jack M. Sasson ed., 1995). *See* William

> Ancient Egypt had several enormous bureaucracies with interlocking directorships, one of which was the government and the others were the major temples. The temples had land holdings and large numbers of dependents, and thus their own agricultural and industrial production remained within their control and was not distributed back to Pharaoh, while Pharaoh and his government likewise controlled huge holdings and large numbers of dependents, the proceeds of which provided for the maintenance of the government, but part of which was voluntarily relinquished to the temples.[36]

The temples controlled vast holdings. Over 90 percent of the land owners listed on the Wilbour Papyrus are temples.[37] Papyrus Harris (from the age of Ramses III (*c.* 1186–1154 B.C.)) indicates that the temples at that time held nearly three-quarters of a million acres (about 15 percent of all useful agricultural land). Additionally, the temples employed about 2 percent of the country's populace (well over 100 thousand people).[38] These figures are

---

A. Ward, *Some Aspects of Private Land Ownership and Inheritance in Ancient Egypt, ca. 2500–1000 B.C., in* Land Tenure and Social Transformation in the Middle East 63, 64 (Tarif Khalidi ed., 1984) ("It is evident that the major land-holders of Egypt were the temples and government institutions, the royal family, and the rich upper strata of the aristocracy") (footnote omitted); Katary, Land Tenure in the Ramesside Period 93–96; S. Allam, *Law Courts in Pharaonic and Hellenistic Times*, 77 J. Egyptian Archaeology 109, 110 ("Such temples occupied themselves with agriculture, commerce and various industries; a considerable portion of the population worked for them and lived on their lands."); Warburton, State and Economy in Ancient Egypt 81; *Id.* at 118 ("The state may have been one of the major land owners in ancient Egypt...."). *But see Id.* at 32 (Citing O'Connor for the proposition that the temples actually were part of the State.).

36. Warburton, State and Economy in Ancient Egypt 302. *See also Id.* at 312–313.

37. *See* Katary, Land Tenure in the Ramesside Period 63.

38. *See* Breasted, History of Egypt 491 ("The records of Ramses III for the first and only time in the course of Egyptian history, enable us to determine the total amount of property owned and controlled by the temples. An inventory in the Papyrus Harris covering almost all the temples of the country shows that they possessed over one hundred and seven thousand slaves; that is, one person in every fifty to eighty of the population was temple property. The first figure is the more probable, so that in all likelihood one person in every fifty was a slave of some temple. The temples thus owned two percent of the population. In lands we find the sacred endowments amounting to nearly three quarters of a million acres, that is, nearly one seventh, or over fourteen and a half percent of the cultivable land of the country; and as some of the smaller temples...are omitted in the inventory it is safe to say that the total holdings of the temples amounted to fifteen percent of the available land of the country.") (footnotes omitted).

especially notable since the temples enjoyed a certain degree of tax exemption.[39] Manning describes the operation of temple estates as follows:

> Land was donated by the king on behalf of the god of each temple in order to maintain the cult as well as the priests and dependents. A large part of the priestly income would have been derived from leasing out such land. In addition, plots of temple land were traditionally exchanged for service to the temple estate and they were certainly treated as private land by those who held them because they were passed on to their heirs.[40]

But although the palace and temples may have held significant interests in real estate, Eyre argues that individual owners and tenants were responsible for substantial agri-business on a different scale. According to Eyre:

> Although evidence is limited, the impression is that large holdings and estates in Egypt were essentially management structures, and not single enterprises: managing individuals running small-to-medium farms on a share-cropping basis, and not running huge farms on the basis of wage/ration labour.[41]

A nomarch could actually own two different types of real property. First, he owned outright the land that had passed to him from his family. Second, he owned the property that he held merely by virtue of his position as nomarch, as a life estate. When a nomarch died, technically, the nomarchy itself reverted to the king who maintained the power to appoint a successor.[42]

---

39. *See Id.* at 492 (All of this temple property "was entirely exempt from taxation....") (footnote omitted); GRIMAL, ANCIENT EGYPT 81. *See also infra* § 5.04[C].

40. J.G. Manning, *Demotic Egyptian Instruments of Transfer as Evidence for Private Ownership of Real Property*, 71 CHICAGO-KENT L. REV. 237, 241 (1995).

41. Christopher J. Eyre, *Peasants and "Modern" Leasing Strategies in Ancient Egypt*, 40 J. ECONOMIC & SOCIAL HIST. ORIENT 367, 379 (1997); *See also Id.* at 380 ("Estates were collections of small plots, not consolidated into large farms. Share-cropping on small units is the characteristic Egyptian style of land management, with landlord and tenant sharing in different degrees the investment and return: One leased land, rather than managed it, and avoided hiring wage-labour.") (footnotes omitted).

42. *See* BREASTED, HISTORY OF EGYPT 161 (Describing Egypt in the Middle Kingdom, Breasted states: "The domains over which the nomarch thus ruled were not all his unqualified possessions. His wealth consisted of lands and revenues of two classes: the 'paternal estate,' received from his ancestors and entailed in his line; and the 'count's estate,' over which the dead hand had no control; it was conveyed as a fief by the Pharaoh anew at the nomarch's death. It was this fact which to some extent enabled the Pharaoh to control the feudatories and to secure the appointment of partisans of his house throughout the country."). *See also Id.* at 229 (Breasted notes that when Ahmose expelled the Hyksos, he seized possession of the land that had belonged to the nobles in the nomes. From that point forward, the king owned those lands.).

The Duties of the Vizier text from Rekhmire's tomb (reign of Thutmose III, *c.* 1479–1425 B.C.) contains special provisions regarding petitions brought to the vizier that concern land disputes. The vizier is told:

> Now anybody who petitions the vizi[e]r about lands, he [the vizi[e]r] should order him (to appear) before him over and above listening to the overseer of farm lands and the assessor of the land register(?); he may grant a delay of two months on his behalf for his lands in the South and in the North; but for his lands which are in the neighbourhood of the Southern City [Thebes] or of the Residence, he should grant a delay for him of three days, which is what the law lays down. He should hear in judgement any petitioner in accordance with this law which is in his hand.[43]

The vizier is also apprised that he should record land transfers ("All conveyances should be brought to him, and it is he who should seal them.") and settle boundary disputes ("In the case of any petitioner who says 'Our boundaries have shifted,' then it should be seen that it has happened under the seal of an official. If it has happened, then he [the vizi[e]r] should take away the plots of lands of the assessors who had them [the boundaries] shifted.").[44] The Law Collection of Hermopolis (*c.* 700 B.C.) also contains provisions that deal with a formal legal procedure used for settling disputes regarding property ownership, the process of "making a public protest."[45]

But see infra §7.04 regarding the hereditary character of the Middle Kingdom nomarchies. *See also infra* §5.02 regarding life estates.

43. T.G.H. JAMES, PHARAOH'S PEOPLE: SCENES FROM LIFE IN IMPERIAL EGYPT 65 (1984). *See also* WARBURTON, STATE AND ECONOMY IN ANCIENT EGYPT 178–79. For other references to Rekhmire, *see supra* §§2.03, 3.04, 4.01, 4.02, *infra* §5.04, note 107.

44. T.G.H. JAMES, PHARAOH'S PEOPLE: SCENES FROM LIFE IN IMPERIAL EGYPT 65 (1984).

45. *See* J.G. Manning, *Demotic Egyptian Instruments of Transfer as Evidence for Private Ownership of Real Property*, 71 CHICAGO-KENT L. REV. 237, 262 (1995) (Manning describes the procedure as follows:

> If a dispute over ownership between two parties arose, there was a clearly defined legal method by which one exerted rightful claim to the property. This method, known as 'making a public protest' (*ir š'r*), is described in some detail in the 'code.' The protest was made by a party who claimed an interest in property, either in the presence of (lit. 'in the face of') the party legally holding the property or in his absence, and had to be done three times in successive years in order to fulfill the requirements associated with the protest.).

See also MATTHA, THE DEMOTIC LEGAL CODE OF HERMOPOLIS WEST 74–76.

§5.02 Some Significant Principles of Property Law

The ancient Egyptians appreciated several rather sophisticated concepts relating to property law. For example, one ostracon from Deir el-Medina (British Museum Ostracon 5625)—a text that records a trial by oracle—may contain an important concept in property law; namely, a natural rights theory of property (*i.e.*, the supposition that a person's labor begets an ownership interest in property). The oracle decided that the plaintiff, Kenna, should be considered the owner of a particular house. The house at issue had originally been owned by another named Peikharu. The oracle awarded ownership to Kenna (rather than a man named Mersekhmet), because Kenna, by himself, had rebuilt the house after it had fallen into disrepair.[46] This principle—that labor can create a property right—is often associated with principles of Roman law (*i.e., accessio*) and later with theories attributed to John Locke.[47] Thus, it is significant that the Egyptians used this precept hundreds of years earlier than the Romans.

Egyptian bailment contracts shed light on a rather subtle facet of the Egyptian law of property.[48] In simple terms, bailment is the modern legal term used to describe a property transfer that involves a transfer of possession but not a transfer of ownership. For example, a contract to store goods in a warehouse is a type of bailment contract. A car rental is also a bailment. The rental company is the bailor and the renter is the bailee. In Roman law, there is a distinction made between the concept called *usus* and the concept known as *usus fructus*. The distinction is actually rather simple. *Usus fructus* was probably the most significant personal servitude in Roman law. *Usus fructus* allowed a person both to use a thing and to reap the benefits of the "fruits" of that thing (*i.e.*, the products of that thing). For example someone who had *usus fructus* of an olive orchard would have both the use of the property itself and would also be entitled to reap the benefits of the olives produced by the trees in the orchard (*e.g.*, to press the olives into oil). Roman law did, however, forbid a person with the right of

---

46. *See* BEDELL, CRIMINAL LAW 257 ("Kenna had stated that he alone rebuilt the ruined house of Peikharu, and therefore, the workman Mersekhmet's claim to part ownership was invalid." The hypothesis regarding labor and its relationship to property ownership is mine, not Bedell's.).
47. *See* J. LOCKE, SECOND TREATISE ON GOVERNMENT ch. 5 (1690).
48. For more on bailment contracts, *see infra* §9.03.

usus fructus to destroy or significantly alter the property.[49] A bailee ordinarily has the right of *usus* but not necessarily *usus fructus*. The Egyptians appreciated this same distinction. In one case from Deir el Medina (Ostracon Gard 54), a plaintiff-bailor complains that the person who was renting his donkey (*i.e.*, the bailee) not only failed to return the animal on time but also had confiscated the donkey's foal (*i.e.*, the "fruits" of the donkey), as well. Consequently, we may assume that the ordinary nature of an Egyptian bailment contract contemplated what the Romans would have called *usus* but not *usus fructus* within its scope (otherwise, absent a particular agreement to the contrary, the bailor would not have had grounds to complain).[50]

The ancient Egyptians also recognized the concept of a life estate.[51] This permitted an Egyptian to transfer property for the term of one's life. But the concept of a life estate in essence also creates a trust[52] because the trans-

---

49. *See* Alan Watson, Roman Law & Comparative Law 50 (1991).

50. *See* McDowell, Jurisdiction 172 (McDowell refers to this case, but the hypothesis regarding the Egyptian recognition of *usus* and *usus fructus* as distinct concepts is mine.); Schafik Allam, *Women as Owners of Immovables in Pharaonic Egypt, in* Women's Earliest Records From Ancient Egypt and Western Asia 123, 133 (Barbara Lesko ed., 1989) ("There seems to be a wide range of personal rights: usufruct...."). *Cf.* J.G. Manning, *Demotic Egyptian Instruments of Transfer as Evidence for Private Ownership of Real Property*, 71 Chicago-Kent L. Rev. 237, 246 (1995) (In discussing "the notion of a public recognition of rights in land or of rights of usufruct of the land", Manning asserts "There was no such legal recognition in pharaonic Egypt....") (footnote omitted); *Id.* at 250–251 (Manning states that "demotic instruments of transfer might record... the transfer of the usufruct"); *Id.* at 265 recognizing a "usufructuary right" in land in some circumstances for "a wife until the children were of age.").

51. *See* Erman, Life in Ancient Egypt 147 (Erman remarks that Ḥapdjefai was careful to declare that his consideration, that is, his payment, was being taken from "that part of his property and revenue which was really hereditary in his family," emphasizing that it was "*not* in any way from the property of the estate of the nomarch" (*Id.* at 146). The point here is that the payment was his personal property, not the property that he held as a life estate by virtue of his official position as nomarch. As regards property law, here we see the recognition of three distinct concepts: 1) a life estate; 2) the concept *nemo dat quod non habet* ("no one grants a greater interest than he owns".); and, 3) public trust.). *See also* Gardiner, Egypt of the Pharaohs 142 (Gardiner also discusses Prince Ḥapdjefai's contracts: "Ḥapdjefai had appointed a 'soul-servant' to attend his funeral cult after his death, endowing him with land, serfs, and cattle as inducement for the loyal discharge of his duties. By a series of exchanges with the priests offerings to his statue were ensured throughout the year. One cannot read the elaborate stipulations of these contracts without realizing that strict rules of property lie behind them, for instance a distinction between what the prince owned by virtue of inheritance and what he owned by virtue of his office.") (citations omitted); *infra* § 9.03.

52. *See infra* § 7.03.

feree must pass along the subject property to someone else at the end of his (*i.e.*, the trustee's) life.

In addition, Egyptian property law understood the concept of easements. An easement is a right to enter another's real property. Often—though not always—adjacent property owners are legally entitled to limited easements that involve a neighbor's land. One text (Ostracon Cairo 25555) refers to the right to use a road for entry and egress.[53] The oracle's decision denied a man named Hay (the defendant in the suit) permission to use a road that belonged to the plaintiff, a man named Pentoere.[54] In an earlier court case, the court had "permitted Hay only the right to use the road for access to an undefined place."[55] Bedell explains that the oracle "overruled the court's decision, and granted Pentoere exclusive rights to the access road."[56]

Lastly, it should be recalled that the offices of nomarch and vizier were considered hereditary even during the Old Kingdom.[57] One of the significant aspects about offices such as the nomarchy and vizierate being considered hereditary is that these—like *usus*, *usus fructus*, and easements—were intangible rights. Thus, in terms of property law, the Egyptians of the Old Kingdom were among the first people to have recognized the existence and alienability of property rights which were intangible.[58]

The Law Collection of Hermopolis contains several provisions that address rights and duties between adjacent landowners. For example, a landowner was required to leave a reasonable amount of space between his neighbor's house and the one that he was constructing.[59] Similarly, a landowner was not permitted to allow his water drain to discharge water onto his neighbor's property,[60] he was not permitted to construct a doorway in a manner that interfered with his neighbor, and he was liable for damage caused when he dug his house foundation too close to his neighbor's house.[61]

---

53. *See* BEDELL, CRIMINAL LAW 245.

54. *See Id.* at 256 ("It is presumed that by the action of walking backwards, the god indicated that a man named Hay would not be permitted to use an access road belonging to the plaintiff Pentoere.").

55. *Id.* at 267.

56. *Id. See also supra* § 4.07 regarding appeal.

57. *See infra* § 7.04.

58. *Id.*

59. *See* MATTHA, THE DEMOTIC LEGAL CODE OF HERMOPOLIS WEST 37, 111.

60. *See Id.* at 38, 113.

61. *See Id.*

§ 5.03 Sale & Lease of Land, Deeds, & Recordation of Real Property

[A] Sales

There were detailed laws concerning the sale of real property. Documents relating to real estate sales and wills were routinely executed in the presence of magistrates.[62] One 17th Dynasty (*c.* 1600–1570 B.C.) stela (Stèle Juridique from Karnak) suggests that a seller and buyer of real estate had one year to complete performance of their transfer, but that they could ask for an extension of time to complete the conveyance if necessary.[63] The Egyptians used a special term, *imyt-pr*, for a certified deed of conveyance of real property.[64] *Imyt-pr* is the same expression used for a valid will (*i.e.*, another legal document which operates to transfer property).[65] These documents ordinarily contain both the price paid and also a description of the property.[66] The seller usually transferred the written deed to the buyer so that the buyer would then have a document to prove his title.[67] Later, in the Ptolemaic Period (*c.* 304–30 B.C.), a seller ordinarily transferred title by using two documents. One was the "document in exchange for money" and the other was a "document of being far" (*i.e.*, a document in which the seller promised not to contest the buyer's rights). Together these documents functioned as memoranda memorializing the oral agreement for sale.[68] According to Manning, "the import of these documents was that they gave proof of legal title to the property in question."[69] Egyptians routinely executed these documents, like their predecessor the *imyt-pr*, in the presence of witnesses and recorded them in some kind of public archive.[70]

---

62. *See* McDowell, Jurisdiction 130 ("sales of real estate and testaments are drawn up before the magistrates.").

63. *See* Aristide Théodorides, *The Concept of Law in Ancient Egypt, in* The Legacy of Egypt 291, 293 (J.R. Harris ed., 2d ed. 1971).

64. *See Id.* at 298 (Explaining the *imyt-pr* as an "expression which designates a certified deed of conveyance".); *Id.* at 304 ("The *imyt-pr* was, during the Old Kingdom, a deed of transfer by gift, but later it became the generic term covering all kinds of conveyance.").

65. *See infra* § 7.02; R.O. Faulkner, A Concise Dictionary of Middle Egyptian 18 (1981) (Defining *imyt-pr* as "will, testament"). *See also infra* § 9.03.

66. *See* Pestman, Marriage & Matrimonial Property 19.

67. *See Id.* at 85; Katary, Land Tenure in the Ramesside Period 221.

68. *See* J.G. Manning, *Demotic Egyptian Instruments of Transfer as Evidence for Private Ownership of Real Property*, 71 Chicago-Kent L. Rev. 237, 251–252 (1995).

69. *Id.* at 252 (footnote omitted).

70. *Id.* at 253–255.

As early as the 4th Dynasty (*c.* 2625–2510 B.C.), the State required that all *inter vivos* (*i.e.*, among the living) transfers of real estate had to be registered with the vizier in the State archives. Thus *imyt-pr* (*i.e.*, deeds of sale) for the transfer of real property had to be taken to the office of the vizier, witnessed, and recorded there in order to be considered valid.[71] Once it was recorded with the vizier, the vizier issued new land titles for the transferee.[72] In sum, then, in sales of real property, the parties filed the contract in a records office as evidence of the transaction. This filing permitted officials to know who was responsible for paying property taxes.[73] The Law Collection of Hermopolis provides an interesting mechanism that permitted a buyer who did not obtain clear title to land at the closing of the sale to legally establish his title. If he executed a written lease for three consecutive years (*i.e.*, if he leased the house to another for three years), at the end of the third year, so long as no one had brought suit against him challenging his ownership, his title was considered valid.[74] If a buyer failed to pay the seller in full (*i.e.*, the buyer had made partial payment but was otherwise in breach), the seller could return the partial payment and rescind the sale within three years.[75] We know of one sale of land from about 1000 B.C. where around six and three-quarters acres in Abydos sold for one deben ("a little over fourteen hundred grains of silver"), a price which Breasted con-

---

71. *See* Aristide Théodorides, *The Concept of Law in Ancient Egypt*, *in* THE LEGACY OF EGYPT 291, 292 (J.R. Harris ed., 2d ed. 1971) (Théodorides notes that the State registered deeds of real estate conveyance. He cites as evidence for this practice "the document called 'the contract for the sale of a small house' (in the pyramid city of Khufu (Cheops) of the early 4th Dynasty)."); *Id.* at 293 (We have a contract to buy and sell a house that "had been prepared before the local council, which registered it, and in the presence of several witnesses...."); *Id.* at 309 ("All land registration comes within the vizier's jurisdiction. That is why the *imyt-pr* have to be sent to him."); J.G. Manning, *Demotic Egyptian Instruments of Transfer as Evidence for Private Ownership of Real Property*, 71 CHICAGO-KENT L. REV. 237, 249 (1995) ("recorded transfers of land in Egyptian history are rare even in the later periods when more documentation is available."); GRIMAL, ANCIENT EGYPT 91 (Describing circumstances in the Old Kingdom, Grimal claims: "The third major department of state, the Royal Archives, looked after the deeds for land ownership."); BREASTED, HISTORY OF EGYPT 82 ("Here all lands were registered, and all local archives centralized and coordinated; here wills were recorded, and when executed the resulting new titles were issued.") (footnote omitted).

72. *See* BREASTED, HISTORY OF EGYPT 82.

73. *See* Janet H. Johnson, *The Legal Status of Women in Ancient Egypt*, *in* MISTRESS OF THE HOUSE MISTRESS OF HEAVEN: WOMEN IN ANCIENT EGYPT 175, 177 (Anne K. Chapel and Glenn E. Markoe eds., 1996). *See also infra* § 5.04.

74. *See* MATTHA, THE DEMOTIC LEGAL CODE OF HERMPOLIS WEST 79, 81.

75. *See Id.* at 107.

76. *See* BREASTED, HISTORY OF EGYPT 524–25.

sidered "very low."[76] Interestingly, it was not until centuries later that the Greeks introduced the concept of a land mortgage into Egypt.[77]

[B] Leases

The Law Collection of Hermopolis contains numerous provisions regarding the rights and obligations of lessors and lessees.[78] This law collection contemplates the lease of a variety of different kinds of property. For example, it articulates rules for the lease of an agricultural field, a house, a clothiery, a brewery, a hatchery, a cabin, and a garden.[79] Leases were ordinarily executed in writing. A typical lease for an agricultural field began by stating the names of the parties followed by a description of the subject property (*i.e.*, the adjacent North, South, East, and West plots were mentioned). It required that the lessor was obligated to provide seed corn (specifying a certain amount of seed corn per aroura (*i.e.*, about two-thirds of an acre) of land) to the lessee and that the lessee was obligated to cultivate the land. Next the lease stipulated the amount of rent that the lessee was required to pay.[80] In many cases, a lessee was allowed to pay his rent (at least in part) with products associated with his lease. For example, a cultivator typically paid his rent in grain from the harvest, a brewer could pay with beer, a clothier could pay with garments, and a gardener could pay with vegetables.[81]

As was mentioned, a landowner who leased fields to a lessee usually was obliged to provide the lessee with a certain amount of seed corn. In turn, the lessee (*i.e.*, cultivator) paid the landowner a percentage of his yield in rent.[82] If the landowner repudiated the lease after the lessee had planted—but before he had undertaken a substantial amount of additional work and harvesting—the landowner was required to pay one-fourth of the yield, as liquidated damages, to the non-breaching lessee.[83] If, on the other hand, a

---

77. *See* Aristide Théodorides, *The Concept of Law in Ancient Egypt, in* THE LEGACY OF EGYPT 291, 319 (J.R. Harris ed., 2d ed. 1971).

78. *See* MATTHA, THE DEMOTIC LEGAL CODE OF HERMOPOLIS WEST xiii–xix.

79. *See Id.* at 24 (Mattha translates "pavilion", "bath"), 25 (cabin, garden). *See also Id.* at 82–83 (I follow Hughes's translation "clothiery" instead of "pavilion"), 84 ("brewery"), 85 ("hatchery" instead of "bath").

80. *See Id.* at XVI, 22–23.

81. *See Id.* at 82–88.

82. Hughes suggests that the normal arrangement required a lessee to pay one-third of the yield to the landowner/lessor. *See* MATTHA, THE DEMOTIC LEGAL CODE OF HERMOPOLIS WEST 73.

83. *Id.* at XIII, 20. According to Hughes: "The awarding of ¼ of the harvest to the cultivator…, after sowing had been done but before tending and harvesting of the

lessee repudiated after irrigation, by refusing to plant the seed corn, he was required to return the seed corn to the lessor and also to pay his full rent.[84] If a lack of inundation caused the lessee's failure to cultivate, then he did not have to pay his rent but he did have to return the seed corn to the lessor.[85]

§ 5.04 Taxation of Property

[A] Introduction

Scholars have debated whether the payments made to the State in association with real property should be characterized as "taxes" or "rents."[86] Fundamentally, the distinction hinges on whether one considers the land to have been privately owned or owned by the State.[87] As was mentioned above,[88] for purposes of this discussion, we shall consider the land as having been privately owned, and, therefore, the payments made as "taxes" rather than as "rents." Although there were other taxes (*e.g.*, a burial tax[89]),

---

crop, would give him somewhat less than half of the probable ⅔ that he would have gotten at harvest...." *Id.* at 73. *See infra* § 9.03 regarding liquidated damages.

84. *Id.* at xiii-xiv, 21.

85. *Id.* at xiv, 21.

86. *See* WARBURTON, STATE AND ECONOMY IN ANCIENT EGYPT 64 ("the basis of [the pharaoh's] power was the right to 'taxation' which in turn implies that people had their private property..."); *Id.* at 140 ("these payments were either a type of 'rent'—if actual possession remained with Pharaoh or the temples—or a tax—if the actual possession of the land was transferred from Pharaoh or the temple to the individual.") (I assume that Warburton's use of the word "possession" in this context ought to be understood more like our modern concept of "ownership in fee simple absolute".); *Id.* at 316 (Noting that the payments made "could be termed either 'taxes'or 'rent' depending upon the definition of ownership...."); KATARY, LAND TENURE IN THE RAMESSIDE PERIOD 172 (Discussing whether the financial transfers recorded in the Wilbour Papyrus should be characterized as "revenue reallocations" or "taxes".); *Id.* at 212 (Noting that "payments...could be termed *either* rent *or* taxes. Documents of this period suggest, moreover, that such a distinction was simply immaterial."); William A. Ward, *Some Aspects of Private Land Ownership and Inheritance in Ancient Egypt, ca. 2500–1000 B.C., in* LAND TENURE AND SOCIAL TRANSFORMATION IN THE MIDDLE EAST 63 (Tarif Khalidi, ed., 1984) ("taxation and rental may not have indicated two different types of payment as they do today".) (footnote omitted); Schafik Allam, *Women as Owners of Immovables in Pharaonic Egypt, in* WOMEN'S EARLIEST RECORDS FROM ANCIENT EGYPT AND WESTERN ASIA 123, 133 (Barbara Lesko ed., 1989).

87. *See supra* § 5.01.

88. *Id.*

89. *See* P.W. Pestman, *The Law of Succession in Ancient Egypt*, 9 STUDIA ET DOCUMENTA AD JURA ANTIQUI PERTINENTIA 58, 64 (1969).

the most common tax levied in ancient Egypt was a property tax.[90] Simply stated, "private land owners were obliged to pay a financial tax to Pharaoh...."[91] Beginning very early in history, the government conducted a fiscal census. At first it was biennial and later annual.[92] Government agents measured fields (*i.e.*, arable land) and counted assets (*e.g.*, cattle, precious metals, etc.) for purposes of assessing taxes.[93] This inventory of real and personal property established the basis for taxes payable. During the Old Kingdom (*c.* 2700–2200 B.C.), and indeed throughout much of antiquity, the Egyptians paid their taxes not with "money" but with grain, their own labor, or other agricultural commodities.[94] Government officials beat de-

---

90. *See* WARBURTON, STATE AND ECONOMY IN ANCIENT EGYPT 68.

91. *Id.* at 319 (Citing the inscription of Mose and Papyrus Valençay I.); *Id.* at 336 ("The taxation of...land-owners and craftsmen was introduced or formalized during the Archaic period and increased during the Old Kingdom.").

92. *See* GRIMAL, ANCIENT EGYPT 81 (Grimal asserts that the census in the 6th Dynasty was "an operation that took place on average every two years or every year and a half."); WILSON, CULTURE OF ANCIENT EGYPT 82 ("Biennially and then later annually, there was a fiscal census, a governmental counting of arable land, cattle, and gold.").

93. *See* Christopher J. Eyre, *Peasants and "Modern" Leasing Strategies in Ancient Egypt*, 40 J. ECONOMIC & SOCIAL HIST. ORIENT 367, 371–72 (1997); WARBURTON, STATE AND ECONOMY IN ANCIENT EGYPT 134–135; J.G. Manning, Gary Greig, and Sugihiko Uchida, *Chicago Oriental Institute Ostracon 12073 Once Again*, 48 J. NEAR EASTERN STUD. 117, 118 (1989) (Citing, in particular, Papyrus Valençay, recto, 9.); Schafik Allam, *Women as Owners of Immovables in Pharaonic Egypt, in* WOMEN'S EARLIEST RECORDS FROM ANCIENT EGYPT AND WESTERN ASIA 123, 128 (Barbara Lesko ed., 1989); David Lorton, *Legal and Social Institutions of Pharaonic Egypt, in* 1 CIVILIZATIONS OF THE ANCIENT NEAR EAST 345 (Jack M. Sasson ed., 1995); GARDINER, EGYPT OF THE PHARAOHS 144 ("Censuses of households were taken and similarly registered. In a word, the busy life of this important local community was regulated by strict administrative measures, the extent and co-ordination of which can only be glimpsed from the surviving debris of manuscripts."); *Id.* at 143 ("Another papyrus fragment of administrative interest was found at Haraga, a 12th Dynasty site only a couple of miles away. This is a memorandum of the days spent in measuring fields, assessing taxes, and reporting on the subject to the overseer of the land of the Northern district."); BREASTED, HISTORY OF EGYPT 237 ("Other royal property, like cattle and asses, was held by people of both classes, subject, like the lands, to an annual assessment for its use. For purposes of taxation all land and other property of the crown, except that held by the temples, were recorded in the tax-registers of the White House, as the treasury was still called. All 'houses' or estates and the 'numbers belonging thereto,' were entered in these registers. On the basis of these, taxes were assessed.") (footnote omitted). *See also* GRIMAL, ANCIENT EGYPT 132–133 (Tax collection depicted in tomb painting.).

94. *See generally* WARBURTON, STATE AND ECONOMY IN ANCIENT EGYPT 159–174 (Translating and discussing The Tax Lists of the Royal Canon of Turin, The Wilbour Papyrus, and the Turin Taxation Papyrus.); WILSON, CULTURE OF ANCIENT EGYPT 82 ("On the basis of this inventory there would be an assessment of taxes, payable in kind—grain, hides, gold, and so on—or in labor."); *Id.* at 270 (Wilson explains that during the time of Ramses III (Papyrus Harris), "The annual income which came to

faulting taxpayers.[95] When the scribe came to record harvest tax collections, certain functionaries (called *iryw-'3*, "doorkeepers") carried staffs and Nubians wielded palm rods with which to beat people who failed to pay their taxes.[96] Because the success or failure of crops was linked closely with the height of the annual Nile inundation, Egyptian officials carefully measured and recorded the flood levels and used that information to adjust tax assessments accordingly.[97] By the end of the Middle Kingdom (*c.* 1674 B.C.) and continuing into the New Kingdom, tax lists were compiled on a routine basis[98] and were recorded in the State treasury called the "White House."[99] The Wilbour Papyrus (*c.* 1188–1069 B.C.) records taxes that property owners owed on their farmland.[100] Warburton concludes that these taxes were an essential feature of the ancient Egyptian economy: "In the end, the fiscal system should be characterized as a taxation system..., as it was the taxation, the forced payments, that permitted the growth of the temples and the construction projects."[101]

We also have documents that indicate that there was a separate tax paid by a buyer when purchasing real estate.[102] Egyptian law seems to have acknowledged the legitimate excuse of *vis maior* (*i.e.*, acts of god) in some circumstances involving tax delinquency. For example, if a third party robbed a

---

the temples through taxes was listed under two headings. Agricultural income was measured in units of grain, 'the grain of the taxes of farmers,' and all other income, whether goods or labor, was measured in units of silver, 'silver, in property and in labor of people, given for the divine offerings.'").

95. *See* T.G.H. JAMES, PHARAOH'S PEOPLE: SCENES FROM LIFE IN IMPERIAL EGYPT 83–84 (1984).

96. *See* MCDOWELL, JURISDICTION 44.

97. *See* Christopher J. Eyre, *Peasants and "Modern" Leasing Strategies in Ancient Egypt*, 40 J. ECONOMIC & SOCIAL HIST. ORIENT 367, 371–72 (1997); BREASTED, HISTORY OF EGYPT 239 ("The taxes were so dependent, as they still are, upon the height of the inundation and the consequent prospects for a plentiful or scanty harvest, that the level of the rising river was also reported to him.") (footnote omitted).

98. *See* BREASTED, HISTORY OF EGYPT 211.

99. *See* GRIMAL, ANCIENT EGYPT 91 (Discussing State organization in the Old Kingdom, Grimal says: "The Treasury was in charge of the economy as a whole, but it was particularly concerned with the collection of taxes, which derived essentially from the second major department: Agriculture."); BREASTED, HISTORY OF EGYPT 237.

100. *See* KATARY, LAND TENURE IN THE RAMESSIDE PERIOD xxi ("Text A of P. Wilbour is an enumeration of what appears to have been the assessment of some 2800 plots of agricultural land located in Middle Egypt during year 4 of Ramesses V (1142 B.C.)."); Janet H. Johnson, *The Legal Status of Women in Ancient Egypt, in* MISTRESS OF THE HOUSE MISTRESS OF HEAVEN: WOMEN IN ANCIENT EGYPT 175, 178 (Anne K. Chapel and Glenn E. Markoe eds., 1996).

101. WARBURTON, STATE AND ECONOMY IN ANCIENT EGYPT 320.

102. *See* PESTMAN, MARRIAGE & MATRIMONIAL PROPERTY 88.

taxpayer so that the taxpayer was unable to pay his taxes, he was excused.[103] We know that during the reign of Amenhotep III (*c.* 1390–1352 B.C.), a significant number of foreign slaves entered Egypt.[104] The government opted to treat many of them as peasants and added them to the tax registers.[105]

[B] Administration

The practical aspects of tax collection must have been arduous to manage. Although other officials (in particular, the "Magnates of the Southern Tens") may have helped with supervision from time to time,[106] the government official principally responsible for taxation in ancient Egypt was the vizier.[107] It is likely that, during the Old Kingdom (*c.* 2700–2200 B.C.), each nome rendered its taxes to the central State government, and that some form of "tax-farming" was used for collection.[108] In the Middle Kingdom (*c.*

---

103. *See* BEDELL, CRIMINAL LAW 170 (Bedell points out that the taxpayer's "crime was unintentional.").

104. *See infra* § 10.04.

105. *See* BREASTED, HISTORY OF EGYPT 339 ("The influx of slaves, chiefly of Semitic race, which had begun under Thutmose III, still continued, and the king's chief scribe distributed them throughout the land and enrolled them among the tax-paying serfs.") (footnote omitted).

106. *See Id.* at 164–65 (Breasted explains that by the Middle Kingdom, officials called the Magnates of the Southern Tens had some responsibility for the census and tax records: "There was now more than one 'Southern Ten,' and 'Magnates of the Southern Tens' were frequently entrusted with various executive and administrative commissions by the king. As we shall see, they had the census and tax records in charge....").

107. Regarding the duties of the vizier in general, *see supra* §§ 3.03, 3.04. *See also* GARDINER, EGYPT OF THE PHARAOHS 105 (Noting that the vizier was in charge of the corvée and taxation.); WILSON, CULTURE OF ANCIENT EGYPT 172 (Stating that the vizier in the New Kingdom "was responsible for taxes from Egypt."); BREASTED, HISTORY OF EGYPT 166 (Referring to circumstances in the Middle Kingdom, Breasted says: "The office of the vizier was thus the central archives of the government as before, and all records of the land-administration with census and tax registration were filed in his bureaus."); *Id.* at 239 ("The great vizier, Rekhmire depicts himself in the gorgeous reliefs in his tomb receiving... the taxes of the officials who appeared before him each year with their dues....") (footnote omitted) ("Of the royal income from all sources in the 18th Dynasty the southern vizier had general charge. The amount of all taxes to be levied and the distribution of the revenue when collected were determined in his office, where a constant balance sheet was kept."). For other references to Rekhmire, *see supra* §§ 2.03, 3.04, 4.01, 4.02, 5.01.

108. *See* Christopher J. Eyre, *Peasants and "Modern" Leasing Strategies in Ancient Egypt*, 40 J. ECONOMIC & SOCIAL HIST. ORIENT 367, 372 (1997); WILSON, CULTURE OF ANCIENT EGYPT 82 (Referring to the Old Kingdom, Wilson relates: "If later evidence is valid, such taxes were rendered by the provinces to the state, so that it is legitimate to suppose that there was a progressive farming-out of taxes."); *Id.* at 279 ("Under Ramses XI, a certain Thut-mose was Clerk of the Great and August Necropolis. One

2040–1674 B.C.), two districts administered the operations of taxation, census records, and public works: one in the south and one in the north.[109] As was mentioned, Egyptians routinely paid their taxes in cattle, grain, wine, oil, honey, and other agricultural products.[110] According to Katary, "Although tax revenues in gold, silver, cattle, and textiles seem to have been handled directly by the vizier, as late as the Middle Kingdom, payments in grain were collected by mayors aided by functionaries of the central bureau of granaries."[111] Thus, in addition to the staff of scribes required to administer this task, the tax officials of necessity had to build and maintain numerous storage facilities.[112]

The Wilbour Papyrus, which dates from the 20th Dynasty (*c.* 1188–1069 B.C.), furnishes many details regarding real property and taxation.[113] Katary asserts that this document is from 1142 B.C., the fourth year of Ramses V.[114] According to Katary:

---

of his functions was to travel around upper Egypt collecting taxes in grain, part of which was allocated to pay the necropolis workers.").

109. *See* BREASTED, HISTORY OF EGYPT 165 ("For the purpose of carrying on public works, as well as for taxation and census records, the country was divided into two administrative districts of the South and the North. . . .").

110. *See* Christopher J. Eyre, *Peasants and "Modern" Leasing Strategies in Ancient Egypt*, 40 J. ECONOMIC & SOCIAL HIST. ORIENT 367, 376 (1997) ("It is characteristic... in the pre-modern context that dues on arable land were calculated in grain, and not necessarily the crop actually grown: it is not then clear whether they were characteristically paid in grain, or to equivalent value in the actual crop.") (footnote omitted); KATARY, LAND TENURE IN THE RAMESSIDE PERIOD 212 (Referring to taxes paid in gold "on a regular basis" in Papyrus Valençay.); BREASTED, HISTORY OF EGYPT 237 ("They were still collected in naturalia: cattle, grain, wine, oil, honey, textiles, and the like."); *Id.* at 80 ("The chief administrative bond which coordinated and centralized these nomes was the organization of the treasury, by the operation of which there annually converged upon the magazines of the central government the grain, cattle, poultry and industrial products, which in an age without coinage, were collected as taxes by the local governors. The local registration of land, or the land-office, the irrigation service, the judicial administration, and other administrative functions were also centralized at the Great House. . . ."); *Id.* at 238 ("All the products which filled these repositories were termed 'labour,' the word employed in ancient Egypt as we use 'taxes.' ").

111. KATARY, LAND TENURE IN THE RAMESSIDE PERIOD 218.

112. *See* BREASTED, HISTORY OF EGYPT 237–238 ("Besides the cattle-yards, the 'granary' was the chief sub-department of the White House, and there were innumerable other magazines for the storage of its receipts."); *Id.* at 238 ("It was collected by the local officials, whom we have already noticed, and its reception in and payment from the various magazines demanded a host of scribes and subordinates, now more numerous than ever before in the history of the country.").

113. *See generally* WARBURTON, STATE AND ECONOMY IN ANCIENT EGYPT 165–169.

114. *See* KATARY, LAND TENURE IN THE RAMESSIDE PERIOD xxi. Katary also discusses the Turin Taxation Papyrus. *See Id.* at 169–184. Katary states that this docu-

> Each paragraph begins with the identification of what is apparently the land-owning institution, religious or secular, under which are ordered a series of assessment lines enumerating plots of various sizes.... Each paragraph specifies the geographic location of each plot.... The assessment lines which follow provide details concerning each plot in question, listing the name and occupation of the responsible party, the size of the plot, and the assessment (if any) levied on the land calculated as a share in the harvest.[115]

Scribes wrote the size of the plots in black ink and the assessed values and tax assessments in red ink.[116] It seems likely that the tax assessors took into account a number of factors when determining property valuation. For example, the location of the property, the owner's occupation (a hint, perhaps, of progressive taxation), the relative irrigability of the land, and "the expected standard yield" appear to have been relevant factors.[117] "[T]he general rate of assessment was actually 30 percent of the standard average grain harvest."[118] As is usually true in modern real property assessments, the assessed value of property for purposes of taxation was typically "low-

---

ment from "year 12 of the reign of Ramesses XI" "detail[s] the collection of grain revenues in several towns south of Thebes, the conveyance of this grain by boat...to Thebes, and the ultimate deposition of the same in appointed storage facilities in the city." *Id.* at 169. In addition, Katary examines a number of other documents that relate to property taxation: 1) P. Amiens (pp. 184–192); 2) P. Harris (pp. 192–193); 3) the Griffith Fragments (pp. 196–200); 4) the Louvre Leather Fragments (pp. 201–207); and, 5) P. Valençay I (pp. 207–216). *See also* WARBURTON, STATE AND ECONOMY IN ANCIENT EGYPT 165 ("the whole text being an office copy relating to a survey carried out in less than four weeks in July and August of perhaps 1140 B.C.") (footnotes omitted); Schafik Allam, *Women as Owners of Immovables in Pharaonic Egypt*, *in* WOMEN'S EARLIEST RECORDS FROM ANCIENT EGYPT AND WESTERN ASIA 123, 128–29 (Barbara Lesko ed., 1989).

115. KATARY, LAND TENURE IN THE RAMESSIDE PERIOD 1. *See also* WARBURTON, STATE AND ECONOMY IN ANCIENT EGYPT 165 ("The main individual entries follow a similar pattern. A group of fields 'under the authority' of a given figure are listed. Each individual plot is listed, followed by a figure giving its size in *arouras* (2735 m²), a rate of assessment of either 5, 7.5 or 10—most probably in *khar* (c. litres)—and the total assessment.") (footnote omitted). *Cf.* WILSON, CULTURE OF ANCIENT EGYPT 271 (According to Wilson, who did not have the benefit of scholars such as Katary and Warburton, even though this document is quite useful, still "we cannot tell whether the figures given are the measures of grain assessed per unit of land or are some kind of data which the assessor would later use to fix the tax.").

116. *See* KATARY, LAND TENURE IN THE RAMESSIDE PERIOD 12, 240. Presumably the red color stood out as a means of making the most important information conspicuous.

117. *See Id.* at 265–266.

118. *Id.* at 21. *See Id.* at 22 ("The actual cultivators...had to pay 30 percent of the yield of their plots to the state.").

balled." For example, for a plot of five arouras (1 aroura (*s‘t3t*) = .66 acres), it was common for the assessed value to be .5 arouras, or 10 percent.[119]

[C] Tax Exemptions

Although most residents and business organizations paid taxes, there were some who were tax exempt (*i.e.*, at least exempt to some degree). Nomarchs, judges, and temples paid either no taxes, or at least reduced taxes, at certain times in ancient Egypt. The nomarchs received a tax exemption for their funerary estates.[120] It is not surprising that State-owned property was exempt from taxation.[121] The judiciary received a tax exemption as well.[122] The 18th Dynasty pharaoh, Horemhab (*c.* 1323–1295 B.C.), exempted judges from taxation.[123] Horemhab wanted to provide an incentive for judges to stop taking bribes. In theory, if the judges were permitted to keep their entire income, they would be less likely to accept bribes.[124] We know that, on occasion, kings exempted certain temples from taxation.[125] For example, a 5th Dynasty (*c.* 2510–2460 B.C.) king completely exempted

---

119. *See Id.* at 83. In fact, over half of the plots assessed on the Wilbour Papyrus are five arouras in size. *See also Id.* at 78.

120. *See* GRIMAL, ANCIENT EGYPT 81 (Mentioning that the 6th Dynasty King Teti exempted the temple at Abydos.); *Id.* at 84 (Noting that Pepi I "issued, in the twenty-first year of his reign, a charter awarding tax immunity to the town that had grown up around Snofru's funerary domain at Dashur."); *Id.* at 92 (Grimal observes that this exemption "was essentially the same as the tax-exemption of temple estates."). *See also* WARBURTON, STATE AND ECONOMY IN ANCIENT EGYPT 191; *Id.* at 321 (Warburton argues "that the temples received taxes" and so he concludes that "it would be relatively logical to suggest that can hardly have been expected to pay them.").

121. *See* BEDELL, CRIMINAL LAW 3 ("Pharaoh's estates...were...exempt from taxes.").

122. *See Id. See also supra* § 3.03[B].

123. *See* WILSON, CULTURE OF ANCIENT EGYPT 237 (Describing the reign of Horemhab, Wilson says: "Pharaoh further made the courts of law free from any tax of silver and gold, in order to prevent an obligation of any kind from being exacted from the courts of Upper and Lower Egypt.'").

124. *See* BREASTED, HISTORY OF EGYPT 405 ("In order to discourage bribery among the local judges he took an unprecedented step. He remitted the tax of gold and silver levied upon all local officials for judicial duties, permitting them to retain the entire income of their offices, in order that they might have no excuse for illegally enriching themselves.") (footnote omitted). *See also* BEDELL, CRIMINAL LAW 203 (Referring to judges accepting bribes.); *supra* § 3.05.

125. *See* David Lorton, *Legal and Social Institutions of Pharaonic Egypt*, *in* 1 CIVILIZATIONS OF THE ANCIENT NEAR EAST 345, 350 (Jack M. Sasson ed., 1995) ("Kings might grant tax exemptions to temples....").

the temple at Abydos from all taxes.[126] Evidently, it was the temples that enjoyed the most extensive tax exemption in ancient Egypt.[127] Some Egyptologists have maintained that the temples paid no taxes whatsoever.[128] Others, on the other hand, have suggested that the exemption only applied to the corvée (*i.e.*, mandatory physical labor).[129] If that is true, then the tax immunity for temples would not have been as costly to the government treasury.

§ 5.05 Chapter Summary

Because ancient Egypt was so heavily dependent upon agricultural productivity, the legal aspects of real property were a vital concern. Although the king may have been considered the legal owner of all land in the early stages of Egyptian history (and, perhaps, technically, later too), by the New Kingdom the Egyptians *treated* real property as if the individuals who possessed and occupied the land (*i.e.*, but obviously not tenants) were its owners. Thus, individuals sold, leased, and bequeathed their land in a manner commensurate with legal ownership. In addition to individual ownership, it was common for certain kinds of property to be owned

---

126. *See* David Lorton, *The Treatment of Criminals in Ancient Egypt*, 20 J. Economic & Social Hist. Orient 2, 6 (1977).

127. *See* Andrea McDowell, *Legal Aspects of Care of the Elderly in Egypt to the End of the New Kingdom, in* The Care of the Elderly in the Ancient Near East 199, 200, 202 (Marten Stol and Sven P. Vleeming eds., 1998) ("as temple property the income was not taxed."); Gardiner, Egypt of the Pharaohs 60 (Gardiner mentions "some royal rescripts which were set up in temples...exempting their priesthoods from taxation....").

128. *See* Breasted, History of Egypt 492 (All of this temple property "was entirely exempt from taxation....") (footnote omitted).

129. *See* Wilson, Culture of Ancient Egypt 271–72 (Wilson discusses the subject of taxation of temples. He cites Gardiner: "He [Gardiner] suggests that the priests themselves and the temple personnel were exempt from forced labor and that the charters of temple immunity forbade civil officials from violating this exemption, but that the temple lands were subject to government taxes. This is a decided amelioration of the situation, since tax-free lands running between 12 and 30 per cent of the arable acreage would have been a crushing burden. On the present evidence, the privilege of the temples was confined to an immunity from the *corvée* which burdened the rest of Egypt.") (Citing A.H. Gardiner, *The Wilbour Papyrus* (London 1948), esp. II, 197 ff.). *See also Id.* at 271 (Explaining that, although the Wilbour Papyrus gives us some details of tax collection in the 20th Dynasty, even this document does not settle the question of whether the temples and their estates were exempt from taxation. Wilson writes: "These are government tax-collectors, and many of the lands are the stated property of the temples.").

jointly, by two or more persons. The State and many temples owned and operated large estates, functioning essentially as corporations managing immense tracts of land.

The vizier(s) maintained records of sales and the taxation of real property. Our data indicates that the government conducted a census for purposes of collecting taxes on real property. Documents such as the Wilbour Papyrus provide a great deal of information relating to property and property taxes. For example, we know that the size, location, irrigability, yield, and owner's occupation affected the rates of taxation. Tax law exempted (at least to some extent) certain entities and individuals, such as nomarchs, judges, and temples.

Egyptian law recognized a number of sophisticated legal concepts and principles relating to property—both tangible and intangible. For example, the Egyptians appreciated: 1) a natural rights theory of property law (*i.e.*, the understanding that labor may create a property interest); 2) a distinction between *usus* and *usus fructus*; 3) life estates; and, 4) easements.

CHAPTER 6

The Family

§6.01 Introduction

One problem we face in interpreting family law matters in ancient Egypt is linguistic. It is often difficult in any given text to know whether words such as son, daughter, brother, and sister were meant literally to indicate blood kinship or whether they were used figuratively as terms to show close bonds of affection or friendship.[1] It is apparent that the ancient Egyptians prized their families.[2] "The basic social unit in ancient Egypt was not an extended kinship group, such as a clan, but rather the nuclear family: father, mother, and children."[3] Men generally had only one legal, principal wife and it was she who was considered the mother of his heirs. Many sculptures and wall paintings depict husbands and wives together showing respect and love towards one another. Artistic representations depict children also as integral parts of the family unit. One word of caution is in order. A great deal of our information about family law—and especially marriage and divorce—comes from the Ptolemaic Period (*c.* 304–30 B.C.), and, therefore, may not necessarily reflect conditions during the Old, Middle, and New Kingdoms.

---

1. *See* GARDINER, EGYPT OF THE PHARAOHS 178 ("[T]he principal difficulty in dealing with Egyptian genealogical problems... [is that] one never knows whether terms like 'son', 'daughter', 'brother', 'sister', and so forth are to be understood literally or not.").

2. *See e.g.*, GRIMAL, ANCIENT EGYPT 98 (Noting that Old Kingdom statuary "evoked family relationships....").

3. David Lorton, *Legal and Social Institutions of Pharaonic Egypt*, *in* 1 CIVILIZATIONS OF THE ANCIENT NEAR EAST 345, 347 (Jack M. Sasson ed., 1995).

§6.02 Marriage

Most scholars believe that the ancient Egyptians had no formal, legal requirements for a valid marriage.[4] They had neither a legal nor religious ritual to commemorate marriage.[5] Eyre explains:

> The sole significant act seems to have been...cohabitation, and, in particular, the entry of one party, usually the woman, into the household of the other. Marriage was referred to simply as the founding of a house (*grg pr*), the entry into the partner's house (*ʿq r pr*), or simply living together (*ḥmsi irm*).[6]

Marriage was, in essence, a private matter that did, however, entail a number of customary social elements. Upon marriage, the man became a *hy* (husband) and the woman became a *ḥm-t* (wife).[7] Ordinarily the bride and groom came from the same social class.[8] We do not have a great deal of evidence regarding the customary age for brides and grooms. The texts that we do possess show that males were often around twenty years old and females were younger, some just barely past fourteen (*i.e.*, just past puberty).[9] Originally marriage involved an agreement between the groom and the bride's father.[10] Beginning in about the 26th Dynasty (*c.* 672–525 B.C.), the agreement was, instead, between the groom and the bride, herself.[11]

Peasants surely could marry. Whether slaves who were captives of foreign conquest had the same right of marriage is doubtful.[12] Although Egyptian nobles ordinarily had only one principal wife (*i.e.*, monogamous

---

4. *See e.g.*, Pestman, Marriage & Matrimonial Property 30 ("a marriage may be concluded without any document being extant.").

5. *See Id.* at 6.

6. C.J. Eyre, *Crime and Adultery in Ancient Egypt*, 70 J. Egyptian Archaeology 92, 100–101 (1984) (footnotes omitted). *See also* Pestman, Marriage & Matrimonial Property 29–30 (Describing one specific type of marriage found in the documents, he says "this marriage is exclusively and solely concluded by taking the girl to the house of her future husband, while presents are sent along with her."); *Id.* at 51 ("the outward sign of a marriage is the cohabitation of husband and wife.") (footnote omitted).

7. *See* Pestman, Marriage & Matrimonial Property 10.

8. *See Id.* at 4, 52.

9. *See Id.* at 5.

10. *See Id.* at 11–12; *Id.* at 51 (Regarding the agreement between the groom and the father of the bride.).

11. *See Id.* at 51.

12. *See* Aristide Théodorides, *The Concept of Law in Ancient Egypt, in* The Legacy of Egypt 291, 307 (J.R. Harris ed., 2d ed. 1971) (Peasant-serfs "seem to have been able to marry easily with free individuals or to be adopted by them, so becoming free themselves....") (footnote omitted).

marriage was clearly the ancient Egyptian norm), we possess convincing evidence that some royalty and nobility had two or more wives; such as the 6th Dynasty kings Teti and Pepi I (*c.* 2460–2200 B.C.) who each had at least two wives apiece.[13] And, in addition to his legitimate legal wife, a noble could have a harem of women who lived in the household.[14] It was the principal wife, however, who legally was considered the mother of the regal line. In this regard, a king's secondary wives essentially constituted a harem. Although the principal wife could be the king's sister,[15] the tradition of purity of royal blood began changing in the 18th Dynasty (*c.* 1552–1295 B.C.).

---

13. *See* PESTMAN, MARRIAGE & MATRIMONIAL PROPERTY 3 ("It is most likely that Herodotus is right and that Egyptian marriage is monogamous.") (footnote omitted); *Id.* at 62 ("polygamy does not occur in Egypt".); C.J. Eyre, *The Adoption Papyrus in Social Context*, 78 J. EGYPTIAN ARCHAEOLOGY 207, 211–212 (1992) ("monogamy is the social norm."). *Also see* GARDINER, EGYPT OF THE PHARAOHS 93 (Gardiner explains that the 6th Dynasty king Teti had two wives: "The existence of two of Teti's spouses is recalled by the great Memphite mastaba of Khuye and the neighboring pyramid of Ipwe....") (footnote omitted); *Id.* at 94 (Gardiner presents further evidence that Pepi I (whom Gardiner calls Piopi) had two wives: "An unpretentious outlook seems indicated by his marriages, doubtless consecutively to two daughters of a local hereditary prince named Khui....").

14. See David Lorton, *Legal and Social Institutions of Pharaonic Egypt, in* 1 CIVILIZATIONS OF THE ANCIENT NEAR EAST 345, 349 (Jack M. Sasson ed., 1995) ("Egyptian men, though, kings as well as commoners, could have concubines."); BREASTED, HISTORY OF EGYPT 85 ("The social unit was as in later human history, the family. A man possessed but one legal wife, who was the mother of his heirs. She was in every respect his equal, was always treated with the greatest consideration, and participated in the pleasures of her husband and her children; the affectionate relations existing between a noble and his wife are constantly and noticeably depicted on the monuments of the time. Such relations had often existed from the earliest childhood of the pair; for it was customary in all ranks of society for a youth to marry his sister. Besides the legitimate wife, the head of his household, the man of wealth possessed also a harem, the inmates of which maintained no legal claim upon their lord. The harem was already at this early day a recognized institution in the East, and nothing immoral was thought of in connection with it. The children of the time show the greatest respect for their parents, and it was the duty of every son to maintain the tomb of his father. The respect and affection of one's parents and family were highly valued, and we often find in the tombs the statement, 'I was one beloved of his father, praised of his mother, whom his brothers and sisters loved.' ") (footnote omitted).

15. *See* WILSON, CULTURE OF ANCIENT EGYPT 97 ("Pharaohs might have many wives, taken from many sources, but the purest line to carry on the seed of the sungod Re would show a mother directly of the royal family. This was the reason for brother-sister marriages by some of the pharaohs, for the purpose of assuring the most divine strain and for the derivative purpose of cutting down on the number of pretenders to the throne."); BREASTED, HISTORY OF EGYPT 75 ("The king's favourite wife became the official queen, whose eldest son usually received the appointment as crown prince to succeed his father. But as at all oriental courts, there was also a royal harem with numerous inmates.").

Indeed, several 18th Dynasty pharaohs married foreign wives who bore princes who later became pharaohs themselves.[16] There are indications that, on occasion, a king may have married his own daughter.[17] Furthermore, it seems quite clear that royal brothers and sisters intermarried. Other than the royalty, however, sibling marriages and father-daughter marriages were probably quite unusual. Indeed, commoners probably were not allowed to marry their full sisters. Marriages between uncles and nieces, cousins, and half-siblings (*e.g.*, persons with the same father but a different mother), however, appear to have been legal.[18]

It was customary for the bride and groom to exchange certain types of property in association with the beginning of their marriage. Technically speaking, these were not really "gifts" in the strict sense of the modern word, but scholars have occasionally referred to them as such. The groom customarily transferred property—called the *šp*—to the bride's father. Its purpose was to sever, symbolically at least, the link between the woman and her family.[19] Pestman interprets the *šp* as a kind of symbolic "consideration" or price paid for the bride.[20] According to Pestman, "By paying the *šp* the legal family tie between the wife and the parental home, as it were, severed and a new legal family bond is formed between her and her husband, founding a new family."[21] Later in Egyptian legal history, it appears that the groom gave his bride the *šp* directly. The *šp* was comprised of wealth (we might be tempted to say "money"); often it was a small amount of corn.[22] The bride's father was likely to give gifts to the couple (including something that was essentially a dowry, called the *ḥd n ir ḥm-t*) and a "wedding party" followed.[23] The

16. *See* WILSON, CULTURE OF ANCIENT EGYPT 201.

17. *See* GARDINER, EGYPT OF THE PHARAOHS 212 (Gardiner mentions the possibility that Amenhotep III married his own daughter, Sitamun.). *See also Id.* at 172 (After quoting a stela discovered by Petrie (BARii, sects. 33–37), Gardiner says: "The important point here is that king Amosis asserts his own parents to have been the children of the same mother and father, a classic example of brother and sister marriage.").

18. *See* GRIMAL, ANCIENT EGYPT 207 (Mentioning a royal marriage involving half-siblings.); PESTMAN, MARRIAGE & MATRIMONIAL PROPERTY 3–4, 52; David Lorton, *Legal and Social Institutions of Pharaonic Egypt*, *in* 1 CIVILIZATIONS OF THE ANCIENT NEAR EAST 345, 349 (Jack M. Sasson ed., 1995).

19. *See* PESTMAN, MARRIAGE & MATRIMONIAL PROPERTY 13, 52.

20. *See Id.* at 19–20.

21. *Id.* at 20. *See also Id.* at 52.

22. *See Id.* at 13–20. For more on the concept of money in ancient Egypt, *see infra* §9.05.

23. *See* PESTMAN, MARRIAGE & MATRIMONIAL PROPERTY 52, 102, 143; Janet H. Johnson, *The Legal Status of Women in Ancient Egypt*, *in* MISTRESS OF THE HOUSE MISTRESS OF HEAVEN: WOMEN IN ANCIENT EGYPT 175, 179 (Anne K. Chapel and Glenn E. Markoe eds., 1996). *See also* David Lorton, *Legal and Social Institutions of*

dowry usually had a much higher value than the *šp*.[24] In addition, the bride typically owned personal items that she brought to the marriage, known as *nkt-w n s-ḥm-t* ("goods of a woman"). These were objects such as ornaments, a bed, mirrors, clothing, and sometimes even a musical instrument. Apparently, however, the most important item in this group was some type of special shawl called the *inšn*.[25] Oddly enough, although the wife technically "owned" these articles, the husband was at liberty to dispose of them as he pleased (*e.g.*, he could even sell them). For, in the event of divorce, he was not obligated to return these precise objects to his wife, but only "similar" ones or even other things of equivalent value.[26] In some marriages, the bride also gave her new husband another type of property, known as the *sʿnḫ*, which was "money" given in return for the husband supporting her during the duration of the marriage. Apparently, if her husband predeceased her, the *sʿnḫ* passed intestate to her directly, while upon her death, her children probably inherited it. Like the other forms of marital property, although it was technically considered the wife's property, the husband was free to administer it as he saw fit, and, in the event of divorce, he was only obligated to return an equivalent amount to his ex-wife.[27] As a rule, a husband was responsible for providing maintenance for his wife during marriage whether or not he had received a *sʿnḫ*.[28] In sum, then, there were three types of property that a wife routinely brought to her marriage: 1) a dowry (*ḥd n ir ḥm-t*); 2) her personal effects (*nkt-w n s-ḥm-t*); and, 3) funds intended for her maintenance and the maintenance of her children (*sʿnḫ*). The wife technically owned these properties but the husband managed them in any way that he desired. His only obligation with respect to these properties was that, as a rule, he had to give to his wife a comparable sum if the couple divorced.[29] In addition, a wife was free to own other types of property that were not considered property either owned or controlled by her husband. She could dispose of such property in any manner that she wished.[30]

Pharaonic Egypt, in 1 CIVILIZATIONS OF THE ANCIENT NEAR EAST 345, 348–49 (Jack M. Sasson ed., 1995); C.J. Eyre, *Crime and Adultery in Ancient Egypt*, 70 J. EGYPTIAN ARCHAEOLOGY 92, 101 (1984) ("there is no doubt that marriages were celebrated by parties and festivities.") (footnote omitted).

24. *See* PESTMAN, MARRIAGE & MATRIMONIAL PROPERTY 102.

25. *See Id.* at 94.

26. *See Id.* at 99–101, 162.

27. *See Id.* at 104–108, 162.

28. *See Id.* at 144.

29. *See Id.* at 108, 162.

30. *See Id.* at 151 ("We see her carrying out all kinds of legal transactions concerning her property, without any restriction, and without the assistance of her husband or other person being necessary.") (footnote omitted).

When a husband acquired property during marriage, Egyptian law—at least by the New Kingdom (*c.* 1552–1069 B.C.)—considered that both husband and wife owned it jointly: two-thirds belonging to the husband and one-third belonging to the wife.[31] Although a husband was permitted to sell or otherwise transfer ownership of property that he jointly owned with his wife, if he did so, he was required to give her equivalent property in its place. The wife did not really have any control over her one-third share during the marriage. It came to her only when the marriage ended—either by divorce or at her husband's death.[32] The same rule operated with respect to any property that the wife had brought to the marriage at its beginning.[33]

Interestingly, we have a number of contracts—most of which date from the Ptolemaic period (*c.* 304–30 B.C.)—that were concluded between husbands and wives that spell out the husband's economic obligations to support his wife and their children.[34] Many of these contracts were even concluded after the couple already had children.[35] Because many bear striking similarities to one another, these contracts appear to have been written by scribes who used the same or similar formulae over and over again (many having the "feel" of modern-day fill-in-the-blank forms).[36] Although some

---

31. *See Id.* at 153; P.W. Pestman, *The Law of Succession in Ancient Egypt*, 9 STUDIA ET DOCUMENTA AD JURA ANTIQUI PERTINENTIA 58, 73 (1969); J. Černý and T. Eric Peet, *A Marriage Settlement of the Twentieth Dynasty*, 13 J. EGYPTIAN ARCHAEOLOGY 30, 36 (1927); C.J. Eyre, *The Adoption Papyrus in Social Context*, 78 J. EGYPTIAN ARCHAEOLOGY 207, 219 (1992); Andrea McDowell, *Legal Aspects of Care of the Elderly in Egypt to the End of the New Kingdom, in* THE CARE OF THE ELDERLY IN THE ANCIENT NEAR EAST 199, 216 (Marten Stol and Sven P. Vleeming eds., 1998); Schafik Allam, *Papyrus Turin 2021: Another Adoption Extraordinary, in* INDIVIDU, SOCIÉTÉ ET SPIRITUALITÉ DANS L'ÉGYPT PHARAONIQUE ET COPTE: MÉLANGES ÉGYPTOLOGIQUES OFFERTS AU PROFESSEUR ARISTIDE THÉODORIDÈS 23, 24 (Christian Cannuyer and Jean-Marie Kruchten eds., 1993).

32. *See* PESTMAN, MARRIAGE & MATRIMONIAL PROPERTY 139, 153; MCDOWELL, JURISDICTION 35 ("This is the usual property settlement after a divorce.") (footnote omitted). Upon her death, the wife's one-third share passed to her children.

33. *See* Janet H. Johnson, *The Legal Status of Women in Ancient Egypt, in* MISTRESS OF THE HOUSE MISTRESS OF HEAVEN: WOMEN IN ANCIENT EGYPT 175, 177 (Anne K. Chapel and Glenn E. Markoe eds., 1996).

34. *See generally* PESTMAN, MARRIAGE & MATRIMONIAL PROPERTY *passim* (Pestman classifies these contracts into four fundamental types and, at length, explains the intricacies of their contents, exploring the similarities and differences.). *See also* C.J. Eyre, *The Adoption Papyrus in Social Context*, 78 J. EGYPTIAN ARCHAEOLOGY 207, 216 (1992); Schafik Allam, *Papyrus Turin 2021: Another Adoption Extraordinary, in* INDIVIDU, SOCIÉTÉ ET SPIRITUALITÉ DANS L'ÉGYPT PHARAONIQUE ET COPTE: MÉLANGES ÉGYPTOLOGIQUES OFFERTS AU PROFESSEUR ARISTIDE THÉODORIDÈS 23, 24–25 (Christian Cannuyer and Jean-Marie Kruchten eds., 1993).

35. *See* PESTMAN, MARRIAGE & MATRIMONIAL PROPERTY 28–29.

36. *See Id.* at 167–181.

Egyptologists have referred to these as "marriage contracts," they were actually *not* a necessary component of a legal marriage.[37] Thus, Johnson calls these instead "annuity contracts."[38] Some scholars speculate that these agreements may have originated earlier as contracts between the groom and the bride's father.[39] At their core, the annuity contracts constitute agreements regarding the disposition of property and property rights related to the marriage (and possible divorce).[40] Indeed, a number of the annuity contracts contemplate the possibility of divorce.[41] Ordinarily, the husband promises that, in the event of divorce initiated by either party, he will give his wife a large sum (an amount equal in value to the property that she brought to the marriage—*i.e.*, her "dowry" (*ḥd n ir ḥm-t*)—plus the value of his bridal gift, the *šp*).[42] If he fails to do so, he will be required to continue to provide, on a monthly basis, a certain specified level of support for his wife and children (*e.g.*, grain, oil, clothing, provisions, silver) until such time that he does, indeed, pay her the preordained sum.[43]

Egyptian law may have recognized a woman's right not to be abused by her husband in marriage. One Deir el-Medina legal text (Ostracon Nash 5 recto) deals with this domestic violence issue, but the text is so badly damaged that we cannot with any certainty state many conclusions.[44] We do

---

37. *See* C.J. Eyre, *The Adoption Papyrus in Social Context*, 78 J. EGYPTIAN ARCHAEOLOGY 207, 210 (1992).

38. *See* Janet H. Johnson, *The Legal Status of Women in Ancient Egypt*, *in* MISTRESS OF THE HOUSE MISTRESS OF HEAVEN: WOMEN IN ANCIENT EGYPT 175, 180 (Anne K. Chapel and Glenn E. Markoe eds., 1996) ("These so-called marriage contracts, however, concern only economic matters—the husband's responsibility to feed and clothe his wife (and their children), and their children's right to inherit his wealth—and are more appropriately called 'annuity contracts.'") (footnote omitted). *See also* MATTHA, THE DEMOTIC LEGAL CODE OF HERMOPOLIS WEST 27–32, 92–103.

39. *See* Janet H. Johnson, *The Legal Status of Women in Ancient Egypt*, *in* MISTRESS OF THE HOUSE MISTRESS OF HEAVEN: WOMEN IN ANCIENT EGYPT 175, 180 (Anne K. Chapel and Glenn E. Markoe eds., 1996) (Citing the work of Pestman.); PESTMAN, MARRIAGE & MATRIMONIAL PROPERTY 12. *See also* David Lorton, *Legal and Social Institutions of Pharaonic Egypt*, *in* 1 CIVILIZATIONS OF THE ANCIENT NEAR EAST 345, 353 (Jack M. Sasson ed., 1995) ("Both husbands and wives brought property into the marriage, and contracts could be drawn up to protect their respective economic interests."); C.J. Eyre, *Crime and Adultery in Ancient Egypt*, 70 J. EGYPTIAN ARCHAEOLOGY 92, 97–99 (1984).

40. *See* PESTMAN, MARRIAGE & MATRIMONIAL PROPERTY 31.

41. *See Id.* at 58.

42. *See Id.* at 102.

43. *See* Janet H. Johnson, *The Legal Status of Women in Ancient Egypt*, *in* MISTRESS OF THE HOUSE MISTRESS OF HEAVEN: WOMEN IN ANCIENT EGYPT 175, 181 (Anne K. Chapel and Glenn E. Markoe eds., 1996).

44. *See* MCDOWELL, JURISDICTION 152, 225.

know that the court in that instance held that the husband's conduct was wrong. We are unable, however, to tell what consequences befell the man as a result of his conduct.[45]

§ 6.03 Divorce

Apparently, as is true in modern America, many marriages in ancient Egypt ended in divorce.[46] The inability to have children may have been one of the common reasons for divorce.[47] Both husband and wife had the right to sue the other for divorce.[48] Our earliest evidence that a husband had this right comes from the 12th Dynasty (*c.* 1991–1785 B.C.), while the first instance of a wife suing her husband for divorce dates to about 500 B.C.[49] The terms of the annuity contracts[50] (which generally seem to have presumed that a man might eventually desire a younger bride), however, probably had a normative effect, and, thus, discouraged some men from divorcing their wives.[51] To begin with, it was common for these annuity contracts to require that a husband return the *šp* if he decided to divorce his wife.[52] But of greater consequence, upon divorce a husband ordinarily was required to return to his wife her dowry (or its equivalent).[53] As a technical matter, she, in order to be entitled to its return, probably needed formally to demand that

---

45. *See Id.* at 155.

46. *See* C.J. Eyre, *Crime and Adultery in Ancient Egypt*, 70 J. EGYPTIAN ARCHAEOLOGY 92, 99 (1984) ("Divorce may have been relatively common at all periods, and for any number of reasons, although it is not often possible to follow the background to specific cases."). *See generally* PESTMAN, MARRIAGE & MATRIMONIAL PROPERTY 58–79 (ch. 3 "Dissolution of the Marriage").

47. *See* C.J. Eyre, *Crime and Adultery in Ancient Egypt*, 70 J. EGYPTIAN ARCHAEOLOGY 92, 99 (1984); C.J. Eyre, *The Adoption Papyrus in Social Context*, 78 J. EGYPTIAN ARCHAEOLOGY 207, 209 (1992).

48. *See* PESTMAN, MARRIAGE & MATRIMONIAL PROPERTY 55 ("both spouses are free to divorce."); *Id.* at 68, 76.

49. *See Id.* at 65.

50. *See supra* § 6.02.

51. *See* PESTMAN, MARRIAGE & MATRIMONIAL PROPERTY 158 ("The wife, thus obtains considerable property if she is repudiated by her husband; the divorced woman is no worse off financially, but for the husband, on the other hand, the repudiation of his wife involves so many financial obligations that, without doubt, these work as a check to rash actions on his part.") (footnotes omitted); C.J. Eyre, *Crime and Adultery in Ancient Egypt*, 70 J. EGYPTIAN ARCHAEOLOGY 92, 99 (1984).

52. *See* PESTMAN, MARRIAGE & MATRIMONIAL PROPERTY 15, 113–114.

53. *See* C.J. Eyre, *The Adoption Papyrus in Social Context*, 78 J. EGYPTIAN ARCHAEOLOGY 207, 209 (1992); PESTMAN, MARRIAGE & MATRIMONIAL PROPERTY 56, 68–69, 104.

he return the dowry. Several annuity contracts provide that, if the husband failed to return the dowry to his ex-wife within thirty days, he had to continue to provide maintenance for her until he did return it. Since the cost of maintenance far exceeded the dowry amount, husbands suing for divorce were likely to return the dowry and be done with it.[54] Quite clearly, however, if a wife was guilty of adultery, the husband generally was not required to repay the *šp* nor did he have to make any other sort of payment to her.[55] As a rule, though, upon divorce without adultery, a husband had to pay his wife (either with the original goods or their equivalent) a great deal: 1) the *šp* (or in some cases one-half of it); 2) her dowry (*ḥd n ir ḥm-t*); 3) her personal effects (*nkt-w n s-ḥm-t*); 4) the funds given to him at the beginning of the marriage for her maintenance and the maintenance of her children (*sʿnḫ*); and, 5) one-third of all property that he had acquired during the marriage.[56] In the absence of adultery, a woman who sued for divorce ordinarily did not have to make any sort of payments; although, as was alluded to above, there are some annuity contracts that required a wife to forfeit one-half of the *šp* if she was the one who initiated divorce.[57] In addition to the property already mentioned (*i.e.*, the property to which she was entitled upon divorce), a wife also ordinarily kept any property that she personally owned.[58] If the party who was sued was found to have been at fault, s/he had to surrender their interest in any property that was jointly owned. Presumably "fault" included adultery.[59] We know of a case, for example, finding a wife at fault in divorce where she seized and sold off joint property and even deserted her husband when he was ill.[60]

---

54. *See* PESTMAN, MARRIAGE & MATRIMONIAL PROPERTY 68–69.
55. *Scc Id.* at 56, 75.
56. *See Id.* at 160.
57. *See Id.* at 109.
58. *See Id.* at 155, 160.
59. *See* Janet H. Johnson, *The Legal Status of Women in Ancient Egypt, in* MISTRESS OF THE HOUSE MISTRESS OF HEAVEN: WOMEN IN ANCIENT EGYPT 175, 183 (Anne K. Chapel and Glenn E. Markoe eds., 1996). *See also* Andrea McDowell, *Legal Aspects of Care of the Elderly in Egypt to the End of the New Kingdom, in* THE CARE OF THE ELDERLY IN THE ANCIENT NEAR EAST 199, 213 (Marten Stol and Sven P. Vleeming eds., 1998); David Lorton, *Legal and Social Institutions of Pharaonic Egypt, in* 1 CIVILIZATIONS OF THE ANCIENT NEAR EAST 345, 358 (Jack M. Sasson ed., 1995) ("In the Third Intermediate Period and later, in the event of a divorce for whatever reason, a woman who had committed adultery during the marriage lost her right to a financial settlement."); C.J. Eyre, *Crime and Adultery in Ancient Egypt*, 70 J. EGYPTIAN ARCHAEOLOGY 92, 98–99 (1984).
60. *See* Janet H. Johnson, *The Legal Status of Women in Ancient Egypt, in* MISTRESS OF THE HOUSE MISTRESS OF HEAVEN: WOMEN IN ANCIENT EGYPT 175, 217, n. 84 (Anne K. Chapel and Glenn E. Markoe eds., 1996).

According to Johnson, "Divorce and remarriage were common in Egypt at all periods...."[61] It was ordinarily the woman who left the home while the husband remained. Where she went thereafter and what became of the children are matters of pure speculation.[62] When a man remarried after a divorce, he was likely to execute a fresh annuity contract with his new bride. This meant that the children of his first marriage were in a position to lose a large portion of their inheritance to his second wife and her family. Not surprisingly, divorce followed by remarriage frequently resulted in acrimonious litigation over wealth and property.[63] Consequently, it became commonplace for the children of a man's first marriage either to sue or to express their acquiescence to the remarriage in writing.[64] In particular, children of the first marriage needed expressly to consent to the forfeiture of their inheritance.[65]

§ 6.04 Roles of Parents and Children

A series of private letters from a man named Hekanakht provides a brief glimpse into family life during the Middle Kingdom (*c.* 2040–1674 B.C.). The letters reveal a controlling, autocratic father who constantly threatens and bullies his sons in order to compel them to do his bidding. It is difficult to say, categorically, whether all 11th Dynasty fathers ruled their households with an iron fist as old Hekanakht did.[66]

It is possible that ancient Egyptian family law permitted a parent unilaterally to dissolve the ties of filial association if he so desired.[67] For example, on his southern boundary stela, the Middle Kingdom monarch Senwosre

---

61. *Id.* at 182. *See also* PESTMAN, MARRIAGE & MATRIMONIAL PROPERTY 3, 77–78; Aristide Théodorides, *The Concept of Law in Ancient Egypt, in* THE LEGACY OF EGYPT 291, 305 (J.R. Harris ed., 2d ed. 1971).

62. *See* PESTMAN, MARRIAGE & MATRIMONIAL PROPERTY 77–78.

63. *See* Janet H. Johnson, *The Legal Status of Women in Ancient Egypt* MISTRESS OF THE HOUSE MISTRESS OF HEAVEN: WOMEN IN ANCIENT EGYPT 175, 182–183 (Anne K. Chapel and Glenn E. Markoe eds., 1996).

64. *See Id.* at 181–182; J. Černý and T. Eric Peet, *A Marriage Settlement of the Twentieth Dynasty*, 13 J. EGYPTIAN ARCHAEOLOGY 30, 37 (1927).

65. *See* PESTMAN, MARRIAGE & MATRIMONIAL PROPERTY 137–139.

66. *See* WILSON, CULTURE OF ANCIENT EGYPT 128–30; GRIMAL, ANCIENT EGYPT 158; Edward Bleiberg, *The Economy of Ancient Egypt, in* 3 CIVILIZATIONS OF THE ANCIENT NEAR EAST 1373, 1383 (Jack M. Sasson ed., 1995); Christopher J. Eyre, *The Market Women of Pharaonic Egypt, in* LE COMMERCE EN ÉGYPT ANCIENNE 173, 184 (Nicolas Grimal and Bernadette Menu eds., 1998).

67. *See infra* § 7.02.

III (Senusert III) (*c.* 1878–1842 B.C.) said: "As for any son of mine who shall maintain this boundary which My Majesty has made, he is my son and was born to me... but he who shall destroy it and fail to fight for it, he is not my son and was not born to me."[68]

Still, ancient Egyptian children were expected to respect both parents with abiding affection. As early as the 6th Dynasty (*c.* 2460–2200 B.C.), we find the eldest son assuming the responsibility of administering the funds of the joint property upon the death of the father,[69] and, generally speaking, when a father died, the eldest son became the new head of the family.[70] Children (at least the "eldest son") also had a legal duty to care for the funerary rights of their deceased parents.[71]

§ 6.05 Chapter Summary

The nuclear family was important to the ancient Egyptians. Most Egyptians were monogamous. Royalty and nobles occasionally had a harem of secondary wives. Only royalty, however, practiced marriage between fathers and daughters or between siblings. There were no legal formalities required for a valid marriage. There were, however, a number of traditions and customs associated with the creation of marital relations. The groom ordinarily gave property called the *šp* to the bride's father. The bride usually brought three special kinds of property to the marriage: 1) a dowry (typically given by her father); 2) certain personal effects—the most important of which was a type of shawl called the *inšn*; and, 3) funds for the bride's maintenance and the maintenance of her children (property known as the *sʿnḫ*). It was the husband, however, who had legal control of the properties during the marriage. The husband and wife shared property that they acquired during the marriage—the husband owned two-thirds and the wife

---

68. GARDINER, EGYPT OF THE PHARAOHS 134.

69. *See* Aristide Théodorides, *The Concept of Law in Ancient Egypt, in* THE LEGACY OF EGYPT 291, 297 (J.R. Harris ed., 2d ed. 1971). *See also infra* § 7.01.

70. *See* Aristide Théodorides, *The Concept of Law in Ancient Egypt, in* THE LEGACY OF EGYPT 291, 297 (J.R. Harris ed., 2d ed. 1971) ("On the death of the eldest in a family, the title and duties of 'eldest son' devolved upon the next in age, though in fact a daughter was not called upon to hold a position equivalent to that of 'eldest son', for she was not 'eldest' in relation to her brothers.").

71. *See* P.W. Pestman, *The Law of Succession in Ancient Egypt*, 9 STUDIA ET DOCUMENTA AD JURA ANTIQUI PERTINENTIA 58, 66 (1969); Janet H. Johnson, *The Legal Status of Women in Ancient Egypt, in* MISTRESS OF THE HOUSE MISTRESS OF HEAVEN: WOMEN IN ANCIENT EGYPT 175, 184 (Anne K. Chapel and Glenn E. Markoe eds., 1996).

owned one-third. Many Egyptian couples entered into annuity contracts that were, in some respects, similar to modern prenuptial agreements. Both husband and wife had legal capacity to sue for divorce. Unless the wife was guilty of serious misconduct (such as adultery), the husband, upon divorce, was required to return the three properties to the bride and pay for her support.

CHAPTER 7

Inheritance & Succession

§7.01 Intestate Succession

Under the ancient Egyptian laws of intestacy (*i.e.*, inheritance in the absence of a valid will), children inherited equal shares of their parents' estate.[1] Thus, property first passed to a decedent's children.[2] If there were no

1. *See* P.W. Pestman, *The Law of Succession in Ancient Egypt*, 9 STUDIA ET DOCUMENTA AD JURA ANTIQUI PERTINENTIA 58, 67 (1969) ("It is remarkable, in such cases, how often all the children receive an equal share in the inheritance".); William A. Ward, *Some Aspects of Private Land Ownership and Inheritance in Ancient Egypt, ca. 2500–1000 B.C., in* LAND TENURE AND SOCIAL TRANSFORMATION IN THE MIDDLE EAST 63, 68 (Tarif Khalidi ed., 1984) (Ward recommends that "It is perhaps best to speak of 'customs' of inheritance rather than 'laws'...." But he concurs regarding the order of intestate succession.); GAY ROBINS, WOMEN IN ANCIENT EGYPT 132 ("[I]t seems that in normal circumstances all children, both male and female, inherited goods equally from their parents."); C.J. Eyre, *The Adoption Papyrus in Social Context*, 78 J. EGYPTIAN ARCHAEOLOGY 207, 218–219 (1992) ("In principle, it is clear that at the death of the head of the household the main inheritance passed to the children...."); Aristide Théodorides, *The Concept of Law in Ancient Egypt, in* THE LEGACY OF EGYPT 291, 292 (J.R. Harris ed., 2d ed. 1971) ("Children were supposed to inherit an equal share of their parents' estate, unless the latter had made other dispositions, for the practice of making a will was known."); *Id.* at 303 ("[T]he right of primogeniture, which...had become the rule after being introduced in the form of a testamentary provision from the 4th Dynasty, fell into disuse." This had happened by the Middle Kingdom.); MATTHA, THE DEMOTIC LEGAL CODE OF HERMOPOLIS WEST 39–41, 116–117; BREASTED, HISTORY OF EGYPT 85–86 (Breasted suggests that the ancient Egyptian law of intestate succession channeled property through the eldest daughter: "As among many other peoples, the natural line of inheritance was through the eldest daughter, though a will might disregard this."); *Id.* at 160 (Referring to circumstances in the Middle Kingdom, Breasted states: "[T]he natural line of succession...was through the eldest daughter...."); Schafik Allam, *Papyrus Turin 2021: Another Adoption Extraordinary, in* INDIVIDU, SOCIÉTÉ ET SPIRITUALITÉ DANS L'ÉGYPT PHARAONIQUE ET COPTE: MÉLANGES ÉGYPTOLOGIQUES OFFERTS AU PROFESSEUR ARISTIDE THÉODORIDÈS 23, 25 (Christian Cannuyer and Jean-Marie Kruchten eds., 1993).

2. *See* P.W. Pestman, *The Law of Succession in Ancient Egypt*, 9 STUDIA ET DOCUMENTA AD JURA ANTIQUI PERTINENTIA 58, 59 (1969); J. Černý and T. Eric Peet, *A Mar-*

children, the decedent's siblings were next in line to inherit on an equal basis.[3] If an intestate decedent left neither children nor siblings, our best evidence suggests that the deceased's parents inherited the estate.[4] Generally speaking, husbands and wives did not inherit from one another.[5] It appears that a woman's children inherited her dowry.[6] Thus, upon the death of her husband, an Egyptian widow retained a life estate in her dowry (*i.e.*, after her death the dowry passed to her children) plus one-third of any property acquired by the couple during their marriage.[7]

There seems to have been some degree of preference in inheritance for the eldest son. As Pestman remarks, "The eldest son has... not only more obligations but also more rights than the other heirs."[8] It was common, for example, for the eldest son to inherit his father's office or position.[9] It was

---

riage Settlement of the Twentieth Dynasty, 13 J. Egyptian Archaeology 30, 36 (1927); J.G. Manning, *Demotic Egyptian Instruments of Transfer as Evidence for Private Ownership of Real Property*, 71 Chicago-Kent L. Rev. 237, 259 (1995).

3. *See* P.W. Pestman, *The Law of Succession in Ancient Egypt*, 9 Studia et documenta ad jura antiqui pertinentia 58, 68–70 (1969); Janet H. Johnson, *The Legal Status of Women in Ancient Egypt, in* Mistress of the House Mistress of Heaven: Women in Ancient Egypt 175, 183 (Anne K. Chapel and Glenn E. Markoe eds., 1996); C.J. Eyre, *The Adoption Papyrus in Social Context*, 78 J. Egyptian Archaeology 207, 216 (1992) ("In the absence of a son, the wife's property should revert to her brother, to *her* family and not that of her husband.") (footnotes omitted, emphasis original).

4. *See* P.W. Pestman, *The Law of Succession in Ancient Egypt*, 9 Studia et documenta ad jura antiqui pertinentia 58, 70 (1969) ("When the deceased leaves no children and no brothers and sisters it is obvious that his estate will fall to his parents. Although not one case is known where such did indeed happen, there are still some signs which point in this direction.").

5. *See Id.* at 73; Schafik Allam, *Papyrus Turin 2021: Another Adoption Extraordinary, in* Individu, Société et Spiritualité dans L'Égypt Pharaonique et Copte: Mélanges égyptologiques offerts au Professeur Aristide Théodoridès 23, 25 (Christian Cannuyer and Jean-Marie Kruchten eds., 1993).

6. *See* Bedell, Criminal Law 19. *See also supra* § 6.02.

7. *See* C.J. Eyre, *The Adoption Papyrus in Social Context*, 78 J. Egyptian Archaeology 207, 219 (1992); Pestman, Marriage & Matrimonial Property 126; J.G. Manning, *Demotic Egyptian Instruments of Transfer as Evidence for Private Ownership of Real Property*, 71 Chicago-Kent L. Rev. 237, 259 (1995); Schafik Allam, *Papyrus Turin 2021: Another Adoption Extraordinary, in* Individu, Société et Spiritualité dans L'Égypt Pharaonique et Copte: Mélanges égyptologiques offerts au Professeur Aristide Théodoridès 23, 25 (Christian Cannuyer and Jean-Marie Kruchten eds., 1993). *See also supra* § 6.02.

8. P.W. Pestman, *The Law of Succession in Ancient Egypt*, 9 Studia et documenta ad jura antiqui pertinentia 58, 66 (1969).

9. *See* Gay Robins, Women in Ancient Egypt 132; C.J. Eyre, *The Adoption Papyrus in Social Context*, 78 J. Egyptian Archaeology 207, 215 (1992). *See also infra* § 7.04.

he who was obligated to make funeral arrangements for his parents.[10] Thus, it is likely that he inherited more as a kind of compensation for shouldering extra filial duty.[11] The Law Collection of Hermopolis[12] actually provides that another child could take over the funerary obligations if the eldest son was unable or unwilling to do so. In such a case, the substitute "eldest son" became entitled to the additional inheritance that had been earmarked for the biological "eldest son."[13] This substitute "eldest son" then administered his father's estate and became a guardian for his mother, brothers, and sisters.[14]

Ordinarily, real estate passed undivided in inheritance. As a practical matter, it made more sense to allow houses and agricultural fields to re-

---

10. *See* GAY ROBINS, WOMEN IN ANCIENT EGYPT 132–133; C.J. Eyre, *The Adoption Papyrus in Social Context*, 78 J. EGYPTIAN ARCHAEOLOGY 207, 215 (1992); J.G. Manning, *Demotic Egyptian Instruments of Transfer as Evidence for Private Ownership of Real Property*, 71 CHICAGO-KENT L. REV. 237, 259 (1995); J.J. Janssen and P.W. Pestman, *Burial and Inheritance in the Community of the Necropolis Workmen at Thebes (Pap. Bulaq X and O. Petrie 16)*, 11 J. ECONOMIC & SOCIAL HIST. ORIENT 168 (1968).

11. *See* Janet H. Johnson, *The Legal Status of Women in Ancient Egypt, in* MISTRESS OF THE HOUSE MISTRESS OF HEAVEN: WOMEN IN ANCIENT EGYPT 175, 183 (Anne K. Chapel and Glenn E. Markoe eds., 1996) ("[T]he child called eldest son bore responsibility for taking care of his parents' funerals and received some of their property in recompense."); J.G. Manning, *Demotic Egyptian Instruments of Transfer as Evidence for Private Ownership of Real Property*, 71 CHICAGO-KENT L. REV. 237, 259 (1995) ("The privileged position of the eldest son derives from the fact that he was legally responsible for both the burial costs and the ritual of burying his parents.") (footnote omitted). *See also* Aristide Théodorides, *The Concept of Law in Ancient Egypt, in* THE LEGACY OF EGYPT 291, 297 (J.R. Harris ed., 2d ed. 1971) ("On the death of the eldest in a family, the title and duties of 'eldest son' devolved upon the next in age, though in fact a daughter was not called upon to hold a position equivalent to that of 'eldest son', for she was not 'eldest' in relation to her brothers."); *Id.* (By the end of the Old Kingdom, "it was no longer necessary, as in earlier times, to insert a special clause in a will so that [a son] should acquire the rights and duties of an elder son."); *Id.* at 305.

12. *See supra* § 1.01, notes 39–41 and accompanying text.

13. *See* MATTHA, THE DEMOTIC LEGAL CODE OF HERMOPOLIS WEST 123; Janet H. Johnson, *The Legal Status of Women in Ancient Egypt, in* MISTRESS OF THE HOUSE MISTRESS OF HEAVEN: WOMEN IN ANCIENT EGYPT 175, 184 (Anne K. Chapel and Glenn E. Markoe eds., 1996); *See also* P.W. Pestman, *The Law of Succession in Ancient Egypt*, 9 STUDIA ET DOCUMENTA AD JURA ANTIQUI PERTINENTIA 58, 64–65 (1969); David Lorton, *Legal and Social Institutions of Pharaonic Egypt, in* 1 CIVILIZATIONS OF THE ANCIENT NEAR EAST 345, 355 (Jack M. Sasson ed., 1995).

14. *See* Aristide Théodorides, *The Concept of Law in Ancient Egypt, in* THE LEGACY OF EGYPT 291, 297 (J.R. Harris ed., 2d ed. 1971) (If a father dies intestate, the eldest son—simply by virtue of that status—"would have administered the property [*i.e.*, the father's estate], and...exercised control over his own mother, as well as over his brothers and sisters."); *Id.* at 298 (He became both administrator of the estate and guardian of the family members. [This evidence comes from the 6th Dynasty will of Tjau]. There is also evidence from the Tjau controversy that the eldest son became the legal guardian/tutor for his mother upon his father's death.).

main intact. Thus, children usually inherited real property jointly.[15] The eldest son, or in some cases another sibling acting as the substitute "eldest son," normally managed the jointly-owned real estate for the group as a whole.[16] Still, heirs could (and occasionally did) ask that such property be divided by the administrator of the estate.[17] If any of his brothers or sisters had predeceased him (so long as those who predeceased had no children), their share of the father's estate reverted to the "eldest son."[18] Interestingly, children even inherited their father's debts.[19]

§ 7.02 Testate Succession

The ancient Egyptians gave legal effect to written wills.[20] In order to avoid intestacy, an ancient Egyptian could use the *imyt-pr* (*i.e.*, the same

15. *See supra* § 5.01. *See also* MATTHA, THE DEMOTIC LEGAL CODE OF HERMOPOLIS WEST 39–41.

16. *See* MATTHA, THE DEMOTIC LEGAL CODE OF HERMOPOLIS WEST 39; Janet H. Johnson, *The Legal Status of Women in Ancient Egypt*, *in* MISTRESS OF THE HOUSE MISTRESS OF HEAVEN: WOMEN IN ANCIENT EGYPT 175, 184 (Anne K. Chapel and Glenn E. Markoe eds., 1996); GAY ROBINS, WOMEN IN ANCIENT EGYPT 136; C.J. Eyre, *The Adoption Papyrus in Social Context*, 78 J. EGYPTIAN ARCHAEOLOGY 207, 215–216 (1992); J.G. Manning, *Demotic Egyptian Instruments of Transfer as Evidence for Private Ownership of Real Property*, 71 CHICAGO-KENT L. REV. 237, 259–260 (1995). *See also infra* § 7.03.

17. *See* MATTHA, THE DEMOTIC LEGAL CODE OF HERMOPOLIS WEST 39; P.W. Pestman, *The Law of Succession in Ancient Egypt*, 9 STUDIA ET DOCUMENTA AD JURA ANTIQUI PERTINENTIA 58, 67 (1969); C.J. Eyre, *The Adoption Papyrus in Social Context*, 78 J. EGYPTIAN ARCHAEOLOGY 207, 216 (1992); J.G. Manning, *Demotic Egyptian Instruments of Transfer as Evidence for Private Ownership of Real Property*, 71 CHICAGO-KENT L. REV. 237, 260 (1995) ("To be sure, family land could be split with the consent of the heirs."). *See also infra* § 7.03.

18. *See* MATTHA, THE DEMOTIC LEGAL CODE OF HERMOPOLIS WEST 39; C.J. Eyre, *The Adoption Papyrus in Social Context*, 78 J. EGYPTIAN ARCHAEOLOGY 207, 216 (1992).

19. *See* Aristide Théodorides, *The Concept of Law in Ancient Egypt*, *in* THE LEGACY OF EGYPT 291, 304 (J.R. Harris ed., 2d ed. 1971).

20. *See Id.* at 298 (Acknowledging that intestate succession could be altered by means of a will.); *Id.* at 320 (Ancient Egyptians had "the freedom to make a will..."); *Id.* at 321 ("There could, indeed, be nothing more simple yet effective than an Egyptian will conceived as a declaration of last intent."); BREASTED, HISTORY OF EGYPT 97–98 (According to Breasted, in the Old Kingdom: "Business had already reached a high degree of development; books and accounts were kept; orders and receipts were given; wills and deeds were made; and written contracts covering long periods of time were entered upon."); *Id.* at 82 (Even as early as the Old Kingdom the ancient Egyptians permitted the making of wills and acknowledged them as valid.); GARDINER, EGYPT OF THE PHARAOHS 90 (Gardiner describes an Old Kingdom inscription regarding "a great Delta magnate named Metjen" who inherited from his father, bought

term that refers to the written document used to validate other types of property transfer) as a "will" to transfer either real or personal property and other forms of wealth either to persons or in proportions that differed from the scheme that would have been supplied by intestate succession.[21] A testator had to record his will with the vizier's office in order for the will to be valid.[22] Both men and women could execute valid wills.[23] A testator was not required to take an oath to validate his will. It is not clear, however, whether wills, like some other legal documents in ancient Egypt, had to be witnessed in order to be valid.[24] We know that the Egyptians occasionally amended their wills. One ostracon from Deir el-Medina (Ostracon Petrie 18) records that a man changed his will to exclude a woman who had failed

---

land, and left a will "for the distribution of his lands...." This appears to be competent evidence for succession, sale of property, and the making a will.).

21. *See* Janet H. Johnson, *The Legal Status of Women in Ancient Egypt, in* MISTRESS OF THE HOUSE MISTRESS OF HEAVEN: WOMEN IN ANCIENT EGYPT 175, 183 (Anne K. Chapel and Glenn E. Markoe eds., 1996) ("The earliest such documents preserved are the *imyt pr* documents...whereby an individual transferred property to someone other than a normal heir—for example, grandchildren rather than children, or wife (and children) rather than children directly."). *See also* P.W. Pestman, *The Law of Succession in Ancient Egypt*, 9 STUDIA ET DOCUMENTA AD JURA ANTIQUI PERTINENTIA 58, 62 (1969) ("An *imy-t pr* is generally used when one wishes to transfer property rights to another person, not only in the case of a bequest of property to an heir but also in the case of a sale of property to a buyer."); Aristide Théodorides, *The Concept of Law in Ancient Egypt, in* THE LEGACY OF EGYPT 291, 304 (J.R. Harris ed., 2d ed. 1971) ("An *imyt-pr*, which provides for a unilateral transfer of property through arrangements consequent upon death, corresponds to what we know as a will."), *Id.* ("The *imyt-pr* was made by declaration to a local council who registered it and recorded it in its archives."); J.J. Janssen and P.W. Pestman, *Burial and Inheritance in the Community of the Necropolis Workmen at Thebes (Pap. Bulaq X and O. Petrie 16)*, 11 J. ECONOMIC & SOCIAL HIST. ORIENT 167 (1968). *See also* David Lorton, *Legal and Social Institutions of Pharaonic Egypt, in* 1 CIVILIZATIONS OF THE ANCIENT NEAR EAST 345, 353 (Jack M. Sasson ed., 1995) ("Private wealth, both goods and real estate, was transmitted from generation to generation by inheritance; many people drew up testaments for this purpose."); BREASTED, HISTORY OF EGYPT 237. *See also infra* § 9.03.

22. GRIMAL, ANCIENT EGYPT 91 (According to Grimal, in the Old Kingdom: "The third major department of state, the Royal Archives, looked after the deeds for land ownership. This department also held copies of documents recording civil actions, consisting essentially of contracts and testaments as well as the texts of royal decrees."). *See also* BREASTED, HISTORY OF EGYPT 240 ("No one might make a will without filing it in the 'vizier's hall.'") (footnote omitted).

23. *See* MCDOWELL, JURISDICTION 152 (McDowell refers to the woman Naunakhte as illustrating a woman's capacity to make a valid will); Schafik Allam, *Women as Owners of Immovables in Pharaonic Egypt, in* WOMEN'S EARLIEST RECORDS FROM ANCIENT EGYPT AND WESTERN ASIA 123, 128 (Barbara Lesko ed., 1989) ("Women could transfer their titles to immovables and dispose of them by several means (sale, adoption, and other inheritance conventions)."). *See also infra* § 10.02.

24. *See* WILSON, CULTURE OF ANCIENT EGYPT 249.

to care for him during a bout of sickness.[25] Egyptian law considered a will revocable, since it did not become effective until the testator's death.[26] An Egyptian could revoke his will by means of a second *imyt-pr*, but we cannot be certain whether other methods of revocation were also valid.[27] In order to manage any real property that was inherited jointly, either the testator might appoint an administrator, or, if he had not done so, the court also could make such an appointment.[28]

As was noted above, under the law of intestate succession, a wife was entitled both to a life estate in her dowry and her one-third share of property acquired by her husband.[29] Apparently, her one-third share came to her upon her husband's death even if he left a will that failed to mention it.[30] As a practical matter, however, a number of wills reveal that husbands routinely left more than the one-third intestate minimum to their wives.[31] For example, one stela (Stela Cairo 34061), dating from about 1458 B.C.—the 21st year of Thutmose III—shows a husband leaving all of his property to his wife first, and then to his children upon her death.[32] It may have been conventional for a father to give his daughter her inheritance as a dowry (we know of situations where this was, in fact, the case).[33] A boy, on the other hand, did not receive his inheritance until the death of his parents.[34]

---

25. *See* McDOWELL, JURISDICTION 155; Andrea McDowell, *Legal Aspects of Care of the Elderly in Egypt to the End of the New Kingdom, in* THE CARE OF THE ELDERLY IN THE ANCIENT NEAR EAST 199, 216 (Marten Stol and Sven P. Vleeming eds., 1998). *See also supra* § 6.03, note 60 and accompanying text.

26. *See* P.W. Pestman, *The Law of Succession in Ancient Egypt*, 9 STUDIA ET DOCUMENTA AD JURA ANTIQUI PERTINENTIA 58, 63 (1969).

27. *See* PESTMAN, MARRIAGE & MATRIMONIAL PROPERTY 138; Aristide Théodorides, *The Concept of Law in Ancient Egypt, in* THE LEGACY OF EGYPT 291, 304 (J.R. Harris ed., 2d ed. 1971) ("The taking of an oath is not required for the drawing up of an *imyt-pr* valid as a will, because it can be revoked, but it is necessary in the case of deeds which involve liabilities for the future."); *Id.* at 304–305 (Noting that one could revoke a will by *imyt-pr*.).

28. *See* P.W. Pestman, *The Law of Succession in Ancient Egypt*, 9 STUDIA ET DOCUMENTA AD JURA ANTIQUI PERTINENTIA 58, 64 (1969).

29. *See supra* § 7.01.

30. *See* PESTMAN, MARRIAGE & MATRIMONIAL PROPERTY 128.

31. *See* C.J. Eyre, *The Adoption Papyrus in Social Context*, 78 J. EGYPTIAN ARCHAEOLOGY 207, 219 (1992).

32. *See* PESTMAN, MARRIAGE & MATRIMONIAL PROPERTY 122.

33. *See* Janet H. Johnson, *The Legal Status of Women in Ancient Egypt, in* MISTRESS OF THE HOUSE MISTRESS OF HEAVEN: WOMEN IN ANCIENT EGYPT 175, 184 (Anne K. Chapel and Glenn E. Markoe eds., 1996) ("Daughters might receive their inheritance as a dowry at the time they married."); C.J. Eyre, *The Adoption Papyrus in Social Context*, 78 J. EGYPTIAN ARCHAEOLOGY 207, 220 (1992).

34. *See* Janet H. Johnson, *The Legal Status of Women in Ancient Egypt, in* MISTRESS OF THE HOUSE MISTRESS OF HEAVEN: WOMEN IN ANCIENT EGYPT 175, 184 (Anne K.

A testator had the ability to "determine the amount of the share to go to his children and, moreover, if he so wishe[d], arrange which assets each child... [would]... receive."[35] Parents could leave property to any child, male or female. Likewise, either parent could disinherit children.[36] We have, for example, the "will" of a woman named Naunakhte who disinherited four of her children on the grounds that they had been neglecting her care. Naunakhte says, "But see, I am grown old,... and see, they are not looking after me in my turn.... [H]e who has not given to me, to him I will not give my property.....As for these four children of mine, they shall (not) participate in the division of any of my property."[37] Naunakhte, who appeared before a court of fourteen persons during the reign of Ramses V[38] (*c.* 1148–1144 B.C.) to formalize the disinheritance, tried to appease these four with the knowledge that, although she was disinheriting them, they still stood to inherit, at least, some property from their father: "They shall not participate in the division of my one-third, but in the two-thirds of their fa-

---

Chapel and Glenn E. Markoe eds., 1996) ("Sons, by contrast, apparently did not receive their inheritance until their parents died....").

35. P.W. Pestman, *The Law of Succession in Ancient Egypt*, 9 STUDIA ET DOCUMENTA AD JURA ANTIQUI PERTINENTIA 58, 67 (1969).

36. *See Id.*; Andrea McDowell, *Legal Aspects of Care of the Elderly in Egypt to the End of the New Kingdom, in* THE CARE OF THE ELDERLY IN THE ANCIENT NEAR EAST 199, 210, 215 (Marten Stol and Sven P. Vleeming eds., 1998); Schafik Allam, *Papyrus Turin 2021: Another Adoption Extraordinary, in* INDIVIDU, SOCIÉTÉ ET SPIRITUALITÉ DANS L'ÉGYPT PHARAONIQUE ET COPTE: MÉLANGES ÉGYPTOLOGIQUES OFFERTS AU PROFESSEUR ARISTIDE THÉODORIDÈS 23, 25 (Christian Cannuyer and Jean-Marie Kruchten eds., 1993); J.J. Janssen and P.W. Pestman, *Burial and Inheritance in the Community of the Necropolis Workmen at Thebes (Pap. Bulaq X and O. Petrie 16)*, 11 J. ECONOMIC & SOCIAL HIST. ORIENT 167 (1968).

37. Jaroslav Černý, *The Will of Naunakhte and the Related Documents*, 31 J. EGYPTIAN ARCHAEOLOGY 29, 31–32 (1945). *See also* PESTMAN, MARRIAGE AND MATRIMONIAL PROPERTY 163; Schafik Allam, *Women as Owners of Immovables in Pharaonic Egypt, in* WOMEN'S EARLIEST RECORDS FROM ANCIENT EGYPT AND WESTERN ASIA 123, 130–31 (Barbara Lesko ed., 1989); J.J. Janssen and P.W. Pestman, *Burial and Inheritance in the Community of the Necropolis Workmen at Thebes (Pap. Bulaq X and O. Petrie 16)*, 11 J. ECONOMIC & SOCIAL HIST. ORIENT 167 (1968); MCDOWELL, JURISDICTION 145 (McDowell notes that Naunakhte's will was brought before a court.).

38. *See* PESTMAN, MARRIAGE & MATRIMONIAL PROPERTY 126 (Pestman places this will in year 3 of Ramses V.); Jaroslav Černý, *The Will of Naunakhte and the Related Documents*, 31 J. EGYPTIAN ARCHAEOLOGY 29, 42 (1945) ("The business connected with Naunakhte carries us back to the reign of Ramesses Skheperenrēʿ, a little-known king of the 20th Dynasty, who is believed to have been the second successor of Ramsses III and whom we consequently count as Ramesses V.") (footnote omitted); Schafik Allam, *Women as Owners of Immovables in Pharaonic Egypt, in* WOMEN'S EARLIEST RECORDS FROM ANCIENT EGYPT AND WESTERN ASIA 123, 130 (Barbara Lesko ed., 1989) (Allam dates Naunakhte's "will" to 1144 B.C.).

ther they shall participate."[39] Interestingly, later in a court hearing these four children expressly agreed to the disinheritance by their mother.[40] Naunakhte's testamentary disposition is also noteworthy for two other reasons. In addition to disinheriting the four "bad" children, she expressly includes the other children who had taken care of her. Furthermore, she singles out one son, Kenherkhepshef for a "special reward" (bequeathing him a particular bronze washing-bowl).[41] It is unlikely, however, that a testator was permitted to disinherit *all* of his children (in favor of, say, his brother) unless the children expressly agreed.[42]

We actually have two wills of princes from the Old Kingdom (one from the 4th Dynasty (*c.* 2625–2510 B.C.) and one from the 5th (*c.* 2510–2460 B.C.)) that were carved into stone on their tomb chapel walls.[43] We also have a will of a man named Heti from the 4th Dynasty who gave assets to his children, but with some restrictions on alienability. In addition, Heti's will provided for funerary offerings each day.[44] This will is an interesting one. Heti, in essence, created an endowment. His will created a type of trust ad-

---

39. Jaroslav Černý, *The Will of Naunakhte and the Related Documents*, 31 J. EGYPTIAN ARCHAEOLOGY 29, 31 (1945). *See also* PESTMAN, MARRIAGE AND MATRIMONIAL PROPERTY 163–164; Andrea McDowell, *Legal Aspects of Care of the Elderly in Egypt to the End of the New Kingdom, in* THE CARE OF THE ELDERLY IN THE ANCIENT NEAR EAST 199, 215–16 (Marten Stol and Sven P. Vleeming eds., 1998); Schafik Allam, *Papyrus Turin 2021: Another Adoption Extraordinary, in* INDIVIDU, SOCIÉTÉ ET SPIRITUALITÉ DANS L'ÉGYPT PHARAONIQUE ET COPTE: MÉLANGES ÉGYPTOLOGIQUES OFFERTS AU PROFESSEUR ARISTIDE THÉODORIDÈS 23, 25 (Christian Cannuyer and Jean-Marie Kruchten eds., 1993); GAY ROBINS, WOMEN IN ANCIENT EGYPT 132. *See also supra* § 6.02 regarding the two-thirds to one-third division of property jointly owned by a married couple.

40. *See* Janet H. Johnson, *The Legal Status of Women in Ancient Egypt, in* MISTRESS OF THE HOUSE MISTRESS OF HEAVEN: WOMEN IN ANCIENT EGYPT 175, 183 (Anne K. Chapel and Glenn E. Markoe eds., 1996).

41. *See* Jaroslav Černý, *The Will of Naunakhte and the Related Documents*, 31 J. EGYPTIAN ARCHAEOLOGY 29, 31, 48–49 (1945); Schafik Allam, *Women as Owners of Immovables in Pharaonic Egypt, in* WOMEN'S EARLIEST RECORDS FROM ANCIENT EGYPT AND WESTERN ASIA 123, 131 (Barbara Lesko ed., 1989); Andrea McDowell, *Legal Aspects of Care of the Elderly in Egypt to the End of the New Kingdom, in* THE CARE OF THE ELDERLY IN THE ANCIENT NEAR EAST 199, 216 (Marten Stol and Sven P. Vleeming eds., 1998).

42. *See* P.W. Pestman, *The Law of Succession in Ancient Egypt*, 9 STUDIA ET DOCUMENTA AD JURA ANTIQUI PERTINENTIA 58, 68 (1969); PESTMAN, MARRIAGE & MATRIMONIAL PROPERTY 47, 137–138.

43. *See* BREASTED, HISTORY OF EGYPT 82 ("The will of a king's son in the 4th Dynasty has been preserved practically complete, and another from the beginnings of the 5th Dynasty, both having been cut in hieroglyphs on the stone wall of the tomb-chapel where they could defy the lapse of nearly five thousand years....") (footnotes omitted).

44. *See* Aristide Théodorides, *The Concept of Law in Ancient Egypt, in* THE LEGACY OF EGYPT 291, 293 (J.R. Harris ed., 2d ed. 1971).

ministered by his eldest son. He did this instead of contracting directly with the priests. According to the terms of the trust, each family member was to receive only the revenue generated by the trust; and the trust was to remain indivisible forever.[45]

In addition to a standard written will, another way to alter the rules of intestacy was to make a testamentary declaration in court. If witnessed and transcribed by the court, this too could operate as a kind of "will."[46] This is actually the type of document that the "will" of Naunakhte was. As Černý states: "[I]t consists of an oral deposition made by the party before the court or witnesses and written down by a professional scribe. Thus it was not the written word alone, but the spoken word subsequently recorded as an actual event on a papyrus or ostracon that conferred upon the document its legal validity."[47]

The Egyptians also used adoption as a means to circumvent the laws of intestate succession.[48] In order to validate an adoption, an adopter merely stated, orally, his intent to adopt in the presence of witnesses.[49] Some couples who had no children felt societal pressure to adopt so that they would

---

45. *See Id.* at 294 ("The deed of foundation makes it clear that each member of said syndicate will himself receive only the revenue from this estate, which has been made indivisible in perpetuity."). *See also supra* § 5.01, *infra* § 7.03.

46. *See* Janet H. Johnson, *The Legal Status of Women in Ancient Egypt, in* MISTRESS OF THE HOUSE MISTRESS OF HEAVEN: WOMEN IN ANCIENT EGYPT 175, 183 (Anne K. Chapel and Glenn E. Markoe eds., 1996); Schafik Allam, *Papyrus Turin 2021: Another Adoption Extraordinary, in* INDIVIDU, SOCIÉTÉ ET SPIRITUALITÉ DANS L'ÉGYPT PHARAONIQUE ET COPTE: MÉLANGES ÉGYPTOLOGIQUES OFFERTS AU PROFESSEUR ARISTIDE THÉODORIDÈS 23, 24 (Christian Cannuyer and Jean-Marie Kruchten eds., 1993).

47. Jaroslav Černý, *The Will of Naunakhte and the Related Documents*, 31 J. EGYPTIAN ARCHAEOLOGY 29, 42 (1945).

48. *See* Alan Gardiner, *Adoption Extraordinary*, 26 J. EGYPTIAN ARCHAEOLOGY 23, 27 (1940) ("Our papyrus provides a particularly clear illustration of a well-known phenomenon, namely the utilization of adoption for testamentary purposes.") (commentary by Prof. de Zulueta); PESTMAN, MARRIAGE & MATRIMONIAL PROPERTY 8; William A. Ward, *Some Aspects of Private Land Ownership and Inheritance in Ancient Egypt, ca. 2500–1000 B.C., in* LAND TENURE AND SOCIAL TRANSFORMATION IN THE MIDDLE EAST 63, 69–72 (Tarif Khalidi ed., 1984); Schafik Allam, *Women as Owners of Immovables in Pharaonic Egypt, in* WOMEN'S EARLIEST RECORDS FROM ANCIENT EGYPT AND WESTERN ASIA 123, 126 (Barbara Lesko ed., 1989); Schafik Allam, *Papyrus Turin 2021: Another Adoption Extraordinary, in* INDIVIDU, SOCIÉTÉ ET SPIRITUALITÉ DANS L'ÉGYPT PHARAONIQUE ET COPTE: MÉLANGES ÉGYPTOLOGIQUES OFFERTS AU PROFESSEUR ARISTIDE THÉODORIDÈS 23 (Christian Cannuyer and Jean-Marie Kruchten eds., 1993); *Id.* at 26 ("Those concerned were solely interested in the effect of the adoption upon the devolution of property; they utilized the fiction of adoption for inheritance purposes."); *Id.* at 27–28.

49. *See* Alan Gardiner, *Adoption Extraordinary*, 26 J. EGYPTIAN ARCHAEOLOGY 23, 25 (1940) ("The procedure of adoption consisted, as in the case of divorce, simply in making a verbal declaration in front of witnesses.").

have a legal heir.[50] We know of a man, a stablemaster named Nebnefer, who lived under Ramses XI (*c.* 1098–1069 B.C.), who adopted his own wife.[51] Thus, since she was technically his "child," she—not his brothers or sisters and not his parents—inherited his wealth.[52] Interestingly, his wife (*i.e.*, daughter by adoption), then, some seventeen years later, adopted three children who belonged to one of their house slaves, so that they, in due course, could inherit from her.[53] It seems likely that those children—two daughters and one son—were fathered by Nebnefer.[54]

---

50. *See* Janet H. Johnson, *The Legal Status of Women in Ancient Egypt, in* MISTRESS OF THE HOUSE MISTRESS OF HEAVEN: WOMEN IN ANCIENT EGYPT 175, 183 (Anne K. Chapel and Glenn E. Markoe eds., 1996) ("Childless individuals were encouraged to adopt children, who would become their legal heirs.") (footnote omitted); William A. Ward, *Some Aspects of Private Land Ownership and Inheritance in Ancient Egypt, ca. 2500–1000 B.C., in* LAND TENURE AND SOCIAL TRANSFORMATION IN THE MIDDLE EAST 63, 69–70 (Tarif Khalidi ed., 1984) (Ward notes: "In one private letter, a man writes to a wealthy friend chiding him for his stinginess and his inability to impregnate his wife.").

51. *See generally* C.J. Eyre, *The Adoption Papyrus in Social Context*, 78 J. EGYPTIAN ARCHAEOLOGY 207–221 (1992). *See also Id.* at 210 (Eyre points out that the document that records these matters is actually "a cross between a marriage settlement, a property settlement, and a will, or rather a mixture of all three."); Alan Gardiner, *Adoption Extraordinary*, 26 J. EGYPTIAN ARCHAEOLOGY 23–29 (1940); William A. Ward, *Some Aspects of Private Land Ownership and Inheritance in Ancient Egypt, ca. 2500–1000 B.C., in* LAND TENURE AND SOCIAL TRANSFORMATION IN THE MIDDLE EAST 63, 70 (Tarif Khalidi ed., 1984) ("The Stable-master Nebnefer, having no children, adopted his own wife so she might inherit all his property and not just the widow's share when he died."); Schafik Allam, *Women as Owners of Immovables in Pharaonic Egypt, in* WOMEN'S EARLIEST RECORDS FROM ANCIENT EGYPT AND WESTERN ASIA 123, 126 (Barbara Lesko ed., 1989); Andrea McDowell, *Legal Aspects of Care of the Elderly in Egypt to the End of the New Kingdom, in* THE CARE OF THE ELDERLY IN THE ANCIENT NEAR EAST 199, 217–19 (Marten Stol and Sven P. Vleeming eds., 1998); Schafik Allam, *Papyrus Turin 2021: Another Adoption Extraordinary, in* INDIVIDU, SOCIÉTÉ ET SPIRITUALITÉ DANS L'ÉGYPT PHARAONIQUE ET COPTE: MÉLANGES ÉGYPTOLOGIQUES OFFERTS AU PROFESSEUR ARISTIDE THÉODORIDÈS 23 (Christian Cannuyer and Jean-Marie Kruchten eds., 1993).

52. *See* Alan Gardiner, *Adoption Extraordinary*, 26 J. EGYPTIAN ARCHAEOLOGY 23, 25 (1940) ("The object was to ensure that the entire property of the stable-master Nebnufer should pass to his wife Nenufer or Rennufer—there has been hesitation over the spelling of the name—and should subsequently be disposed of in accordance with her desires.").

53. *See Id.* at 25–26; Janet H. Johnson, *The Legal Status of Women in Ancient Egypt, in* MISTRESS OF THE HOUSE MISTRESS OF HEAVEN: WOMEN IN ANCIENT EGYPT 175, 183 (Anne K. Chapel and Glenn E. Markoe eds., 1996); P.W. Pestman, *The Law of Succession in Ancient Egypt*, 9 STUDIA ET DOCUMENTA AD JURA ANTIQUI PERTINENTIA 58, 74 (1969); William A. Ward, *Some Aspects of Private Land Ownership and Inheritance in Ancient Egypt, ca. 2500–1000 B.C., in* LAND TENURE AND SOCIAL TRANSFORMATION IN THE MIDDLE EAST 63, 70 (Tarif Khalidi ed., 1984); Schafik Allam, *Women as Owners of Immovables in Pharaonic Egypt, in* WOMEN'S EARLIEST RECORDS FROM ANCIENT EGYPT AND WESTERN ASIA 123, 126 (Barbara Lesko ed., 1989).

54. *See* Alan Gardiner, *Adoption Extraordinary*, 26 J. EGYPTIAN ARCHAEOLOGY 23, 25–26 (1940); C.J. Eyre, *The Adoption Papyrus in Social Context*, 78 J. EGYPTIAN AR-

§ 7.03 The Concept of a Trustee for an Estate

The role of an estate administrator was recognized as early as the 6th Dynasty (*c.* 2460–2200 B.C.). The estate administrator was to "consume the fruits of the assets" but without causing any loss.[55] Generally speaking, an administrator was legally bound to preserve the principal of the estate as if he were the deceased father himself.[56] It was also during the 6th Dynasty that it became common practice for the eldest son to assume the responsibility of administering the funds of the joint property upon the death of the father.[57]

The lawsuit concerning Mose[58] (dating from late in the 18th Dynasty—*c.* 1552–1295 B.C.), in which the ownership of an estate was contested, provides an example of a woman being appointed trustee for property in dispute. In that case, one of the potential heirs (also a woman) objected to the trustee appointment, and she persuaded the magistrate to remove the trustee and to divide the estate equally among the six heirs instead.[59] Another example of an appointment of a trustee occurs in a text from the time of Ramses II (*c.* 1279–1212 B.C.). Papyrus Berlin 3047 (dating from year 46 of Ramses II) describes a property dispute in which one family member administered the subject property "as trustee (*rw'dw*) on behalf of coheirs...."[60] Heti's will, mentioned above, also created a trust with his son acting as trustee.[61]

CHAEOLOGY 207, 210 (1992) ("Although the text does not state explicitly who the father of the children was, the text seems fairly clearly to represent an arrangement well attested elsewhere among the propertied classes in the ancient Near East. Where a wife is unable (or unwilling) to provide a legitimate heir, her social and economic status as a married woman can be protected by provision of a surrogate mother, typically a slave-woman bought for the purpose.") (footnote omitted).

55. *See* Aristide Théodorides, *The Concept of Law in Ancient Egypt, in* THE LEGACY OF EGYPT 291, 300 (J.R. Harris ed., 2d ed. 1971). *See also supra* § 5.02 regarding the concepts *usus* and *usus fructus*.

56. *See* Aristide Théodorides, *The Concept of Law in Ancient Egypt, in* THE LEGACY OF EGYPT 291, 300 (J.R. Harris ed., 2d ed. 1971) ("[H]e is to handle it like a good father of the family.").

57. *See Id.* at 297.

58. *See supra* § 4.01.

59. *See* GARDINER, EGYPT OF THE PHARAOHS 268–269 ("In the time of Horemhab the Great Court sitting in Hēliopolis and presided over by the Vizier sent a commissioner to the locality where the property was, whereupon a lady named Wernero was appointed to cultivate the land as trustee for her brothers and sisters. Objection to this arrangement having been raised by a sister named Takharu, a new division was made whereby the estate, hitherto indivisible, was parcelled out between the six heirs." Ultimately, even this decision was overturned.). *See supra* § 4.01.

60. KATARY, LAND TENURE IN THE RAMESSIDE PERIOD 224.

61. *See supra* § 7.02, text accompanying notes 44–45.

§7.04 Inheritance of Office

Certain government offices became hereditary as early as the Old Kingdom (*c.* 2700–2200 B.C.). We have clear evidence for two such offices: nomarch and vizier.[62] Technically, the king retained the right to appoint a successor who was unrelated to a recently deceased nomarch. But as a practical matter, the king rarely ignored the late nomarch's rightful heir. We cannot be entirely certain whether the nomarch's eldest son succeeded to his father's nomarchy or whether the nomarch's eldest grandson—born of his eldest daughter—was the rightful successor (there is conflicting evidence). If it was the latter, it is possible that a nomarch's eldest daughter herself could have ruled a nome as rightful nomarch until her son reached an age at which he could govern in his own stead.[63] Like the nomarchy, the office of vizier seems to have been hereditary even in the Old Kingdom. For example, we know that when the government changed hands at the outset of the 5th Dynasty (*c.* 2510–2460 B.C.), the vizierate also changed hands and became hereditary with a new family.[64]

---

62. *See generally* Andrea McDowell, *Legal Aspects of Care of the Elderly in Egypt to the End of the New Kingdom, in* THE CARE OF THE ELDERLY IN THE ANCIENT NEAR EAST 199, 203 (Marten Stol and Sven P. Vleeming eds., 1998).

63. *See* GRIMAL, ANCIENT EGYPT 89, 92 (Grimal claims that the nomarchs in the Old Kingdom became hereditary, "even though it was still non-hereditary in legal terms."); William A. Ward, *Some Aspects of Private Land Ownership and Inheritance in Ancient Egypt, ca. 2500–1000 B.C., in* LAND TENURE AND SOCIAL TRANSFORMATION IN THE MIDDLE EAST 63, 69 (Tarif Khalidi ed., 1984); J.G. Manning, *Demotic Egyptian Instruments of Transfer as Evidence for Private Ownership of Real Property*, 71 CHICAGO-KENT L. REV. 237, 240 (1995) (Manning notes that children often inherited land as part of their father's office); BREASTED, HISTORY OF EGYPT 161 (Referring to circumstances in the Middle Kingdom, Breasted says: "The domains over which the nomarch thus ruled were not all his unqualified possessions. His wealth consisted of lands and revenues of two classes: the 'paternal estate,' received from his ancestors and entailed in his line; and the 'count's estate,' over which the dead hand had no control; it was conveyed as a fief by the Pharaoh anew at the nomarch's death. It was this fact which to some extent enabled the Pharaoh to control the feudatories and to secure the appointment of partisans of his house throughout the country. Nevertheless he could not ignore the natural line of succession, which was through the eldest daughter; and...she might even rule the domain after the death of her father until her son was old enough to assume its government.") (footnotes omitted); *Id.* at 126 ("This hereditary succession, so striking in the highest office of the central government, was now common in the nomes, and the local governors were each gaining stronger and stronger foothold in his nome as the generations passed, and son succeeded father in the same nome.").

64. *See* BREASTED, HISTORY OF EGYPT 126 (Referring to the 5th Dynasty, Breasted says: "The change in royal line is also evident in the organization of the government. The eldest son of the king is no longer the most powerful officer in the state, but the position which he held in the 4th Dynasty as vizier and chief judge is now the prerogative of another family, with whom it remains hereditary.").

§7.05 Chapter Summary

When an ancient Egyptian died without a will, the laws of intestate succession dictated to whom his property would pass. As a rule, a decedent's children inherited equal shares of his estate. Ordinarily, real estate passed to the heirs as undivided property which they then owned jointly. If there were no children, the decedent's siblings inherited the estate. In the event that the decedent had neither children nor siblings, his parents inherited instead. Husbands and wives did not inherit from one another. A woman's children inherited her dowry. The eldest son had both more rights and obligations than his siblings. He inherited his father's office (especially in the case of a nomarch or vizier), he may have been entitled to select his share of the estate first, he bore the burden of caring for the funeral and cult obligations for his deceased parents, and he served as administrator of his parents' estate. In some instances a child who was not the biological eldest son assumed the eldest son's rights and responsibilities.

The Egyptians recognized the validity of wills. They used a document called the *imyt-pr* to function as a will, and the testator was required to record the *imyt-pr* with the vizier in order for it to be considered valid. Wills were considered revocable and served to dispense property to designated legatees in just about any manner that the testator desired. A testator could even disinherit children by means of a will. Some Egyptian wills operated to create rather sophisticated trusts. The Egyptians also used adoption as a vehicle for creating an heir.

CHAPTER 8

Crime & Tort (Damage to Persons & Things)

§8.01 Introduction

There is no compelling evidence to indicate that the ancient Egyptians formally recognized or even abstractly appreciated a general theory of legal recovery remotely similar to modern tort law. Rather, for them it appears that criminal laws fulfilled some of the functions that modern tort law serves. As is true in many ancient legal systems, the Egyptians did not distinguish between tort and crime in the same fashion that modern societies do.[1] The legal term for "wrong" or "crime" was *bt3*.[2] In many instances, either a victim or his family bore the responsibility to initiate legal action.[3] To

1. *See* David Lorton, *The Treatment of Criminals in Ancient Egypt*, 20 J. ECONOMIC & SOCIAL HIST. ORIENT 2, 7, 45–46 (1977); Jac Janssen, *Rules of Legal Proceeding in the Community of Necropolis Workmen at Deir el-Medina*, 32 BIBLIOTHECA ORIENTALIS 291, 294 (1975); MCDOWELL, JURISDICTION 208 (Referring to the similarities between torts and crimes.); *Id.* at 246–247 (Referring to problems inherent in defining "crime."); *Id.* at 247 (Referring to the difficulty of separating crime from tort.). For a general discussion of ancient Egyptian criminal law, *see generally* Taylor, *Law Under the Pharaohs*, 6 POL'Y REV. 66, 70 (1980). One of the most ancient criminal trials is described in the Pyramid Texts of the Old Kingdom: the mythological trial of Set for the murder of Osiris. *See* BREASTED, DEVELOPMENT OF RELIGION AND THOUGHT 33–36; 175–76. For a more detailed account of criminal law and procedure in the New Kingdom, *see* ERMAN, LIFE IN ANCIENT EGYPT 130–38.

2. *See* FAULKNER, A CONCISE DICTIONARY OF MIDDLE EGYPTIAN 85 (Defining *bt3* as "wrong, crime."); MCDOWELL, JURISDICTION 26 ("In everyday settings *bt3* can mean 'wrong,' 'fault,' or 'harm'; an unpleasant or even offensive action but not necessarily the sort of thing one would take to court. On the other hand, in denunciations, verdicts and the like, *bt3* means 'crime'; at any rate, many of the most blatant crimes are called *bt3* or *bt3 n mwt*, 'crime worthy of death....'") (footnotes omitted).

3. *See* Janet H. Johnson, *The Legal Status of Women in Ancient Egypt*, *in* MISTRESS OF THE HOUSE MISTRESS OF HEAVEN: WOMEN IN ANCIENT EGYPT 175 (Anne K. Chapel and Glenn E. Markoe eds., 1996).

be sure, today it is, as a practical matter, virtually impossible for us to distinguish ancient Egyptian tort law from criminal law in any meaningful way. One theoretical means of distinguishing tort from crime is to categorize laws and legal situations based on types of punishments (*i.e.*, the legal consequences).[4] Monetary payments madc by a wrongdoer to his victim as compensation are usually associated with torts whereas corporal punishments and fines paid to the State are hallmarks of criminal law. For convenience, this chapter (like the book as a whole) uses modern legal categories as points of reference. Thus, I have relied on modern American legal classifications of crime and tort to discuss analogous conduct in ancient Egypt. Before examining crimes and torts in detail, however, it will be helpful first to consider the consequences of such conduct; namely, punishments and penalties.

§ 8.02 Punishment: An Overview[5]

[A] General

The term used for "punishment" was ordinarily *sb3yt*. More often than not, *sb3yt* involved some form of corporal punishment.[6] According to Erman, in ancient Egypt "[p]unishment was regarded as the necessary consequence of crime...."[7] Jurisprudentially speaking, it seems clear that the Egyptians understood the deterrent function that punishment could serve. About thirty years after the thieves who were convicted in the Great Tomb Robberies had been executed,[8] for example, a suspect in a fresh case testified: "I saw the punishment that was inflicted on the thieves in the time of the vizier Khaemwse. Is it then likely that I should seek such a death?"[9] And James tells us:

---

4. *See* McDowell, Jurisdiction 247 (Noting that the type of punishment imposed may be used as a method of categorizing a wrong as a crime as opposed to a tort or civil action.).

5. This section provides an overview of punishment for wrongs. I have noted more specifically the punishments associated with individual wrongs in the appropriate sections that follow.

6. *See* McDowell, Jurisdiction 29; R.O. Faulkner, A Concise Dictionary of Middle Egyptian 219 (Entry for *sb3yt* meaning "teaching", "instructions".).

7. Erman, Life in Ancient Egypt 141. *See* Bedell, Criminal Law 179 ("[T]hose who committed crimes against the state were always subject to corporal punishment.") (footnote omitted). *See also Id.* at 191.

8. *See infra* § 8.04[B].

9. Jacke Phillips, *Tomb-robbers and their Booty in Ancient Egypt, in* Death and Taxes in the Ancient Near East 157, 160 (Sara E. Orel ed., 1992) (footnote omitted).

> Summary punishment was common in cases where the facts of the matter were not in dispute or, perhaps even more common, thought not to be in dispute. A felon brought before a local magistrate would have found little in the way of legal process before punishment was enacted, unless the crime was something which required investigation.[10]

In the Old and Middle Kingdoms, some criminal penalties were not as physically brutal as later in the New Kingdom. For example, a 5th Dynasty (*c.* 2510–2460 B.C.) text states that government officials found guilty of misusing their office were removed from office, forced to do labor, and had their property confiscated. Although these were stiff consequences, no bodily mutilation was involved. Other documents from the 6th Dynasty (*c.* 2460–2200 B.C.) as well as others from the 16th or 17th (*c.* 1600 B.C.) show officials punished by forfeiting their jobs and property in similar circumstances.[11] Thus, divesting a criminal of his civic status (which included deprivation of ritual burial, and hence loss of status in the afterlife) coupled with forfeiture of property and forced labor were typical of early Egyptian criminal punishments.[12] Beating became a criminal punishment in the Middle Kingdom (*c.* 2040–1674 B.C.).[13] One commentator summarizes punishments in ancient Egypt during this period by saying that they "typi-

---

10. T.G.H. JAMES, PHARAOH'S PEOPLE, SCENES FROM LIFE IN IMPERIAL EGYPT 82 (1984). *See also supra* § 4.01 regarding due process.

11. *See* David Lorton, *Legal and Social Institutions of Pharaonic Egypt*, *in* 1 CIVILIZATIONS OF THE ANCIENT NEAR EAST 345 (Jack M. Sasson ed., 1995) (Referring to punishments such as "loss of civic status in this life and the next—namely, loss of office and property, forced labor, and denial of ritual burial."); WILSON, CULTURE OF ANCIENT EGYPT 241–42 ("The severity of these punishments contrasts markedly with the penalties in earlier decrees. A 5th Dynasty enactment...provided that the guilty official should be removed from his office and put upon any kind of work, with his servants and property confiscated." Wilson also gives examples of the 6th Dynasty, and 16th or 17th Dynasty where the guilty official lost his job and had property confiscated.) (footnote omitted).

12. *See* David Lorton, *The Treatment of Criminals in Ancient Egypt*, 20 J. ECONOMIC & SOCIAL HIST. ORIENT 2, 50 (1977) (Lorton summarizes these Old Kingdom penalties "for infringement upon temple immunities" as having involved "loss of civic status in life and death (i.e., loss of the right to a ritual burial and enjoyment of a blessed afterlife), and quite possibly assignment to labor...."). *See also* BEDELL, CRIMINAL LAW 164 (Referring to denial of ritual burial as a means of punishment.); KATARY, LAND TENURE IN THE RAMESSIDE PERIOD 186 (Mentioning that P. Amiens refers to a domain that was "'established for (?)' convicted criminals" and suggesting that that "may have been related to the practice of having convicted criminals serve their sentences as agricultural laborers....").

13. *See* David Lorton, *The Treatment of Criminals in Ancient Egypt*, 20 J. ECONOMIC & SOCIAL HIST. ORIENT 2, 51 (1977).

cally consist of (1) deprivation of burial; (2) bodily destruction (*e.g.* by burning); (3) exclusion from divine communication (offering) and social memory, a kind of 'excommunication' including outlawry."[14] Later, New Kingdom (*c.* 1552–1069 B.C.) penalties commonly consisted of "a complex set of punishments for various offenses, including beatings, mutilations, and impalement, as well as reduction to unfree status...."[15] Much punishment in the New Kingdom was corporal in nature—and brutal by today's standards; although some economic sanctions did exist, especially for theft. And, in lieu of fines (or money damages), since ancient Egypt was really a "non-monetary society," punishment could take the form of conscription for public service.[16] Convicted criminals routinely lost their freedom and their right to inherit office.[17] In circumstances where a convicted criminal lost his freedom, he may also, on occasion, have been branded.[18] Evidence suggests that the death penalty was imposed for murder, conspiracy to assassinate the king (treason), robbery of royal tombs, perjury, and judicial bribery.[19] In the Nauri Decree of Seti I (*c.* 1294–1279 B.C.), the punishment

---

14. Jan Assman, *When Justice Fails: Jurisdiction and Imprecation in Ancient Egypt and the Near East*, 78 J. Egyptian Archaeology 149, 154 (1992) (footnote omitted).

15. David Lorton, *The Treatment of Criminals in Ancient Egypt*, 20 J. Economic & Social Hist. Orient 2, 50 (1977). *See also* McDowell, Jurisdiction 29, n. 107 (Referring to death, beating, and mutilation as punishments.); *Id.* at 173 (Referring to beating as a punishment.); Bedell, Criminal Law 174 ("In the Edict of Horemhab there are crimes for which both mutilation and exile are prescribed."); *Id.* at 175–176 ("[T]here is one recorded case in which cutting off the hand was the specific punishment.") (Bedell also notes that this was a punishment that Diodorus Siculus mentioned, as well.); *Id.* at 178 ("Indeed, the concept of forced labor as reparation for various types of crimes was thoroughly entrenched in Egyptian legal practice."); *Id.* ("The usual number of blows was a hundred, but there were many crimes requiring two hundred blows.") (footnote omitted).

16. *See* T.G.H. James, Pharaoh's People: Scenes From Life in Imperial Egypt 83, 85–87 (1984). For more on the topic of money, *see infra* § 9.05.

17. *See* David Lorton, *The Treatment of Criminals in Ancient Egypt*, 20 J. Economic & Social Hist. Orient 2, 11–12, 52 (1977) ("the removal of an individual from office must have had a devastating effect on the criminal's family."); Janet H. Johnson, *The Legal Status of Women in Ancient Egypt*, *in* Mistress of the House Mistress of Heaven: Women in Ancient Egypt 175 (Anne K. Chapel and Glenn E. Markoe eds., 1996).

18. *See* David Lorton, *The Treatment of Criminals in Ancient Egypt*, 20 J. Economic & Social Hist. Orient 2, 18 (1977).

19. *See* David Lorton, *Legal and Social Institutions of Pharaonic Egypt*, *in* 1 Civilizations of the Ancient Near East 345, 356 (Jack M. Sasson ed., 1995); David Lorton, *The Treatment of Criminals in Ancient Egypt*, 20 J. Economic & Social Hist. Orient 2, 11–14 (1977). *See also* Breasted, History of Egypt 500; McDowell, Jurisdiction 223 (Remarking that those found guilty in the Great Tomb Robbery

prescribed for corrupt judges was 100 blows, removal from office, and to be "placed as a cultivator in the Foundation."[20] The Edict of Horemhab punished a corrupt judge with the death penalty ("it shall be (reckoned) to him (for) a great capital crime.").[21] A number of Egyptologists have theorized that the pharaoh was the only individual in Egypt who had the authority to impose either mutilation or death as a penalty for criminal conduct.[22] McDowell, however, suggests that the pharaoh did not reserve the right to impose the death penalty in all cases.[23] In the Nauri Decree, for example, the local courts seem to have been given the authority to impose the mandated penalties—which included a death penalty.[24] We are unsure whether a small, local court had the power to impose either death or amputation on its own accord (*i.e.,* in the absence of the authorization of a royal decree, like the Nauri Decree or the Edict of Horemhab).[25] Beyond these harsh punishments, the Greek historian Diodorus relates several other cruel and unusual penalties: cutting off a hand, for forgery; cutting out the tongue, for "treachery"; and, for infanticide, holding the dead child's corpse for three days (a punishment which many Egyptologists believe dubious).[26] In

---

trials were executed.); BEDELL, CRIMINAL LAW 14 (Noting that "tomb robbery was punishable by death."); *Id.* at 145–153 (Referring to the death penalty.); ERMAN, LIFE IN ANCIENT EGYPT 141 (Noting that, according to Diodorus, the death penalty was given for murder of either a free man or a slave, and also for perjury.); James Hoch and Sara E. Orel, *Murder in Ancient Egypt, in* DEATH AND TAXES IN THE ANCIENT NEAR EAST 87, 107 (Sara E. Orel ed., 1992) ("Another magical text to ward off murderers is found in the **Armytage Ostracon** which dates to the 19th or 20th Dynasty. A spell would have the murderer fall victim to his own plot.") (footnote omitted); *Id.* at 112 ("In most cases it seems the expectation was that murderers would be punished with death."). *See infra* §§8.04, 8.05, 8.07. For more on judicial bribery, *see supra* §3.05.

20. William F. Edgerton, *The Nauri Decree of Seti I. A Translation and Analysis of the Legal Portion*, 6 J. NEAR EASTERN STUD. 219, 227 (1947). *See also* BEDELL, CRIMINAL LAW 30–31.

21. BEDELL, CRIMINAL LAW 152 (footnote omitted).

22. *See Id.* at 21–22 (Bedell cites Černý and Peet for this proposition; a proposition with which she disagrees. Bedell states that the vizier had the authority to sentence a criminal to death.); *Id.* at 22 (She contends: "There is reason to believe that in some instances the local courts could order the punishment of mutilation, exile or death without referring the case to the vizier or the king."). *See also* MCDOWELL, JURISDICTION 216 ("The choice of punishment for those found guilty was apparently left to the Pharaoh, but there can be no doubt that in these very serious cases the guilty paid with their lives."). *See also supra* §§3.03[B], 3.04, 4.06, *infra* §8.04[B], note 96.

23. *See* MCDOWELL, JURISDICTION 223. *See also* BEDELL, CRIMINAL LAW 14–15 (Referring to the vizier as having the ultimate decision regarding capital punishment.).

24. *See* BEDELL, CRIMINAL LAW 23.

25. *See Id.* at 175.

26. *See* ERMAN, LIFE IN ANCIENT EGYPT 141.

the Old Kingdom (*c.* 2700–2200 B.C.), decapitation was a common method of execution.[27] Although artistic representations from the New Kingdom show prisoners of war being decapitated, there is no similar proof regarding it as type of death penalty.[28] The Egyptians used impalement as a means of execution at least by the 19th Dynasty (*c.* 1295–1188 B.C.). And, during the New Kingdom, impalement is the only method of State execution for which we have hard evidence.[29] The Nauri Decree of Seti I (*c.* 1294–1279 B.C.), for example, mentions impalement as a penalty twice.[30] There are also a handful of references to casting convicted criminals to the crocodiles.[31] Death by crocodile may have been used as a literary device to denote either State sanctioned or divinely sanctioned capital punishment. In the *Book of the Dead*, a beast who is one-third crocodile inflicts capital punishment upon those whose hearts are heavier than the symbol of *Ma'at*: "a grotesque monster called the 'Devouress,' *with the head of a crocodile*, fore quarters of a lion and hind quarters of a hippopotamus, wait[s] to devour the unjust soul."[32] Execution by crocodile is significant for another reason as well. As is true with death by burning or drowning, when a criminal was eaten by a crocodile, he lost the opportunity for a ritual burial.[33] Indeed, a Middle

27. *See* BEDELL, CRIMINAL LAW 157.

28. *See Id.* at 158.

29. *See* David Lorton, *The Treatment of Criminals in Ancient Egypt*, 20 J. ECONOMIC & SOCIAL HIST. ORIENT 2, 51 (1977); BEDELL, CRIMINAL LAW 153–159 (Referring to impalement as a means of execution.).

30. *See* William F. Edgerton, *The Nauri Decree of Seti I: A Translation and Analysis of the Legal Portion*, 6 J. NEAR EASTERN STUD. 219, 224, 226 (1947). *See also* BEDELL, CRIMINAL LAW 155.

31. *See* MCDOWELL, JURISDICTION 174 (Referring to throwing a convicted criminal to a crocodile as a method execution.). *See also* BEDELL, CRIMINAL LAW 162–164 (Referring to execution by "being thrown to the crocodiles," Bedell discusses the story of adultery told in Papyrus Westcar.). *See infra* § 8.06.

32. BREASTED, DEVELOPMENT OF RELIGION AND THOUGHT 305 (emphasis added). *See also* JON MANCHIP WHITE, EVERYDAY LIFE IN ANCIENT EGYPT 75–76 (Discussing the trial in the underworld and the fate of those whose hearts are heavier than the ostrich feather of *Ma'at*). *See also supra* § 2.01.

33. *See* BEDELL, CRIMINAL LAW 164 ("[D]eath by drowning, crocodile, or fire deprived the victim of a ritual burial in a country where preservation of the body was thought essential for an afterlife.") (footnote omitted). *See also Id.* at 166–167 (Referring to burning as a form of execution for criminals; but noting that there is no direct evidence of it in the Ramesside Period.) (Citing the Decree of Neferhotep and Papyrus Westcar.); *Id.* at 159–162 (Referring to the slight possibility that one tax collector drowned a man who could not pay. Thus, a very slight possibility exists that drowning could have been used as a means of execution in this circumstance. Bedell's also suggests that taking someone to the riverbank was a prelude to drowning as a means of execution. *See supra* § 4.03. McDowell, however, persuasively argues to the contrary. *See* MCDOWELL, JURISDICTION 219–223. *See also* BEDELL, CRIMINAL LAW 163–164 (Referring also to drowning in Egyptian mythology.); James Hoch and Sara E. Orel,

Kingdom stela (Cairo 20538) relates that a certain type of criminal (*i.e.*, executed by having "his corpse... thrown in the river") was also denied burial.[34]

[B] Incarceration

Although prisons existed,[35] they were usually used as means either for detaining suspects before trial or for holding convicted criminals while awaiting their sentences.[36] Even some smaller towns may have had prison facilities. The Egyptians ordinarily did not build prisons but rather used existing buildings for incarceration.[37] Criminals, for example, were routinely held in temples used to serve as makeshift prisons. Tomb robbers, for instance, were imprisoned in the temple of *Ma'at* on at least one occasion.[38] In Deir el-Medina, it is possible that persons suspected of theft were imprisoned at the *ḫtm*.[39] Nevertheless, because we have Middle Kingdom documents that list "escaped criminals" and a few that mention imprisonment as a punishment, it is possible that the ancient Egyptians used incarceration

Murder in Ancient Egypt, in DEATH AND TAXES IN THE ANCIENT NEAR EAST 87, 102–03 (Sara E. Orel ed., 1992)(Discussing the Demotic Literary Papyrus from Saqqâra (Text I), wherein "The punishment, proclaimed by Pharaoh, is death by burning."); *Id.* at 113.

34. David Lorton, *The Treatment of Criminals in Ancient Egypt*, 20 J. ECONOMIC & SOCIAL HIST. ORIENT 2, 14 (1977).

35. *See* David Lorton, *The Treatment of Criminals in Ancient Egypt*, 20 J. ECONOMIC & SOCIAL HIST. ORIENT 2, 63, n. 3 (1977) ("Arrest and imprisonment can be traced back to the 6th Dynasty....").

36. *See* MCDOWELL, JURISDICTION 23 ("P Leopold/Amherst 4, 11 records that the prisoners were locked up...'until Pharaoh our lord...(decides) their punishment.'") (footnote omitted). *See also* BEDELL, CRIMINAL LAW 82 (Referring to keeping an accused in prison "for an unlimited period."); *Id.* at 183 (Referring to prisons as holding pens: "Although prisons were utilized to detain suspects before and during their trial and until their sentence was executed, a term in prison was not a specific punishment."); *Id.* at 185 (same proposition); *Id.* at 184 ("Apparently suspects could be detained in prison for as long as the court wished."); BREASTED, HISTORY OF EGYPT 239–240 ("the southern vizier...maintained a criminal docket of prisoners awaiting trial or punishment....")(footnote omitted); *Id.* at 236 ("The punishment of condemned criminals was determined by him [*i.e.*, the pharaoh], the documents in the case being sent up to him for a decision while the victims awaited their fate in the dungeon.") (footnote omitted); ERMAN, LIFE IN ANCIENT EGYPT 133 (Explaining that the thieves who were involved in the Great Tomb Robberies trial under Ramses IX remained in the custody of the high priest of Amon and were held "in the prison of the temple....").

37. *See* BEDELL, CRIMINAL LAW 185–188.

38. *See Id.* at 78–79. *See also Id.* at 63 (Referring to incarceration.).

39. *See* MCDOWELL, JURISDICTION 100. *See also supra* § 3.03[C].

as a means of punishment on some, albeit limited, scale.[40] Also in support of the supposition that imprisonment could be a punishment in and of itself, it is useful to note that the prince Merikare (*c.* 2100 B.C.) was instructed to "punish by beating and imprisonment..." in an effort to maintain order.[41] There were also some instances where members of an escaped criminal's family were imprisoned either to substitute for the escapee or in cases where the crime involved was military desertion.[42] By the second century B.C., there is more solid evidence. Documents of that time specifically refer to taking convicted criminals to prison.[43]

§ 8.03 The Landscape of Egyptian Crime & Tort

One useful starting point for considering crime and tort is the well-known *Book of the Dead*. As has been mentioned,[44] by the New Kingdom, scribes routinely produced copies of the *Book of the Dead* on papyrus scrolls which were then placed alongside the corpse of a deceased individual at burial. The text of the *Book of the Dead* was a formulaic précis intended to persuade Osiris and the other judges of the Hereafter that the departed should be allowed to enter the blessed land of the West (*i.e.*, the afterlife). Although not as specific as a legal brief, the *Book of the Dead* pre-

---

40. *See* David Lorton, *The Treatment of Criminals in Ancient Egypt*, 20 J. ECONOMIC & SOCIAL HIST. ORIENT 2, 17 (1977); Janet H. Johnson, *The Legal Status of Women in Ancient Egypt, in* MISTRESS OF THE HOUSE MISTRESS OF HEAVEN: WOMEN IN ANCIENT EGYPT 175, 175–176 (Anne K. Chapel and Glenn E. Markoe eds., 1996).

41. T.G.H. JAMES, PHARAOH'S PEOPLE: SCENES FROM LIFE IN IMPERIAL EGYPT 73 (1984).

42. *See* David Lorton, *Legal and Social Institutions of Pharaonic Egypt, in* 1 CIVILIZATIONS OF THE ANCIENT NEAR EAST 345, 347 (Jack M. Sasson ed., 1995) ("We know of cases where the family of a criminal was imprisoned in a labor camp or was held hostage in an attempt to catch the fugitive from justice."); David Lorton, *The Treatment of Criminals in Ancient Egypt*, 20 J. ECONOMIC & SOCIAL HIST. ORIENT 2, 17, 37, 52 (1977); Janet H. Johnson, *The Legal Status of Women in Ancient Egypt, in* MISTRESS OF THE HOUSE MISTRESS OF HEAVEN: WOMEN IN ANCIENT EGYPT 175, 215, n. 8 (Anne K. Chapel and Glenn E. Markoe eds., 1996) ("When a prisoner escaped, family members were forced to serve in the escapee's place."); GAY ROBINS, WOMEN IN ANCIENT EGYPT 137–138.

43. *See* S. Allam, *Egyptian Law Courts in Pharaonic and Hellenistic Times*, 77 J. EGYPTIAN ARCHAEOLOGY 109, 120 (1991).

44. *See supra* § 4.03. *See also* GRIMAL, ANCIENT EGYPT 131 ("From the New Kingdom onwards funerary texts were also included in the bandages, fulfilling the same purpose as the amulets and jewels; a *Book of the Dead*, for instance was often inserted between the legs of the mummy.").

sents arguments on behalf of the deceased.[45] Perhaps because of its general nature, it is more like an attorney's trial summation than a pleading. In the *Book of the Dead*, the speaker—the deceased—claims to have lived an exemplary life and professes not to have done many, many different acts. Presumably, each act that the speaker claims not to have done represents conduct thought to be socially unacceptable: either a criminal or civil wrong (or both). Among those acts listed are the following: murder; conspiracy to commit murder; diminishing food in the temples; stealing the food offerings of the dead; adultery; "self-pollution in the pure precinct of... [the] city god;" misrepresenting the grain measure; misrepresenting measurements of length in commercial transactions; misrepresenting measurements of land in real estate transactions; misrepresenting weights in commercial transactions; stealing cattle; snaring sacred birds; catching fish in pools (*i.e.,* instead of from the river?); diverting water from a neighbor's property to one's own; withholding herds of the temple endowments; "interfer[ing] with god in his payments...." Many of the wrongs enumerated read like a list of crimes including: homicide; theft; making threats; inciting riot; falsehood; eavesdropping; adultery; "self-pollution"; blaspheming the gods; stealing from temples; and, killing sacred animals.[46]

In addition to the catalogue of wrongs identified in the *Book of the Dead*, there is independent evidence regarding a great deal of criminal conduct in ancient Egypt.[47] As regards "mainstream" or everyday criminal law, there were several aspects of the ancient Egyptian criminal law system that were similar to modern American law. For example, they seem to have established a police force[48] and, as was mentioned above, some kind of a prison

---

45. *See generally* THE BOOK OF THE DEAD: PAPYRI OF ANI, HUNEFER, ANHAI (1979) (Commentaries by Evelyn Rossiter); James Hoch and Sara E. Orel, *Murder in Ancient Egypt, in* DEATH AND TAXES IN THE ANCIENT NEAR EAST 87, 108–09 (Sara E. Orel ed., 1992). *See also supra* § 4.03.

46. *See* GRIMAL, ANCIENT EGYPT 151; BREASTED, DEVELOPMENT OF RELIGION AND THOUGHT 302–03; *Id.* at 173 (Explaining that in the Judgment of the Dead, the deceased pleads not guilty to forty-two "sins." "They may be summed up as murder, stealing, especially robbing minors, lying, deceit, false witness and slander, reviling, eaves-dropping, sexual impurity, adultery, and trespass against the gods or the dead as in blasphemy or stealing of mortuary offerings.").

47. *See* C.J. Eyre, *Crime and Adultery in Ancient Egypt*, 70 J. EGYPTIAN ARCHAEOLOGY 92, 93 (1984) (Eyre remarks that "Egyptian material does not provide evidence for the legal treatment of homicide and wounding, the most obvious of offences against the person.").

48. GARDINER, EGYPT OF THE PHARAOHS 224 (Describing the situation in Akhetaton, Gardiner says: "A captain of police was required to keep order in the city."); WILSON, CULTURE OF ANCIENT EGYPT 138 (Noting that as early as the Old Kingdom the government employed foreigners to serve as a police force.).

system.[49] The prisons do not appear to have been extensive, but there were buildings that functioned as prisons nonetheless.[50] Officials maintained criminal records.[51] And some laws created specific punishments that were mandatory for certain offenses. Criminal sanctions were available for wrongs as diverse as murder and infanticide, perjury,[52] "treachery," forgery,[53] and judicial misconduct (including bribery).

Conduct that contravened a royal edict was considered criminal. And initiating a lawsuit under false pretenses ("false litigation") was also a criminal act.[54] The penalty for this crime was 100 blows.[55] One text also mentions the possibility of the infliction of wounds in addition to the 100 blows. In the Salt Papyrus 124 we learn of a lawsuit alleging a variety of claims that we today would consider criminal. One of the Deir el-Medina workmen accused a foreman of: 1) robbing both royal tombs and temples; 2) assigning government laborers to work on his personal ventures; 3) physically abusing workers; and, 4) sexual misconduct that encompassed either rape or adultery (or perhaps both). Unfortunately, we do not have the portion of the papyrus that reveals the outcome of the case, but the accused appears to have evaded punishment.[56] In another enigmatic case (Papyrus Deir el-Medina 27), a workman accused of rape (or adultery) merely swears some sort of oath but it is his accuser who is punished with 100 blows for having brought the complaint in the first place.[57] In addition, we also have extensive accounts of several extraordinary criminal trials; trials where special commissions were formed. In these extraordinary criminal

---

49. *See supra* § 8.02[B].

50. *See* GARDINER, EGYPT OF THE PHARAOHS 119 (Gardiner discusses a stela of Waḥ-ʿnkh (an 11th Dynasty king) who says "that he captured the whole of Abydos territory and opened up all its prisons.").

51. *See* Aristide Théodorides, *The Concept of Law in Ancient Egypt, in* THE LEGACY OF EGYPT 291, 309 (J.R. Harris ed., 2d ed. 1971).

52. *See* David Lorton, *The Treatment of Criminals in Ancient Egypt*, 20 J. ECONOMIC & SOCIAL HIST. ORIENT 2, 7 (1977); *See also* BEDELL, CRIMINAL LAW 125–127 (Referring to punishment for perjury.). *See also supra* § 4.05[B].

53. *See* David Lorton, *Legal and Social Institutions of Pharaonic Egypt, in* 1 CIVILIZATIONS OF THE ANCIENT NEAR EAST 345, 347 (Jack M. Sasson ed., 1995).

54. *See* David Lorton, *The Treatment of Criminals in Ancient Egypt*, 20 J. ECONOMIC & SOCIAL HIST. ORIENT 2, 11, 41 (1977).

55. *See Id.* at 24, 41.

56. *See Id.* at 38–41. *See also* James Hoch and Sara E. Orel, *Murder in Ancient Egypt, in* DEATH AND TAXES IN THE ANCIENT NEAR EAST 87, 96–97 (Sara E. Orel ed., 1992).

57. *See* Janet H. Johnson, *The Legal Status of Women in Ancient Egypt, in* MISTRESS OF THE HOUSE MISTRESS OF HEAVEN: WOMEN IN ANCIENT EGYPT 175, 179 (Anne K. Chapel and Glenn E. Markoe eds., 1996).

trials, special procedures were established for certain high crimes such as treason and robbery of royal tombs.[58] Among the particular wrongs for which we have more extensive evidence are the following: theft/conversion; conspiracy/treason and homicide; certain kinds of sexual conduct; judicial misconduct; and, extortion.

§ 8.04 Theft/Conversion

[A] General

The account of a man named Weni[59] furnishes textual proof from the 6th Dynasty (*c.* 2460–2200 B.C.) that the State was prepared to intervene in matters where theft was concerned. Weni says that he was sent "to prevent any one of them (i.e. the army) from taking bread or sandals from a wayfarer, to prevent any one of them from taking a loin-cloth from any village, to prevent any one of them from taking any goat from any people."[60] There were many problems with theft in ancient Egypt in general[61] and at Deir el-Medina in particular.[62] The term used for "theft" in our documents from Deir el-Medina is usually *'t3wt*.[63] The Deir el-Medina *ḳnbt* handled two especially curious criminal cases involving theft. In one (Ostracon Nash 1), a woman named *Ḥri3* was initially accused of stealing a copper chisel. According to the testimony in the case, this act alone (*i.e.*, stealing a copper object) was considered an "abomination" (*bwt*).[64] When the court ordered

58. *See supra* § 4.06.
59. *See supra* § 3.03[D], note 80 and accompanying text.
60. GARDINER, EGYPT OF THE PHARAOHS 96.
61. *See* BEDELL, CRIMINAL LAW 25 (Referring to the Great Tomb Robberies, Bedell states that the pharaoh "did retain the right to make the final decision."). *See also Id.* at 28–29 (Referring to a woman who "made large thefts from the great stable of Pharaoh."); *Id.* at 6 (Referring to a temple theft from Elephantine.); MCDOWELL, JURISDICTION 222 (Referring to a non-Deir el-Medina case of embezzlement from a storehouse.); GRIMAL, ANCIENT EGYPT 287.
62. *See* MCDOWELL, JURISDICTION 134, 227–228, 248–249 (Referring to the numerous thefts in Deir el-Medina.). *See also Id.* at 210 (Referring to embezzlement: "borrowing a chisel from the official stores".); *Id.* (Referring to having workers work on a superior's own projects.); *Id.* at 217 (Referring to embezzlement.).
63. *See Id.* at 38; FAULKNER, A CONCISE DICTIONARY OF MIDDLE EGYPTIAN 303 (Defining *'t3wt* as "theft"; and, incidentally, citing its use in *The Eloquent Peasant* as an illustration.).
64. *See* MCDOWELL, JURISDICTION 156. *See also* BEDELL, CRIMINAL LAW 64 (Referring to the theft of copper objects having been "a crime punishable by death."); Janet H. Johnson, *The Legal Status of Women in Ancient Egypt*, *in* MISTRESS OF THE

a search of *Ḥri3*'s home, they discovered, in addition to the missing copper chisel, a censer of the god Amon (it had been stolen too). This was notable because the censer was property that the State owned. It may have been because State-owned property was involved that three scribes of the vizier *and* the police chief were all on the panel of judges that heard this case.[65] There is a second case (Ostracon Nash 2) involving chisel theft in Deir el-Medina, but in that case the chisels themselves were State-owned (*i.e.*, "belonged to Pharaoh").[66] We know that the court conducted a thorough investigation into the matter, but we do not know how the case was resolved.[67] Interestingly, Horemhab's Edict contains several obscure provisions relating to theft of crops (a certain kind of herb, corn, flax, and vegetables).[68]

As a rule, a convicted thief had to return stolen goods to the individual to whom they belonged, and, in addition, pay damages to the victim of double or triple (the cases vary) the value of the stolen goods (what modern law might call "punitive damages").[69] In some cases of theft, damages

---

HOUSE MISTRESS OF HEAVEN: WOMEN IN ANCIENT EGYPT 175, 179 (Anne K. Chapel and Glenn E. Markoe eds., 1996).

65. *See* MCDOWELL, JURISDICTION 156 (According to McDowell, this was "an exceptionally high-powered *ḳnbt*...."). *See also Id.* at 159 (Noting that the *ḳnbt* adjudicated a few isolated cases dealing with criminal law—mostly theft.); BEDELL. CRIMINAL LAW 14–15 (Referring to the case of *Ḥri3* and the stolen chisels.).

66. *See See* MCDOWELL, JURISDICTION at 157. *See also* Janet H. Johnson, *The Legal Status of Women in Ancient Egypt, in* MISTRESS OF THE HOUSE MISTRESS OF HEAVEN: WOMEN IN ANCIENT EGYPT 175, 179 (Anne K. Chapel and Glenn E. Markoe eds., 1996). The defendant's perjury may have been significant. For more on perjury as a crime, *see* David Lorton, *The Treatment of Criminals in Ancient Egypt*, 20 J. ECONOMIC & SOCIAL HIST. ORIENT 2, 7, 44 (1977); *supra* §4.05[B].

67. *See* MCDOWELL, JURISDICTION 157.

68. *See Id.* at 264.

69. *See Id.* at 230 (McDowell cites Černý for the proposition that the normal punishment for theft was to return the stolen goods and to pay, in addition, two or three times the value of the objects stolen: "[W]e have the material collected by Černý to demonstrate that the thief had to return the stolen property and pay an additional penalty of two or three times its value.") (footnote omitted); *Id.* at 231 ("[T]heft was at least sometimes punished with a two- or three-fold penalty, though we still cannot say who imposed that penalty."); *Id.* at 233 (Referring to three or four times penalty for theft.); *Id.* at 29 (Explaining that, in many cases, the penalty for theft was to pay either two or three times the value of the object that was stolen.). *See also* Jaraslav Černý, *Restitution of, and Penalty Attaching to, Stolen Property in Ramesside Times*, 23 J. EGYPTIAN ARCHAEOLOGY 186, 189 (1937) ("A convicted thief was obliged to give the stolen property back to the person robbed, and in addition to pay him a penalty which amounted to double or treble its value."); David Lorton, *The Treatment of Criminals in Ancient Egypt*, 20 J. ECONOMIC & SOCIAL HIST. ORIENT 2, 47 (1977) ("[T]heft from a private person was considered a civil wrong, and...a guilty party was required to return the stolen object, and in ad-

were three or four times the value of the stolen object(s).[70] If, on the other hand, the thief had stolen from the State rather than from a private individual, his penalties were far more severe: usually eighty to one hundred-times the value of objects stolen from the State.[71] In a few texts, the same term used for theft, *'t3wt*, is also used to describe the "fine" that a thief had to pay.[72] In one Deir el-Medina theft case (Ostracon Turin 57455), imprisonment was used as a penalty for theft. Apparently, this was a more serious theft than the sort for which a defendant was ordered merely to return the goods and pay an additional two to three-times the value of the stolen goods.[73] For robbery of a *royal* tomb, the penalty was death.[74] Neither the status of the thief nor the status of the victim appears to have been relevant in fixing penalties for theft. Thieves received the same punishments regardless of their social standing.[75] Furthermore, it appears that Egyptian law did not consider the mere *purchase* of stolen goods as a particularly serious offense. The court was, however, keenly interested in securing the return of the things stolen.[76]

The Nauri Decree of Seti I (*c.* 1294–1279 B.C.) imposed ear and nose amputation plus forced labor as punishments both for direct and indirect

---

dition, to pay a penalty of two or three times its value."); David Lorton, *Legal and Social Institutions of Pharaonic Egypt, in* 1 CIVILIZATIONS OF THE ANCIENT NEAR EAST 345, 358 (Jack M. Sasson ed., 1995); C.J. Eyre, *Crime and Adultery in Ancient Egypt*, 70 J. EGYPTIAN ARCHAEOLOGY 92, 93 (1984); BEDELL, CRIMINAL LAW 180–183 (Explaining that, for conversion, Egyptian law required that the tortfeasor pay two or three times the value of the converted property as damages.). It should be noted that scholars disagree as to whether the converter/thief was required to return the stolen property in addition to paying the double or triple damages/fine. Bedell, for example, argues that there was no return of converted property. *See* BEDELL, CRIMINAL LAW 68, 182.

70. *See* MCDOWELL, JURISDICTION 138.

71. *See* David Lorton, *The Treatment of Criminals in Ancient Egypt*, 20 J. ECONOMIC & SOCIAL HIST. ORIENT 2, 47 (1977). *See also* BEDELL, CRIMINAL LAW 176 ("In one case of theft from a state institution a fine was assessed at a certain amount times the value of the item stolen.").

72. *See* MCDOWELL, JURISDICTION 29; R.O. FAULKNER, A CONCISE DICTIONARY OF MIDDLE EGYPTIAN 232 (Referring to a *'t3wt* as "a fine" in certain contexts.).

73. *See* MCDOWELL, JURISDICTION 231–233 (Referring to one text recording prison as the penalty for theft.).

74. *See* David Lorton, *The Treatment of Criminals in Ancient Egypt*, 20 J. ECONOMIC & SOCIAL HIST. ORIENT 2, 31–33 (1977). *See also infra* § 8.04[B].

75. *See* David Lorton, *The Treatment of Criminals in Ancient Egypt*, 20 J. ECONOMIC & SOCIAL HIST. ORIENT 2, 47–48 ("[T]he fact that the penalties were the same for the slave-woman and the free man suggests that Egyptian law did not recognize the respective status of the two parties involved as a criterion for fixing the penalty, as was the case in the Asiatic systems.") (footnote omitted).

76. *See* BEDELL, CRIMINAL LAW 172.

forms of theft: 1) stealing an animal of the estate (an offense to sacred animals);[77] and, 2) moving a boundary marker of the god's estate (an offense to sacred real property).[78] In addition, the thief's family suffered penal servitude on the estate as part of the punishment.[79] Other minor offenses that resulted in a loss of production on the estate (*i.e.*, other indirect kinds of theft) were punished by a specific number of blows (typically 200 or 100), "pierced wounds" (typically five), and forced labor.[80] Also, in the Nauri Decree, one theft crime imposed death as its penalty when a person entrusted with an animal sacred to Osiris allowed it to be offered to a different god or gave it away.[81] Independent evidence shows that theft of a

---

77. *See* William F. Edgerton, *The Nauri Decree of Seti I: A Translation and Analysis of the Legal Portion*, 6 J. NEAR EASTERN STUD. 219, 224 (1947).

78. *See Id.* at 223.

79. *See Id.* at 224. *See also* BEDELL, CRIMINAL LAW 173; WILSON, CULTURE OF ANCIENT EGYPT 241 (Noting that those who shifted the boundaries of the fields belonging to the religious foundation at Abydos had their ears and noses chopped off as punishment.). For more on the Nauri Decree of Seti I, *see* T.G.H. JAMES, PHARAOH'S PEOPLE: SCENES FROM LIFE IN IMPERIAL EGYPT 80–82 (1984).

80. *See* William F. Edgerton, *The Nauri Decree of Seti I: A Translation and Analysis of the Legal Portion*, 6 J. NEAR EASTERN STUD. 219, 223–227 (1947); BEDELL, CRIMINAL LAW 178. Wilson summarizes a portion of the Nauri Decree as follows:

> Anyone who arbitrarily and illegally took away one of the foundation's herdsmen, so that a loss of cattle resulted, was punished by two hundred blows and the exaction from him of the lost cattle at a rate one hundred to one. Any herdsman who disposed of the foundation's cattle to his profit, was impaled upon a stake, his wife, children, and all his property were confiscated by the foundation, and the cattle had to be returned by the purchaser at the rate of one hundred to one.

WILSON, CULTURE OF ANCIENT EGYPT 241.

See also BEDELL, CRIMINAL LAW 6 (Referring to the Nauri Decree and the death penalty.); *Id.* at 22 (Referring to the punishments imposed by the Nauri Decree: mutilation, impalement, family sent to forced servitude.); David Lorton, *The Treatment of Criminals in Ancient Egypt*, 20 J. ECONOMIC & SOCIAL HIST. ORIENT 2, 25–27 (1977); WILSON, CULTURE OF ANCIENT EGYPT 242 ("Why are the decrees of Horemhab and Seti I so much harsher in punishment than...earlier acts? Why do they add cruel physical abuse and the repayment of property in high proportion on top of the earlier removal from office and confiscation of property? It would seem that the word of the king no longer had the same effectiveness in maintaining order; pharaoh was no longer respected and feared as he had been in the more sacred state of earlier times. Now a harsh and impersonal law had to take the place of the older discipline which had been based upon the acceptance of the rule of a god-king."). On Horemhab's punishments, *see also Id.* at 238.

81. *See* William F. Edgerton, *The Nauri Decree of Seti I: A Translation and Analysis of the Legal Portion*, 6 J. NEAR EASTERN STUD. 219, 224 (1947). *See also* BEDELL, CRIMINAL LAW 151; *Id.* at 148 ("In at least some instances theft of property belonging to Pharaoh or one of the numerous Egyptian divinities was also a crime punishable by death.") (Citing British Museum Ostracon 5631.).

State-owned ox could be punished by exile.[82] Under Horemhab's Edict, a soldier who stole hides from citizens received, as punishment, "one hundred blows, opening five wounds and taking away the hides which he took."[83]

[B] The Great Tomb Robberies

The most celebrated robbery trial—indeed these are often referred to as "the Great Tomb Robberies"—occurred during the reign of Ramses IX (*c.* 1125–1107 b.c.).[84] Papyrus Abbott describes this infamous lawsuit and offers what is perhaps the most vivid narrative of criminal law in ancient Egypt.[85] The State instigated charges against a group accused of robbing

---

82. *See* Bedell, Criminal Law 174.

83. Breasted, History of Egypt 404 (footnote omitted). *See also* David Lorton, *The Treatment of Criminals in Ancient Egypt*, 20 J. Economic & Social Hist. Orient 2, 25–27 (1977); Wilson, Culture of Ancient Egypt 237 (Wilson describes Horemhab's edict as "not a code of law, but rather a series of police regulations directed against specific malpractices and also a reorganization of the administrative machinery in the land, in order to control future abuses."); Gardiner, Egypt of the Pharaohs 244–45 (Gardiner describes Horemhab's penalties for theft as follows: "The penalties imposed were of great severity, the malefactors in the worst cases being docked of their noses and banished to the fortress town of Tjel on the Asiatic boarder, and in the lesser cases punished with a hundred strokes and five open wounds."); McDowell, Jurisdiction 158 (Referring to blows as a type of punishment.).

84. *See* Grimal, Ancient Egypt 289 ("The robberies took place in the sixteenth year of Ramesses IX's reign."). *See generally Id.* at 289–290.

85. For an overview of the Great Tomb Robberies, *see generally* McDowell, Jurisdiction 189–200. In particular, *see Id.* at 194 (McDowell reconstructs the sequence of events relating to the investigation of the Great Tomb Robberies as follows: "[T]he events are recorded in the order that they occurred, namely: 1) examination of the thieves; 2) taking the thieves to the Necropolis by the vizier and butler on day 19; 3) report of the investigation sent to Pharaoh; 4) handing over of the thieves to the High Priest of Amon at the *ḳnbt*-session for imprisonment pending Pharaoh's instructions."). *See also* David Lorton, *The Treatment of Criminals in Ancient Egypt*, 20 J. Economic & Social Hist. Orient 2, 30–37 (1977); Bedell, Criminal Law 5–6 (Referring to the Great Tomb Robberies under Ramses IX and tomb robbery trials under Ramses XI.); James Hoch and Sara E. Orel, *Murder in Ancient Egypt, in* Death and Taxes in the Ancient Near East 87, 108 (Sara E. Orel ed., 1992); Jacke Phillips, *Tomb-robbers and their Booty in Ancient Egypt, in* Death and Taxes in the Ancient Near East 157, 161 (Sara E. Orel ed., 1992); Gardiner, Egypt of the Pharaohs 300–301; Grimal, Ancient Egypt 90 (Grimal says: "Eventually the affair was taken to the vizier himself, in the form of a criminal trial."); *Id.* ("Most of the seventeen guilty persons were sentenced to be impaled."); *Id.* at 188, 206, 289–290; Wilson, Culture of Ancient Egypt 282–287; Breasted, History of Egypt 510.

tombs in Thebes.[86] The court was comprised of "the superintendent of the town and governor" and he was "assisted by two other high officials, the *scribe* and the *speaker* of Pharaoh...."[87] These three "sent out a commission of inquiry" (police officers, scribes, priests, and others) to inspect the tombs. This was really a special task force created to investigate the facts of this extraordinary case.[88] Upon investigation, they discovered that, of the ten *royal* tombs that they feared had been broken into, only one had, in fact, been entered.[89] One defendant, named Amenpnefer "admitted that he and his gang rifled the tomb and burned the mummies of king Sekhemre-shed-taui, 'Son of Re,' Sebkemsaf and Queen Nubkhaas."[90] But the robbers had also penetrated several private tombs, and they had ransacked the mummies in order to snatch the jewelry contained in the wrappings.[91] The task force sent its written report to the three judges assigned to the case.[92] The authorities apprehended eight suspects, most of whom were servants in the temple of Amon. They were "examined" by beating them on their hands and feet with sticks. Upon being tortured in this manner, they confessed that they had broken into the burial chamber.[93] After having confessed, they were compelled to identify the scene of their crime.[94] While the thieves were held in the temple of Amon, the judges then sent a written report to Ramses concerning their investigation.[95] It was Ramses who then pronounced the sentence for the guilty robbers.[96] Quite clearly, execution—

---

86. *See* David Lorton, *The Treatment of Criminals in Ancient Egypt*, 20 J. ECONOMIC & SOCIAL HIST. ORIENT 2, 30–37 (1977); ERMAN, LIFE IN ANCIENT EGYPT 130.

87. ERMAN, LIFE IN ANCIENT EGYPT 131.

88. *See* MCDOWELL, JURISDICTION 190; ERMAN, LIFE IN ANCIENT EGYPT 131. *See also supra* § 4.06.

89. *See* MCDOWELL, JURISDICTION 190; ERMAN, LIFE IN ANCIENT EGYPT 132.

90. BEDELL, CRIMINAL LAW 25 (footnote omitted). *See* Jacke Phillips, *Tomb-robbers and their Booty in Ancient Egypt, in* DEATH AND TAXES IN THE ANCIENT NEAR EAST 157, 158 (Sara E. Orel ed., 1992).

91. *See* MCDOWELL, JURISDICTION 192 (Referring to the fact that both royal and private tombs were involved in the Great Tomb Robberies.); ERMAN, LIFE IN ANCIENT EGYPT 132. For more on the types of loot that tomb robbers preferred, *see* Jacke Phillips, *Tomb-robbers and their Booty in Ancient Egypt, in* DEATH AND TAXES IN THE ANCIENT NEAR EAST 157, 163–65 (Sara E. Orel ed., 1992).

92. ERMAN, LIFE IN ANCIENT EGYPT 132.

93. *See* MCDOWELL, JURISDICTION 190 (Referring to the imprisonment of suspects.); ERMAN, LIFE IN ANCIENT EGYPT 132. On the torture of suspects and witnesses, *see supra* § 4.05[B].

94. ERMAN, LIFE IN ANCIENT EGYPT 133.

95. *See* MCDOWELL, JURISDICTION 192; *Id.* at 196 (Explaining that at one point some thieves seem to have been kept at "the granary of the temple of Maʿat.").

96. *See* David Lorton, *The Treatment of Criminals in Ancient Egypt*, 20 J. ECONOMIC & SOCIAL HIST. ORIENT 2, 32 (1977); J. Capart, A.H. Gardiner, and B. van de

apparently by impalement—was the customary penalty for robbing royal tombs.[97]

Additional evidence soon came to light suggesting that thieves had entered other tombs in the section of the necropolis nearest the tombs of the royal relatives. But upon further inspection, it appeared that none had really been pilfered. And in order to dispel rumors, government officials did their best to inform the public that the tombs had not been robbed. One official, who did not care for the overseer of the necropolis, still smelled a rat, and thought that there had been a cover-up. Consequently, he told others that he was prepared to share his suspicions with the Pharaoh. The overseer of the necropolis sent a letter to the governor in an effort to forestall the other official.[98] At this point, in the wake of these threats and squabbling among officials, the whole affair seems to have ended. Thieves continued to loot tombs in the ensuing years. For example, during the first year of Ramses X (*c.* 1107–1098 B.C.), officials made nearly sixty arrests for tomb robbery.[99] Robbers made their way into the outer chambers of the tombs of Ramses II and Seti I, and later sold the valuables that they had stolen.[100] Thefts continued unabated and officials ultimately gathered the mummies of the most renowned pharaohs and hid them together in one place in an effort to conceal the bodies (at least) of the deceased kings from the rapacious bandits of the necropolis. Luckily for modern scholars, that hiding place at Deir el-Bahri went undiscovered until the late nineteenth century A.D. Thus, indirectly, the thievery of ancient tomb robbers caused the royal mummies of

---

Walle, *New Light on the Ramesside Tomb-Robberies*, 22 J. EGYPTIAN ARCHAEOLOGY 169, 190 (1936); MCDOWELL, JURISDICTION 242 (Referring to the pharaoh as approving the punishments in the Great Tomb Robberies.); ERMAN, LIFE IN ANCIENT EGYPT 133; BEDELL, CRIMINAL LAW 147–148 (Bedell states that the pharaoh made the ultimate decision about sentencing tomb robbers.). *See also supra* §§3.03[B], 3.04, 4.06, §8.02[A], notes 22–25 and accompanying text.

97. *See* David Lorton, *The Treatment of Criminals in Ancient Egypt*, 20 J. ECONOMIC & SOCIAL HIST. ORIENT 2, 31–33 (1977); BEDELL, CRIMINAL LAW 146 (Noting that the death penalty was common for "serious offenses against the state, such as an attempt against the life of Pharaoh or theft of property belonging to a god." "It is clear that tomb robbery was included in this group...."); *See Id.* at 191 ("Only the most serious crimes, such as tomb robbery, were punishable by death, and the method of execution was probably impaling."); Jacke Phillips, *Tomb-robbers and their Booty in Ancient Egypt, in* DEATH AND TAXES IN THE ANCIENT NEAR EAST 157, 160 (Sara E. Orel ed., 1992) ("their ultimate fate probably would be execution or some form of mutilation.") (footnote omitted).

98. *See* ERMAN, LIFE IN ANCIENT EGYPT 133–35.

99. *See Id.* at 137 ("[I]n the first year of Ramses X., about sixty arrests were made of persons supposed to be thieves.") (footnote omitted).

100. *See Id.*

the New Kingdom to be preserved. When Gaston Maspero finally discovered the cache of royal mummies in 1881, museum officials were able to collect them and transfer them to the Cairo Museum.[101]

[C] International (The Report of Wenamun)

One especially interesting glimpse of theft as a crime in an international context comes from the late 20th Dynasty report of Wenamun (*c.* 1100 B.C.).[102] Wenamun sailed from Egypt to the land of Dor. Someone on Wenamun's ship stole a number of valuables from him. When he reported the theft to the local prince, the prince replied that, if the thief had been from his country, he would have replaced the stolen articles for him from his storehouse; at least until the thief was found. As matters stood, however, the prince told Wenamun: "But in fact the thief who robbed you, he is yours, he belongs to your ship. Spend a few days here with me, that I may search for him."[103]

From this exchange, it is apparent that the local prince would have been willing to make restitution to Wenamun from the State treasury if the thief had been from Dor.[104] Since, however, the thief was another Egyptian on Wenamun's ship—and thus the dispute was actually between two Egyptians—the prince of Dor was unable to do anything for Wenamun beyond helping him try to locate the thief. Thus, the fact that the thief was not a local affected the extent of the legal remedy that the prince was willing to offer. But it does seem significant that the prince at least offers to help Wenamun locate the thief.

---

101. *See* Breasted, History of Egypt 525–26 (Breasted recounts the concealment of the New Kingdom pharaohs and modern discovery.); Jacke Phillips, *Tombrobbers and their Booty in Ancient Egypt, in* Death and Taxes in the Ancient Near East 157, 167 (Sara E. Orel ed., 1992). *See also* Grimal, Ancient Egypt 190, 200, 268, 291 (Mentioning also Loret's excavation in 1898 of Amenhotep II's tomb containing the royal mummies of other 18th and 19th Dynasty pharaohs.).

102. *See* James Hoch and Sara E. Orel, *Murder in Ancient Egypt, in* Death and Taxes in the Ancient Near East 87, 102 (Sara E. Orel ed., 1992).

103. Gardiner, Egypt of the Pharaohs 307 (Gardiner's translation).

104. *Cf.* Laws of Hammurabi ¶23: "If the robber should not be seized, the man who has been robbed shall establish the extent of his lost property before god; and the city and the governor in whose territory and district the robbery was committed shall replace his lost property to him". Martha T. Roth, Law Collections from Mesopotamia and Asia Minor 85 (1995).

§ 8.05 Conspiracy/Treason & Homicide

Records of two ancient conspiracy trials—conspiracies to assassinate an Egyptian king—have survived: one from the 6th Dynasty (*c.* 2460–2200 B.C.) and the other from the 19th (*c.* 1295–1188 B.C.). This type of crime necessitated extraordinary procedures, not merely the judicial machinery of routine criminal operations.[105] In each case the plot to assassinate the king originated in the royal harem. In each case the king desired to distance himself from the decision making process. Interestingly, apart from these two cases relating to political assassinations, there is precious little evidence regarding ordinary murder or homicide. As was mentioned above,[106] the *Book of the Dead* indicates that the Egyptians treated homicide as wrongful conduct. McDowell suggests that one text (Ostracon Deir el-Medina 126) could refer to a murder. But she admits that there is really not much on which to rely.[107] Nevertheless, we have no texts relating to a murder trial from the Ramesside Period.[108] Bedell bluntly asserts: "We do not know how murder was treated in this period."[109] A 21st Dynasty (*c.* 1069–945 B.C.) stela (the obscure Stela of Banishment) shows that the Egyptians punished murder with the death penalty.[110] Hoch and Orel note both that "[t]here is an apparent lack of evidence concerning murder (as distinct from simple homicide) in ancient Egypt"[111] and that "there is no comprehensive discussion... of what constituted murder in that society."[112] Nevertheless, there were specific terms used for murder: *sm3 m nf* (Middle Egyptian) and *'hḏb m grg* (Late Egyptian).[113] "Both phrases may be translated as 'to kill wrongfully.'"[114] As near as we can tell, the ancient Egyptians considered homicide as murder if it was wrongful or unjustifiable. They did not, necessarily, focus on the issue of premeditation as a determining factor.[115] But according to Diodorus Siculus ancient Egyptian law under the Ptolemies (c.

105. *See supra* § 4.06.
106. *See supra* § 8.03.
107. *See* MCDOWELL, JURISDICTION 225–226.
108. *See* BEDELL, CRIMINAL LAW 179.
109. *Id.* at 143–143a.
110. *See Id.* at 179 (Citing J.H. BREASTED, ANCIENT RECORDS OF EGYPT, IV, no. 658, p.320.); James Hoch and Sara E. Orel, *Murder in Ancient Egypt, in* DEATH AND TAXES IN THE ANCIENT NEAR EAST 87, 91 (Sara E. Orel ed., 1992).
111. *See* James Hoch and Sara E. Orel, *Murder in Ancient Egypt, in* DEATH AND TAXES IN THE ANCIENT NEAR EAST 87 (Sara E. Orel ed., 1992).
112. *Id.* at 88.
113. *See Id.* at 92.
114. *Id.*
115. *Id.*

304–30 B.C.) appreciated the difference between premeditated and unpremeditated murder.[116]

When the royal harem hatched a plot to assassinate King Pepi I in the 6th Dynasty (*c.* 2325 B.C.), Pepi immediately appointed an individual named Weni to act alone as a special prosecutor to hear evidence and to issue a written report of his findings. According to Weni's first-person account, this was the first time that a person had been specially appointed to hear a matter of such significance:[117]

> When there was litigation in private in the king's harem against the Queen, His Majesty caused me to go to hear (the matter) alone without there being any vizier or any other official there, only myself alone, because of my excellence and of my being firmly planted in the heart of His Majesty, and because His Majesty had confidence in me. It was I who put it in writing alone with one magistrate, though my rank was that of an Overseer of the tenants of the Palace. Never before had the like of me heard a secret matter of the king's harem, but His Majesty caused me to hear it, because I was excellent in the heart of His Majesty beyond any official of his, beyond any noble of his, beyond any servant of his.[118]

We know more details of a similar conspiracy that occurred during the reign of Ramses III (*c.* 1186–1154 B.C.).[119] As soon as the scheme was uncovered, Ramses appointed a special commission to investigate. In doing so, Ramses admonished this ad hoc council to take great care to exercise exacting impartiality. He wished to ensure that justice would be served—not merely vengeance.[120] Ramses selected fourteen members for this special investigatory

---

116. *See* BEDELL, CRIMINAL LAW 179 (Citing Diodorus Siculus I,77,6.).

117. *See* GARDINER, EGYPT OF THE PHARAOHS 94–95 ("So quickly did he win the confidence of the king that he was next appointed a judge, in which capacity he was called upon, as sole assessor of the vizier, to hear cases of conspiracy that had arisen in the royal harem and the Six Great Houses."); GRIMAL, ANCIENT EGYPT 82–83.

118. GARDINER, EGYPT OF THE PHARAOHS 95. *See* GRIMAL, ANCIENT EGYPT 82–83. *See also supra* §§ 3.03[D], 4.06.

119. *See* GRIMAL, ANCIENT EGYPT 275–276; David Lorton, *The Treatment of Criminals in Ancient Egypt*, 20 J. ECONOMIC & SOCIAL HIST. ORIENT 2, 28–30 (1977); BREASTED, HISTORY OF EGYPT 498–500; WILSON, CULTURE OF ANCIENT EGYPT 267–69; GARDINER, EGYPT OF THE PHARAOHS 289–292; BEDELL, CRIMINAL LAW 175; James Hoch and Sara E. Orel, *Murder in Ancient Egypt, in* DEATH AND TAXES IN THE ANCIENT NEAR EAST 87, 120–21 (Sara E. Orel ed., 1992). *See also supra* §§ 3.03[D], 4.06.

120. *See* BREASTED, HISTORY OF EGYPT 499 ("The old Pharaoh... appointed a special court for the trial of the conspirators." His charge to the court "lay upon the judges a responsibility for impartial justice on the merits of the case, with a judicial objectivity which is remarkable in one who held the lives of the accused in his unchal-

commission. When two of the judges and several other court officials were found to have "caroused with" some of the accused harem women, they were immediately tried and found guilty of judicial misconduct.[121] A third judge was accused but was acquitted. The guilty were punished by having their ears and noses cut off. One of the convicted judges immediately committed suicide after having endured his gruesome punishment. The trials of the conspirators proceeded. Each conspirator (including those who merely *knew about* the conspiracy)—thirty-two people in all—received the death penalty.[122]

In the cases involving treason, it appears that the pharaoh usually—if not exclusively—made the ultimate decision whether to impose the death penalty.[123] In the courts at Deir el-Medina, for example, the local judges routinely referred "the death penalty and other penalties for high treason" to the king.[124] As was just noted, in the famous harem conspiracy trial under Ramses III, the guilty were executed.[125] The defendants who were part of the royal family were permitted to commit suicide.[126] This is our only evidence for convicted criminals being allowed to commit suicide rather than being executed by other means. Those allowed to take their own lives probably had a higher social standing than the others who were executed.[127] Clearly, as a serious malfeasance against the State, conspiracy to assassinate the monarch was always punished by death.[128]

---

lenged power and had himself just been the victim of a murderous assault at their hands." Among the charges, Ramses III reminded the court: "Give heed and have a care lest ye execute punishment upon [anyone] unjustly....") (Breasted's brackets).

121. *See infra* § 8.07.

122. *See* David Lorton, *Legal and Social Institutions of Pharaonic Egypt*, *in* 1 Civilizations of the Ancient Near East 345, 356 (Jack M. Sasson ed., 1995) ("Those with knowledge of the assassination attempt against Ramesses (Ramses) III were executed or forced to commit suicide, the same penalties suffered by the actual conspirators."); Breasted, History of Egypt 500 ("Immediately following the execution of the sentence, one of the unfortunate judges committed suicide. The trials of the conspirators continued with regularity, and from the records of three different prosecutions, we are able to trace the conviction of thirty two officials of all ranks including the unhappy young pretender himself....") (footnotes omitted).

123. *See* McDowell, Jurisdiction 27, 242–243; *Id.* at 243 ("There is... not yet sufficient evidence to refute the theory that Pharaoh alone could order executions.").

124. David Lorton, *Legal and Social Institutions of Pharaonic Egypt*, *in* 1 Civilizations of the Ancient Near East 345, 356 (Jack M. Sasson ed., 1995).

125. *See* Bedell, Criminal Law 23.

126. Janet H. Johnson, *The Legal Status of Women in Ancient Egypt*, *in* Mistress of the House Mistress of Heaven: Women in Ancient Egypt 175, 176 (Anne K. Chapel and Glenn E. Markoe eds., 1996).

127. *See* Bedell, Criminal Law 167–169.

128. *See Id.* at 146 (Noting that the death penalty was common for "serious offenses against the state, such as an attempt against the life of Pharaoh or theft of property belonging to a god.").

We also know of a case involving treason of a somewhat different sort. A priest (Tety) of the temple of the god Min about 1630 B.C. allowed a traitor to stay in the temple. Tety was expelled from his position at the temple, and his heirs were expelled forever.[129]

§ 8.06 Sexual Conduct: Homosexuality; Prostitution; Rape; Adultery

Homosexual relations between consenting partners was not subject to legal sanctions in ancient Egypt.[130] Similarly, there is very little evidence relating to any criminalization of prostitution.[131] In addition, unmarried, consenting adults were free to have sex with one another (at least legally speaking).[132] Both rape and adultery, on the other hand, were considered wrongful conduct.[133] Johnson explains, however, that it is difficult to distinguish rape from adultery in Egyptian law: "In the cases we have, we cannot be certain whether the woman was a willing participant or not—that is, whether it was a case of rape or adultery."[134] It is possible that the Egyptians

---

129. *See* David Lorton, *The Treatment of Criminals in Ancient Egypt*, 20 J. ECONOMIC & SOCIAL HIST. ORIENT 2, 18–23 (1977); David Lorton, *Legal and Social Institutions of Pharaonic Egypt*, *in* 1 CIVILIZATIONS OF THE ANCIENT NEAR EAST 345, 346 (Jack M. Sasson ed., 1995).

130. *See* S. Allam, *Legal Aspects in the 'Contendings of Horus and Seth'*, *in* STUDIES IN PHARAONIC RELIGION AND SOCIETY IN HONOUR OF J. GWYN GRIFFITHS 137, 141 (Alan B. Lloyd ed., 1992) (According to Allam, "it would appear that homosexuality was not considered a punishable offence, provided that it was practised with mutual consent and without using any violence.").

131. *See* C.J. Eyre, *Crime and Adultery in Ancient Egypt*, 70 J. EGYPTIAN ARCHAEOLOGY 92, 96 (1984) ("[A]ctual evidence for prostitution in the New Kingdom is slight."); C.J. Eyre, *The Adoption Papyrus in Social Context*, 78 J. EGYPTIAN ARCHAEOLOGY 207, 211–212 (1992).

132. *See* Janet H. Johnson, *The Legal Status of Women in Ancient Egypt*, *in* MISTRESS OF THE HOUSE MISTRESS OF HEAVEN: WOMEN IN ANCIENT EGYPT 175, 216, n. 47 (Anne K. Chapel and Glenn E. Markoe eds., 1996) ("Apparently there were no strictures against sex between 'consenting adults' as long as neither was married to someone else, and it was as offensive for a married man to have sex outside marriage as for a married woman."); C.J. Eyre, *Crime and Adultery in Ancient Egypt*, 70 J. EGYPTIAN ARCHAEOLOGY 92, 95 (1984) ("It may thus be presumed that copulation with an unmarried and willing woman was of relatively neutral implication socially and legally, at least for the man.").

133. *See* David Lorton, *The Treatment of Criminals in Ancient Egypt*, 20 J. ECONOMIC & SOCIAL HIST. ORIENT 2, 38 (1977).

134. Janet H. Johnson, *The Legal Status of Women in Ancient Egypt*, *in* MISTRESS OF THE HOUSE MISTRESS OF HEAVEN: WOMEN IN ANCIENT EGYPT 175, 216, n. 47

treated adultery not as an issue for courts to deal with but rather as a family law matter—something that a husband and wife had to resolve privately.[135] The Deir el-Medina documents contain some examples of oaths taken by women, proclaiming their innocence to charges of adultery.[136] In one such declaration from a much later period (*i.e.,* Ptolemaic or, perhaps, even Roman) a wife declares: "I did not have any extramarital intercourse, I have had no intercourse with anybody, since I was married to you...."[137] Recall also that the *Book of the Dead* specifically states: "I did not commit adultery."[138] Divorce was the most likely consequence of adultery.[139] And, if the wife was guilty of adultery, she forfeited to her husband her one-third share of their marital property, her *šp*, and any dowry.[140]

The Middle Kingdom story, *King Cheops and the Magicians* (Papyrus Westcar), provides a fictional account of adultery. In the second tale in the narrative, a man named Webaoner discovers that his wife has been committing adultery on a routine basis with a townsman. Without a trial of any sort, Webaoner summons a magical crocodile to attack the townsman. The crocodile snatches the adulterous townsman and descends to the bottom of a lake for seven days. In the meanwhile, Webaoner brings King Nebka for assistance.[141] The king, upon hearing the facts of the adultery, instructs the

---

(Anne K. Chapel and Glenn E. Markoe eds., 1996). *See* McDOWELL, JURISDICTION 210 (Referring to "a possible case of rape.").

135. *See* David Lorton, *Legal and Social Institutions of Pharaonic Egypt, in* 1 CIVILIZATIONS OF THE ANCIENT NEAR EAST 345, 358 (Jack M. Sasson ed., 1995); C.J. Eyre, *Crime and Adultery in Ancient Egypt,* 70 J. EGYPTIAN ARCHAEOLOGY 92, 102 (1984) ("cases of adultery should have been matters for the injured husband to pursue as best he could, within the limits of public order."). *See also supra* § 6.03 regarding the relationship between adultery and divorce.

136. *See* McDOWELL, JURISDICTION 67 (Referring to the adultery case of a young man who found his wife in bed with Mry-sẖmt but was beaten by the *srw*. The foreman referred to the beating as "a great outrage".). *See also Id.* at 155–156; 170; *Id.* at 208 (Referring to another case of adultery—a man who allegedly "slept with three married women...." Here McDowell states: "Adultery does not even seem to have been a punishable offense....") (footnote omitted); *Id.* at 210 (Referring to "the possibility that adultery was criminal under some circumstances."); BEDELL, CRIMINAL LAW 74 (Referring to the adultery/rape case of Peneb.).

137. PESTMAN, MARRIAGE & MATRIMONIAL PROPERTY 56.

138. BREASTED, DEVELOPMENT OF RELIGION AND THOUGHT 300. *See also supra* § 8.03.

139. *See* C.J. Eyre, *Crime and Adultery in Ancient Egypt,* 70 J. EGYPTIAN ARCHAEOLOGY 92, 98 (1984); PESTMAN, MARRIAGE & MATRIMONIAL PROPERTY 55–56; McDOWELL, JURISDICTION 35–36.

140. *See supra* §§ 6.02—6.03.

141. *See* GRIMAL, ANCIENT EGYPT 63 (According to Grimal, "there are reasonable grounds for suggesting that the first 3rd Dynasty king would actually have been Nebka, who is mentioned in Papyrus Westcar.").

crocodile to take the body of the townsman away.[142] Thus, the king expressly approves the way that Webaoner handled the situation. This story seems to imply, then, that under Egyptian law, a husband had the right to kill an adulterer whom he discovered with his wife.[143] As for Webaoner's adulteress wife, the king ordered that she be burned alive. In fact, the king, himself, apparently acted as the executioner: "His [Majesty the King of Upper] and Lower Egypt, Nebka, the vindicated, had the wife of Webaoner taken to a plot north of the capital, and he set / fire to her [...in] the river."[144] This suggests (although it is unlikely) that capital punishment—in this case, death by burning—could have been the penalty for a woman who committed adultery.[145] In fact, Eyre concludes:

> [A]n adulterer who was effectively caught in the act might expect to be killed by the enraged husband or his circle on the spur of the moment. Such action is, of course, tolerated quite widely in societies

---

142. *See* SIMPSON, THE LITERATURE OF ANCIENT EGYPT 18. It is unlikely that the townsman was still alive after the crocodile had had its way with him for seven days "in the [lake without] breathing." *Id.* This is, however, consistent with what Erman says about the role of the king in criminal law: "In these cases also the sentence was not always pronounced by the court. It sufficed for the court to declare the guilt of the prisoner, to 'find him guilty'; the deed was then sent to the Pharaoh, and it was left for him to decide what punishment should be inflicted." ERMAN, LIFE IN ANCIENT EGYPT 141 (footnotes omitted).

143. *But see* David Lorton, *Legal and Social Institutions of Pharaonic Egypt, in* 1 CIVILIZATIONS OF THE ANCIENT NEAR EAST 345, 358 (Jack M. Sasson ed., 1995) ("While literary texts intimate that a jealous husband might kill his wife and the other man, the 'real life' texts...do not suggest that such acts of vengeance were the norm....").

144. SIMPSON, THE LITERATURE OF ANCIENT EGYPT 18.

145. *But see* David Lorton, *The Treatment of Criminals in Ancient Egypt*, 20 J. ECONOMIC & SOCIAL HIST. ORIENT 2, 15 (1977) ("we need see here no more than a reference to branding...or, perhaps less likely, torture."). *See* JON MANCHIP WHITE, EVERYDAY LIFE IN ANCIENT EGYPT 167 (In discussing criminal punishments, White, quite obviously referring to these punishments from the story, *Cheops and the Magicians*, remarks: "There is little evidence that the more startling punishments—*burning women for adultery, or throwing traitors to the crocodiles*—were often carried out.") (emphasis added). *See also* SIMPSON, THE LITERATURE OF ANCIENT EGYPT 166, who says:

In *The Maxims of Ptahhotpe*, Ptahhotpe advises his son:

> If you desire to preserve friendship in a home into which you enter, whether as lord or as brother or as friend, at any place into which you enter, beware of approaching the women, / for no good comes to a place where this is done, nor is it clever to reveal them; a thousand men are turned aside from what is good for them. A little moment, the semblance of a dream, and death reaches you because of knowing them.(footnote omitted).

For a good general discussion of *The Maxims of Ptahhotpe*, *see* Georges Posener, *Literature, in* THE LEGACY OF EGYPT 220, 226–27 (J.R. Harris ed., 2d ed. 1971).

> where adultery is not otherwise punished severely, if at all, just as it is often permissible to kill a thief caught in the act, when otherwise the punishment for theft would not be particularly severe.[146]

Still, one must remember that the example of Webaoner is fictional.[147] Other evidence suggests that "such acts of vengeance" for adultery were *not* common.[148] The later account of the Greek historian Diodorus reports that Egyptian law punished a man convicted of rape by castration; and that a man found guilty of adultery was punished by a thousand lashes, while an adulteress had her nose amputated.[149]

§ 8.07 Judicial Misconduct

Judicial misconduct was especially problematic. During the reign of Horemhab (*c.* 1323–1295 B.C.) at the close of the 18th Dynasty, the Pharaoh made judicial bribery a capital offense, with a mandatory death penalty.[150] In the case of the harem conspiracy during the reign of Ramses III (*c.* 1186–1154 B.C.),[151] several judges were arrested for becoming friendly with a number of the defendants. As punishment, their ears and noses were cut off.[152]

---

146. C.J. Eyre, *Crime and Adultery in Ancient Egypt*, 70 J. EGYPTIAN ARCHAEOLOGY 92, 102 (1984) (footnotes omitted). *See* James Hoch and Sara E. Orel, *Murder in Ancient Egypt, in* DEATH AND TAXES IN THE ANCIENT NEAR EAST 87, 89 (Sara E. Orel ed., 1992) ("In ancient Egypt a revenge homicide committed by a cuckolded husband was apparently considered justifiable."); *Id.* at 90.

147. *See* C.J. Eyre, *Crime and Adultery in Ancient Egypt*, 70 J. EGYPTIAN ARCHAEOLOGY 92, 97 (1984) ("The literary norm in Egypt was that adultery resulted in death.").

148. David Lorton, *Legal and Social Institutions of Pharaonic Egypt, in* 1 CIVILIZATIONS OF THE ANCIENT NEAR EAST 345, 358 (Jack M. Sasson ed., 1995).

149. *See* C.J. Eyre, *Crime and Adultery in Ancient Egypt*, 70 J. EGYPTIAN ARCHAEOLOGY 92, 96 (1984).

150. *See* BREASTED, HISTORY OF EGYPT 405 ("But he went still further; while organizing the local courts throughout the land he passed a most stringent law against the acceptance of any bribe by a member of a local court or 'council'....") (footnote omitted); *Id.* at 406 (In fact he made accepting a judicial bribe a capital offense: "Behold my majesty has done this to improve the laws of Egypt."). *See also* GARDINER, EGYPT OF THE PHARAOHS 296; *supra* § 3.05.

151. *See supra* §§ 3.03[D], 4.06, and 8.05.

152. *See supra* § 8.05. *See also* Janet H. Johnson, *The Legal Status of Women in Ancient Egypt, in* MISTRESS OF THE HOUSE MISTRESS OF HEAVEN: WOMEN IN ANCIENT EGYPT 175, 215, n. 12 (Anne K. Chapel and Glenn E. Markoe eds., 1996) (Explaining that three members of the six-person subcommittee were arrested because they were becoming friendly with the harem women.); ERMAN, LIFE IN ANCIENT EGYPT 144

§ 8.08 Extortion by Officials & Tax Collectors

The Egyptian government developed an extensive system for collecting taxes.[153] As part of that process, the government prohibited tax collectors from overcharging the taxpayers, and made tax extortion a criminal offense. Clearly there were tax collectors who, on occasion, overcharged taxpayers, and kept more than their legitimate share. The law provided criminal penalties for tax extortion of this sort. In particular, Thutmose III (*c.* 1479–1425 B.C.) and Horemhab (*c.* 1323–1295 B.C.) (both 18th Dynasty pharaohs) are credited with taking exceptional measures to crack down on dishonest tax collectors.[154] Horemhab, for example, was struggling to reassert pharaonic authority in the wake of the relative laissez-faire laxity that had existed under Akhenaton (*c.* 1352–1348 B.C.). During the reign of Akhenaton, local government officials had become rapacious. They were enriching themselves at the expense of the citizens in their communities. Thus, when Horemhab became king, he took steps to punish the corrupt local officials. In his Edict, Horemhab promulgated a series of laws designed to thwart specific misconduct.[155] Remarkably, according to the Edict, when a commoner attempted but failed to deliver goods ("dues") by boat to the pharaoh, he was excused without consequence if the failure was due to theft or other loss beyond his control. If, for example, an official or a member of the military prevented the commoner's delivery, the wrongdoer's (*i.e.*, the official's or military man's) punishment was severe: his nose was cut off and he was banished to Tjel (a remote military town on the

("[T]heir punishment was fulfilled by cutting off their noses and ears."); Bedell, Criminal Law 31 ("[T]hree judges, a police chief, and an officer of the infantry were found guilty of carousing with some of the guilty harem women and probably taking a bribe."); *Id.* at 32 (Noting that the guilty judges were punished by dismissal and mutilation (their ears and noses were amputated), and that one judge committed suicide in the wake of his conviction.); *Id.* at 171 (Referring to several of the judges in the harem conspiracy "carousing with" some of the defendants, and being punished by amputation of their ears and noses.).

153. *See supra* § 5.04[B].

154. *See* Breasted, History of Egypt 320 (Breasted refers to Thutmose III as having "crushed the extortionate tax-gatherer."). *See also Id.* at 309.

155. *See* Kurt Pflüger, *The Edict of Horemhab*, 5 J. Near Eastern Stud. 260 (1944); David Lorton, *The Treatment of Criminals in Ancient Egypt*, 20 J. Economic & Social Hist. Orient 2, 24–25 (1977); Bedell, Criminal Law 12 (Referring to the decrees of pharaohs (such as Horemhab and Seti I), Bedell states: "These decrees contained criminal statutes for certain crimes against a particular estate of a god."); T.G.H. James, Pharaoh's People: Scenes From Life in Imperial Egypt 81–82 (1984). *See also supra* §§ 1.01, 3.03[B], 3.05, 8.02[A], 8.04[A], and 8.07.

eastern edge of the empire).[156] If a soldier looted a taxpayer's farm and stole his hides, the taxpayer was excused and the soldier was punished "by inflicting upon him a hundred blows, causing five open wounds, and taking from him the hide which he has seized as (being) something that has been unlawfully acquired."[157]

§ 8.09 Miscellaneous Wrongs

[A] Battery

In modern American law, battery is intentional harmful or offensive contact with another. A few texts suggest that ancient Egyptian law also regarded such conduct as a wrong worthy of punishment. One document (Papyrus Geneva MAH 15274 verso III), for example, records that a man who struck three others on the head was punished.[158] There are a few other cases in which a person was accused of conduct that we today would char-

---

156. *See* Kurt Pflüger, *The Edict of Horemhab*, 5 J. NEAR EASTERN STUD. 260, 261 (1944) (The penalty mandated in Horemhab's law was twofold: the guilty had his nose cut off and he was banished to a remote location in the Arabian desert.). *See also supra* §§ 1.01, 3.03[B], 3.05, 8.02[A], 8.04[A], and 8.07; BREASTED, HISTORY OF EGYPT 404–405 (The severing of one's ears and nose was known as a punishment for tax extortion, and the extortionate tax collector was also banished to the Arabian desert.).

157. Kurt Pflüger, *The Edict of Horemhab*, 5 J. NEAR EASTERN STUD. 260, 263 (1944) (footnote omitted). *See also* BREASTED, HISTORY OF EGYPT 404 (According to Breasted: "they [*i.e.*, the provisions in Horemhab's Edict] were all directed against the practice of extortion upon the poor by fiscal and administrative officials. The penalties were severe. A tax collector found guilty of thus practising upon the poor man was sentenced to have his nose cut off, followed by banishment to Tharu, the desolate frontier city far out in the sands of the Arabian desert toward Asia.") (footnote omitted); *Id.* at 405 ("For the collection of all the various produce of the land by the different departments of the treasury, laws were framed to prevent robbery and extortion on the part of the officials. In the introduction and application of the new laws Horemhab went personally from end to end of the kingdom.") (footnote omitted).

158. *See* MCDOWELL, JURISDICTION 187 (McDowell refers to this conduct as "assault." I prefer to use the technical term "battery" as it is used in the American law of torts (*i.e.*, intentional harmful or offensive contact with another's person). On this distinction *see infra* § 8.10, notes 171 and 173. *See also* MCDOWELL, JURISDICTION 210 (Referring to another possible case of battery ("attacking workmen").).

acterize as battery. In one case (Papyrus Salt 124 2, 17), the wrongdoer (who beat nine different men) received a beating himself as punishment. And in two other instances, including the case of the man who hit three others on the head mentioned above (Papyrus Geneva MAH 15274 verso III and Papyrus Turin 1977), the batterers were punished by forced labor (cutting stone and "compulsory labor" (*h3yt*)).[159] Given the nature of the consequences, this conduct seems to have been dealt with as if it were criminal rather than tortious—since there is no mention of compensatory payment, but rather, only corporal punishment.

[B] Trespass to Land

One case recorded on a papyrus suggests that Egyptian law (at least in Deir el-Medina) recognized the legal theory of trespass to land.[160]

[C] Trespass to Chattels/Vandalism (Criminal Mischief)

One case from Deir el-Medina (RAD 57, 8-58, 6) involves conduct that is analogous to what we might be tempted to call either trespass to chattels (in a civil law context) or vandalism—or criminal mischief (in a criminal law context). A workman named Pn-ʿnḳt reports "that two workmen... stripped the boulder on top of the tomb of Ramesses II...."[161] Another possible reference to what modern law would consider trespass to chattels, vandalism, or criminal mischief involved a man named P3-nb who was accused of "urinating in a private tomb".[162]

---

159. *See* MCDOWELL, JURISDICTION 226–227. *See also Id.* at 218–219 (Referring to the possibility of battery (Again McDowell says "assault") as a wrong that could be dealt with as a criminal matter—but there is not much hard evidence. In fact, this particular instance is probably merely the fabrication of Christophe.); *Id.* at 233 (Referring to battery and "compulsory labor or beatings" constituting the penalty for battery.); James Hoch and Sara E. Orel, *Murder in Ancient Egypt, in* DEATH AND TAXES IN THE ANCIENT NEAR EAST 87, 96–97 (Sara E. Orel ed., 1992); GRIMAL, ANCIENT EGYPT 287.

160. *See* MCDOWELL, JURISDICTION 129 (Citing Papyrus Berlin 10496.); *Id.* at 156 (Also citing Papyrus Berlin 10496, McDowell comments that in this case "the court was seen to uphold the rights to a tomb granted by an oracle three years earlier."); *Id.* at 228 (Referring to breaking and entering.).

161. *See Id.* at 208.

162. *See Id.* at 210; *Id.* at 228.

[D] Defamation

Egyptian law had a cause of action for some form of defamation, but we know very little regarding the particulars. In one Deir el-Medina case (Ostracon Cairo 25556), a foreman named *Ḥ3y* complained that a woman and several workmen had slandered him.[163] According to *Ḥ3y*, the defendants said that he had cursed or insulted Seti I (*c.* 1294–1279 B.C.), the reigning pharaoh.[164] Those found guilty of this defamation received a beating as punishment (100 blows).[165] The facts recorded in this case do, however, suggest that truth could be an effective defense in defamation cases; for it was only after the defendants admitted that their statements about the plaintiff were false that the defendants were found guilty.[166] After the defendants admitted that they had committed perjury, the judges demanded that they take an oath that invoked mutilation (*i.e.*, amputation of nose and ears) if they repeated their defamatory allegations. What is interesting here is that they were not punished with mutilation for their initial perjury. Rather, the court threatened that punishment only if they lied again![167] In another case (Papyrus Deir el-Medina 26 A) that appears to have involved defamation, a foreman named *Ḫnsw* alleged that one of his men had cursed someone (or perhaps something). The defamer was punished with 100 blows of a stick.[168]

---

163. *See Id.* at 152; David Lorton, *The Treatment of Criminals in Ancient Egypt*, 20 J. Economic & Social Hist. Orient 2, 42 (1977) (Citing Ostracon Cairo 25556.).

164. *See* McDowell, Jurisdiction 175 (In McDowell's words, he had "cursed the reigning king."); Bedell, Criminal Law 71 (According to Bedell, the accusation was that "He said insults against Seti.") (footnote omitted).

165. *See* McDowell, Jurisdiction 156.

166. *See Id.* at 160 ("[T]he foreman Ḥ3y accuses three men and a woman of slandering him, and under questioning these at first vacillate, then admit that stories they had exchanged about Ḥ3y were groundless. For that they get a sound thrashing."). *See also* Bedell, Criminal Law 87 ("their accusations had been false".); *Id.* at 118 ("the judges discovered that the accuser and his witnesses had lied...."); *Id.* at 138 (Noting that "the accusers admitted that they were lying."). This theory regarding the role of truth in the substantive Egyptian law of defamation is mine, not McDowell's or Bedell's. To be sure, this conclusion may simply be an example of my having fallen prey to a *post hoc ergo propter hoc* fallacy, but I'm willing to take a slight risk here given the facts of this case and the surrounding context.

167. *See* Bedell, Criminal Law 138.

168. *See* McDowell, Jurisdiction 176–177.

§8.10 Crime & Tort in *The Tale of the Eloquent Peasant*

The Tale of the Eloquent Peasant offers an interesting literary perspective on criminal and tort law in ancient Egypt.[169] Both principal characters, Khunanup and Nemtynakhte, act in ways that today could (potentially) be considered criminal or tortious. Nemtynakhte's barrier of cloth across the road may constitute something like a public nuisance.[170] His beating of Khunanup could be considered battery.[171] His taking of Khunanup's asses might constitute theft, trespass to chattels, or conversion.[172] And Nemtynakhte's threat to kill the peasant (after he complained about the beating

---

169. *See supra* § 1.02 for a summary of the tale.

170. A public nuisance is an unreasonable interference with a right common to the general public. *See generally* RESTATEMENT (SECOND) OF TORTS §821B (1979). That a property owner is not privileged to obstruct a public way adjacent to his property has been recognized for a long time. In ancient Roman law, the *actio de posito et suspenso* (literally "an action concerning that which has been placed and that which has been hung") made property owners strictly liable for damage caused by objects, such as signs, that endangered travellers. *See* J.A.C. THOMAS, TEXTBOOK OF ROMAN LAW 378–379 (1976).

171. Today,

> An actor is subject to liability to another for battery if (a) he acts intending to cause a harmful or offensive contact with the person of the other or a third person, or an imminent apprehension of such a contact, and (b) a harmful contact with the person of the other directly or indirectly results.

RESTATEMENT (SECOND) OF TORTS §13 (1979). *See also* W. PAGE KEETON ET AL., PROSSER AND KEETON ON THE LAW OF TORTS §9, at 39–42 (5th ed. 1984).

172. The difference between the torts of trespass to chattels and conversion is basically one of degree. A person converts another's property when she intentionally interferes with the property of another in such a manner that the property is rendered useless or valueless to the owner. Simple theft is usually deemed conversion. When a defendant exercises substantial dominion and control over another's property, she converts it. If the defendant's interference with the plaintiff's property is not especially serious (or falls short of substantial dominion and control), that interference is considered trespass to chattels. Generally, damages for conversion are the value of the chattel at the time of conversion (plus interest). Damages for trespass to chattel are actual damage to the property. *See generally* RESTATEMENT (SECOND) OF TORTS §§216–244 (1979). Nemtynakhte's intent is quite plain from the text: "Now this Nemtynakhte said, when he saw the asses of this peasant, which were pleasing to his heart: O that I had some potent idol, that I might steal this peasant's goods from him!" SIMPSON, THE LITERATURE OF ANCIENT EGYPT 32. As regards the degree of dominion and control that Nemtynakhte exercised, we note that he took Khunanup's asses and apparently had no intention of returning them to Khunanup: "Thereupon, he took a rod of green tamarisk-wood to him and belabored all his limbs with it; he took away his asses and drove them to his estate." *Id.* at 33.

and the theft) could be either assault or intentional infliction of emotional harm.[173] For his part, Khunanup may be liable for either conversion or trespass to chattels[174] for the damage that his donkey did to the Nemtynakhte's barley.

Undoubtedly, however, neither Nemtynakhte nor Khunanup analyzed their conflict in terms like these. Rather, Nemtynakhte apparently assumed that he, as the one in possession of realty, had the right to block the "public road" adjacent to the land that he possessed and, thereby, to force the peasant to choose among: 1) driving his herd into the river; 2) trespassing upon the barley field; or, 3) damaging the garment that he used to block the road.[175] Furthermore, in addition to believing that he could legally force the peasant into such a decision, Nemtynakhte evidently believed

---

173. The general standards today are:

> (1) An actor is subject to liability to another for assault if (a) he acts intending to cause a harmful or offensive contact with the person of the other or a third person, or an imminent apprehension of such a contact, and (b) the other is thereby put in such imminent apprehension. (2) An action which is not done with the intention stated in Subsection (1, a) does not make the actor liable to the other for an apprehension caused thereby although the act involves an unreasonable risk of causing it and, therefore, would be negligent or reckless if the risk threatened bodily harm.

RESTATEMENT (SECOND) OF TORTS §21 (1979). *See also* W. PAGE KEETON ET AL., PROSSER AND KEETON ON THE LAW OF TORTS § 10, at 43–46 (5th ed. 1984).

> (1) One who by extreme and outrageous conduct intentionally or recklessly causes severe emotional distress to another is subject to liability for such emotional distress, and if bodily harm to the other results from it, for such bodily harm. (2) Where such conduct is directed at a third person, the actor is subject to liability if he intentionally or recklessly causes severe emotional distress.

RESTATEMENT (SECOND) OF TORTS §46 (1979). *See also* W. PAGE KEETON ET AL., PROSSER AND KEETON ON THE LAW OF TORTS § 12, at 54–66 (5th ed. 1984). "The peasant/ wept very much at the pain of what had been done to him, and Nemtynakhte said: Do not raise your voice, peasant; look you are on your way to the city of the Lord of Silence!" SIMPSON, THE LITERATURE OF ANCIENT EGYPT 33 (footnote omitted).

174. *See supra* §§ 8.04 and 8.09[C].

175. Such damage would either be trespass to chattels or conversion under modern American tort principles. *See supra* §§ 8.04 and 8.09[C]. Assuming that the entire herd would have trampled the garment, perhaps the damage to the garment would have been sufficiently extensive to constitute conversion. *See also* Nili Shupak, *A New Source For the Study of the Judiciary and Law of Ancient Egypt: "The Tale of the Eloquent Peasant"*, 51 J. NEAR E. STUD. 1, 6–8 (1992) (Discussing the magical significance of Nemtynakhte's conduct with his garment.); *Id.* at 8 (Shupak says, in addition: "By spreading his garment on the public way, Nemty-nakht was indicating to the peasant that this section of the road was his private property, and no one could trespass. He was indeed wrong in trying to appropriate a public road, but the peasant, realizing the significance of the official's act, neither touched nor trod on the garment.").

that *he* was the party wronged when Khunanup's donkey took a bite of barley, and he argued that the appropriate measure of damages was payment of the donkey.[176]

Since Khunanup ultimately wins his case against Nemtynakhte, it may be reasonable to conclude that ancient Egyptian law considered Nemtynakhte liable and acquitted Khunanup.[177] Possibly, Egyptian law, like modern American tort law, provided Khunanup with a defense of "necessity."[178] Prosser cites necessity as a defense in cases "permitt[ing] a traveler on a public highway to turn out to avoid a temporary obstruction, and pass over the adjoining land."[179] If the necessity were deemed "public" (and arguably since the road was public it could be considered a "public necessity"), necessity would be a complete defense for Khunanup. If the necessity were deemed private, Khunanup would only be liable for—as he argues—actual damages (*i.e.*, the cost of the barley actually eaten) but not for the trespass.[180]

On the other hand (again assuming for the sake of discussion that Egyptian law was analogous, at least partially, to modern American tort principles), Nemtynakhte might have argued that Khunanup should have been liable for his donkey's damage on a theory of strict liability for damage caused by domesticated animals.[181] However, strict liability of this nature in modern law is generally excused when damage is "done by animals straying onto abutting land while driven on the highway; or . . . brought about by the . . . intentional, reckless or negligent conduct of a third person."[182] To be sure, this principle seems applicable since quite plainly it was Nemtynakhte's conduct that caused Khunanup's donkey to enter the barley field.

---

176. Nili Shupak, *A New Source For the Study of the Judiciary and Law of Ancient Egypt: "The Tale of the Eloquent Peasant"*, 51 J. NEAR E. STUD. 1, 8 (1992) (Shupak suggests that Nemtynakhte confiscation of Khunanup's ass was as "surety for payment of a debt.").

177. *See* GRIMAL, ANCIENT EGYPT 148–149 (Grimal makes inconsistent statements about the Peasant. First he says that the conduct of the Peasant's donkey makes it so that "Nemtynakht[e] is then *legally* empowered to seize the donkey and all of the goods that it is carrying." Then, when he concludes his discussion, he characterizes the king's disposition of the case as right: "[T]he justice of his cause is recognized by the king, who recompenses him with the goods of the dishonest steward." Logically, both statements cannot be correct.).

178. *See* W. PAGE KEETON ET AL., PROSSER AND KEETON ON THE LAW OF TORTS § 24, at 146 (5th ed. 1984).

179. *Id.*

180. *See Id.* § 24, at 146–148.

181. *See* RESTATEMENT (SECOND) TORTS § 504 (1979), "Liability for Trespass by Livestock."

182. *Id.*

Indeed, Khunanup's argument certainly sounds more appealing to the contemporary sense of remedies. He contended that he owed Nemtynakhte only the value of barley eaten.[183] Khunanup seems not to have intended any harm whatsoever. Thus, this is hardly a situation that would justify an award of anything like punitive damages (*i.e.*, anything beyond the actual diminution in value to Nemtynakhte's wisp of barley).[184]

When Rensi first contacts the king to relate to him the account of Khunanup's pleas, he already believes the truth of Khunanup's allegations. He comes right out and says to the king: "I have found one of these peasants who is really eloquent; *his goods have been stolen*, and see, he has come to appeal to me about it."[185]

When Khunanup wins his case, the remedy for all of Nemtynakhte's wrongs is payment of everything he owns.[186] Although this may seem severe, it may not be very far out of line either with punishment in ancient Egypt (where forfeiture of property was not uncommon as a penalty) or with many damage awards given in tort litigation today for that matter. For indeed, if he were liable for public nuisance, conversion, assault, battery, and intentional infliction of emotional harm, damages today could run in the millions of dollars. It is unfortunate for legal scholars that Rensi fails to articulate any legal analysis to explain how he reached his decision that Nemtynakhte was liable to Khunanup. It is equally unfortunate that he fails to reveal how he arrived at the measure of damages.[187]

---

183. *See* SIMPSON, THE LITERATURE OF ANCIENT EGYPT 33 (The Peasant argues: "one (wisp only) has been damaged. It is for its (the wisp's) price that I will buy back my ass if you take possession of it/ for a (mere) filling of its mouth with a wisp of barley."). Khunanup immediately recognized that Nemtynakhte might carry out his threat to take away the donkey in retaliation for its having taken a bite of barley. Nevertheless, he believed that he would have the right to buy back the donkey for the value of one bite of barley. Although the mechanics of such a remedy may sound strange and cumbersome (Defendant's animal damages Plaintiff's crop; Plaintiff seizes Defendant's animal; Defendant buys back his animal at a price equal to the value of damage done to Plaintiff's crop.), the outcome would simply be that the defendant would end up paying the plaintiff the value of the damage to the plaintiff's crop.

184. *See generally* W. PAGE KEETON ET AL., PROSSER AND KEETON ON THE LAW OF TORTS § 2, at 9–15 (5th ed. 1984).

185. SIMPSON, THE LITERATURE OF ANCIENT EGYPT 35 (emphasis added). *See supra* § 8.04.

186. *See supra* § 8.02 regarding forfeiture of property as a form of punishment in ancient Egypt.

187. *See* Nili Shupak, *A New Source For the Study of the Judiciary and Law of Ancient Egypt: "The Tale of the Eloquent Peasant"*, 51 J. NEAR E. STUD. 1, 13 (1992) (Shupak, however, does explain that the verb *'db3* ("recompense" or "compensation") is an ancient Egyptian technical legal term. He notes that "Rensi's advisors thought that the

The text does, however, suggest a plausible defense for Nemtynakhte. When Rensi, the High Steward, confers with the *srw*, the other magistrates, regarding this case, they submit to him that Nemtynakhte was probably privileged to act as he did: "Surely it is a peasant of his who has gone to someone else beside him. That is what they do to peasants of theirs who go to others beside them. That is what they do."[188] Lichtheim comments that "[t]he magistrates exculpate Nemtynakht[e] by surmising that the peasant was a serf of his who had tried to do business with another landlord and was being punished for it."[189] The magistrates make it sound as though it is customary for landlords to beat peasant-serfs and take their possessions when the peasant-serfs attempt to "go to others besides themselves."[190] Therefore, the legal analysis which explains why Nemtynakhte's conduct is justifiable and why Khunanup should be denied recovery is rather simple. If such pummelings and confiscations were both customary and legal in the Middle Kingdom, then Nemtynakhte apparently would have been entitled to do just what he did, *if Khunanup had been his peasant-serf.*[191] The facts, nonetheless, make it highly unlikely that Khunanup was a peasant-serf of Nemtynakhte. Khunanup and Nemtynakhte lived very far apart from each other—too far for a master-serf relationship to have been feasible. The first sentence of the tale indicates that Khunanup lived with his wife in the Wadi Natrun.[192] Furthermore, the facts of the story also tell us that "the peasant traveled south to Ninsu," a distance of approximately 100 miles.[193] Thus, factually, the magistrates' attempt at ratiocination cannot withstand scrutiny. Nevertheless, the magistrates continue their counsel and advise Rensi that, under these circumstances (*i.e.*, assuming that Khunanup is Nemtynakhte's peasant-serf who has tried to go to work with an-

---

avaricious official should give compensation (*'d̲b3*) to the peasant for his property."). *See also* Faulkner, A Concise Dictionary of Middle Egyptian 321 (Defining *'d̲b3* as "make repayment").

188. Lichtheim, Ancient Egyptian Literature 171.

189. *Id.* at 183, n.9.

190. Simpson, The Literature of Ancient Egypt 34. *See also infra* § 10.04.

191. This concept is analogous to the modern American tort defense of the privilege of "discipline." *See* W. Page Keeton et al., Prosser and Keeton on the Law of Torts § 27, at 157–159 (5th ed. 1984).

192. *See* Simpson, The Literature of Ancient Egypt 31 ("There once was a man called Khunanup, who was a peasant of the Wadi Natrun, and he had a wife named [Maryet].").

193. *Id.* at 32. *See also Id.* at n. 3 (In the footnote, Faulkner, the translator of this story in Simpson's anthology, explains that Ninsu was "Herakleopolis in Middle Egypt."). For a measure of the distance from the Wadi Natrun to Herakleopolis, *see* Gardiner, Egypt of the Pharaohs 29 (map and scale of miles).

other landlord), Nemtynakhte should not be punished: "Is it a case for punishing Nemtynakhte on account of a trifle of natron and a trifle of salt?"[194] Rather, they suggest that he simply be ordered to return the goods: "If he be commanded to replace them, he will replace them."[195] Their suggested remedy, that is, to exact no punishment but merely order Nemtynakhte to return the goods (*i.e.*, simple restitution), may tell us something about ancient Egyptian remedies and punishments. To the extent that Nemtynakhte's transgressions are tortious, the magistrates' suggestion recommends incomplete compensatory damages—merely returning the property taken. This remedy, however, does not contemplate any compensation for Khunanup's physical or mental pain and suffering. Their recommendation that Nemtynakhte not be punished also, *ipso facto*, suggests that he not be assessed punitive damages.

To the extent that Rensi considers the case of Khunanup and Nemtynakhte as a criminal case, the magistrates recommend extreme clemency: merely a return of stolen property but no fines or corporal punishment.[196] The list of Nemtynakhte's crimes is at least as long as the list of his torts. The physical abuse that he inflicts upon Khunanup would be considered criminal assault and battery in most modern jurisdictions,[197] and his confiscation of Khunanup's property would be robbery.[198]

Given the numerous crimes that he committed, Nemtynakhte's punishment does not necessarily seem excessive when compared to other accounts of criminal penalties in ancient Egypt (*e.g.*, torture, mutilation, exile, forfeiture of property, forced labor, and heavy fines).

---

194. Simpson, The Literature of Ancient Egypt 34 (Evidently, the "trifle of natron" and "trifle of salt" refer to Khunanup's goods that Nemtynakhte took away.).

195. *Id.*

196. Such clemency contrasts with the harsh punishments inflicted upon other criminals in the New Kingdom; such as death and amputation. *See supra* § 8.02. Lenience is also inconsistent with the ideal expressed in *The Man Who Was Tired of Life* where it is hoped that the future king will be someone "[a]verting the ill of him who does it." Simpson, The Literature of Ancient Egypt 208. Breasted refers to this story as *The Dialogue of a Misanthrope with His Own Soul*, and translates the passage saying that the future king will "inflict the punishment of wickedness on the doer of it...." Breasted, Development of Religion and Thought 196.

197. *See generally* Wayne R. LaFave & Austin W. Scott, Criminal Law §§ 7.15–7.16 (2d ed. 1986).

198. *See generally id.* at § 8.11. *See also supra* § 8.04. In another Middle Kingdom story, *The Man Who Was Tired of Life*, the protagonist laments the sad state of affairs in Egypt: "Robbery is practised, every man seizes his neighbor's (goods)." Breasted, Development of Religion and Thought 193.

§8.11 Chapter Summary

There was little if any distinction between criminal law and tort law in ancient Egypt. Typical punishments that did not entail abject brutality included forced labor, confiscation of property, loss of office (*i.e.*, civic status), and loss of ritual burial. Punishments progressively became more brutal and included some grotesque penalties in the New Kingdom. Among the more harsh penalties that convicted criminals suffered were beatings, mutilation (*e.g.*, amputation of nose and/or ears), branding, and death by impalement. The Egyptians used prisons mostly as places either for confining the accused while they awaited trial or for holding convicts for sentencing. The *Book of the Dead* enumerates a long list of wrongful conduct recognized by Egyptian society such as murder, commercial fraud, theft, waste, adultery, rape, and battery.

For ordinary theft, a thief had to return the stolen goods and pay double or triple their value, as a kind of punitive damages. The punishment was markedly higher if the stolen objects were either sacred or owned by the State, and the penalty was death in the case of theft from a royal tomb. We have very little evidence relating to ordinary homicide. But those found guilty of conspiracy to assassinate a monarch (*i.e.*, treason) received the death penalty (*e.g.*, the harem conspiracies to assassinate Pepi I and Ramses III). Rape was treated as a crime, but there is less conclusive proof regarding adultery—which may have been considered more of a private, family law matter to be worked out between husband and wife. Judges were not allowed to accept bribes nor to associate inappropriately with criminal defendants. Judicial misconduct of this nature was punished by death. Tax collectors and other government officials guilty of extortion were banished to remote areas and could also suffer amputation of their ears and nose. The Egyptians usually punished battery by beatings or forced labor. They also recognized trespass to land, vandalism (or trespass to chattels/criminal mischief), and defamation (*e.g.*, the case involving *Ḥ3y*) as wrongful conduct.

CHAPTER 9

Trade, Contracts, & Commercial Law

§9.01 Trade

The ancient Egyptians developed extensive domestic and international trade. Even in the predynastic age (*c.* 4500–3150 B.C.):

> There was commerce the whole length of Egypt, and somehow goods trickled in from other areas: gold and copper from the eastern mountains, ivory and myrrh from the distant south, olive oil from Lybia and from Palestine, cedar woods from the Phoenician coast, lapis lazuli and obsidian from lands far to the east. Such goods may have passed only from community to community, but the means were already present, in shipping, for more direct contact and thus for greater influence of one culture on another. It is already possible to see a remarkable similarity of form between Egypt and Palestine in the shapes of pots, stone vessels, and stone palettes.[1]

1. WILSON, CULTURE OF ANCIENT EGYPT 26 (footnote omitted). *See also Id.* at 81 (Discussing Egyptian commerce and traffic on the Nile.); *Id.* at 35 ("Further, predynastic Egypt saw an increasing amount of commerce and thus an increasing interweaving of persons and communities which were not related by blood. Basically, the economy of any one unit was that of self-sufficiency, but the role of the market was already strong...."); *Id.* at 24 (Wilson suggests that the predynastic Egyptians probably had to trade for metal implements.); *Id.* at 41 (Using evidence of "boats of Mesopotamian type on monuments in the Nile valley", Wilson suggests that, as early as the predynastic era, "the Babylonians or some people in close touch with the Babylonians came as sailing merchants to Egypt."); WARBURTON, STATE AND ECONOMY IN ANCIENT EGYPT 69 (Describing Egypt's "long distance trade connections with Palestine and Mesopotamia.") (footnote omitted); GRIMAL, ANCIENT EGYPT 27 ("By the end of the Predynastic period the Nile valley was obliged to open itself up to the outside world, for it had very few natural resources.").

The Nile facilitated the transport of goods and provided ready access to the Mediterranean. Consequently, at least as early as recorded history (roughly 3000 B.C.), Egyptian merchants actively bought and sold goods throughout the Nile valley and beyond.[2] Commerce flourished and developed in the Old Kingdom (*c.* 2700–2200 B.C.).[3] As Egyptian merchants plied the Nile's waters, they also kept books and accounts, gave purchase orders and receipts, and entered into long-term written contracts.[4] The 4th Dynasty King Snefru (*c.* 2600 B.C.) imported wood from abroad.[5] And other evidence indicates that the Egyptians of the pyramid age traded with Lybia, Byblos, the Sudan, Punt, Asia, and even the Aegean world.[6] Apparently, even at this early date, the king established a royal "monopoly" on all for-

---

2. *See generally* Edward Bleiberg, *The Economy of Ancient Egypt, in* 3 CIVILIZATIONS OF THE ANCIENT NEAR EAST 1373–1385 (Jack M. Sasson ed., 1995); *Id.* at 1373 ("Throughout the period of pharaonic civilization, the need for products from abroad led to government-organized long-distance trading expeditions."); GARDINER, EGYPT OF THE PHARAOHS 41 ("The most beneficent factor in the Egyptian economic structure was the river itself. All distant travel within the country was by boat, and the ancient people were as expert as ship-builders as they were in all other practical techniques."); *Id,* at 31–32 (Given that ancient Egyptian society was primarily agricultural and dependent on transportation on the Nile, it seems probable that such a society must have had elaborate rules concerning the sale of goods and the risk of loss of goods while they were in transit on the river.); BREASTED, HISTORY OF EGYPT 7 ("The wealth of commerce which the river served to carry, it was equally instrumental in producing."); GRIMAL, ANCIENT EGYPT 28–29, 50.

3. *See* GARDINER, EGYPT OF THE PHARAOHS 134; *Id.* at 98 (Evidence of international trade with Nubia—corn, oil, honey, clothing, etc.); WILSON, CULTURE OF ANCIENT EGYPT 100, 108, 110 (Regarding foreign commerce and its effect on Old Kingdom government.); WARBURTON, STATE AND ECONOMY IN ANCIENT EGYPT 65 (Citing Kemp for the existence of "widespread" "commerce and manufacturing" during the Old and Middle Kingdoms."); BREASTED, HISTORY OF EGYPT 115 (Regarding trade with Phoenicia.); *Id.* at 136 (Explaining that near the end of the Old Kingdom, Egyptian king, Mernere (Pepi I's son), expanded trade routes to Nubia in the south: "The country was furthermore the only gateway to the regions of the south, with which constant trade was now maintained. Besides gold, the Sudan sent down the river ostrich feathers, ebony logs, panther skins and ivory; while along the same route, from Punt and the countries further east, came myrrh, fragrant gums and resins and aromatic woods. It was therefore an absolute necessity that the Pharaoh should command this route."); *Id.* at 142–143 (Noting that in the Old Kingdom there was commerce with the Aegean.).

4. *See* BREASTED, HISTORY OF EGYPT 98.

5. *See* GARDINER, EGYPT OF THE PHARAOHS 42 ("forty seafaring vessels laden with *'ash* were brought into Egypt in a single year of king Snofru of the 4th Dynasty (*c.* 2620 B.C.)."(Citing BAR i, sect. 146.); GRIMAL, ANCIENT EGYPT 68–69.

6. *See* WILSON, CULTURE OF ANCIENT EGYPT 82 ("The Old Kingdom sent commercial and military expeditions into Lybia, the Sudan, and Asia."); GRIMAL, ANCIENT EGYPT 68–69, 76 ("The first known contacts—probably commercial—between Egypt and the Aegean world can also be dated to Userkaf's reign...."); *Id.* at 77–79.

eign trade. It is difficult to say with certainty whether this "monopoly" entailed actual control of foreign commerce or whether the government merely charged some kind of customs duty.[7] In any event, the government continued to exercise a degree of control over foreign trade on the Nile throughout most of antiquity. During the Middle Kingdom (*c.* 2040–1674 B.C.), we see a significant increase in the activity of the merchant class. More tradesmen, artisans, and artificers were producing and selling their wares than ever before.[8] As might be expected, trade in the Middle Kingdom expanded beyond what would have been imaginable in the Old Kingdom. Foreign markets which the Egyptians had only begun exploring in the Old Kingdom now took on exceptional prominence.[9]

Foreign trade during the New Kingdom (*c.* 1552–1069 B.C.) burgeoned.[10] Egyptians bought, sold, and traded goods with foreign lands and peoples such as Nubia, the Sudan, Sinai, Lybia, Babylonia, Assyria, Crete, Mycenae, Rhodes, Palestine, Cyprus, Phonecia, the Hittites, and other locations throughout the Aegean and Mediterranean.[11] Foreign trade became

---

7. *See* WILSON, CULTURE OF ANCIENT EGYPT 81 (Discussing the Old Kingdom, Wilson states: "It is likely that the major movement of goods—thereby resorting to the Nile traffic—was controlled by the royal Sealbearer and thereby by the king. If so, we do not know whether the state's advantage was one of control only or of an exacted price for such traffic. Foreign commerce was probably a royal monopoly, although our evidence is slight. . . ."); *See also Id.* at 134; WARBURTON, STATE AND ECONOMY IN ANCIENT EGYPT 309 (Questioning the validity of this assertion.); GRIMAL, ANCIENT EGYPT 87 (Describing the expeditions of Harkhuf.).

8. *See* BREASTED, HISTORY OF EGYPT 168. On middle class merchants, *see infra* §§ 10.01, 10.03.

9. *See* WILSON, CULTURE OF ANCIENT EGYPT 138–39 (Noting that the government actively sought trade in the south during the Middle Kingdom.); BREASTED, HISTORY OF EGYPT 185 (Mentioning trade with the Sudan.); *Id.* at 188 (Evidence for trade with Babylon and the Aegean during the 12th Dynasty.); *Id.* at 188–189 (Referring to commerce with the Aegean in Middle Kingdom.); GRIMAL, ANCIENT EGYPT 157 (Mentioning military efforts to guard "the ancient caravan trading routes" and expeditions sent by Mentuhotep III to Punt.); *Id.* at 164–165 (Noting that commercial links with Kerma and "with Syria-Palestine extended as far north as Ugarit during this period.").

10. *See* Christopher J. Eyre, *The Market Women of Pharaonic Egypt, in* LE COMMERCE EN ÉGYPT ANCIENNE 173 (Nicolas Grimal and Bernadette Menu eds., 1998); E.W, Castle, *Shipping and Trade in Ramesside Egypt,* 35 J. ECONOMIC & SOCIAL HIST. ORIENT 239 (1992).

11. *See* WILSON, CULTURE OF ANCIENT EGYPT 273 ("The Egyptian Empire had been able to exploit the gold mines of Nubia and the Sudan and the copper mines of Sinai. Egypt had no silver and relied upon her foreign trade to gain that metal, probably from the Hittite country."); *Id.* at 251 (Wilson mentions trade with the Mediterranean under Ramses II.); *Id.* at 183 (Significant commerce with the Hittites, Babylonia, and Assyria under Thutmose III.); *Id.* at 189–91 (Extensive trade with the Mediterranean, Aegean, Crete, Mycenae, Rhodes, Syria, Palestine, and other areas in

so extensive under Amenhotep III (*c.* 1390–1352 B.C.) that he established a kind of coast guard or marine police who patrolled the Delta and turned back unauthorized boats. They also staffed customs houses in the Delta and collected duties for all goods (except those which were being remitted to the pharaoh).[12] With commerce developed to such a degree, it was crucial for Egypt to establish a coherent jurisprudence of business, contract, and commercial law.

§ 9.02 Business Organizations

Early in their legal development, the Egyptians recognized the concept of corporate identity for legal purposes. For example, the State was considered to be its own business entity.[13] There were also associations of people

---

the 18th Dynasty.); BREASTED, HISTORY OF EGYPT 337–338 (Vigorous commerce with the Mediterranean world.); *Id.* at 447–448 (Trade with Palestine.); *Id.* at 337 (Trade with the island of Rhodes.); *Id.* at 447 (Under Ramses II: "The tide of commerce that ebbed and flowed through the Isthmus of Suez was even fuller than under the 18th Dynasty, while on the Mediterranean the Egyptian galleys must have whitened the sea."); *Id.* at 322 (At the peak of the New Kingdom: "The wealth of Asiatic trade, circulating through the eastern end of the Mediterranean, which once flowed down the Euphrates to Babylon, was thus diverted to the Nile Delta, centuries earlier united by canal with the red sea. All the world traded in the Delta markets."); *Id.* at 338 (Under Amenhotep III: "Trade now developed as never before. The Nile, from the Delta to the cataracts, was alive with the freight of all the world, which flowed into it from the Red sea fleets and from long caravans passing back and forth through the Isthmus of Suez, bearing the rich stuffs of Syria, the spices and aromatic woods of the east, the weapons and chased vessels of the Phoenicians, and a myriad of other things, which brought their Semitic names into the hieroglyphic and their use into the life of the Nile-dwellers." There was also commerce with the Mediterranean, Mycenae, Cnossos, Rhodes, and Cyprus.); *Id.* at 448 (In the era of Ramses II, "Phoenician and other alien merchants were so numerous that there was a foreign quarter in Memphis, with its temples of Baal and Astarte...."); *Id.* at 337–338 (Commerce with the Aegean in the New Kingdom.); GRIMAL, ANCIENT EGYPT 188, 200, 212, 219.

12. *See* BREASTED, HISTORY OF EGYPT 338–39.

13. *See* Aristide Théodorides, *The Concept of Law in Ancient Egypt, in* THE LEGACY OF EGYPT 291, 294 (J.R. Harris ed., 2d ed. 1971). *See generally* WARBURTON, STATE AND ECONOMY IN ANCIENT EGYPT 315 ("The state basically consists of an independent social organization within a territorial entity, with a population, and a legitimate government which administers, and makes laws."). *See also Id.* at 37 (Discussing the State as "a specific legal entity."); *Id.* at 70 (Asserting that the State in the late New Kingdom "was probably the single most important economic player in the Two Lands...."); *Id.* at 302; *Id.* at 318 ("The Egyptian state was ultimately responsible for justice and security."). *But see Id.* at 31 ("Efforts to study and understand the state have revealed that there is no general agreement about what is meant by the term 'state.'").

deemed to be business entities, such as the family syndicate created in Heti's will.[14] Heti's family syndicate was an association of individuals comprising a business organization with its own legal personality.[15] Temples and statue cults also were regarded as business entities (although the gods probably were deemed the actual owners of the temples).[16] In all likelihood, corporate identity in ancient Egypt was important in terms of liability in the same way that today we use a corporation as a shield for liability and for accounting purposes. An association had its own life so to speak. Many scholars have asserted that the large estates owned and managed by the government and temples collected taxes—in goods—and channeled their yield to the workers and inhabitants. A number of modern scholars have referred to this as a "redistributive economy."[17] Warburton, however, maintains that this is an erroneous assumption:

> The degree of private enterprise demonstrated by the records stands in clear contrast to the absence of any recorded "redistribution" on a large scale. The state was collecting and constructing, but it does not seem to have been redistributing, primarily because the population had their own sources of income in the private sector.[18]

---

14. *See supra* §§7.02, 7.03.

15. *See* Aristide Théodorides, *The Concept of Law in Ancient Egypt, in* THE LEGACY OF EGYPT 291, 294 (J.R. Harris ed., 2d ed. 1971).

16. *See supra* §5.01; WARBURTON, STATE AND ECONOMY IN ANCIENT EGYPT 32 (Discussing potential relationships between the State and temples.); *Id.* at 70; Andrea McDowell, *Legal Aspects of Care of the Elderly in Egypt to the End of the New Kingdom, in* THE CARE OF THE ELDERLY IN THE ANCIENT NEAR EAST 199, 204–207 (Marten Stol and Sven P. Vleeming eds., 1998); Aristide Théodorides, *The Concept of Law in Ancient Egypt, in* THE LEGACY OF EGYPT 291, 294 (J.R. Harris ed., 2d ed. 1971) (Noting that other legal entities/personalities included temples "whose estates are regarded as belonging to the gods to whom they are dedicated. . . .").

17. *See* Edward Bleiberg, *The Economy of Ancient Egypt, in* 3 CIVILIZATIONS OF THE ANCIENT NEAR EAST 1373, 1375 (Jack M. Sasson ed., 1995) ("In a redistributive economic organization, all goods are collected by a central authority and channeled to others on the basis of social status or kinship."); David Lorton, *Legal and Social Institutions of Pharaonic Egypt, in* 1 CIVILIZATIONS OF THE ANCIENT NEAR EAST 345, 353 (Jack M. Sasson ed., 1995) ("They collected part of what their tenants raised as taxes and used some of the proceeds to pay their employees, a system that is called 'redistributive.'"). *See also supra* §5.04. *But see* WARBURTON, STATE AND ECONOMY IN ANCIENT EGYPT 31 ("The evidence of fiscal activity does however also indicate that ancient Egypt cannot be understood as either a redistribution or command economy, and that it has features characteristic of market economy."); *Id.* at 32; *Id.* at 72, 82 (Citing Polanyi.).

18. WARBURTON, STATE AND ECONOMY IN ANCIENT EGYPT 69. *See also Id.* at 79–80.

Indeed, Warburton asserts that "other sources suggest that the ancient Egyptian economy could even be classified as a kind of nascent capitalism, for we have wage-labour, a market for land, production for the market, and state involvement."[19]

§9.03 Contracts

Most early trade (both domestic and foreign) was probably conducted by simple barter, an exchange of one kind of goods for another.[20] Even in the New Kingdom (*c.* 1552–1069 B.C.), records show that workers at Deir el-Medina, for example, continued to transact much of their daily business by simply swapping goods (*i.e.*, barter).[21] Nevertheless, the Egyptians also formulated basic principles of true contracts—that is, mutual exchanges dependent upon bilateral promises for future performance, as opposed to merely a contemporaneous swap.[22] For example, we know of a contract

---

19. WARBURTON, STATE AND ECONOMY IN ANCIENT EGYPT 80. *See Id.* at 92–99 (Refuting Polanyi's theory of a redistributive economy in ancient Egypt.); *Id.* at 300 ("Egypt can be understood as a pre-capitalist market economy."); *Id.* at 328 ("There is...not only no 'redistribution', but the market is the primary means of allocating goods.").

20. For more about barter in ancient Egypt, *see* Edward Bleiberg, *The Economy of Ancient Egypt, in* 3 CIVILIZATIONS OF THE ANCIENT NEAR EAST 1373, 1376 (Jack M. Sasson ed., 1995). *See also* BREASTED, HISTORY OF EGYPT 97 (Breasted describes commerce in the Old Kingdom as follows: "The Nile was alive with boats, barges, and craft of all descriptions, bearing the products of these industries, and of field and pasture, to the treasury of the Pharaoh, or to the markets where they were disposed of. Here barter was the common means of exchange...."); GARDINER, EGYPT OF THE PHARAOHS 44, 134; WILSON, CULTURE OF ANCIENT EGYPT 82 (Referring to the Old Kingdom: "Commercially and fiscally it was an age of barter, whether in the market place or through the payment of taxes in kind."); Aristide Théodorides, *The Concept of Law in Ancient Egypt, in* THE LEGACY OF EGYPT 291, 314 (J.R. Harris ed., 2d ed. 1971) (Under Amenhotep III: In Messuia's slave rental contracts "payment" is often done with oxen, cows, calves, grain, silver, bronze, fabrics, or clothes.).

21. *See* GARDINER, EGYPT OF THE PHARAOHS 275 (Gardiner mentions records of barter and lawsuits on the ostraca of the workers at Deir el-Medina.).

22. For an explanation of the technicalities of the vocabulary relating to purchase and sale in ancient Egypt, *see* Edward Bleiberg, *The Economy of Ancient Egypt, in* 3 CIVILIZATIONS OF THE ANCIENT NEAR EAST 1373, 1376–77 (Jack M. Sasson ed., 1995). *See also* WARBURTON, STATE AND ECONOMY IN ANCIENT EGYPT 75 (Noting that "the existence of contracts dealing with commercial transactions" was evidence of a "market economy."); Aristide Théodorides, *The Concept of Law in Ancient Egypt, in* THE LEGACY OF EGYPT 291, 292–293 (J.R. Harris ed., 2d ed. 1971) ("[F]rom the Old Kingdom, sale in Egypt could be done by consent."); *Id.* at 293 (Regarding sales contracts, Théodorides states: "there are clear indications of the bilateral nature of such transactions.").

that involved bilateral promises for future performance that was the subject of litigation (in either the late 19th or early 20th Dynasty (*c.* 1200 B.C.)). This contract provided that a scribe would make a coffin for a woman's dead husband. In return, the woman promised to give the scribe a particular hut.[23] Similarly, the lease agreements detailed in the Law Collection of Hermopolis typically recite, for example, that the lessee promises to pay rent to the lessor and that, in return, the lessor promises that he will allow the lessee to have possession of the premises.[24] Erman refers to ancient Egyptian contract law as "a complete system."[25] As was the case with many aspects of Egyptian law, there was basic equality between men and women; women had legal capacity to enter into binding agreements on par with men.[26]

We have an ostracon (Ostracon Chicago, Oriental Institute 12.073, 3) dating from the 20th Dynasty, in the reign of Ramses IV (*c.* 1148–1144 B.C.), that uses the word *snḥ*, "tie" or "bind" in the legal sense of "obligation."[27] But the term *imyt-pr*, which even in the Old Kingdom meant "a certified deed of conveyance,"[28] later evolved into a generic term for all kinds of conveyance.[29] The phrase *imyt-pr* literally translates as "that which is in

---

23. *See* MCDOWELL, JURISDICTION 121–122; Schafik Allam, *Women as Owners of Immovables in Pharaonic Egypt, in* WOMEN'S EARLIEST RECORDS FROM ANCIENT EGYPT AND WESTERN ASIA 123, 126–27 (Barbara Lesko ed., 1989). Unfortunately, the details of the litigation are too obscure to interpret with any certainty.

24. *See e.g.*, MATTHA, THE DEMOTIC LEGAL CODE OF HERMOPOLIS WEST 22.

25. ERMAN, LIFE IN ANCIENT EGYPT 147. *See* Taylor, *Law Under the Pharaohs*, 6 POL'Y REV. 66, at 69 (1980) ("Simplicity governed the law of contract and it was invariably documented in terms such as, 'A will give this to B; B will give that to A: behold, A and B are therewith content.'"). *See also* Aristide Théodorides, *The Concept of Law in Ancient Egypt, in* THE LEGACY OF EGYPT 291, 303, 313 (J.R. Harris ed., 2d ed. 1971); *Id.* at 315 (Théodorides notes that the word *snḥ*, originally meaning tie, bind," had come to mean "legal obligation" by the 20th Dynasty.). *See also* BREASTED, DEVELOPMENT OF RELIGION AND THOUGHT 67 (Discussing "ten elaborate contracts on the inner wall of . . . [a] . . . tomb-chapel.. . ."); *Id.* at 260–61, 268–69; GARDINER, EGYPTIAN GRAMMAR 23.

26. *See* GAY ROBINS, WOMEN IN ANCIENT EGYPT 129; WILSON, CULTURE OF ANCIENT EGYPT 203 ("[S]uch business documents as we possess from the Empire show that women had their own rights... to buying and selling...."). *See also infra* § 10.02.

27. *See* Aristide Théodorides, *The Concept of Law in Ancient Egypt, in* THE LEGACY OF EGYPT 291, 315 (J.R. Harris ed., 2d ed. 1971). *See also* R.O. FAULKNER, A CONCISE DICTIONARY OF MIDDLE EGYPTIAN 233 (Entry for *snḥ* meaning "bind".).

28. Aristide Théodorides, *The Concept of Law in Ancient Egypt, in* THE LEGACY OF EGYPT 291, 298 (J.R. Harris ed., 2d ed. 1971).

29. *See* PESTMAN, MARRIAGE & MATRIMONIAL PROPERTY 18; Aristide Théodorides, *The Concept of Law in Ancient Egypt, in* THE LEGACY OF EGYPT 291, 304 (J.R. Harris ed., 2d ed. 1971); Schafik Allam, *Women as Owners of Immovables in Pharaonic Egypt, in* WOMEN'S EARLIEST RECORDS FROM ANCIENT EGYPT AND WESTERN ASIA 123, 125 (Barbara Lesko ed., 1989). *See also* R.O. FAULKNER, A CONCISE DICTIONARY

the house." These *imyt-pr* documents often reflect the transfer of land in situations where the transferor wished to alienate property to someone who otherwise would not have inherited it under the laws of intestacy.[30] Although some Egyptologists once believed that these were wills, it seems more likely now that these transfers were effective prior to the transferor's death. In most circumstances, the parties saw to it that the *imyt-pr* was filed in a municipal records facility of some sort.[31] We know of one such document in which a woman named Nebsenet, the mother of a 3rd Dynasty (*c.* 2700–2625 B.C.) nobleman named Metjen, transferred land to her grandchildren. Examples from the Middle Kingdom (*c.* 2040–1674 B.C.) illustrate the flexibility of this type of document for transfer. These Middle Kingdom *imyt-pr* typically operate to transfer property to persons such as brothers and wives. The types of property transferred include real property, personal property, and even intangible property, such as the right to live in a house and the right to be buried in a tomb.[32]

In order to form a contract, an offerer orally presented his offer to an offeree in the presence of witnesses. Once the offeree had signified his acceptance, the agreement bound both parties. A scribe was responsible for writing down the content of the agreement.[33] In one contract for the sale of a slave girl, the offeror states his offer as follows: "Buy this girl and give me a price for her." According to the offeree's own account, he concluded the purchase by doing just that: "And I bought the girl and gave him a [price] for her."[34] In Egyptian sales law, a number of agreements called for an express warranty of title to be made by the seller.[35] Title itself passed from

---

OF MIDDLE EGYPTIAN 18 (Entry for *imt-pr* meaning "will, testament".). *See supra* §§5.03[A], 7.02.

30. *See supra* §7.01.

31. *See* Janet H. Johnson, *The Legal Status of Women in Ancient Egypt, in* MISTRESS OF THE HOUSE MISTRESS OF HEAVEN: WOMEN IN ANCIENT EGYPT 175, 177 (Anne K. Chapel and Glenn E. Markoe eds., 1996) ("These documents were sealed and filed or recorded in a central government office....") (footnote omitted); GRIMAL, ANCIENT EGYPT 91. *See also supra* §7.02.

32. *See* Janet H. Johnson, *The Legal Status of Women in Ancient Egypt, in* MISTRESS OF THE HOUSE MISTRESS OF HEAVEN: WOMEN IN ANCIENT EGYPT 175, 177–178 (Anne K. Chapel and Glenn E. Markoe eds., 1996). For further mention of intangible property rights, *see supra* §5.02.

33. *See* Janet H. Johnson, *The Legal Status of Women in Ancient Egypt, in* MISTRESS OF THE HOUSE MISTRESS OF HEAVEN: WOMEN IN ANCIENT EGYPT 175, 177 (Anne K. Chapel and Glenn E. Markoe eds., 1996).

34. *See* BEDELL, CRIMINAL LAW 45.

35. *See* MCDOWELL, JURISDICTION 37 ("a person transferring ownership of a possession, usually a donkey but in one case servants, guarantees that no one will challenge the new owner's rights to the object by swearing that...'no other will stand behind him.'"); *Id.* at 99 (McDowell describes a legal dispute where a man who sold an

seller to buyer only when the buyer paid the seller.[36] Many of the contracts which have survived were written in the same formulaic pattern:

> Contract concluded between A and B,
> that B should give *x* to A,
> whilst A should give *y* to B.
> Behold, B was therewith content.[37]

Menu illustrates "the ancient pattern" of Egyptian contracts with the Cairo Stela from Thebes, dating about 660 B.C.:

> *on this day;* definition of the juridical act (*smn*); designation of the contracting parties (the representative of the divine Adoratrice and a Recluse Singer of Amun); description of what is sold (ten arouras of private fields; high lands in Amun's domain in such and such a district); specification of the price received; signature of the scribe and the witness; boundaries of the field sold which seems surrounded by canals; finally the beginning of an imprecatory formula.[38]

Some of the most illuminating examples of Egyptian contracts from antiquity are contracts for funerary services.[39] Typically, such contracts were

---

ox swears that the ox was his own, not one that had belonged to the High priest of Amon. This case also demonstrates that warranty of title was probably an essential part of a sales contract.).

36. *See* PESTMAN, MARRIAGE & MATRIMONIAL PROPERTY 18 ("[T]he vendor of a slave remains owner of this slave, even if the latter is already in the possession of the purchaser, until the purchase-money is paid.").

37. ERMAN, LIFE IN ANCIENT EGYPT 145. *See also* Bernadette Menu, *Women and Business Life in the First Millennium B.C., in* WOMEN'S EARLIEST RECORDS FROM ANCIENT EGYPT AND WESTERN ASIA 193, 195, 200–202 (Barbara S. Lesko ed., 1989) (Suggesting that significant changes in contract law occurred during the reign of "Psametichus (circa 660–640 B.C.)").

38. Bernadette Menu, *Women and Business Life in the First Millennium B.C., in* WOMEN'S EARLIEST RECORDS FROM ANCIENT EGYPT AND WESTERN ASIA 193, 200 (Barbara S. Lesko ed., 1989); *See also* Andrea McDowell, *Legal Aspects of Care of the Elderly in Egypt to the End of the New Kingdom, in* THE CARE OF THE ELDERLY IN THE ANCIENT NEAR EAST 199, 215 (Marten Stol and Sven P. Vleeming eds., 1998) (Noting the necessity for including dates and party names in legal documents.).

39. *See* David Lorton, *Legal and Social Institutions of Pharaonic Egypt, in* 1 CIVILIZATIONS OF THE ANCIENT NEAR EAST 345, 353 (Jack M. Sasson ed., 1995); ERMAN, LIFE IN ANCIENT EGYPT 145 (Of course these are not the only kind of contracts from ancient Egypt. There are also "more detailed business provisions."). *See also* William A. Ward, *Some Aspects of Private Land Ownership and Inheritance in Ancient Egypt, ca. 2500–1000 B.C., in* LAND TENURE AND SOCIAL TRANSFORMATION IN THE MIDDLE EAST 63, 65–67 (Tarif Khalidi ed., 1984) (Mentioning such contracts from the 4th and 5th Dynasties, as well as Ḥapdjefai.); Andrea McDowell, *Legal Aspects of Care of the Elderly in Egypt to the End of the New Kingdom, in* THE CARE OF THE ELDERLY IN THE ANCIENT NEAR EAST 199, 220 (Marten Stol and Sven P. Vleeming eds., 1998).

concluded between a noble and a group of priests. The noble promised to give the priests a fixed payment (of foodstuffs for example) in return for their promise to provide offerings, after the noble had deceased, and to light candles at the noble's tomb on designated days throughout the year.[40] These contracts (which involved a mutual exchange—what we today call "consideration," a *quid pro quo*) were written, signed, witnessed and, like wills and land deeds, had to be filed in the office of the vizier in order to be valid.[41] Among the best examples of this genre of contracts are a series of ten such agreements that were concluded between a 12th Dynasty (*c.* 1991–1785 B.C.) noble named Ḥapdjefai and the priesthood of the temple of Asyûṭ.[42] In one of these funerary contracts, Ḥapdjefai contracted with "the great priest of Anubis" for the lighting of lamps of Anubis' temple on three specific festival days every year, including New Year's day. According to the contract, Ḥapdjefai promised to give the priests "1000 field measures from the estate of his fathers, as the price for these three wicks...."[43] Other contracts in this Ḥapdjefai series specify amounts of the offering of bread and beer and how they were to be allotted to different priests (staff of the temple).[44]

---

40. *See* BREASTED, HISTORY OF EGYPT 70 (Even in the Old Kingdom: "Very specific contracts were made with...persons [who provided daily offerings for the deceased], requiting them for their services with a fixed income drawn from endowments legally established and recorded for this purpose by the noble himself, in anticipation of his death.") (footnote omitted).

41. We do not know whether witnesses were mandatory for a contract to be considered valid. In the 12th Dynasty, for example, Ḥapdjefai "drew up various contracts with the priesthood of the temple of Siut, all for the benefit of his personal cult." The text adds that the temple council was present when the contracts were written and signed to serve as a witness to the contract. Aristide Théodorides, *The Concept of Law in Ancient Egypt, in* THE LEGACY OF EGYPT 291, 303 (J.R. Harris ed., 2d ed. 1971). *See also* WILSON, CULTURE OF ANCIENT EGYPT 249 ("The final section of the treaty, like other ancient legal documents, listed the witnesses who attested to the compact, but in this case they were divine."); GRIMAL, ANCIENT EGYPT 91 (Describing the Old Kingdom, Grimal states: "[T]he Royal Archives...held copies of...contracts...."); ERMAN, LIFE IN ANCIENT EGYPT 145.

42. *See* William A. Ward, *Some Aspects of Private Land Ownership and Inheritance in Ancient Egypt, ca. 2500–1000 B.C., in* LAND TENURE AND SOCIAL TRANSFORMATION IN THE MIDDLE EAST 63, 66 (Tarif Khalidi ed., 1984) ("The most elaborate arrangements now known made for a private mortuary cult are those of Ḥapdjefai...."); GARDINER, EGYPT OF THE PHARAOHS 142 ("One cannot read the elaborate stipulations of these contracts without realizing that strict rules of property lie behind them, for instance a distinction between what the prince owned by virtue of inheritance and what he owned by virtue of his office."); Aristide Théodorides, *The Concept of Law in Ancient Egypt, in* THE LEGACY OF EGYPT 291, 303 (J.R. Harris ed., 2d ed. 1971).

43. ERMAN, LIFE IN ANCIENT EGYPT 146.

44. *See Id.*

There are two aspects of the Ḥapdjefai contracts which deserve special comment. First, because Ḥapdjefai himself was a member of the priesthood with which he was contracting (*i.e.*, in one respect he was contracting with himself!), he had to delineate his roles and separate his obligations. As a consequence of this duality, he was able to pay his colleagues, at least in part, with rations from the temple to which he and his heirs would have otherwise been entitled.[45] Second, Ḥapdjefai emphasized that the real property that he promised to give to the priesthood as consideration (in addition to temple rations) was property that derived from his family's inheritance, not property in which he had a life estate by virtue of being a nomarch.[46] These two aspects of the Ḥapdjefai contracts illustrate that the Egyptians reached a sophisticated level of legal abstraction. As Erman remarks: "A people who could so clearly grasp the double nature of an individuality as to allow him to conclude contracts with himself, was certainly long past the time of judicial infancy, and had attained to a highly developed legal status."[47]

Another example of service contracts of a different sort are the contracts of Messuia which span almost a quarter of a century during the reign of Amenhotep III (*c.* 1390–1352 B.C.). Mussuia ran an agricultural enterprise and weaving industry. These contracts deal mostly with the terms under which Messuia rented slaves for a certain number of days' work; a "hire of services."[48] They basically are "sale of labor" agreements, and include a

---

45. *See Id.* at 145.

46. For more regarding the ancient Egyptian life estate, *see supra* § 5.02. *See also* William A. Ward, *Some Aspects of Private Land Ownership and Inheritance in Ancient Egypt, ca. 2500–1000* B.C., *in* LAND TENURE AND SOCIAL TRANSFORMATION IN THE MIDDLE EAST 63, 66 (Tarif Khalidi ed., 1984); J.G. Manning, *Demotic Egyptian Instruments of Transfer as Evidence for Private Ownership of Real Property*, 71 CHICAGO-KENT L. REV. 237, 242 (1995) ("Temple property... may have been transferred by right of the priests' office and not by right of a personal holding of land that the priest would have been able to cede, presumably, permanently."); ERMAN, LIFE IN ANCIENT EGYPT 146–147 (Erman remarks how Ḥapdjefai is careful to declare that his consideration, that is, his payment, is being taken from "that part of his property and revenue which was really hereditary in his family," emphasizing that it was "*not* in any way from the property of the estate of the nomarch." The point here is that the payment is his personal property, not the property that he holds as a life estate by virtue of his official position as nomarch.

47. ERMAN, LIFE IN ANCIENT EGYPT 147.

48. *See* Aristide Théodorides, *The Concept of Law in Ancient Egypt*, *in* THE LEGACY OF EGYPT 291, 314–315 (J.R. Harris ed., 2d ed. 1971) (Théodorides speculates that a town may have actually owned some slaves "being then placed at the disposal of the inhabitants at the rate of so many days per month or year. It would then be their right to days of the slaves' work that the inhabitants of the Faiyum were selling to Messuia....") (footnote omitted). *See also* BEDELL, CRIMINAL LAW 7 (Referring to contracts from the 18th Dynasty that related to rental of a female slave's services.).

guarantee, given under oath, that the services will be provided. Théodorides suggests that this guarantee provision required an accompanying oath because it contemplated future performance rather than merely a contemporaneous swap.[49] There is simply not enough corroborating evidence, however, to conclude that, as a rule, a promisor had to swear an oath in order to make an ancient Egyptian contract enforceable.

One of the most interesting aspects of the guarantee in the Messuia contracts, at least from the perspective of substantive contract law, is that "[t]he guarantee provides for compensation in case the work cannot be done as agreed."[50] This is equivalent to what we today call "liquidated damages": an express agreement to pay a fixed sum in the event of breach of contract. We see similar liquidated damages provisions in a number of the contracts from Deir el-Medina. In one such contract, a donkey seller promises to replace the beast with another if a third party successfully proves title to it (*i.e.*, in the event the seller breaches his warranty of title). In another, a donkey seller promises double (*i.e.*, presumably two donkeys) if a third party successfully proves title. In yet another agreement, a buyer on credit stipulates that if he fails to pay, he will return the goods and, in addition, pay the court costs of his brothers who had served as witnesses to the transaction.[51] As a general rule, the 18th Dynasty texts, including the Messuia slave-rental contracts, reveal that the breaching party was expected to provide the other party with either equivalent goods or services as compensation.[52] This is often expressed as an equivalent number of work days ("day for day").[53] As such, this measure of contract damages approximates what modern law calls expectation damages. In other words, the breaching party is obligated to pay an amount to the aggrieved party that will put him (*i.e.*, the non-breaching party) into an economic position equivalent to that which he would have been in had there been no breach. The cases described in the Law Collection of Hermopolis that involve breach of an annuity contract routinely grant specific performance (*i.e.*, the breacher is required to pay the contract amount).[54] This too is a

---

49. *See* Aristide Théodorides, *The Concept of Law in Ancient Egypt, in* THE LEGACY OF EGYPT 291, 313 (J.R. Harris ed., 2d ed. 1971) (Théodorides seems to think that an oath is required whenever a contract deals with some future performance instead of just a contemporaneous swap.).

50. *Id.*

51. *See* David Lorton, *The Treatment of Criminals in Ancient Egypt*, 20 J. ECONOMIC & SOCIAL HIST. ORIENT 2, 49 (1977).

52. *See Id.* at 46–47, 49.

53. *See Id.* at 47.

54. *See* MATTHA, THE DEMOTIC LEGAL CODE OF HERMOPOLIS WEST 30, 99.

method—albeit a specialized method, an equitable remedy—of compensating for expectation loss.

Other texts from Deir el-Medina reveal a truly curious treatment of breach of a debtor-creditor contract. These texts suggest that when a debtor failed to repay his debt on time, his creditor could take him to court, where the debtor would be required to promise to pay in full by a specific date. As part of his promise—which was under oath—the debtor also pledged to undergo 100 blows and/or to repay twice the amount of the original loan if he failed to pay by the date specified.[55] This consequence actually appears to be more criminal than civil in nature. In essence, the process initially contemplates the same type of contract damages that we see in the other 18th Dynasty texts; namely, simply payment of the amount that was owed (*i.e.*, the breaching party's promise to pay by a specific date). Perhaps the 100 blows and the double damages are actually criminal penalties for perjury (*i.e.*, for the debtor's failure to keep his promise of payment made under oath in court), not technically "contract damages" *per se*.[56]

In bailment agreements (such as the rental of a donkey), the term for "rent" was usually *iʿt3y*.[57] Egyptian bailment contracts seem to presume that a bailee was strictly liable (*i.e.*, liable regardless of fault) for loss or

---

55. *See* David Lorton, *The Treatment of Criminals in Ancient Egypt*, 20 J. ECONOMIC & SOCIAL HIST. ORIENT 2, 43 (1977). For more on the legal aspects of the payment of debts in Deir el-Medina, *see* MCDOWELL, JURISDICTION 163 (Discussing the unusual character, "the chief of policemen Mnʿtw-ms, a hardened debtor who was singularly unimpressed by the dictates of the local court. In O Or. Inst. 12073 he ignores three successive orders to pay spanning 18 years...and he does eventually pay."); *Id.* at 175 (Referring to a case where blows were given as punishment in a case of failure to repay a debt. Here the defendant had already been found liable four times before—so this was the fifth time that he had been found liable for the same debt.); J.G. Manning, Gary Greig, and Sugihiko Uchida, *Chicago Oriental Institute Ostracon 12073 Once Again*, 48 J. NEAR EASTERN STUD. 117, 119, 120–23 (1989) (These authors analyze the transactions as having involved middlemen acting as go-betweens for persons outside of the community doing business with persons on the inside: "We would suggest that this is evidence of the use of middlemen in transactions between workmen and outsiders." (*Id.* at 121)).

56. *See* J.G. Manning, Gary Greig, and Sugihiko Uchida, Chicago Oriental Institute Ostracon 12073 Once Again, 48 J. NEAR EASTERN STUD. 117, 122 (1989) (Mentioning double damages.). For more on perjury and the penalties therefore, *see supra* § 4.05[B].

57. *See* MCDOWELL, JURISDICTION 38. *See also* R.O. FAULKNER, A CONCISE DICTIONARY OF MIDDLE EGYPTIAN 34 (Entry for *iʿti* meaning "take," and "take possession of."). For more on bailment contracts in Deir el-Medina (especially the rental of donkeys) *see Id.* at 137; William A. Ward, *Some Aspects of Private Land Ownership and Inheritance in Ancient Egypt, ca. 2500–1000 B.C.*, *in* LAND TENURE AND SOCIAL TRANSFORMATION IN THE MIDDLE EAST 63, 75 n. 22 (Tarif Khalidi ed., 1984). For a further explanation of the concept of bailment, *see supra* § 5.02.

damage to bailed property. In particular, in the Deir el-Medina donkey rental cases, the parties accepted that the bailee was always responsible whenever the donkey died while in his possession.[58] A bailee, then, as a rule, was liable for damage to the bailed property while in his possession.[59] As was mentioned above, many bailment contracts included what modern law characterizes as a liquidated damages provision. This type of contract clause specified the payment that the bailee would make if he failed to return the object that had been bailed.[60] Since these ancient liquidated damages provisions normally imposed corporal punishment (*e.g.*, 100 blows) and two times the original payment, modern contract law would probably invalidate such provisions as "penalty clauses". Nevertheless, we ought not allow our contemporary sensibilities to cloud our view. It is entirely possible that the Egyptians considered these as reasonable measures necessary to promote their concept of how contracts should operate. It is not, therefore, imperative that we interpret these breach of bailment contract cases as criminal matters rather than civil.[61]

One particular bailment contract (Ostracon Deir el-Medina 433) illustrates two important points. The bailee (named Imn-m-ipt) paid certain quantities of both oil and copper to the bailor (named Knr) for the use of an ox. When Knr, the bailor, failed to deliver the ox as promised, Imn-m-ipt, the bailee, complained to the local authorities. The defaulting bailor then swore that he would either deliver the ox within one month or endure 100 blows and give twice the value of the ox rental to the bailee.[62] The first important point is this: often (and routinely) a debtor's promise to undergo 100 blows and double his payment was unrealized.[63] Probably, the lit-

---

58. *See* McDowell, Jurisdiction 151, 155. For more on rental of donkeys at Deir el-Medina, *see* Warburton, State and Economy in Ancient Egypt 241.

59. *See* McDowell, Jurisdiction 6 (McDowell mentions a case where a bailee "admitted that he owed... [the bailor] the value of a donkey and her foal which had died in his possession.").

60. *See* Bedell, Criminal Law 120 (Referring to situations such as these, Bedell says: "When a person borrowed something, a legal document was drawn up between the two parties stating the terms of repayment." Interestingly, Bedell explains these cases as "theft" cases. I disagree. They simply look like breach of contract cases to me. *See also Id.* at 121 (Bedell states: "[T]hese agreements often stated the penalty for defalcation, so that the court's function in the matter was to force the party at fault to pay the penalty." Again Bedell explains these clauses in terms of criminal law and labels them as penalties rather than the way that I interpret them, namely, as contract remedies.).

61. *See Id.* at 121.

62. *See* McDowell, Jurisdiction 8.

63. *See Id.* at 182 ("In short, I can find no case in which the penalty of a double debt invoked in so many oaths is unquestionably imposed."). *See also Id.* at 147 (Mc-

igants were so familiar with one another—given the limited size of the community in Deir el-Medina—that they frequently wished to work out their problems with a degree of understanding, compassion, and flexibility.[64] Secondly, this donkey rental case involving Knr and Imn-m-ipt serves as an illustration of a contract modification that modern law might characterize as a substituted contract or an accord.[65] In fact, in the Deir el-Medina contract disputes, it was very common for a creditor and debtor to agree to what we today would label as a substituted contract or an accord. In other words, the creditor would refrain from insisting on immediate payment of a debt, and instead accepted the debtor's new promise to pay his debt by some later date.[66]

§ 9.04 Foreign & International Aspects

We occasionally catch glimpses of both private and public international law in our sources. For example, the extensive foreign trade carried on by Egyptian merchants necessitated a viable law merchant for international shipping and sale of goods.[67] Under Ramses II (*c.* 1279–1212

Dowell refers to another case of a bailment contract; another donkey rental case. The decision was that 81 days' rental was worth 20 copper deben (it appears that the bailee had only paid 3 deben).).

64. *See Id.* at 178–179.

65. *See generally* E. ALLAN FARNSWORTH, CONTRACTS § 4.24, at 300–306 (2d ed. 1990).

66. *See* McDOWELL, JURISDICTION 178. The interpretation of this practice as analogous to the modern concepts of substituted contracts or accords is mine, not McDowell's.

67. *See* GARDINER, EGYPT OF THE PHARAOHS 134 (On methods of foreign trade with Nubia and the Sudan; gold and "a number of other much-prized commodities." "Most of these things were obtained by barter from the natives...."); *Id.* at 98 (Evidence of international trade with Nubia—corn, oil, honey, clothing, etc.); *Id.* at 44 ("In a land where natural resources were so abundant, and where craftsmanship of so high an order was rapidly developed, it was natural that much should be available for barter with foreigners."); *Id.* at 42 (Early evidence of international trade: "forty seafaring vessels laden with '*ash* were brought into Egypt in a single year of king Snofru of the 4th Dynasty (*c.* 2620 B.C.)." (Citing BAR i, § 146.); WILSON, CULTURE OF ANCIENT EGYPT 183 (Under Thutmose III, the Egyptian government held a monopoly on "the coniferous woods of Asia, which we lump together in the translation 'cedar'...."); *Id.* at 134 ("We assume that commerce with foreign countries may still have been a royal monopoly, and the 12th Dynasty was assiduous in courting neighbors abroad."); *Id.* at 251 (Wilson mentions trade with the Mediterranean under Ramses II.); *Id.* at 24 (Wilson suggests that the predynastic Egyptians probably had to trade for metal implements.); *Id.* at 26 (Also discussing predynastic Egypt, Wilson says: "There was

B.C.), we know that there was an Egyptian law court located in Nubia.[68]

We must always bear in mind that ancient expectations regarding relations with foreign nations were generally not benign. The threat of invasion was a simple fact of life. Aggression was common. Even in the Old King-

---

commerce the whole length of Egypt, and somehow goods trickled in from other areas: gold and copper from the eastern mountains, ivory and myrrh from the distant south, olive oil from Lybia and from Palestine, cedar woods from the Phoenician coast, lapis lazuli and obsidian from lands far to the east. Such goods may have passed only from community to community, but the means were already present, in shipping, for more direct contact and thus for greater influence of one culture on another. It is already possible to see a remarkable similarity of form between Egypt and Palestine in the shapes of pots, stone vessels, and stone palettes.") (footnote omitted); *Id.* at 35 ("Further, predynastic Egypt saw an increasing amount of commerce and thus an increasing interweaving of persons and communities which were not related by blood."); *Id.* at 81 (In the Old Kingdom: "It is likely that the major movement of goods—thereby resorting to the Nile traffic—was controlled by the royal Sealbearer and thereby by the king. If so, we do not know whether the state's advantage was one of control only or of an exacted price for such traffic. Foreign commerce was probably a royal monopoly, although our evidence is slight...."); *Id.* at 82 ("The Old Kingdom sent commercial and military expeditions into Lybia, the Sudan, and Asia."); *Id.* at 41 (Using evidence of "boats of Mesopotamian type on monuments in the Nile valley", Wilson suggests that, as early as the predynastic era, "the Babylonians or some people in close touch with the Babylonians came as sailing merchants to Egypt."); *Id.* at 100, 108, 110 (Foreign commerce and its effect on Old Kingdom government.); *Id.* at 134 ("We assume that the commerce with foreign countries may still have been a royal monopoly, and the 12th Dynasty was assiduous in courting neighbors abroad."); *Id.* at 138–139 (The government actively sought trade in the south during the Middle Kingdom.); *Id.* at 183 (Significant commerce with the Hittites, Babylonia, and Assyria under Thutmose III.); *Id.* at 189–191 (Extensive trade with the Mediterranean, Aegean, Crete, Mycenae, Rhodes, Syria, Palestine, and other areas in the 18th Dynasty.); BREASTED, HISTORY OF EGYPT 304; *Id.* 337–338 (Vigorous commerce with the Mediterranean world.); *Id.* at 447–448 (Trade with Palestine.); *Id.* at 115 (Trade with Phoenicia.); *Id.* at 337 (Trade with the island of Rhodes.); *Id.* at 185 (With the Sudan.); *Id.* at 447 (Under Ramses II: "The tide of commerce that ebbed and flowed through the Isthmus of Suez was even fuller than under the 18th Dynasty, while on the Mediterranean the Egyptian galleys must have whitened the sea."); *Id.* at 322 (At the peak of the New Kingdom: "The wealth of Asiatic trade, circulating through the eastern end of the Mediterranean, which once flowed down the Euphrates to Babylon, was thus diverted to the Nile Delta, centuries earlier united by canal with the red sea. All the world traded in the Delta markets."); *Id.* at 337 (Under Amenhotep III: "Trade now developed as never before. The Nile, from the Delta to the cataracts, was alive with the freight of all the world, which flowed into it from the Red sea fleets and from long caravans passing back and forth through the Isthmus of Suez, bearing the rich stuffs of Syria, the spices and aromatic woods of the east, the weapons and chased vessels of the Phoenicians, and a myriad of other things, which brought their Semitic names into the hieroglyphic and their use into the life of the Nile-dwellers." There was also commerce with the Mediterranean, Mycenae, Cnossos, Rhodes, and Cyprus.); *Id.* at 338–339.

68. *See* ERMAN, LIFE IN ANCIENT EGYPT 504 (Under Ramses II, in Nubia, "there was even an Egyptian court of justice, with the viceroy as chief judge.").

dom (*c.* 2700–2200 B.C.), Egyptian kings did not hesitate to attack and plunder foreign nations.[69] By the New Kingdom (*c.* 1552–1069 B.C.), Egyptian militancy was responsible for a tremendous increase in foreign captive slaves.[70] It was also during the New Kingdom that many subjugated countries routinely sent tribute to the Egyptian pharaohs.[71] It was then too that the Egyptians controlled and exploited mines in conquered lands.[72] In contrast to this general acceptance of international aggression is the Hittite peace treaty—an international contract of unique significance.

In the eighteenth year of his reign, Ramses II concluded an international treaty with the Hittites. This treaty marks one of the first international accords between two sovereign nations in the history of human civilization. First, the treaty pledges non-aggression. Each state promised not to attack the other. Secondly, the two nations created an alliance; each promising to come to the aid of the other in the event of an attack by a third party. In addition, they agreed to extradite refugees, and agreed that anyone so extradited would not be subject to mistreatment upon his return to his home country.[73]

---

69. *See* GARDINER, EGYPT OF THE PHARAOHS 78 (Regarding international law, we can observe that in the 4th Dynasty Egyptian kings apparently had no hesitation to invade and plunder a foreign nation.).

70. *See* WILSON, CULTURE OF ANCIENT EGYPT 187 ("Military successes under the Empire brought into Egypt thousands of captives, taken in battle." "Many of the foreigners were mere slaves of the palace, of the domains of the nobles, or of the temple estates. However, slavery was not then the sharply and legally delimited category which it was in more modern times. The household slave was much better off than the native Egyptian peasant."). *See also* BREASTED, HISTORY OF EGYPT 253; *infra* § 10.04.

71. *See* BREASTED, HISTORY OF EGYPT 307 (Under Thutmose III, Breasted describes tribute coming into Egypt, some in the form of "gold and silver in large commercial rings, some of which weighed as much as twelve pounds each, while others for purposes of daily trade were of but a few grains weight.").

72. *See* WILSON, CULTURE OF ANCIENT EGYPT 273 ("The Egyptian Empire had been able to exploit the gold mines of Nubia and the Sudan and the copper mines of Sinai. Egypt had no silver and relied upon her foreign trade to gain that metal, probably from the Hittite country.").

73. *See* GRIMAL, ANCIENT EGYPT 257 (Grimal calls this "the first state-to-state treaty in history..." and notes that "a copy of... [the treaty] was kept in both capitals, transcribed into the language of each of the empires." Grimal also states: "This treaty, which included extradition clauses for political opponents, provided the basis for a lasting peace...."); GARDINER, EGYPT OF THE PHARAOHS 264 (Gardiner's discussion of the Hittite treaty in the time of Ramses II is as follows: "Neither is to encroach upon the territory of the other, and each is pledged to render assistance in the case of attack from any other quarter. Provision is made for the extradition of refugees in either direction, but these are not to be treated as criminals on their return. The Egyptian document differs from the Hittite by invoking as witnesses many gods of both countries, and by describing the silver tablets which are to be exchanged; no doubt

§ 9.05 Commercial Law: Credit, Security, & Standard Media of Exchange

One important aspect of commercial law in ancient Egypt was that it allowed sales on credit terms.[74] Credit, of course, can facilitate economic growth because it allows buyers to obtain goods without needing the full purchase price immediately, and, as a general rule, it increases business for tradespeople. A concept related to credit, namely, security for loans, was also known and employed in ancient Egypt (especially in the Ptolemaic period—304–30 B.C.).[75] The use of security also encourages commercial transactions because it increases the likelihood that lenders will be willing to make loans. As a consequence, more individuals are able to share purchasing power. And at least by the 20th Dynasty (*c.* 1188–1069 B.C.), Egyptian law recognized and permitted suretyship for debts.[76]

---

similar perorations would have been found in the Hittite tablets had these been preserved in their entirety."); WILSON, CULTURE OF ANCIENT EGYPT 248–250 (Wilson's version of the Hittite-Egyptian treaty under Ramses II.); *Id.* at 249 (Regarding the extradition provisions which ensured that a returned fugitive would not be maltreated upon his return, Wilson hypothesizes: "Apparently there was an accepted code of international law, which protected the person and property of such refugees, although not their former positions or privileges." "The final section of the treaty, like other ancient legal documents, listed the witnesses who attested to the compact, but in this case they were divine."); *Id.* at 239 ("The reign of the Hittite king Mursilis coincided fairly well with that of Horemhab, and it may be that these two kings concluded the first Egyptian-Hittite treaty."); BREASTED, HISTORY OF EGYPT 437–439 (Breasted's description of the treaty between Ramses II and the Hittites.); *Id.* at 438 (The principal provisions of which were as follows: "the renunciation by both rulers of all projects of conquest against the other, the reaffirmation of the former treaties existing between the two countries, a defensive alliance involving the assistance of each against the other's foes; cooperation in the chastisement of delinquent subjects, probably in Syria; and the extradition of political fugitives and immigrants. A codicil provides for the humane treatment of these last.").

74. *See* Christopher J. Eyre, *Peasants and "Modern" Leasing Strategies in Ancient Egypt*, 40 J. ECONOMIC & SOCIAL HIST. ORIENT 367, 383 (1997); Aristide Théodorides, *The Concept of Law in Ancient Egypt, in* THE LEGACY OF EGYPT 291, 294 (J.R. Harris ed., 2d ed. 1971) ("[W]e are faced at this early date with a remarkable system of credit."); *See also Id.* at 304 (Explaining that sales could be made on credit.). Unfortunately, we have insufficient information about interest rates to draw many meaningful conclusions. *See* WARBURTON, STATE AND ECONOMY IN ANCIENT EGYPT 118, n. 323. But it is entirely possible that "the lack of interest" contributed to stable prices in ancient Egypt "where prices changed very little over hundreds or perhaps even a thousand years." *Id.* at 126–127 (footnote omitted).

75. *See* PESTMAN, MARRIAGE & MATRIMONIAL PROPERTY 45, 87, 115, 117.

76. *See* Aristide Théodorides, *The Concept of Law in Ancient Egypt, in* THE LEGACY OF EGYPT 291, 315 (J.R. Harris ed., 2d ed. 1971).

As has been mentioned, a significant degree of trade was conducted by means of barter.[77] Beyond this, however, the ancient Egyptians were among the first people to employ fixed standards of economic exchange value.[78] We have a text that describes the sale of a house near the Great Pyramid at Giza in the Old Kingdom (*c.* 2700–2200 B.C.). The buyer exchanged a bed and two different lots of linen for the house. What distinguishes this transaction from ordinary barter is that each item (*i.e.*, the bed and the linen lots) was designated as having a specific, fixed value. The bed was worth four "pieces" and each batch of linen was worth three "pieces." It appears that a "piece" had an established correlation to a particular weight and type of precious metal (of some sort). Thus, the buyer paid a total of ten "pieces" but he paid by transferring property whose total value equalled ten pieces.[79] Wilson observes:

> Thus there was a fixed and accepted unit of value for price quotations, even though a transaction might be carried entirely through with goods in kind and without the "piece" being handled by either party. This was an economic advance, and the unit of value was a precursor of money proper, which would not appear for another two thousand years.[80]

It was during the Old Kingdom that the Egyptians developed the use of copper rings (*š‘t*) to use as a medium of exchange.[81] There is evidence

77. *See supra* § 9.03.

78. *See* David Lorton, *Legal and Social Institutions of Pharaonic Egypt*, *in* 1 CIVILIZATIONS OF THE ANCIENT NEAR EAST 345, 353 (Jack M. Sasson ed., 1995). *See also* WARBURTON, STATE AND ECONOMY IN ANCIENT EGYPT 19 (Discussing specific units of value: *khar*, *deben*, and *kite*.); *Id.* at 84 ("The mere fact that tombs were robbed for their precious materials makes clear that the ancient Egyptians were conscious of the fact that in their economy silver and gold were money equivalents, and confirms that they were interested in accumulating wealth.").

79. *See* WILSON, CULTURE OF ANCIENT EGYPT 82–83 ("Although transactions were conducted by barter, there was already a referable medium of exchange in the Old Kingdom, a 'piece' of metal of fixed material and weight—not a coin, because it was not stamped. A man sold a house near the Great Pyramid and received ten 'pieces' for it. What he actually received was a bed valued at four pieces and two different lots of linen valued at three pieces each.").

80. *Id.* at 83 (footnote omitted).

81. *See* David Lorton, *Legal and Social Institutions of Pharaonic Egypt*, *in* 1 CIVILIZATIONS OF THE ANCIENT NEAR EAST 345, 352–53 (Jack M. Sasson ed., 1995) ("As early as the Old Kingdom, Egypt had an object, a ring of metal known as the *š‘t* (*shat*) that was employed as a unit of exchange. It was evidently of copper at first, but could be of silver in the Middle Kingdom or of gold in the New Kingdom."). *See also* Edward Bleiberg, *The Economy of Ancient Egypt*, *in* 3 CIVILIZATIONS OF THE ANCIENT NEAR EAST 1373, 1376 (Jack M. Sasson ed., 1995) ("Though the Egyptians used copper, bronze, and silver as units of exchange and standards of value, they never developed the concept of money to store and transport wealth.").

showing that there were some high-priced transactions in the Old Kingdom using such rings.[82] In the Middle Kingdom (*c.* 2040–1674 B.C.), the rings were often silver and, by the New Kingdom (*c.* 1552–1069 B.C.), gold.[83] In fact, in the New Kingdom under Thutmose III (*c.* 1479–1425 B.C.), one foreign nation used silver rings weighing almost 100 lbs. each as a means of commercial exchange.[84] Eyre emphasizes the importance of cloth as a medium of exchange also. According to Eyre:

> Cloth is an important form of capital, that the substantial household could itself manufacture on the basis of its lands and household labour. For relatively high value transactions and capital exchanges cloth played as important—if not more important—a role as metal.[85]

Still, Warburton advises that we must be cautious when interpreting units of value in ancient Egypt as anlogous to the modern concept of money:

> Money is assumed to possess three basic attributes, as (1) a unit of value, (2) a store of value, and (3) an exchange value. In ancient Egypt, the copper *deben* was a unit of value and evidently a store of value, but it was not normally employed in transactions, and thus fails to meet all three criteria. The *khar* of grain was used both as a unit of value and a unit of exchange, but storing grain is not a realis-

82. *See* BREASTED, HISTORY OF EGYPT 97–98 (Breasted describes commerce in the Old Kingdom as follows: "In some transactions, however, presumably those involving larger values, gold and copper in rings of a fixed weight, circulated as money, and stone weights were already marked with their equivalents in such rings. This ring-money is the oldest currency known. Silver was rare and more valuable than gold.").

83. *See* David Lorton, *Legal and Social Institutions of Pharaonic Egypt, in* 1 CIVILIZATIONS OF THE ANCIENT NEAR EAST 345, 352–53 (Jack M. Sasson ed., 1995); WARBURTON, STATE AND ECONOMY IN ANCIENT EGYPT 138.

84. *See* BREASTED, HISTORY OF EGYPT 304 (Breasted describes these rings as "commercial rings of silver, weighing nearly ninety eight pounds...."). *See also Id.* at 307 (Under Thutmose III, Breasted describes tribute coming into Egypt, some in the form of "gold and silver in large commercial rings, some of which weighed as much as twelve pounds each, while others for purposes of daily trade were of but a few grains weight.").

85. Christopher J. Eyre, *The Market Women of Pharaonic Egypt, in* LE COMMERCE EN ÉGYPT ANCIENNE 173, 180 (Nicolas Grimal and Bernadette Menu eds., 1998) (footnotes omitted). *See also Id.* at 182–83 ("The local records of transactions [in Deir el-Medina] frequently include cloth among the commodities used to make payments....") (footnote omitted). *See also* WARBURTON, STATE AND ECONOMY IN ANCIENT EGYPT 68 (Citing Roth for the proposition that "cloth was used 'as compensation for labor'" "'with well-known values.'"); *Id.* at 330 ("in the peculiar nature of the Egyptian economy, precious metals and textiles, etc. were both 'money' and 'articles'....").

> tic method of keeping one's savings, so that it likewise fails to meet all three criteria. Beds and other articles could be used for exchange purposes, and perhaps as a store of value, but they could not be regarded as a unit of value. In any case, there was no government controlled money or currency, which could be used as a tool of monetary policy....[86]

Warburton concludes, however, that grain was Egypt's principal medium of exchange:

> Egypt was...basically on the grain standard, and this particular commodity was the basis on which the entire economy flourished. It was grain which was used to pay the workers who built the monuments of the land, and by withdrawing labour from the agricultural sector, demand was actually increased, along with employment.[87]

§ 9.06 Customs Tax & Tax on Municipal Office

In addition to the ubiquitous property tax and the tax on real estate sales,[88] there were two other kinds of taxes routinely collected by the Egyptian government, namely, a customs tax and a tax on holding municipal office. At the time when commerce on the Nile was waxing—especially during the New Kingdom (*c.* 1552–1069 B.C.)—the government established customs houses in the Delta region at the mouths of the Nile. Thus, merchants paid a customs duty on most imported goods.[89] According to Breasted: "The income from this source must have been very large, but we have no means of estimating it. All the land-routes leading into the country were similarly policed, and foreigners who could not satisfactorily explain

86. WARBURTON, STATE AND ECONOMY IN ANCIENT EGYPT 116.

87. *Id.* at 120; *Id.* at 122 ("[A]lthough most people interested in Egyptian economics would not claim that Egypt had money, many economists could be persuaded to believe that emmer and barley were in fact money...."); *Id.* at 326 ("The evidence of P. Louvre E 3226 suggests that during the 18th Dynasty the state organs used grain as a medium of exchange to acquire other goods.") (footnote omitted).

88. *See supra* § 5.04.

89. *See* BREASTED, HISTORY OF EGYPT 338 ("Such trade required protection and regulation." "Amenhotep was therefore obliged to develop a marine police which patroled the coast of the Delta and constantly held the mouths of the river closed against all but lawful comers. Custom houses were also maintained by these police officials at the same places, and all merchandise not consigned to the king was dutiable.") (footnote omitted).

their business were turned back, while legitimate trade was encouraged, protected and properly taxed."[90]

The tax on holding municipal office was basically a tax for having the privilege of being an official. The amounts appear to have been substantial. Breasted offers the following example:

> This tax on officials consisted chiefly of gold, silver, grain, cattle and linen; the mayor of the old city of El Kab, for example, paid some 5,600 grains of gold, 4,200 grains of silver, one ox and one 'two-year old' into the vizier's office every year, while his subordinate paid 4,200 grains of silver, a bead necklace of gold, two oxen and two chests of linen.[91]

§ 9.07 Chapter Summary

Beginning even before the historical period, Egypt developed an active trade, both foreign and domestic. A number of business entities, such as the State, temples, and various associations of individuals prospered. Ancient Egyptians used the *imyt-pr* to formalize bilateral agreements (*i.e.*, contracts) in which both parties promised mutual exchanges. Archaeologists have unearthed many different types of contracts, including contracts for funerary services, slave sales, slave rental, donkey rental, and sales of houses, fields, and sales of goods. In bailment agreements, Egyptian law seems to have presumed that bailees were strictly liable for damage to bailed property. Some contracts included provisions for liquidated damages (often requiring specific performance of a promise) and warranties of title. In a number of circumstances, damages for breach of contract approximated what we today would call expectation damages (giving the non-breaching party the benefit of his bargain). Quite a few contract disputes were resolved by the parties agreeing to what was essentially a substituted contract or accord (*i.e.*, a brand new deal for payment). The Hittite Peace Treaty provides an example of a contract of international proportions. As regards general commercial law, we know that the Egyptians allowed sales on credit and established standard values for purposes of exchange. And, in addition to property taxes, there were also import or customs taxes.

---

90. *Id.* at 338–339.
91. *Id.* at 238.

CHAPTER 10

Personal Status

§ 10.01 General

Some Egyptologists believe that ancient Egypt was a place where people of relatively humble birth could advance in society. In other words, it is possible that the system was not completely a rigid caste system.[1] Nevertheless, there were distinct citizen classes: nobles, middle class merchants, and peasant-serfs. Grimal reminds us that "the social hierarchy was [even] perpetuated after death, with the nobles, courtiers and officials guaranteed their eternal reward alongside the king."[2] The term *pꜥt*, nobles, was used to describe the citizens who were the civil administrators, priests, and military officers. The term *sr* was also used for an administrator. The terms *rhyt* (Old Kingdom), *nḏs* (Middle Kingdom), and *nmḥy* (New Kingdom) were used for the commoners.[3] Lorton suggests that, for convenience, it may be best to conceptualize ancient Egyptian society as having been divided into two fundamental categories: "elite" and "nonelite": essentially equivalent to the groups represented by the terms *pꜥt* and *rhyt*. But admittedly, there was also a group that

---

1. *See* Wilson, Culture of Ancient Egypt 75. *But see* Grimal, Ancient Egypt 11 (Describing pharaonic Egypt as having had a "rigid social system....").
2. Grimal, Ancient Egypt 128.
3. *See* David Lorton, *Legal and Social Institutions of Pharaonic Egypt*, *in* 1 Civilizations of the Ancient Near East 345, 351 (Jack M. Sasson ed., 1995); Katary, Land Tenure in the Ramesside Period 211 (Katary claims that "As early as the Middle Kingdom, the word *nmḥ* was used to refer to 'freemen' as opposed to 'slaves' (*b3k*)...."); Christopher J. Eyre, *Peasants and "Modern" Leasing Strategies in Ancient Egypt*, 40 J. Economic & Social Hist. Orient 367, 377–78 (1997) ("In the Middle Kingdom a class of *nḏs* 'little man' may be parallel independent holders, while in the New Kingdom and after the term *nmḥw* (*n p3 t3 n pr* '3) literally 'orphan (of the Land of Pharaoh)' was used to indicate 'free' status...."); Warburton, State and Economy in Ancient Egypt 19.

was, in many respects, analogous to what we call a middle class.[4] From top to bottom, then, we see the following. First, the king was, by and large, in a social class unto himself. The nobles (*pꜥt*) ranked highest (other than the king himself). A middle class comprised of artisans and tradespeople prospered in the towns. And the lower class of peasant-serfs (*mrt*) worked on the nobles' estates.[5] According to Katary, "[t]he *nmḥ* was clearly a smallholder of land rather than a great land-owner.... [The] *nmḥw* were smallholders whose lands were independent of temple lands."[6] By the Middle Kingdom (*c.* 2040–1674 B.C.), all free citizens were routinely listed on rolls and were thereby subject to a draft for military or public service.[7] Foreigners, it should be noted, occasionally received land as rewards for fighting as mercenaries in the Egyptian military.[8] And finally, it should be remembered that the Egyptians recognized the need for a degree of social justice and conceptualized individual rights for all persons, whether noble, merchant, or peasant-serf.[9]

§ 10.02 Women

There is some evidence to suggest that early in the Old Kingdom women were considered more as valuable property than as people.[10] It appears,

---

4. *See* David Lorton, *Legal and Social Institutions of Pharaonic Egypt, in* 1 CIVILIZATIONS OF THE ANCIENT NEAR EAST 345, 351–52 (Jack M. Sasson ed., 1995); GRIMAL, ANCIENT EGYPT 167.

5. *See* Christopher J. Eyre, *Peasants and "Modern" Leasing Strategies in Ancient Egypt*, 40 J. ECONOMIC & SOCIAL HIST. ORIENT 367, 379 (1997); BREASTED, HISTORY OF EGYPT 44 ("In all probability the land all belonged to the estate of the king, by whom it was entrusted to a noble class. There were large estates conducted by these nobles, as in the period which immediately followed; but on what terms they were held we can not now determine. The people, with the possible exception of a free class of artificers and tradesmen, will have been slaves on these estates.").

6. KATARY, LAND TENURE IN THE RAMESSIDE PERIOD 211. *See also* WARBURTON, STATE AND ECONOMY IN ANCIENT EGYPT 19.

7. *See* BREASTED, HISTORY OF EGYPT 167–168 ("All free citizens, whether priests or not, were organized and enrolled in 'generations,' a term designating different classes of youth, which were to become successively liable to draught for military or public service.").

8. *See* William A. Ward, *Some Aspects of Private Land Ownership and Inheritance in Ancient Egypt, ca. 2500–1000* B.C., *in* LAND TENURE AND SOCIAL TRANSFORMATION IN THE MIDDLE EAST 63, 71 (Tarif Khalidi ed., 1984) ("foreigners could also be rewarded with land for military service.").

9. *See* WILSON, CULTURE OF ANCIENT EGYPT 140 ("The Egyptians had carried into the Middle Kingdom an emphasis on social justice and the rights of the common man, but they still thought the Egyptians were the only proper humans and that foreigners were akin to the animals.").

10. *See Id.* at 96 ("[I]t could be argued that women were basically chattels, although

however, that by the 4th Dynasty (*c.* 2625–2510 B.C.) women held a more elevated social position. But in the 6th Dynasty (*c.* 2460–2200 B.C.), the status of women may have fallen again and was quite low. A woman's husband legally controlled her, and when he died, either her son or a designated person named in her late husband's will assumed that legal management.[11] As the Middle Kingdom (*c.* 2040–1674 B.C.) approached, the wives of the nobility were moving toward greater equality with their husbands.[12] And, by the 13th Dynasty (*c.* 1785 B.C.), significant change had occurred. We see, for example, one married woman acting in a manner that is entirely independent. She sues her father in a property dispute.[13] By the New Kingdom (*c.* 1552–1069 B.C.), women appear to have gained a legal status basically equal to men.[14] Although artistic representations of married couples in the Old Kingdom often portrayed wives as much smaller and less significant figures than their husbands, in the New Kingdom husband and wife generally appear as a balanced pair, with the wife depicted as an equal partner.[15] Thus, in contrast to circumstances in ancient Athens and Rome, women in ancient Egypt—certainly by the New Kingdom—possessed a legal status

---

perhaps the most valuable of chattels."); Schafik Allam, *Women as Owners of Immovables in Pharaonic Egypt, in* WOMEN'S EARLIEST RECORDS FROM ANCIENT EGYPT AND WESTERN ASIA 123, 123 (Barbara Lesko ed., 1989).

11. Some legal historians (Théodorides and Pirenne) believe that, at least during the 6th Dynasty (*i.e.*, the late Old Kingdom), a woman "no longer enjoyed more than a reduced legal status, which, in particular, placed her under the tutelage of her husband, and after his death under that of his eldest son, or, indeed, of a third party designated by her husband in a will." Aristide Théodorides, *The Concept of Law in Ancient Egypt, in* THE LEGACY OF EGYPT 291, 296 (J.R. Harris ed., 2d ed. 1971). *See also Id.* (Théodorides remarks that this is an "evolution which has taken place in public and family law since the 4th Dynasty."); *Id.* at 298 (Noting also evidence that the eldest son became the legal guardian, or tutor, for his mother upon his father's death.).

12. *See* WILSON, CULTURE OF ANCIENT EGYPT 98 (Regarding the evolving equality of status between man and wife as the Middle Kingdom approached.).

13. *See* Aristide Théodorides, *The Concept of Law in Ancient Egypt, in* THE LEGACY OF EGYPT 291, 303 (J.R. Harris ed., 2d ed. 1971). *See also* David Lorton, *Legal and Social Institutions of Pharaonic Egypt, in* 1 CIVILIZATIONS OF THE ANCIENT NEAR EAST 345, 349 (Jack M. Sasson ed., 1995).

14. *See* Schafik Allam, *Women as Owners of Immovables in Pharaonic Egypt, in* WOMEN'S EARLIEST RECORDS FROM ANCIENT EGYPT AND WESTERN ASIA 123, 133 (Barbara Lesko ed., 1989); PESTMAN, MARRIAGE AND MATRIMONIAL PROPERTY 182.

15. *See* WILSON, CULTURE OF ANCIENT EGYPT 203 ("This acknowledged importance of women was not restricted to queens—who were, after all, daughters or wives or mothers of gods. It has been pointed out that the artistic convention of a married couple under earlier periods gave priority to the husband and made the wife his attaché, whereas the Empire presented the couple as a balanced pair in equal prominence.") (footnote omitted).

that was on equal footing with men.[16] Women could participate in legal relations and legal transactions on their own.[17] They could execute wills[18] and enter into binding contracts on their own behalf.[19] They could own, buy, sell, and inherit property and real estate.[20] They were permitted to take part in all legal proceedings. For example, women could sue and be sued in court,[21] serve as witnesses for contracts and wills, and could testify in court

---

16. *See* Janet H. Johnson, *The Legal Status of Women in Ancient Egypt, in* MISTRESS OF THE HOUSE MISTRESS OF HEAVEN: WOMEN IN ANCIENT EGYPT 175 (Anne K. Chapel and Glenn E. Markoe eds., 1996) (Johnson takes the position that women were the equals of men even in the Old Kingdom).

17. *See Id. See also* PESTMAN, MARRIAGE & MATRIMONIAL PROPERTY 54; David Lorton, *Legal and Social Institutions of Pharaonic Egypt, in* 1 CIVILIZATIONS OF THE ANCIENT NEAR EAST 345, 349 (Jack M. Sasson ed., 1995); Christopher J. Eyre, *The Market Women of Pharaonic Egypt, in* LE COMMERCE EN ÉGYPT ANCIENNE 173, 183 (Nicolas Grimal and Bernadette Menu eds., 1998).

18. *See* MCDOWELL, JURISDICTION 152 (McDowell refers to the woman Naunakhte as illustrating a woman's capacity to make a valid will.); Schafik Allam, *Women as Owners of Immovables in Pharaonic Egypt, in* WOMEN'S EARLIEST RECORDS FROM ANCIENT EGYPT AND WESTERN ASIA 123, 128 (Barbara Lesko ed., 1989) ("Women could transfer their titles to immovables and dispose of them by several means (sale, adoption, and other inheritance conventions)."). *See also supra* § 7.02.

19. *See* GAY ROBINS, WOMEN IN ANCIENT EGYPT 129.

20. *See Id.* at 131–137; Schafik Allam, *Women as Owners of Immovables in Pharaonic Egypt, in* WOMEN'S EARLIEST RECORDS FROM ANCIENT EGYPT AND WESTERN ASIA 123, 134 (Barbara Lesko ed., 1989); KATARY, LAND TENURE IN THE RAMESSIDE PERIOD 16 ("there is a very real possibility that some of these women may have been smallholders in their own right rather than simply by title of inheritance".) (footnote omitted); *Id.* at 211 (Referring to Naunakhte, Katary states that "she was free to dispose of her property as she saw fit".); David Lorton, *Legal and Social Institutions of Pharaonic Egypt, in* 1 CIVILIZATIONS OF THE ANCIENT NEAR EAST 345, 349 (Jack M. Sasson ed., 1995); PESTMAN, MARRIAGE & MATRIMONIAL PROPERTY 87–88, 151–152; C.J. Eyre, *The Adoption Papyrus in Social Context,* 78 J. EGYPTIAN ARCHAEOLOGY 207, 219 (1992); WILSON, CULTURE OF ANCIENT EGYPT 203 ("[S]uch business documents as we possess from the Empire show that women had their own rights to property, to buying and selling, or to testifying in court."); Christopher J. Eyre, *Peasants and "Modern" Leasing Strategies in Ancient Egypt,* 40 J. ECONOMIC & SOCIAL HIST. ORIENT 367, 380 (1997); Bernadette Menu, *Women and Business Life in the First Millennium B.C., in* WOMEN'S EARLIEST RECORDS FROM ANCIENT EGYPT AND WESTERN ASIA 193, 199 (Barbara S. Lesko ed., 1989) ("In short women of the 21st to 23rd Dynasties seem to have enjoyed an important legal capacity, although they are mainly entitled to land rights (land property in ruling families, simple holding among small farmers or peasant soldiers)."). *See also Taylor, Law Under the Pharaohs,* 6 POL'Y REV. 66, at 68 (1980) (Regarding inheriting property.).

21. *See* GAY ROBINS, WOMEN IN ANCIENT EGYPT 129 (Describing a case that "shows that a woman could initiate a lawsuit on her own behalf."). *See also* MCDOWELL, JURISDICTION 152 ("On the whole, however, women appear in relatively few cases either as claimants or defendants, probably because they were involved in fewer substantial economic transactions.").

trials. In addition, they were considered competent to serve as judges.[22] Seti I's Nauri Decree specifically claims that it is designed to protect and promote freedom for both men and women.[23]

Women played a more prominent role in the political developments of the 18th (*c.* 1552–1295 B.C.) and 19th (*c.* 1295–1188 B.C.) Dynasties than ever before. To be sure, women had wielded political influence in earlier times, but never before had Egypt seen the likes of Queen Hatshepsut (*c.* 1478–1458 B.C.), who ruled as "pharaoh" for over twenty years, nor queens Tiy (wife of Amenhotep III (*c.* 1390–1352 B.C.)) and Nefertiti (wife of Akhenaton/Amenhotep IV (*c.* 1352–1348 B.C.)).[24] In the Amarna Age under Akhenaton (Amenhotep IV), women actively participated in public life to a degree beyond what Egypt had previously experienced. Wilson boldly remarks: "It was an age of strong feminism."[25]

§ 10.03 Middle Class

During the Middle Kingdom (*c.* 2040–1674 B.C.), we see a significant increase in the number of persons whom we would label as middle class.[26] This middle class was gradually gaining wealth and prosperity. In particular, there was significant growth in the number of tradesmen, artisans, and artificers.[27] The handicrafts of this middle class soon appeared in the mar-

22. *See* Janet H. Johnson, *The Legal Status of Women in Ancient Egypt, in* Mistress of the House Mistress of Heaven: Women in Ancient Egypt 175 (Anne K. Chapel and Glenn E. Markoe eds., 1996) ("they could sit on juries...."). *See also* S. Allam, *Legal Aspects in the 'Contendings of Horus and Seth', in* Studies in Pharaonic Religion and Society in Honour of J. Gwyn Griffiths 137, 142 (Alan B. Lloyd ed., 1992).

23. *See* William F. Edgerton, *The Nauri Decree of Seti I: A Translation and Analysis of the Legal Portion*, 6 J. Near Eastern Stud. 219, 221–222 (1947).

24. *See* Wilson, Culture of Ancient Egypt 202 ("One feature of the imperial age of Egyptian history was the prominence of women." Wilson says that this is not necessarily new, and gives examples from earlier times, but he says: "The 18th Dynasty, however, surpassed previous ages in the acknowledged influence of women." He gives as examples Queen Hatshepsut, Tiy, and Nefertiti.).

25. *Id.* at 214.

26. *See* Grimal, Ancient Egypt 167.

27. *See* Warburton, State and Economy in Ancient Egypt 19 (Citing Drenkhahn for the vitality of an appreciable number of "independent craftsmen."); *Id.* at 126 (Discussing the increase in the numbers of private sector craftsmen.); Breasted, History of Egypt 168; *Id.* at 169 (In the Middle Kingdom (*c.* 2040–1674 B.C.), we begin to see the emergence of "a prosperous and often well-to-do middle class in the provinces, sometimes owning their own slaves and lands and bringing

kets throughout Egypt.[28] Later, in the New Kingdom (*c.* 1552–1069 B.C.), the more well-to-do of the old middle class climbed into the lower tier of what may be called an "official class." These, along with the relatives and dependents of the landed nobility (who comprised the upper tier of the "official class") held administrative offices in local bureaucracies. The tradespeople, merchants, and craftspeople continued to thrive as well.[29]

§ 10.04 Peasant-Serfs and Slaves

The fundamental social hierarchy that defined ancient Egypt was established and in place early in the Old Kingdom. The nobles operated large agricultural estates and the majority of the population—the landless peasants (*smdt*)—worked on those estates.[30] The peasants performed the manual labor and menial tasks. Many historians have analogized the life of an ancient Egyptian peasant to that of a "serf" who worked on a lord's feudal estate in Medieval Europe.[31] Peasants, however, could own property, testify in court, and could marry.[32]

---

their offerings of first fruits to the temple of the town as did the nomarch himself.") (footnote omitted).

28. *See* BREASTED, HISTORY OF EGYPT 170.

29. *See Id.* at 246 (In the New Kingdom (*c.* 1552–1069 B.C.), Breasted identifies: an "official class": "its lower ranks drawn from the old middle class, while on the other hand its upper strata were the relatives and dependents of the old landed nobility, by whom the higher and more important local offices were administered." "The old middle class of merchants, skilled craftsmen and artists also survived and continued to replenish the lower ranks of the official class. Below these were the masses who worked the fields and estates, the serfs of the Pharaoh.") (footnote omitted).

30. *See* David Lorton, *Legal and Social Institutions of Pharaonic Egypt, in* 1 CIVILIZATIONS OF THE ANCIENT NEAR EAST 345, 351 (Jack M. Sasson ed., 1995); WARBURTON, STATE AND ECONOMY IN ANCIENT EGYPT 19.

31. *See e.g.,* BREASTED, HISTORY OF EGYPT 84 (Regarding land ownership, Breasted says: "The land which was thus administered must to a large extent have belonged to the crown. Under the oversight of the local governors' subordinates it was worked and made profitable by slaves or serfs, who formed the bulk of the population. They belonged to the ground and were bequeathed with it.") (footnote omitted).

32. *See* Aristide Théodorides, *The Concept of Law in Ancient Egypt, in* THE LEGACY OF EGYPT 291, 307 (J.R. Harris ed., 2d ed. 1971) ("They enjoyed a legal status which made them more like serfs. They could acquire property and bear witness at law, even against their masters.... they seem to have been able to marry easily with free individuals or to be adopted by them, so becoming free themselves, the process of manumission being unknown.") (ellipses original) (footnotes omitted); *See also* David Lorton, *Legal and Social Institutions of Pharaonic Egypt, in* 1 CIVILIZATIONS OF THE ANCIENT NEAR EAST 345, 352 (Jack M. Sasson ed., 1995) ("As to slaves, they could acquire property of their own, and they could marry free people, be freed, or be adopted by free people.").

In addition to the class of peasant-serfs, foreign captives came to Egypt as slaves when the kings of the New Kingdom invaded other nations. This influx of foreign slaves resulted directly from the policy of aggression and expansion promoted by the 18th and 19th Dynasty pharaohs. Thutmose III (*c.* 1479–1425 B.C.), for example, brought many foreign slaves to Egypt as captives of war. He rewarded his generals by giving them slaves. And he used many other slaves to work on his estates and to construct his building projects in Thebes.[33] These captive-slaves did not enjoy the technical, legal independence that the peasant-serfs had (at least in theory), although, generally speaking, both slave and serf status usually resulted either from being taken as a prisoner of war, from debt, or from pursuing protection under another's wing.[34] Foreign slaves legally were treated as personal property, chattels. Owners could sell them, rent them, and leave them to another in a will.[35] We have, for example, one will (Flinders Petrie found it in El-Lahun) in which a noble bequeaths his wife four Asiatic slaves.[36] We also know of one town that owned slaves. The town itself then allotted slaves to its citizens for a certain number of days per month or per year. We are aware of this practice because of extant contracts in which citizens sold their rights (*i.e.*, rights to the town's slaves) to a man—already mentioned above—named Messuia.[37] Many such slaves who worked for the palace or in the

---

33. *See* BREASTED, HISTORY OF EGYPT 309.

34. *See* Janet H. Johnson, *The Legal Status of Women in Ancient Egypt, in* MISTRESS OF THE HOUSE MISTRESS OF HEAVEN: WOMEN IN ANCIENT EGYPT 175 (Anne K. Chapel and Glenn E. Markoe eds., 1996) ("Some, especially in the New Kingdom, were prisoners of war; some bound themselves (and their children) to an individual, or more frequently, to a temple because of debts or to secure protection.") (footnote omitted).

35. *See* Aristide Théodorides, *The Concept of Law in Ancient Egypt, in* THE LEGACY OF EGYPT 291, 307 (J.R. Harris ed., 2d ed. 1971) (Slaves "were not very numerous in Egypt...." They "were bought and transferred from owner to owner like chattels....").

36. *See* GARDINER, EGYPT OF THE PHARAOHS 144 (Gardiner discusses wills found in El-Lahun, excavated by Petrie and translated by F. Ll. Griffith: "Then there are wills from which we learn that a man was able to bequeath pretty well as he chose not only his house and chattels, but also such an office as that of director of a phylē of lay-priests. In another case a wife was left, among other things, four 'Aamu, Asiatic slaves.").

37. *See* David Lorton, *Legal and Social Institutions of Pharaonic Egypt, in* 1 CIVILIZATIONS OF THE ANCIENT NEAR EAST 345, 354 (Jack M. Sasson ed., 1995) ("According to the documents, members of his community sold him workdays of slaves in exchange for animals, grain, cloth, and silver or bronze. It has been guessed that Messuia had his own weaving establishment, but he must have obtained the metal from other transactions not recorded in the preserved documents."); Aristide Théodorides, *The Concept of Law in Ancient Egypt, in* THE LEGACY OF EGYPT 291, 314–315 (J.R. Harris ed., 2d ed. 1971) (Théodorides speculates that a town may have actually owned some slaves "being then placed at the disposal of the inhabitants at the rate of so many days

households of nobles probably had a more comfortable life than the average peasant.[38] Under Amenhotep III (*c.* 1390–1352 B.C.), in many respects the pinnacle of the New Kingdom, a great many slaves entered Egypt from foreign countries. But at that time the pharaoh's chief scribe was responsible for distributing them throughout Egypt, and for granting them peasant-serf status (*i.e.*, they were liable for payment of taxes). By then, Egypt had become something of a melting pot with more and more intermarriages between native Egyptians and foreigners.[39] Other slaves, however, probably would have been happy to have traded places with a peasant-serf: such as the Canaanites who were forced to work in the copper and turquoise mines in the Sinai, or those who labored on construction projects in Thebes or Karnak, or the slaves whom Ramses III (*c.* 1186–1154 B.C.) branded and compelled to fight in his army.[40]

§ 10.05 Chapter Summary

The king was clearly at the apex of the legal and social pyramid in ancient Egypt. After the king, there was a significant group of persons whom

---

per month or year. It would then be their right to days of the slaves' work that the inhabitants of the Faiyum were selling to Messuia....") (footnote omitted). *See also supra* § 9.03.

38. *See* WILSON, CULTURE OF ANCIENT EGYPT 187 ("Military successes under the Empire brought into Egypt thousands of captives, taken in battle." "Many of the foreigners were mere slaves of the palace, of the domains of the nobles, or of the temple estates. However, slavery was not then the sharply and legally delimited category which it was in more modern times. The household slave was much better off than the native Egyptian peasant.").

39. *See* BREASTED, HISTORY OF EGYPT 339 ("The influx of slaves, chiefly of Semitic race, which had begun under Thutmose III, still continued, and the king's chief scribe distributed them throughout the land and enrolled them among the tax-paying serfs.") (footnote omitted); *Id.* ("As this host of foreigners intermarried with the natives, the large infusion of strange blood began to make itself felt in a new and composite type of face, if we may trust the artists of the day.").

40. *See* GRIMAL, ANCIENT EGYPT 271–272 ("These mercenaries, marked with a branding iron as a sign of their servitude, were taken into captivity along with their wives and children; their goods, particularly their herds, were confiscated and transferred to the estate of Amun."); WILSON, CULTURE OF ANCIENT EGYPT 191 (Wilson remarks that, in the 18th Dynasty, "Some time within the range of the early fifteenth century B.C., Canaanites were used as the miners for turquoise and copper at Serabit el-Khadem in Sinai. Presumably they were captives held in the Delta and brought out seasonally, under armed escort, for the mining."); BREASTED, HISTORY OF EGYPT 496 (Relating that Ramses III used slaves, "branded with the name of the king," in his army.); GARDINER, EGYPT OF THE PHARAOHS 253 (Stating that in the 19th Dynasty war captives became "slaves in the workshops of the temple of Karnak.").

historians usually call nobles. The nobles constituted an elite circle who were the principal land owners. An appreciable number of merchants, craftspeople, and, eventually, local government administrators comprised what came to be a thriving middle class. The peasant-serfs typically worked on large estates owned by nobles. During the New Kingdom, foreign slaves were brought into Egypt as captives of war. In contrast to many other ancient civilizations, women in ancient Egypt—at least by the New Kingdom—enjoyed a status that was the legal equivalent of men.

Bibliography

Allam, Schafik, *Egyptian Law Courts in Pharaonic and Hellenistic Times*, 77 J. Egyptian Archaeology 109 (1991).

———, *Legal Aspects in the 'Contendings of Horus and Seth'*, *in* Studies in Pharaonic Religion and Society in Honour of J. Gwyn Griffiths 137 (Alan B. Lloyd ed., 1992).

———, *Papyrus Turin 2021: Another Adoption Extraordinary, in* Individu, Société et Spiritualité dans L'Égypt Pharaonique et Copte: Mélanges égyptologiques offerts au Professeur Aristide Théodoridès 23 (Christian Cannuyer and Jean-Marie Kruchten eds., 1993).

———, *Women as Owners of Immovables in Pharaonic Egypt, in* Women's Earliest Records From Ancient Egypt and Western Asia 123 (Barbara S. Lesko ed., 1989).

Anthes, Rudolf, *The Legal Aspect of the Instruction of Amenemhet*, 16 J. Near Eastern Stud. 176 (1957).

Assman, Jan, *When Justice Fails: Jurisdiction and Imprecation in Ancient Egypt and the Near East*, 78 J. Egyptian Archaeology 149 (1992).

Bedell, Ellen, Criminal Law in the Egyptian Ramesside Period (Brandeis University, Ph.D. Dissertation) (1973).

Bleiberg, Edward, *The Economy of Ancient Egypt, in* 3 Civilizations of the Ancient Near East 1373 (Jack M. Sasson ed., 1995).

Breasted, James H., A History of Egypt (1905).

———, The Development of Religion and Thought in Ancient Egypt (1912).

Camilleri, Marijane, Comment, *Lessons in Law From Literature: A Look at the Movement and a Peer at Her Jury*, 39 Cath. U. L. Rev. 557 (1990).

Castle, E.W., *Shipping and Trade in Ramesside Egypt*, 35 J. Economic & Social Hist. Orient 239 (1992).

Capart, J, Gardiner, A.H., and van de Walle, B., *New Light on the Ramesside Tomb-Robberies*, 22 J. Egyptian Archaeology 169 (1936).

Černý, Jaraslav, *Restitution of, and Penalty Attaching to, Stolen Property in Ramesside Times*, 23 J. Egyptian Archaeology 186 (1937).

———, *The Will of Naunakhte and the Related Documents*, 31 J. Egyptian Archaeology 29 (1945).

Černý, J. and Peet, T. Eric, *A Marriage Settlement of the Twentieth Dynasty*, 13 J. Egyptian Archaeology 30 (1927).

Cunningham, Roger A., Stoebuck, William B., and Witman, Dale A., The Law of Property (1993).

Edgerton, William F., *The Nauri Decree of Seti I: A Translation and Analysis of the Legal Portion*, 6 J. Near Eastern Stud. 219 (1947).

Erman, Adolf, Life in Ancient Egypt (original English trans. 1894 by H.M. Tirard, 1971).

Eyre, Christopher J., *Crime and Adultery in Ancient Egypt*, 70 J. Egyptian Archaeology 92 (1984).

———, *Peasants and "Modern" Leasing Strategies in Ancient Egypt*, 40 J. Economic & Social Hist. Orient 367 (1997).

———, *The Adoption Papyrus in Social Context*, 78 J. Egyptian Archaeology 207 (1992).

———, *The Market Women of Pharaonic Egypt, in* Le commerce en Égypt ancienne 173, (Nicolas Grimal and Bernadette Menu eds., 1998).

Farnsworth, E. Allan, Contracts (2d ed. 1990).

Faulkner, R.O., A Concise Dictionary of Middle Egyptian (1981).

Fed. R. Civ. P. 8(a) (1991).

Fed. R. Civ. P. 38 (1991).

Fed. R. Civ. P. 39 (1991).

Gardiner, Sir Alan, *Adoption Extraordinary*, 26 J. Egyptian Archaeology 23 (1940).

———, Egypt of the Pharaohs (1961).

———, Egyptian Grammar (3d ed. 1978).

Griffiths, J. Gwyn, *Isis as Maat, Dikaiosune, and Iustitia, in* 3 Hommages a Jean Leclant 255 (1994).

Grimal, Nicolas, A History of Ancient Egypt (Ian Shaw trans. 1992).

HALL, JEROME, FOUNDATIONS OF JURISPRUDENCE (1973).

Hoch, James, and Orel, Sara, *Murder in Ancient Egypt, in* DEATH AND TAXES IN THE ANCIENT NEAR EAST 87 (Sara Orel ed., 1992).

HORNBLOWER, SIMON AND ANTONY SPAWFORTH, eds. THE OXFORD CLASSICAL DICTIONARY 1047 (1996, 3d ed.).

Iversen, Erik, *The Hieroglyphic Tradition,* in The Legacy of Egypt 170 (J.R. Harris ed., 2d ed. 1971).

JAMES, T.G.H, PHARAOH'S PEOPLE: SCENES FROM LIFE IN IMPERIAL EGYPT (1984).

Janssen, Jac, *Rules of Legal Proceeding in the Community of Necropolis Workmen at Deir el-Medina,* 32 Bibliotheca Orientalis 291 (1975).

Janssen, J.J., and Pestman, P.W., *Burial and Inheritance in the Community of the Necropolis Workmen at Thebes (Pap. Bulaq X and O. Petrie 16),* 11 J. ECONOMIC & SOCIAL HIST. ORIENT 168 (1968).

Johnson, Janet H., *The Legal Status of Women in Ancient Egypt, in* MISTRESS OF THE HOUSE MISTRESS OF HEAVEN: WOMEN IN ANCIENT EGYPT 175 (Anne K. Chapel and Glenn E. Markoe eds., 1996).

KATARY, SALLY L.D., LAND TENURE IN THE RAMESSIDE PERIOD (1989).

KEETON, W. PAGE ET AL., PROSSER AND KEETON ON THE LAW OF TORTS (5th ed. 1984).

Kemp, Barry J., *Old Kingdom, Middle Kingdom and Second Intermediate Period c. 2686–1552 B.C., in* Ancient Egypt: A Social History 83 (Trigger *et al* eds., 1983).

LAFAVE, WAYNE R., AND SCOTT, AUSTIN W., CRIMINAL LAW (2d ed. 1986).

Levinson, Sanford, *Law as Literature,* 60 TEX. L. REV. 373 (1982).

LEXIKON DER ÄGYPTOLGIE, Vol. 5 (1984), "Recht" 185.

LICHTHEIM, MIRIAM, ANCIENT EGYPTIAN LITERATURE VOLUME I: THE OLD AND MIDDLE KINGDOMS (1975).

LOCKE, J., SECOND TREATISE ON GOVERNMENT (1690).

Lorton, David. *Legal and Social Institutions of Pharaonic Egypt, in* 1 CIVILIZATIONS OF THE ANCIENT NEAR EAST 345 (Jack M. Sasson ed., 1995).

———, *The Treatment of Criminals in Ancient Egypt,* 20 J. ECONOMIC & SOCIAL HIST. ORIENT 2 (1977).

LURKER, MANFRED, THE GODS AND SYMBOLS OF ANCIENT EGYPT (Barbara Cummings trans., 1980).

McDOWELL, ANDREA, JURISDICTION IN THE WORKMEN'S COMMUNITY OF DEIR EL-MEDINA (1990).

———, *Legal Aspects of Care of the Elderly in Egypt to the End of the New Kingdom, in* THE CARE OF THE ELDERLY IN THE ANCIENT NEAR EAST 199 (Marten Stol and Sven P. Vleeming eds., 1998).

MATTHA, GIRGIS, THE DEMOTIC LEGAL CODE OF HERMOPOLIS WEST (1975, preface, additional notes, and glossary by George R. Hughes).

Manning, J.G., *Demotic Egyptian Instruments of Transfer as Evidence for Private Ownership of Real Property*, 71 Chicago-Kent L. Rev. 237 (1995).

Manning, J.G., Gary Greig, and Sugihiko Uchida, *Chicago Oriental Institute Ostracon 12073 Once Again*, 48 J. NEAR EASTERN STUD. 117 (1989).

Meltzer, Edmund S., Book Review, 104.2 J. AM. ORIENTAL SOC'Y 363 (Reviewing ROBERT PARANT, L'AFFAIRE SINOUHE. TENTATIVE D'APPROACHE DE LA JUSTICE REPRESSIVE ÉGYPTIENNE AU DEBUT DU II MILLENAIRE AV. J.C. (1982).).

Menu, Bernadette, *Women and Business Life in the First Millennium B.C., in* WOMEN'S EARLIEST RECORDS FROM ANCIENT EGYPT AND WESTERN ASIA 193 (Barbara S. Lesko ed., 1989).

PESTMAN, PIETER WILLEM, MARRIAGE AND MATRIMONIAL PROPERTY IN ANCIENT EGYPT (1961).

———, *The Law of Succession in Ancient Egypt*, 9 Studia et documenta ad jura antiqui pertinentia 58 (1969).

Pflüger, Kurt, *The Edict of Horemhab*, 5 J. NEAR EASTERN STUD. 260 (1944).

Phillips, Jacke, *Tomb-robbers and their Booty in Ancient Egypt, in* DEATH AND TAXES IN THE ANCIENT NEAR EAST 157 (Sara Orel ed., 1992).

Posener, Georges, *Literature, in* THE LEGACY OF EGYPT 220 (J.R. Harris ed., 2d ed. 1971).

POSNER, RICHARD, LAW AND LITERATURE: A MISUNDERSTOOD RELATION (1988).

RESTATEMENT (SECOND) OF TORTS § 13 (1979).

RESTATEMENT (SECOND) OF TORTS § 21 (1979).

RESTATEMENT (SECOND) OF TORTS § 46 (1979).

RESTATEMENT (SECOND) OF TORTS §§ 216-244 (1979).

RESTATEMENT (SECOND) TORTS § 504 (1979)

RESTATEMENT (SECOND) OF TORTS § 821B (1979).

ROBINS, GAY, WOMEN IN ANCIENT EGYPT (1993).

ROSSITER, EVELYN, THE BOOK OF THE DEAD: PAPYRI OF ANI, HUNEFER, ANHAI (1979).

ROTH, MARTHA T., LAW COLLECTIONS FROM MESOPOTAMIA AND ASIA MINOR (1995).

Shupak, Nili, *A New Source For the Study of the Judiciary and Law of Ancient Egypt: "The Tale of the Eloquent Peasant"*, 51 J. NEAR E. STUD. 1 (1992).

SIMPSON, WILLIAM K. ed., THE LITERATURE OF ANCIENT EGYPT (1972).

Taylor, David, *Law under the Pharaohs* 6 Pol'y Rev. 66 (1980).

Théodorides, Aristide, *The Concept of Law in Ancient Egypt*, *in* THE LEGACY OF EGYPT 291 (J.R. Harris ed., 2d ed. 1971).

THOMAS, J.A.C., TEXTBOOK OF ROMAN LAW (1976).

Tobin, Vincent, *Ma'at and Dike: Some Comparative Considerations of Egyptian and Greek Thought*, 24 J. AM. RESEARCH CENTER IN EGYPT 113 (1987).

VAN DEN BOORN, G.P.F., THE DUTIES OF THE VIZIER: CIVIL ADMINISTRATION IN THE EARLY NEW KINGDOM (1988).

VerSteeg, Russ *Law in Ancient Egyptian Fiction*, 24 Ga. J. Int'l & Comp. L. 37 (1994).

Ward, William A., *Some Aspects of Private Land Ownership and Inheritance in Ancient Egypt, ca. 2500–1000 B.C.*, *in* Land Tenure and Social Transformation in the Middle East 63 (Tarif Khalidi ed., 1984).

WARBURTON, DAVID A., STATE AND ECONOMY IN ANCIENT EGYPT: FISCAL VOCABULARY OF THE NEW KINGDOM (1997).

WATSON, ALAN, ROMAN LAW & COMPARATIVE LAW (1991).

Weisberg, Richard, *Coming of Age Some More: "Law and Literature" Beyond the Cradle*, 13 NOVA L. REV. 107 (1988).

———, *Family Feud: A Response to Robert Weisberg on Law and Literature* 1 YALE J.L. & HUMAN. 69 (1988).

Weisberg, Robert H., *The Law-Literature Enterprise*, 1 YALE J.L. & HUMAN. 1 (1988).

WHITE, JAMES B., THE LEGAL IMAGINATION: STUDIES IN THE NATURE OF LEGAL THOUGHT AND EXPRESSION (1973).

WHITE, JON MANCHIP, EVERYDAY LIFE IN ANCIENT EGYPT (1963).

Wilson, John A., *Authority and Law in Ancient Egypt*, Supplement to 40 J. AM. ORIENTAL SOC. 1 (1954).

———, THE CULTURE OF ANCIENT EGYPT (1951).

General Index

Accessio, 109
Accomplices, 76
Accord, 155, 201, 208
Accused, 32, 34, 44, 50, 60, 65, 69, 72, 74–75, 78–81, 83–85, 87–88, 157, 160–161, 165, 170–171, 177–178, 186
Actio de Posito et Suspenso, 180
Adjacent Landowners, 111
Adj-Mer, 39
Admonitions of an Egyptian Sage, 11, 16, 26
Admonitions of Ipuwer, 3
Adoption, 104, 127, 130–132, 137–146, 149, 172, 212, 219–220
Advocates, 34, 71, 75, 94, 100
Affidavits, 74
Agents, 57, 116
Agricultural, 4, 48, 99, 103, 106, 114, 116–117, 119, 122, 139, 153, 188, 197, 207, 214
Akkadian, 8
Amarna Period, 6, 39
Amiens, 120, 153
Amputation, 155, 163, 176, 179, 185–186
'nḫ, 80
  'nḫ n nb, 80
  'nḫ '3 n nb, 80
Animals, 16, 28, 103, 159, 164, 182, 210, 215
Annuity Contracts, 131–133, 136
Appeal, 27–28, 64, 67, 87–89, 92–94, 183
Appellate Courts, 88
Archives, 10, 24, 39, 50–51, 64, 67, 99, 113, 118, 141, 196
Army, 161, 216
Armytage Ostracon, 155
Arrest, 72, 86, 157
Assassinate, 85–86, 154, 169–171, 186
Assault, 44, 85, 171, 177–178, 181, 183, 185
Asyûṭ, 196
Aroura, 114, 121
3'tw, 55
3ṯw, 57

B3k, 209
Bailee, 109–110, 199–201
Bailiffs, 57, 69
Bailment, 109–110, 199–201, 208
Balance, 11, 13, 19, 21, 31–32, 36, 118
Banishment, 80, 169, 177
Barge, 89
Barter, 6, 102, 192, 201, 205
Battery, 177–178, 180, 183, 185–186
Beam, 31
Beatings, 56, 76, 78–79, 154, 178, 186
Birds, 159
Blackmarket, 76

Boat, 35, 90, 120, 176, 188
Book of the Dead, The, 3, 20, 71, 91, 156, 158–159, 169, 173, 186, 223
Boundaries, 24, 42, 99, 108, 134–135, 164, 195
Branded, 154, 216
Bribery, 23, 29, 41, 46, 53–54, 58, 121, 154–155, 160, 175–176, 186
Bride, 126, 128–129, 131–132, 134–136
British Museum Ostracon 5631, 164
British Museum Ostracon 5625, 109
Brother, 34–35, 125, 128, 138, 144, 174
Brothers, 64, 127–128, 135, 138–140, 146–147, 194, 198
Bt3, 151
Buildings, 60, 157, 160
Burial, 45, 115, 139, 141, 143, 153–154, 156–158, 166, 186, 221
Burning, 154, 156–157, 174
Business Entity, 190
Business Organization, 191
Business, 10, 61, 78, 93, 103–104, 121, 140, 143, 184, 190–193, 195, 199, 204, 208, 212, 222
Bwt, 161

Cairo 20538, 157
Cairo Stela, 61, 195
Cairo Stela jd'E 43649, 61
Capital Offense, 53–54, 175
Captives, 126, 203, 215–217
Castration, 175
Cattle, 17, 39–40, 105, 110, 116, 119, 159, 164, 208
Census, 42, 50–51, 116, 118–119, 123
Chief Justice, 39–40, 50–51
Children, 32, 82, 110, 125, 127–135, 137–138, 140–149, 164, 215–216
Citizens, 17–18, 42, 55, 59, 72, 80, 165, 176–177, 209–210, 215
Civil Trials, 74, 77
Civil Procedure, 63, 70, 90–93
Cloth, 16, 180, 206, 215
Code, 4, 6–10, 65, 77–78, 83, 108, 111, 113–114, 131, 137, 139–140, 165, 193, 198, 204, 222
Coffin, 20, 34, 193
Coffin Texts, 20, 34
Collection of laws, 7, 9
Commerce, 47, 103, 105–106, 134, 187–190, 192, 201–202, 206–207, 212, 220
Commercial Law, 187, 189–191, 193, 195, 197, 199, 201, 203–205, 207–208
Commissions, 37, 42, 62, 118, 160
Complaint, 15, 26, 28, 70, 72–74, 90, 94, 160
Consideration, 9, 52, 74, 110, 127–128, 196–197
Conspiracy, 37–38, 44, 85–86, 154, 159, 161, 169–171, 175–176, 186
Conspirators, 44, 85–86, 170–171
Contracts, 6, 10–12, 14, 17, 39, 94, 109–110, 130–133, 136, 140–141, 187–189, 191–193, 195–201, 203, 205, 207–208, 212, 215, 220
Copper, 76, 88, 161–162, 187, 189, 200–203, 205–206, 216
Corn, 76, 114–115, 128, 162, 188, 201

Corporal Punishment, 152, 178, 185, 200
Corvée, 118, 122
Court Calendar, 66
Courts of Hearers, 46
Courts, 6–7, 10, 18, 23–24, 26, 37–51, 54–58, 60–62, 64–68, 71–75, 77–81, 83–85, 87–88, 90–91, 94–95, 106, 121, 127, 155, 158, 171, 173, 175, 219
Credit, 27, 198, 204, 208
Crime Scene, 82, 84
Crimes, 7, 37–38, 44, 46, 51–52, 69, 81, 84, 86, 151–152, 154, 159, 161, 167, 176, 185
Criminal Trials, 10, 51, 74, 80, 151, 160
Criminal Procedure, 52, 69, 89
Criminal Law, 5, 7, 10–11, 21, 23–24, 37–38, 44–48, 50–52, 54–60, 64–67, 69, 72–74, 76–80, 83–84, 88, 109, 111, 118, 121, 138, 151–157, 159–167, 169–171, 173–174, 176, 178–179, 185–186, 194, 197, 200, 219, 221
Criminal Mischief, 178, 186
Criminals, 3, 7, 9–10, 19, 38, 44, 52, 71–72, 75–76, 85–86, 122, 151, 153–154, 156–158, 160, 162–167, 170–172, 174, 176, 179, 185–186, 198–199, 203, 221
Crocodile, 32, 156, 173–174
Crop, 103, 115, 119, 183
Custom, 4, 6, 13, 17, 22, 43, 67, 90, 100, 190, 207
Customs Duty, 189, 207
(See also Customs Tax)
Customs Tax, 207
Cut Off, 80, 86, 171, 175–177
Dam, 33
Death, 3, 7, 9, 12, 20, 26, 84, 86, 93, 107, 110, 129–130, 135, 137–139, 141–142, 147–148, 151–157, 159–161, 163–171, 174–175, 178, 185–186, 194, 196, 209, 211, 221–222
Death Penalty, 154–156, 164, 167, 169, 171, 175, 186
Debtor-Creditor, 199
Debts, 140, 199, 204, 215
Decapitation, 156
Decedent, 137–138, 149
Decree of Neferhotep, 156
Deeds, 4, 10, 12, 19, 23, 36, 39, 83–84, 94, 112–113, 140–142, 196
Defamation, 179, 186
Defendant, 70–77, 79–81, 83–84, 88, 94, 111, 162–163, 166, 180, 183, 199
Deir el-Bahri, 167
Delta, 45–46, 88, 140, 190, 202, 207, 216
Demotic, 4, 8–9, 77–78, 83, 99–100, 102–104, 107–108, 110–114, 131, 137–140, 148, 157, 193, 197–198, 222
Dependent, 34, 117, 122, 188, 192
Deposition, 72, 83, 120, 145
Detectives, 57, 84
Devourer, The, 19
Devouress, 156
Disihnerit, Disinheritance, 143–144
Divorce, 125, 129–134, 136, 145, 173
Divorcee, 34–35
Ḏb3, 183–184
Documents, 4, 6, 8, 10–12, 39, 43–44, 47–48, 50–52, 54, 63–64, 68, 71, 77–78, 82–84,

Documents, *continued*, 94–95, 99, 102–104, 112, 115, 117, 120, 123, 126, 141, 143–145, 153, 157–158, 161, 173, 193–196, 204, 212, 215, 220
Domestic Violence, 131
Donkey, 16, 26, 110, 181–183, 194, 198–201, 208
Dowry, 45, 128–129, 131–133, 135, 138, 142, 149, 173
Drowning, 35, 156
Due Process, 44, 65, 94, 153
Duties of the Vizier, 50–51, 108, 118, 223
2nd Dynasty, 50, 101–102
4th Dynasty, 7, 39–40, 50, 113, 137, 144, 148, 188, 201, 203, 211
5th Dynasty, 20, 40, 50–51, 121, 144, 148, 153
6th Dynasty, 40, 85, 116, 121, 127, 135, 139, 147, 153, 157, 161, 169–170, 211
7th, 8th, and 9th Dynasties, 3
11th Dynasty, 134, 160
12th Dynasty, 8–9, 42, 116, 132, 189, 196, 201–202
13th Dynasty, 27, 67, 211
17th Dynasty, 92, 112, 153
18th Dynasty, 6, 12, 43, 63, 118, 121, 127–128, 147, 175–176, 190, 197–199, 202, 207, 213, 216
19th Dynasty, 3, 14, 47, 58, 156, 168, 215–216
20th Dynasty, 48, 85–86, 119, 122, 143, 155, 168, 193, 204
21st Dynasty, 58–59, 169
22nd Dynasty, 89
24th Dynasty, 9–10
26th Dynasty, 126

Easement, 111
Edict, 6–7, 17, 45–47, 62, 154–155, 160, 162, 165, 176–177, 222
Eldest Son, 40, 127, 135, 138–140, 145, 147–149, 211
Elephantine, 7, 161
Enforcement, 56–57, 72, 93
Equality, 11, 23, 26–27, 102, 193, 211
Equilibrium, 21, 36
Ethiopia, 80
Evil, 19, 23, 30, 71
Execute, 41, 44, 85–86, 134, 141, 171, 212
Execution, 87, 93, 156, 166–167, 171
Exempt, 107, 121–122
Exempted, 47, 53, 121, 123
Exemptions, 7, 121
Expectation Damages, 198, 208
Extortion, 161, 176–177, 186

Fairness, 11, 26
Falsehood, 22, 30, 32, 79–80, 159
Family, 10–13, 28, 32, 34, 40, 49, 61, 83, 104, 106–107, 110, 125, 127–129, 131, 133–135, 138–140, 145, 147–148, 151, 154, 158, 164, 171, 173, 186, 191, 197, 211, 223
Family Law, 10–11, 13, 49, 125, 134, 173, 186, 211
Father, 23, 34–35, 59, 64, 83, 88, 125–128, 131, 134–135, 138–140, 142–144, 147–149, 211
Festival, 58, 66, 196
Fines, 152, 154, 185
First Intermediate Period, 3, 11, 13, 25–26
Fish, 159

Flood, 33, 117
Flooding, 24, 32–33
Food, 26, 32, 159
Foreign Trade, 189, 201, 203
Foreigners, 105, 159, 201, 203, 207, 210, 216
Forgery, 83, 155, 160
Fraud, 186
Fugitives, 9, 204
Funeral, 110, 139, 149
Funerary Rights, 135

Gifts, 27, 128
God, 5, 8, 19–20, 23–24, 27, 33–34, 42, 52–53, 58–60, 62, 67, 71, 93, 107, 111, 117, 159, 162, 164, 167–168, 171–172, 176
Goddess, 19–21, 36, 51
Gold, 41, 47, 53, 76, 84, 116, 119, 121, 187–189, 201–203, 205–206, 208
Goods of a Woman, 129
Government, 22, 27, 37–40, 42, 46, 49–51, 100, 105–106, 109, 116, 118–119, 122–123, 148, 153, 159–160, 167, 176–177, 186, 188–191, 194, 201–202, 207, 217, 221
Governor, 39, 76, 91, 166–168
Grain, 16, 39–40, 102, 105, 114, 116–117, 119–120, 131, 159, 192, 206–208, 215
Granary, 83, 119, 166
Great House, 119
Great Tomb Robberies, 57, 62, 66, 78, 80, 84, 86–87, 152, 157, 161, 165–167
Great Court, 37–38, 42, 45–46, 51, 55–56, 63–64, 69, 74, 76, 81, 83, 147
Greeks, 3, 8, 27, 39, 114
Griffith Fragments, The, 120
Groom, 126, 128, 131, 135
Guarantee, 198

H3n, 59
Harem, 37, 44, 50, 62, 85–86, 127, 135, 169–171, 175–176, 186
Harem Conspiracy, 37, 44, 85–86, 171, 175–176
Haraga, 116
Harvest, 103, 114–115, 117, 120
H3yt, 178
Hearsay, 82
Heart, 19–20, 32, 36, 65, 170, 180
Hebrews, 27
Heir, 23, 86, 141, 146–149, 176
Heirs, 64, 102, 107, 125, 127, 138, 140, 146–147, 149, 172, 197
Heliopolis, 19, 43–46, 51–52, 63–64
Hermopolis, 4, 8–10, 77–78, 83, 103, 108, 111, 113–114, 131, 137, 139–140, 193, 198, 222
Hermopolis Legal Code, 9
Hieraconpolis, 53
Hittite, 8, 189, 203–204, 208
Hittites, 9, 11, 189, 202–204
Ḥm-t, 126
Homes, 84
Homicide, 38, 159, 161, 169, 175, 186
Homosexual Relations, 172
Houses, 39, 42–43, 60, 84, 94, 105, 116, 139, 170, 190, 207–208
Hp, 4–5, 9
hepw, 39
(see also Hp)
Ḫtm, 48, 157
Hu, 6, 53
Human, 11–12, 22, 27, 34, 52, 77, 127, 203, 223

Husband, 10, 23, 34–35, 82, 126–136, 138, 142, 173–175, 186, 193, 211
Hut, 65, 84, 193
Hy, 126
Hyksos, 104, 107

Impalement, 80, 154, 156, 164, 167, 186
Impartiality, 23, 26, 31, 53, 170
Imprisoned, 86–87, 157–158
Imyt-pr, 112–113, 140–142, 149, 193–194, 208
Incarcerated, 78
Incarceration, 157
Inheritance, 10, 13, 44–45, 48–49, 59–60, 63, 77, 83, 99–106, 110, 115, 134, 137–139, 141–143, 145–149, 195–197, 199, 210, 212, 221, 223
Inšn, 129, 135
Instructions for Merikare, 4
Intangible rights, 111
Intentional Infliction of Emotional Harm, 181, 183
Inter Vivos, 113
International Trade, 187–188, 201
International Law, 11, 201, 203–204
Intestacy, 137, 140, 145, 194
Inundation, 24, 31, 33, 35, 99, 103, 115, 117
Investigation, 69, 72, 85–87, 95, 153, 162, 165–166
Irrigation, 115, 119
Ir š‘r, 108
Iryw-‘3, 117
Israel, 9
I‘t3y, 199

Jointly, 104, 123, 130, 133, 140, 142, 144, 149
Judge, 4–6, 8–9, 23, 28–35, 39–40, 42–43, 45, 47–55, 61–62, 65–66, 70–71, 74–75, 85, 90–91, 148, 155, 170–171, 176, 202
Judgment of the dead, 19, 36, 159
Jurisdiction, 4, 14, 20–21, 37–38, 42, 45–49, 51–52, 54–55, 57–61, 64–69, 72–80, 84, 87–88, 90, 93, 110, 112–113, 117, 130–131, 141–143, 151–152, 154–157, 161–163, 165–167, 169, 171, 173, 177–179, 193–194, 199–201, 212, 219, 222
Jurisprudence, 5, 13, 19–21, 23, 25, 27–29, 31, 33, 35–36, 54, 67, 92, 190, 221
Jurors, 54
Jury, 4, 12, 54, 91, 219
Justice, 1, 3–6, 12–13, 15, 18–23, 25–36, 38–44, 50–51, 53, 58, 65–67, 73, 85–86, 89, 93, 154, 158, 170, 182, 190, 202, 210, 219, 222

Karnak, 7, 59, 112, 216
King Cheops and the Magicians, 173
Kings, 3, 5–8, 39, 60–61, 85, 121, 127, 167, 203–204, 215
Ḳnbt, 46–49, 54–57, 59–62, 66, 68, 72, 74, 76, 87–88, 93, 161–162
Kush, 80

Labor, 25, 88, 109, 116–117, 122–123, 153–154, 158, 163–164, 178, 185–186, 197, 206, 214

Lamps, 65, 196
Landlords, 184
Lashes, 175
Law of the Pharaoh, 67
Law Merchant, 201
Lawyers, 71–72, 94
Lease, 103, 112–114, 193
Leasing, 10, 24, 83, 99–100, 102–103, 105, 107, 116–119, 204, 209–210, 212, 220
Legal Philosophy, 23, 28
Legislation, 5, 24
Lessee, 114–115, 193
Lessees, 114
Lessor, 114–115, 193
Lessors, 114
Life Estate, 107, 110, 138, 142, 197
Liquidated Damages, 114–115, 198, 200, 208
Literary Evidence, 11–12
Litigation, 46, 48–49, 54, 60–61, 63–64, 68, 70, 75, 77, 82, 134, 160, 170, 183, 193
Litter, 58–59, 62
Livestock, 28, 105, 182
Louvre Leather Fragments, The, 120
Lower Egypt, 7, 39, 45–47, 121, 174
Lying, 22, 81, 159, 179

M'd3yw, 57
(See also Medjay)
Ma'at, 5–6, 13, 17, 19–24, 27–29, 32, 36, 40, 50, 53, 62, 65, 156–157, 166, 223
Ma'e, 51
(See also Ma'at)
Magic, 13–14, 29
Magistrates, 42, 46, 54, 61, 90–92, 112, 184–185
Magnates of the Southern Tens, 42–43, 118
Man Who Was Tired of Life, The, 185
Marriage, 9–11, 13, 82, 112, 117, 125–135, 138, 142–146, 172–173, 193, 195, 204, 211–212, 220, 222
Mayor, 56, 208
Maxims of Ptahhotpe, The, 174
Mdw, 64
Medinet Habu, 84
Mediterranean, 188–190, 201–202
Medjay, 57
Memphis, 7, 41, 83, 104, 190
Merchants, 187–190, 201–202, 207, 209, 214, 217
Mesopotamia, 6–7, 9, 65, 168, 187, 223
Middle Kingdom, 3–7, 11–13, 15, 25–27, 29, 31, 34, 41–43, 51, 61, 65, 68, 107–108, 117–119, 134, 137, 148, 153, 157, 173, 184–185, 189, 194, 202, 205–206, 209–211, 213, 221
Military, 56, 86, 104–105, 158, 176, 188–189, 202–203, 209–210, 216
Misrepresenting, 159
Money, 39, 112, 116, 128–129, 154, 205–207
Mtrw, 77
Mutilation, 78–80, 153–155, 164, 167, 176, 179, 185–186

Natural Law, 23, 31
Natural Rights, 109, 123
Nature, 10–12, 20–21, 24, 29, 31–32, 38, 50, 59, 72, 75, 82, 84, 91, 94, 99, 110, 154, 159, 178, 182, 186, 192, 197, 199, 206, 223

Nauri Decree, 7, 62, 69, 154–156, 163–164, 213, 220
Nḏs, 209
Necessity, 119, 182, 188, 195
Necropolis, 4, 10, 14, 38, 57, 60, 69, 86–87, 118–119, 139, 141, 143, 151, 165, 167, 221
Neighbor, 42, 111, 159, 185
Nekhen, 38, 50, 52–53
Neo-Babylonian, 8
New Kingdom, 3, 6, 18, 20, 37, 41, 43–45, 47–48, 50–51, 54, 57–58, 61–62, 67, 73, 78, 89, 100–101, 103–105, 117–118, 122, 130, 133, 142–144, 146, 148, 151, 153–154, 156, 158, 168, 172, 185–186, 189–192, 195, 202–203, 205–207, 209, 211, 214–217, 222–223
Nḥm, 25–26
Nile, 8, 10, 24, 28, 31, 33, 35–36, 65, 81, 99, 117, 187–190, 192, 202, 207
Ninsu, 15, 28, 89, 184
Nmḥ, 210
Nmḥw, 209–210
Nmḥy, 209
Nobles, 38, 101, 107, 126, 135, 203, 209–210, 214, 216–217
Nomarch, 39, 61, 107, 110–111, 148–149, 197, 214
Nomes, 39–40, 107, 119, 148
Nubia, 7, 57, 188–189, 201–203

O Or. Inst. 12073, 199
O. Petrie 16, 139, 141, 143, 221
Oar, 31, 35
Oath, 66, 69, 72–73, 75–76, 78, 80–81, 87, 92, 141–142, 160, 179, 198–199
Office, 6, 10, 21, 27, 42–43, 50–51, 53–54, 59–60, 67, 69–70, 110, 113, 118, 120, 138, 141, 148–149, 153–155, 164, 186, 194, 196–197, 207–208, 215
Old Kingdom, 5–7, 11, 17, 24, 32–33, 37–39, 41–43, 52, 61, 70, 88–89, 102, 111–113, 116–118, 125, 139–141, 144, 148, 151, 153, 156, 159, 188–189, 192–193, 196, 202, 205–206, 209–212, 214, 221
Oracle, 56, 58–61, 65–66, 68, 87–89, 93, 109, 111, 178
Oracular, 58–59, 61–62
Oriental Institute Ostracon 12073, 116, 199, 222
Orphan, 34–35, 209
Ostraca, 6, 48, 61, 68, 74, 192
Ostracon, 88, 109–111, 116, 131, 141, 145, 155, 161–164, 169, 179, 193, 199–200, 222
Ostracon British Museum 5631 Recto, 88
Ostracon Cairo 25556, 179
Ostracon Cairo 25555, 111
Ostracon Chicago, Oriental Institute 12.073, 3, 193
Ostracon Deir el-Medina 126, 169
Ostracon Deir El-Medina 433, 200
Ostracon Gard 54, 110
Ostracon Nash 1, 161
Ostracon Nash 2, 162
Ostracon Nash 5 Recto, 131
Ostracon Petrie 18, 141
Ostracon Turin 57455, 163
Ostrich Feather, 19–20, 156

P.Leopold/Amherst, 157
P. Wilbour, 103, 117
P. Berlin 3047, 103
P. Amiens, 120, 153
Palace, 45, 107, 170, 203, 215–216

Papyrus, 9, 15, 34, 51, 56, 65, 68, 74, 78–79, 81–83, 85, 91, 104–106, 115–117, 119, 121–123, 127, 130–132, 137–140, 142–147, 156–158, 160, 165, 172–173, 177–179, 212, 219–220
Papyrus Abbott, 165
Pap. Bulaq X, 139, 141, 143, 221
Papyrus B.M. 10052, 79
Papyrus Berlin 3047, 147
Papyrus Berlin 10496, 178
Papyrus British Museum 10052, 81
Papyrus British Museum 10335, 56
Papyrus Cairo 65739, 78
Papyrus Deir el-Medina 26, 65, 68, 179
Papyrus Deir el-Medina 26 A, 65, 179
Papyrus Deir el-Medina 27, 160
Papyrus Deir el-Medina 26 A Recto, 65
Papyrus Geneva, 177–178
Papyrus Harris, 106, 116
Papyrus Mayer A, 82–83
Papyrus Salt 124 2, 17, 178
Papyrus Turin 1977, 178
Papyrus Westcar, 156, 173
P't, 209–10
Patience, 29
Peace Treaty, 203, 208
Peasants, 24, 83, 99–100, 102–103, 105, 107, 116–119, 126, 183–184, 204, 209–210, 212, 214, 220
Penalties, 80, 94, 152–155, 163, 165, 171, 176–177, 185–186, 199–200
Perjury, 80–81, 94, 154–155, 160, 162, 179, 199
Pharaoh, 6, 12–13, 17, 20, 22–23, 29, 37–38, 40, 44–45, 47–48, 50–54, 56, 60–64, 66–68, 76, 83–88, 100–101, 104, 106–108, 115–117, 121, 148, 153–155, 157–158, 161–162, 164–167, 170–171, 174–176, 179, 188, 190, 192, 209, 213–214, 216, 221
Pi-Ra'messe, 83
Plot, 44, 63, 85–86, 99, 101, 120–121, 155, 169–170, 174
Plumbline, 31
Police, 6, 51, 55, 57, 69, 81, 159, 162, 165–166, 176, 190, 207
Precedent, 5, 20, 24, 36, 41, 66–68, 92, 94
Predynastic, 100, 187, 201–202
Premeditation, 169
Price, 16, 59, 112–113, 128, 183, 189, 194–196, 202, 204–205
Priests, 6, 21, 41–42, 46–47, 59, 62, 104–105, 107, 110, 122, 145, 166, 196–197, 209–210
Prisoners, 44, 51–52, 79, 156–157, 215
Prisons, 157, 160, 186
Privately Owned, 100–103, 115
Procedure, 1, 5, 8, 11, 13, 28, 52, 59, 63–65, 67–75, 77, 79, 81, 83–85, 87, 89–95, 108, 145, 151
Property, 7, 9–11, 13–14, 17, 24, 37, 45, 49, 59–64, 72, 75, 77–78, 82–84, 88, 91, 94, 99–117, 119–123, 126–135, 137–149, 153, 159, 162–164, 167–168, 171, 173, 180–181, 183–186, 193–197, 200, 204–205, 207–208, 210–212, 214–215, 220, 222
Prosecution, 69, 73, 75, 78, 81–82
Prosecutors, 69, 74, 76
Prostitution, 172

Ptolemaic, 9, 103–104, 112, 125, 130, 173, 204
Public Protest, 108
Public Nuisance, 180, 183
Punishment, 17, 30, 44, 51–52, 76, 80, 85–87, 94, 152–158, 160, 162, 164–165, 171, 174–179, 183, 185–186, 199–200
Punishments, 7, 44, 62, 75, 80–81, 87, 152–155, 160, 163–164, 167, 174, 185–186
Punitive Damages, 162, 183, 185–186
Punt, 188–189
Pyramid Texts, 33, 151

RAD, 57, 8-58, 6, 178
Rape, 38, 160, 172–173, 175, 186
Real Property, 60–62, 88, 99–105, 107–108, 110–113, 115, 119–120, 122–123, 138–140, 142, 148, 164, 194, 197, 222
Real Estate, 10, 41, 59–61, 100, 103, 107, 112–113, 117, 139–141, 149, 159, 207, 212
(See also Real Property)
Redistributive Economy, 191–192
Real Property, 60–62, 88, 99–105, 107–108, 110–113, 115, 119–120, 122–123, 138–140, 142, 148, 164, 194, 197, 222
Religion, 13, 15, 19–21, 29, 31, 33–34, 38, 53, 65, 70–71, 73, 88, 91, 94, 151, 156, 159, 172–173, 185, 193, 213, 219
Remarriage, 134
Rent, 49, 101, 103, 114–115, 193, 199, 215
Res Judicata, 64
Retainer of the Court, 56
Rhetorical, 4, 23, 26, 30
Rhyt, 209
Right, 4, 16, 20, 22, 27, 29, 52, 60, 65–66, 70, 73, 89, 91, 94, 100, 102, 104, 109–111, 115, 126–127, 131–133, 137, 148, 153–155, 161, 174, 180–183, 194, 197, 212, 216
Rings, 203, 205–206
River, 16, 24, 31–33, 65, 117, 157, 159, 174, 181, 188, 207
River Ordeal, 65
Riverbank, 68–69, 156
Robber, 33, 168
Romans, 4, 102, 109–110
Royal Butler, 56
Royal Tomb Robbers, 37
Rw'ḏw, 57
Rw'dw, 147

S'nḫ, 129, 133, 135
Sakkara, 104
Sale, 10, 49, 76, 101–103, 112–113, 141, 188, 192, 194, 197, 201, 205, 212
Salt Papyrus 124, 160
Sb3yt, 152
Scale, 21, 31–32, 107, 158, 184, 191
Scribes, 6, 17, 19, 28, 38, 41, 48, 51, 54–56, 62, 71, 76, 94, 104–105, 119–120, 130, 158, 162, 166
Seal, 108
Security, 22, 24, 190, 204
Sentencing, 44, 52, 76–77, 85, 167, 186
Serf, 184, 214–215
Serfs, 101, 110, 118, 214, 216
Servant of Choice, 28, 90
Servants, 17, 41, 82, 153, 166, 194
Servitude, 109, 164, 216
Settle, 70, 108, 122
Settlement, 130, 133–134, 138, 146, 220

Sexual Misconduct, 160
Sexual, 49, 159–161, 172
Shade, 32
Share-Cropping, 107
Shelter, 32–33, 35
Ship, 25–26, 35, 63, 90, 103–104, 168
Shipwrecked Sailor, The, 25–26
Šmsw, 56–57, 72
Šmsw n ḳnbt, 56–57
Šp, 128–129, 131–133, 173
Šʿt, 205
Sia, 6, 53
Siblings, 135, 138, 149
Signature, 78, 195
Sisters, 64, 127–128, 138–140, 146–147
Six Great Courts, 39–40, 61
Slave, 41, 84, 106, 155, 192, 194–195, 197, 203, 208, 215–216
Slaves, 46, 78, 82, 105–106, 118, 126, 146, 197, 203, 209–210, 213–217
Smallholders, 104–105, 210, 212
Smi, 73
Smtr, 78
Snḥ, 193
Social Justice, 15, 26–27, 29, 210
Soldier, 165, 177
Son, 17, 23, 40, 50, 64, 89–90, 92, 104, 125, 127, 135, 138–140, 144–149, 166, 174, 188, 211
Soul, 19, 21, 31, 156, 185
Southern Tens, 42–43, 61, 118
Speech, 4, 15–16, 25, 28, 30–31, 54
Sr, 54, 209
Srw, 54–55, 89, 91–92, 173, 184
Sʿt3t, 121
Stare Decisis, 67
State, 3, 5, 11, 14, 21–23, 37–40, 45–51, 54–57, 59–61, 69, 72, 74–75, 84, 88, 90, 94, 100–106, 108, 113, 115–121, 123, 131, 141, 147–148, 152, 156, 161–165, 167–168, 171, 185–192, 200, 202–210, 213–214, 223
Status Quo, 22
Status, 3–5, 9–10, 22, 37–38, 67, 70, 74, 81, 84, 104, 113, 117, 128, 130–131, 133–135, 138–142, 144–147, 151, 153–154, 158, 160–163, 171–172, 175, 186, 191, 194, 197, 209, 211–217, 221
Statutes, 8, 10, 21, 176
Stela, 7, 61, 92, 112, 128, 134, 142, 157, 160, 169, 195
Stela Cairo 34061, 142
Stela of Banishment, 169
Stèle Juridique from Karnak, 112
Strict Liability, 182
Strictly Liable, 180, 199, 208
Substituted Contract, 201, 208
Succession, 11, 115, 130, 135, 137–149, 222
Sudan, 188–189, 201–203
Suicide, 86, 93, 171, 176
Sumerian, 8
Sun, 20, 28, 33
Suretyship, 204
Suspects, 68–69, 72, 75, 78–79, 82, 84, 86–87, 157, 166

Ṯ3wt, 161, 163
Tale of the Eloquent Peasant, The, 9–11, 13, 15–17, 21–22, 28–29, 31, 34, 36, 89–93, 180–183, 223
Tax Exemption, 53, 107, 121–122
Taxes, 3, 7, 9, 11–12, 39–40, 47, 83–84, 100, 105, 113, 115–119, 121–123, 152, 155,

Taxes, *continued*, 157, 159–160, 165–170, 175–176, 178, 191–192, 207–208, 216, 221–222
Teaching for Merikare, The, 25
Temple, 7, 20, 22, 45, 76, 84, 106–107, 115, 121–122, 153, 157, 159, 161, 166, 172, 196–197, 203, 210, 214–216
Tenants, 102, 107, 122, 170, 191
Testate Succession, 140
Testimony, 77–84, 94, 161
Thebes, 7, 41, 45–46, 51, 55–56, 58, 72, 74, 76, 81, 87, 108, 120, 139, 141, 143, 166, 195, 215–216, 221
Thief, 33, 46, 59–60, 65, 76, 162–164, 168, 175, 186
Thieves, 60, 72, 76, 79, 81–82, 87, 152, 157, 163, 165–167
Third Intermediate Period, 9, 133
Thirty, The 11, 39, 43, 61
Thirty Great Men of the South, 39, 61
Tjaty, 50
Tjebnet, 46
Tomb, 10, 23, 37–38, 52, 57, 62, 65–66, 75–76, 78, 80–82, 84, 86–87, 104, 108, 116, 118, 127, 144, 152, 154–155, 157, 161, 163, 165–168, 178, 186, 194, 196
Tombs, 6, 37, 46, 49, 57, 86, 127, 154, 160–161, 166–167, 205
Torts, 14, 151–152, 177, 180–185, 221–223
Torture, 56, 75, 78–79, 166, 174, 185
Tradition, 6, 9, 20–24, 34, 36, 39, 44, 52, 58, 61–62, 127, 221
Treason, 37, 50, 154, 161, 169, 171–172, 186
Treasury, 40, 43, 83, 105, 116–117, 119, 122, 168, 177, 192
Trespass to Land, 178, 186
Trespass to Chattels, 178, 180–181, 186
Trial, 44, 49, 51–52, 56–58, 66–67, 69–70, 72–73, 75–76, 79–80, 82, 85–86, 88, 91, 93–94, 104, 109, 151, 156–157, 159, 165, 169–171, 173, 186
Trials, 10, 17, 37–39, 49, 51, 54–55, 62, 68, 74, 77, 80, 94, 151, 155, 160–161, 165, 169, 171, 213
Trust, 33, 110, 144–145, 147, 216
Trustee, 64, 111, 147
Truth, 19–22, 30, 36, 51, 75, 78–81, 90, 179, 183
Turin, 85, 116, 119, 130, 137–138, 143–146, 163, 178, 219

Underworld, 19, 91, 156
Unreasonable Searches and Seizures, 84
Upper Class, 56
Upper Egypt, 39, 45, 119
Usus Fructus, 109–111, 123, 147
Usus, 109–111, 123, 147

Valençay, Recto, 9, 116
Values, 21, 23, 36, 60, 120, 206, 208
Vandalism, 178, 186
Victim, 44, 60, 85, 151–152, 155–156, 162–163, 171
Vis Maior, 117
Vizier, 6, 8, 23–24, 26–27, 31–32, 34, 36–37, 40–46, 48, 50–56, 59–60, 62–63, 65, 67–72, 74, 76, 81, 83, 86–87, 89, 92, 108, 111, 113, 118–119, 123, 141, 147–149, 152, 155, 157, 162, 165, 170, 196, 208, 223

W'b, 75
Wadi Natrun, 15, 184
Warmth, 32, 34
Warranty of Title, 194–195, 198
Waste, 186
Water, 23, 31–32, 35, 111, 159
White House, 105, 116–117, 119
Widow, 23, 29, 34–35, 64, 81–82, 138, 146
Wilbour Papyrus, 105–106, 115–117, 119, 121–123
Will, 6, 13–14, 16, 27, 29–31, 35, 49–50, 53, 79, 92–93, 101–102, 112, 131, 137–147, 149, 152, 183, 185, 191, 193–194, 198, 204, 210–212, 215, 220
Wills, 10–12, 17, 39, 50, 77, 82, 94, 112–113, 140–142, 144, 149, 194, 196, 212, 215
Wind, 28, 31
Witness, 56, 69, 75, 78, 80–84, 93, 159, 195–196, 214
Witnesses, 56–57, 60, 63–64, 75–83, 94–95, 103, 112–113, 145, 166, 179, 194, 196, 198, 203–204, 212
Wives, 32, 125, 127–128, 130–132, 135, 138, 142, 149, 194, 211, 216
Woman, 19, 45, 64, 76, 80, 126, 128–129, 131–134, 138, 141, 143, 147, 149, 161, 172, 174, 179, 193–194, 211–212
Wood , 15, 188
Written Laws, 5–10, 47, 53

Index of Names

Ahmose I, 59
Ahmose, 59, 104, 107
Akhenaton, 176–177, 213
Amenhotep I, 58–59, 62
Amenhotep II, 168
Amenhotep III, 118, 128, 190, 192, 197, 202, 213, 216
Amenhotep IV, 7 (see also Akhenaton)
Amenhotep (sailor named), 75
Amenophis IV, 7
Amenpnefer, 166
Amon, 56, 88, 157, 162, 165–166, 195 (see also Amun)
Amun, 195, 216 (see also Amon)
Amon-Re, 59
Amos, 26
Anubis, 92–93, 196
Ahmose, 59, 104, 107
Amosis, 104, 128
Astarte, 190
Baal, 190
Bak-en-renef, 9
Bocchoris, 8–9
Cheops, 113, 173–174 (see also Khufu)
Degay, 84
Deir el-Medina, 4, 6, 10, 14, 18, 37–38, 45, 47–49, 51, 54–56, 58–62, 65, 68–69, 74, 87–88, 93, 109, 131, 141, 151, 157, 160–163, 169, 171, 173, 178–179, 192, 198–201, 206, 221–222
Diodorus Siculus, 3, 154, 169–170
Ese, 84
Gaston Maspero, 168
Hapdjefai, 110, 195–197
Hapy, 33
Harkhuf, 189
Hatshepsut, 213
Ḥ3y, 75, 179
Hay, 111
Hekanakht, 134
Heti, 144, 147, 191
Ḫnsw, 179
Horemhab, 3, 6–7, 17–18, 45–48, 53–54, 62, 121, 147, 154–155, 162, 164–165, 175–177, 204, 222
Horus, 19, 38, 53, 65, 70–71, 73, 88, 94, 104, 172, 213, 219
Hosea, 26
Howtenefer, 83–84
Ḥri3, 161, 162
Huy, 64
Ibana, 104
Imn-m-ipt, 200–201
Irinefer, 84
Isis, 20, 91, 220
Kenherkhepshef, 144
Kenna, 109
Khaʿy, 64, 83
Khnum, 7
Khufu, 113 (see also Cheops)
Khunanup, 15–17, 28–35, 89–92, 180–185
King Khety III, 25

King Nebirierau, 92
Knr, 200–201
Mentuhotep, 8, 189
Merikare, 4, 25–26, 158
Mernere, 188
Mersekhmet, 109
Mes, 64
(see also Mose)
Messuia, 192, 197–198, 215–216
Metjen, 102, 140, 194
Min, 172
Mnʿtw-ms, 199
Mose, 63–64, 70, 77, 80, 83, 102–104, 116, 147
(see also Mes)
Mry-sḫmt, 173
Naunakhte, 141, 143–145, 212, 220
Nebka, 173–174
Nebkaure, 28
Nebnefer, 146
Nebsenet, 194
Nefertiti, 213
Nemtynakhte, 15–17, 28, 89–91, 180–185
Nenufer, 146
Nephthys, 91
Nesamon, 81
Neshi, 63, 83, 103–104
Nubkhaas, 166
Nubnofre, 64, 83
Osiris, 5, 7, 19, 52, 71, 91, 151, 158, 164
P3-nb, 178
Peikharu, 76, 81, 109
Peneb, 173
Pennestytauy, 82
Pentoere, 111
Pepi I, 49, 85, 121, 127, 170, 186, 188
Perpethew, 82
Pn-ʿnḳt, 178
Psametichus, 195
Ptahhotpe, 174
Ramesses, 117, 120, 143, 165, 171, 178
Skheperenre, 143
Ramses II, 11, 48, 59, 63, 76, 147, 167, 189–190, 201–204
Ramses III, 7, 44, 76, 85–86, 106, 116, 170–171, 175, 186, 216
Ramses IV, 193
Ramses V, 119, 143
Ramses IX, 78, 85–87, 157, 165
Ramses X, 167
Ramses XI, 56, 118, 146, 165
Re, 20, 33, 127, 166
Rekhmire, 23, 52, 65, 67, 108, 118
Rensi, 15, 17, 28–35, 89–92, 183–185
Sebkemsaf, 166
Sekhemre-shedtaui, 166
Senusert III, 135
Senwosre III, 134
(see also Senusert III)
Set, 7, 9, 19, 21, 25, 38, 47, 75, 104, 122, 151, 154, 174
Seti I, 7, 14, 18, 62, 154–156, 163–164, 167, 176, 179, 213, 220
Shepsekaf, 7
Sitamun, 128
Snefru, 188
Snofru, 121, 188, 201
(see also Snefru)
Taaper, 76
Takharu, 147
Teti, 121, 127
Tety, 172
Thoth, 8, 19, 33–34
Thutmose III , 52, 65, 74, 108, 118, 142, 176, 189, 201–203, 206, 215–216
Tiy, 213
Userkaf, 188

Waḥ-ʿnkh, 160
Webaoner, 173–175
Wenamun, 168
Weni, 49–51, 85, 161, 170
Wernero, 64, 147
William the Conqueror, 101